The Uncrowned Queen of Ireland

ALSO BY JOYCE MARLOW

The Tolpuddle Martyrs
The Peterloo Massacre
The Life and Times of George I
Captain Boycott and the Irish

The Uncrowned Queen of Ireland

The Life of
'Kitty' O'Shea

JOYCE MARLOW

SATURDAY REVIEW PRESS

E. P. DUTTON & CO., INC.

New York

Library of Congress Cataloging in Publication Data
Marlow, Joyce.
The uncrowned queen of Ireland.

Bibliography: p.
Includes index.
1. Parnell, Katharine Wood.   2. Parnell, Charles
Stewart, 1846–1891. I. Title.
DA958.P2M27   1975   941.58'092'4 [B]   74-28356

First U.S. Edition

10 9 8 7 6 5 4 3 2 1

ISBN: 0-8415-0374-5
Designed by The Etheredges

For Julian

Illustrations

Acknowledgments

I should like to thank the following people for the help they have given during the preparation of this book: the staff of the Reading Room and Department of Manuscripts of the British Museum (now retitled the British Library); the staff of the Public Records Offices in London and Ashridge, Herts; the staff of the library of the University of Birmingham; the staff of the Catholic Information Office in London, as always most helpful in answering queries, and the Reverend Louis Jester of St Joseph's College, Mill Hill, for his assistance on specific questions; Mr J. S. Hicks of Eltham Public Library for his advice on local history and for showing me the O'Shea/Wood landmarks in the town; the Secretary of the Royal Blackheath Golf Club for giving me access to the clubhouse, formerly the home of Aunt Ben; Father Chapeau of St Mary of the Angels, Bayswater, and of Angers University for allowing me to inspect the surviving papers of Cardinal Manning, now in his custody; David McLoughlin of Oscott College, Sutton Coldfield, for his work in tracing Willie O'Shea's career at the college; Mrs Maureen Sibley of Littlehampton for her considerable help in regard to Katie O'Shea/Parnell's grave in Littlehampton cemetery and for other local information; Sir Richard Barrett Lennard for his help on family history; Miss Margaret Rawlings for loaning me her precious scrapbooks accrued during the period when she played Katie O'Shea on Broadway and in

[xi]

London in the late 1930s, and for the information contained therein; and last but very much not least to Mrs Christine Fitzgerald, Katie O'Shea's great-niece, for her invaluable knowledge of Wood family history, for allowing me to borrow the family books and letters, for giving me permission to use the photographs and drawings in her possession, and for the whole-hearted enthusiasm she showed throughout the research and writing of the book.

The Uncrowned Queen of Ireland

Chapter One

In 1890 the previously unknown name of 'Kitty' O'Shea rang round the world, and among other things she was called 'a proved British prostitute' and 'the were-wolf woman of Irish politics'; when she died it was said that she had done more to affect Anglo-Irish history than any female of the nineteenth century, Queen Victoria excepted. The life that led to such world-wide notoriety and to the sweeping if not unjustified statements of the obituaries started peacefully and in great respectability on 30 January 1845, when Emma, the wife of Sir John Page Wood, Bart, bore him their thirteenth and last child. It was in a house called Glazenwood which lay in the hamlet of Bradwell in Essex, some forty-five miles from London, that the child christened Katharine was born, and though from an early age she was known as Kate or Katie, nobody ever called her 'Kitty'. The diminutive under which she passed into history was not used until 1890, and then by people who did not personally know her.

Sir John Page Wood was the Anglican vicar of nearby Cressing and had inherited the baronetcy two years before the birth of his last child. He was descended from a noted West Country family, the Woods of Tiverton, whose lineage could be traced back to the days of Edward III, though his branch of the family had settled in Gloucestershire. His uncle, Benjamin Wood, was a rich man who had made a fortune out of brewing and then become a Liberal MP, but it was his father, Matthew Wood, who was perhaps the most renowned and interesting of Katharine's immediate forebears. He was twice Lord Mayor of London and like his brother Benjamin was also a Liberal MP. His reputation was acquired initially during the stormy years of 1815 and 1816 when he earned a name as champion of the oppressed, but Matthew's greater fame resulted from his devotion to Queen Caroline. In 1820 Caroline, the long-estranged wife of the Prince Regent, newly become George IV, returned to England to claim her rights as Queen. Her husband was determined to divorce her and was supported by the current Tory Government, which meant that Caroline gathered the support of the Whig Opposition, and as the Government popularly equalled repression and oppression, she temporarily became the people's favourite. Matthew Wood, Whig and Populist (within reason), was Caroline's devoted champion, putting his London house at her disposal, and escorting her on the famous ride to the coronation ceremony at Westminster Abbey when she hammered on the door demanding admittance as the Queen of England, only to be refused.

While Matthew Wood battled by the Queen's side, his son John was newly down from Cambridge University, where he had studied for holy orders, and he decided to spend a brief holiday in Cornwall. There he fell in love—apparently at first sight—with a young lady called Emma Michell, but when he told his father that he wished to marry Miss Michell, Matthew Wood considered they were both too young and impoverished to marry, and being himself involved in Queen Caroline's affairs, he sent his brother Benjamin to prevent the match. But Benjamin Wood promptly fell in love with Emma's older sister Maria, with the result that he married one Michell daughter while his nephew married another. Matthew Wood used his influence with Queen Caroline to have his son appointed her private chaplain and secretary, while his new daughter-in-law Emma became a Lady of the Bedchamber. For the Wood family, Caroline was the martyred, ill-used, injured Queen of England, and when she died in 1821, it was her youthful spiritual adviser, John Page Wood, who performed the last offices, while both he and his father accompanied the body back to its native Brunswick for burial. The young Katie grew up in a household filled with treasured mementoes of the Queen and in which her memory was sacrosanct. Among the souvenirs was an ill-spelled letter in Caroline's handwriting addressed to 'The Revd John Wood, my Chapplain' in which she sent him 'the half years Sallery inclosed in this Papear', a lace cap and coat personally worked for Emma Wood's first child, and a gold ring whose crown opened to reveal a lock of her hair and whose inner band bore the inscription 'With affectionate regards to Matthew Wood from Caroline, the Injured Queen of England'. (Incidentally, it was the young Queen Victoria who conferred the baronetcy on Matthew Wood in his old age.)

After his brief tenure of royal office John Page Wood settled for a more humdrum but better remunerated living, for however cherished her memory, his 'sallery' as chaplain to Queen Caroline had been small and erratically paid, and with his family increasing apace he needed a good income. In 1824 the living of St Peter's, Cornhill, became vacant and, according to a contemporary newspaper, 'The Rev John Page Wood, Ll.B. of Trinity College, was, on the 28th ult., elected Rector of St Peter's, Cornhill, by the Common Council of the City of London. There were four candidates. The living is stated to be worth from £700 to £800 a year.' In 1824 that was a good salary—many families in England were existing on eight shillings a week, which gave them a yearly gross of £20-odd—but throughout his life John Page Wood was beset with financial difficulties. This was not because his income was poor—indeed in 1833 he was appointed vicar of Cressing, so hencefor- ward he had two salaries—but because of his temperament and back- ground. He was a generous man and his family needed money in a way that an urban working-class or an agricultural labourer's did not, because such families were not accustomed to gracious living. His two incomes did not provide sufficiently large sums to enable his wife and children to live in the style which they considered their natural right, and the Woods were constantly supplementing their incomes in any possible way; a gift from another member of the family was acceptable, as was involvement in the world of the arts.

From 1833 onwards the Woods settled in Essex, first living in the vicarage at Cressing, and when this proved to be an excessively damp dwelling, moving to the house called Glazenwood, where Katharine was born. But as Sir John remained the rector of St Peter's, Cornhill, the metropolitan links were kept in being. In Essex Sir John took his duties seriously and cared for his parishioners' welfare within the limits of what was possible without too radical an upheaval of the existing laws, customs and class stratifications which he took for granted. He also involved himself in local government and politics—he was chairman of the Board of Guardians and a magistrate, acting as visiting magistrate to the Chelmsford gaol and as chairman of the nearby Witham Bench, and at General Elections he campaigned for the Whig candidate. To supplement his income, Sir John also acted as a reader for the London publishers Chapman and Hall. Thus his life was well-filled. He was 'a cultured man, a good classical scholar, interested in literature, painting and music. His particular enthusiasm was for botany, and his youngest daughter later wrote of the many happy hours she spent in her father's company, wandering through the Essex countryside searching the fields and hedgerows for wild flowers which they then pressed into books and catalogued. For Katie, her father had an unblemished character and was the ideal parent, but another of his daughters suggested that he was not without his faults, which included irritability when crossed (particularly by his sons), a fair degree of masculine selfishness and a tendency to complain about the slings and arrows of outrageous fortune rather than to endure them with Christian forbearance.

The stronger character and the dominant partner in the Wood marriage was Emma. Like her husband she came from a West Country family, whose name derived from the Cornish village of Michell, which lies between Bodmin and Truro (the name was always pronounced 'Mitchell', and the village is now spelled with the 't'). The Michells were of the squirearchy and boasted an ancestor who had been an MP in the reign of Elizabeth I, another who had been High Sheriff of Cornwall, another who had been Mayor of Truro and another who was the grandmother of Percy Bysshe Shelley. Emma Michell was born in 1802, and the first few years of her life were spent not in Cornwall but in Lisbon because her father, Sampson Michell, had been seconded from the British to the Portuguese navy, of which latter fleet he eventually became the Commander-in-Chief. In their early days the Michell children lived a pleasant life in a fine house in Lisbon, but when Napoleon's troops invaded Portugal the family fled back to England and Sampson Michell decided it was his duty to follow the Portuguese King into exile. He left his wife and family in Truro and sailed for the Brazils, where he died shortly after his arrival in 1809. Thus only the first few years of Emma's life were spent in style and comfort in Lisbon, while the rest of her childhood was passed in more straitened circumstances in Cornwall. Among her siblings was a brother who rose to be Admiral Sir Frederick Michell (in the British, not Portuguese, navy), another brother, Charles, who became the first Surveyor-General of the

[4]

Cape of Good Hope, in which capacity he was mainly responsible for the opening-up of the colony's interior, while her sister Maria (the one who married Benjamin Wood) played a large part in the lives of the Woods of Cressing, most crucially in that of Katharine.

Members of the family attributed to Emma Wood a spark of genius, and while this might seem a misapplication of that overworked word, she was certainly a woman of vitality, determination and concentration, with a deep capacity for love, a considerable amount of talent and a strongly developed sense of duty which (unlike her husband) made her bear her burdens with a Spartan lack of complaint. From her parents she inherited a good singing voice and she was an accomplished amateur musician, but her ability as an artist reached a higher standard. When the New Water Colour Society was established in the 1830s she was among its first exhibitors and thereafter started to illustrate books professionally, a task she continued for the rest of her life. Emma Wood was also the mother of a large brood of children and she was a good one—her offspring were not banished from her presence to be cared for by nannies and governesses. To an extent, the lack of staff was due to the financial exigencies, but she herself was not the sort of woman who thought her children should be totally entrusted to strangers. In addition to her maternal duties and her money-earning artistic actvities, she was the wife of the parish priest, and her sister Maria—who having married Benjamin Wood was always known as Aunt Ben—described her ability to cope thus: 'Emma's capabilities are as general as my incapabilities. It is surprising how much she does. Her characters of surgeon and physician to the poor are added to those of *belle esprit* and artist, all of which she is. *Dei gratia,* she proves the truth of the saying, that time gives to every man an hour for everything, unless he chooses to yawn it away.'

Emma Wood did not choose to yawn away a single minute, and while her life can be said to have been comparatively easy and blessed with good fortune, it was not without its trials and real sorrows, and with these she coped in as able a manner as with her daily round. She had six children in quick succession, of whom only two were alive in 1827, and of the four infant deaths Emma Wood had to bear, the most shattering was that of her second-born son, christened John Page Wood after his father and said to be a prodigy who could read Latin and Greek at the age of four. Within two years of the birth of her last child, Katharine, fate dealt Lady Wood more blows with the deaths of her first-born son, Frederick, and of her seventeen-year-old daughter, Cla-

[5]

rissa. Of these two deaths, that of Clarissa was the more shattering as she was a most beautiful child, a veritable angel according to the Wood family, whose character matched her physical loveliness. Emma Wood was generally an affectionate mother but she seemed to need one child on whom she could focus her store of emotion and maternal pride. First it was young John, then Clarissa and, when she died so suddenly and tragically, it was Emma's last-born son, Evelyn, who became the apple of his mother's eye.

Katharine was the thirteenth and last child*, and according to family history, Sir John and Lady Wood decided that the arrival of the new baby necessitated a larger residence. Consequently, their son Charles was sent out on his pony to reconnoitre the area and returned with the news that he had found the ideal empty house which artistic Mama would love 'because it has a waterfall down the front stairs'. This ideal house, which was in a state of total disrepair, was Rivenhall Place, which still stands about six miles from Braintree, closer to Witham than to the village of Cressing which was Sir John's parish. Rivenhall belonged to Lord Western, an Essex neighbour and friend, and his lordship was only too delighted to lease the leaking ruin for a peppercorn rent to the Woods who, despite their ever-present financial difficulties, promised (and managed) to spend hundreds of pounds on repairs. Rivenhall Place stands on a slight undulation looking out over open countryside, with its own lake fed from a nearby stream. The building dates back to Tudor times but it had been mainly rebuilt in the eighteenth century, before being allowed to go to seed in the nineteenth century, so the aspect is Georgian. It has forty rooms and halls in all but it is not a rambling house, the construction being compact, and it was therefore manageable without the army of servants Emma Wood could not afford to employ.

It was this comfortable, spacious, yet charming and friendly house which figured in Katharine's first conscious memories and in which she spent her youth. As the last child born when her mother was aged forty-three, she suffered to the extent that there were no playmates of her immediate age and because her mother's attention was focussed on the seven-year-old Evelyn. The lack of maternal devotion was mini-

---

* Katie herself recorded that her mother bore thirteen children while Wood family history states that she had ten. She would seem to be correct. There were eight children alive when she was born, four had died by 1827, add on Katie herself and that makes thirteen.

mal, at her least Lady Wood had more to offer than most mothers, and it was compensated by her father's affection. If Evelyn was the new jewel in Lady Wood's quiverful of children, the last-born daughter filled the same function for Sir John, and she was the constant companion of his middle-aged and declining years. Bedecked in the ribbons of the party, she accompanied him when he campaigned for the Whig candidate at the General Elections, and when he visited his Cornhill parish or his friends and relations she went too. In these various processes Katie was thoroughly spoiled and absorbed the information that it was from men that she obtained the most pleasures and comforts and to them she should therefore devote her attention. Among the relatives she visited was her father's brother, William Page Wood, who had already made a mark in the world, and who was to become Lord Chancellor of England in Gladstone's first ministry, be created Baron Hatherley and prove a useful connection for the adult Katie.

Katharine had no formal education, she never went to school—even her brother Evelyn's schooling was limited by financial exigencies until he went to Marlborough at the age of nine—but the Wood household was filled with life, there were musical evenings and everybody played word games. They were particularly fond of capping quotations, punning, and riddles such as, *Question:* How is it that the Athanasian Creed reminds you of a Bengal tiger? *Answer:* Because of its damnation claws, or *Question:* Who is the smallest man in the Bible? *Answer:* Bildad the Shuhite. All the Wood children were encouraged to develop their individual talents; Katie's then lay in a musical direction, and she was so pleased with her setting of Longfellow's poem *Weariness* that she sent the author a copy. Longfellow replied saying it was the best setting of *Weariness* that he had heard, and thus encouraged, Katie persuaded Boosey's, the London music firm, to publish it and two other of her songs, but she lacked sufficient talent or the concentrated drive to continue and that was the limit of her artistic success. In addition to the home-made entertainments, her mother's personality and artistic interests brought many visitors to Rivenhall, among them Edward Landseer, Anthony Trollope and George Meredith. As a member of the household, however young, Katie was expected to participate in its social and intellectual life. The Victorian precept that children should be seen and not heard (or neither seen nor heard) had not rooted in her childhood, and in any case the Woods were not that sort of family. Katie matured in an atmosphere in which intelligent conversation was the order of the

[7]

day, in which she heard what Tennyson had said at dinner the other night, and in which because of the participation expected of her she acquired an early confidence.

Apart from the cerebral pleasures to be had at Rivenhall there was plenty of physical enjoyment, chiefly riding. Katharine had her own pony from an early age, originally because she was considered to be a delicate child, with a weakness of the spine and lungs, and it was thought the healthy outdoor exercise would strengthen both. It appears to have done so because she survived an immense amount of stress and lived to a good old age. Hunting was another pastime followed at Rivenhall, with the hounds meeting frequently at the house, and it was as much for the hunting as for the intellectual delights that Anthony Trollope paid his visits. Despite his skill as a horseman Trollope was not the most welcome of equestrian guests as he was so short-sighted that he rode dangerously close to the preceding horse and an accident was always feared. Katie herself, much as she enjoyed riding, was not an enthusiastic fox-hunter because she felt sorry for the foxes, and while the hunt was meeting at the house she would slip away and try to spoil the scent by tramping over the day's intended covers, and once the hunt was up she would shout 'View Hulloa' in the wrong direction. Katie was not dependent for company on visitors coming to Rivenhall, there were the visits to London with her father, there were other visits to the capital *en famille* when Sir John and Lady Wood would stay at the fashionable Thomas's Hotel in Berkeley Square, and there were frequent visits to her sister Emma's house at Belhus which was always overflowing with a variety of guests.

As Katie grew up her surviving siblings numbered six, Maria, Francis, Charles, Evelyn, Emma and Anna. Maria—known to the family as Polly—was years older; she married an army officer two years after Katharine was born and went with him to India. There she had some hair-raising adventures during the Mutiny and in adversity she displayed some of the Wood initiative by walking herself and her children several hundred miles to safety, bearing a phial of poison for each in case of capture. Otherwise she was described as 'sweet, placid and rather stout', and on her return to England she lived in Oxford where her husband, Colonel Chambers, became Professor of Hindustani. She suffered much heart-break with the early deaths of several of her children—not as stoically as Lady Wood would have wished—and her influence on Katie's life was minimal. Francis, or Frank, was an officer in the 17th

Foot. He married when Katie was nine and his influence on his youngest sister's life was similarly not great. However, it was on a visit in 1860 to Aldershot, where Frank was stationed, that Katie was first introduced to another young army officer, a Cornet in the 18th Hussars whose name was William Henry O'Shea, so he affected her life to that degree. The next brother Charles, or Charlie as he was known in the current fashion for 'ie' endings to Christian names, was a good classical scholar, but he suffered from poor health and became a farmer, on the premise that an outdoor life would be good for him. He did not marry until 1864 and as he farmed at Wakes Colne Hall, near Mark's Tey in Essex, Katie saw a fair amount of him and their relationship was then most amicable.

The three siblings with whom she had the greatest contact were Emma, Evelyn and Anna. Emma married Sir Thomas Barrett Lennard when Katharine was eight, but despite the age gap the two sisters then had a great rapport and as Emma's husband was a rich man who adored her and adored entertaining, and as the Barrett Lennard country seat was near Rainham in Essex, they saw a good deal of each other. The Barrett Lennard house was a historic mansion called Belhus—Queen Elizabeth I was reputed to have slept there en route from London to Tilbury to deliver her Armada speech. It lay in hundreds of acres of parkland, and the young Katie spent a considerable amount of time in its beautiful environment, enjoying the lavish Barrett Lennard hospitality; it was at a Belhus week-end party that she remet William Henry O'Shea. By all accounts, Emma Barrett Lennard was the sweetest-natured of the Wood children, she was also a talented lady who inherited her mother's musical ability. She wrote hundreds of songs such as 'Plymouth Hoe' which achieved great popularity in their day, she set to music an equal number of poems, including some written by her mother and her sister Anna, Tennyson's 'Crossing the Bar', William Allingham's verses 'Up the airy mountain, Down the rushy glen, We daren't go a-hunting for fear of little men', as well as works by Bret Harte, Henry Newbolt, Charles Kingsley and H. de Vere Stacpole. In Emma's case, lack of money was not the driving force for her prolific output.

Anna was perhaps the most talented member of the family, and she was said to be one of the cleverest women in England. While this statement, like the one about her mother's genius, might be called an exaggeration, Anna nonetheless had a good brain. In 1865 she and her mother jointly published a book of poems called *Ephemera,* with charming line drawings by Lady Wood, which enjoyed a considerable success (it was originally published under the names of Helen and Gabrielle Carr but later the ladies revealed their true identities). Two years later, encouraged by her mother, Anna published her first novel, *Gardenhurst*, which was an even greater success and ran to several cheap editions. It was swiftly followed by *Broken Toys* and *So Runs the World Away;* both of which were similarly successful, with requests coming in for serial rights in England and overseas. *Gardenhurst,* which was dedicated to 'My Sister Katie (Mrs O'Shea)', is the story of the trials and tribulations (particularly financial) of a large upper-middle-class family living in an unnamed English county resembling Essex, and it remains the most readable of Anna's books. She had a nice clear style and a certain ironic humour, and her characters are well observed and delineated. What is lacking in her writing, as in most people's, is the depth of originality, observation or passion that makes it imperishable, but in her day Anna was a highly regarded author and had many eminent friends with whom she retained contact over the years. Among her eminent associates—nearly all men, despite her affecting to despise the male sex—were George Meredith, Lord Lytton (beloved in Victorian literary circles as 'Owen Meredith'), Sir Garnet Wolseley and W. M. Rossetti.

It was as Anna Steele, not as Anna Wood, that she earned her literary reputation, because in 1858 she married Lieutenant Colonel Steele. Within a week of the marriage she had returned to Rivenhall, and legend within the Wood family says that it was because Anna, sexually ignorant like all well-bred young ladies of the day, was so appalled by what her husband suggested they do together that she bolted back home. Despite Colonel Steele's efforts over a prolonged period to reclaim his wife, she refused to have anything more to do with him, and on occasion his efforts verged on the violent, with Evelyn Wood knocking over a persistent Colonel Steele (and being sued for assault), and Anna being forced to escape via the back door of the house while her husband broke down the front. The Steeles were never divorced or legally separated, and consequently she was always known as Mrs Anna or Mrs Anna C. (for Caroline) Steele. Her family backed her refusal to cohabit with her legal husband and regarded his character without enthusiasm, but Anna herself was not the most agreeable of ladies. She could be charming, she could be excellent company—like most members of her family she loved talking and had an enquiring, not to say inquisitive mind, and was reputed to be a brilliant conversationalist—but Anna had no inclination to please. If she was in a bad mood everybody suffered and even her mother, with whom she had a close bond, said that frequently she was 'as cross as old Scratch'.

Anna adopted a sharply cynical attitude towards life, notably towards the male sex (other than the chosen few), stating, 'All men can be won by flattery and liqueurs', and 'Man is a very limited creature, very limited; I find infinitely more variety in woman.' With regard to her sexual relationship with this limited creature, legend within the family again asserts that as a result of her disastrous honeymoon encounter with Colonel Steele, Anna lived and died a virgin. Whether or not she did remains her secret, but it was not the view taken by her sister Katharine in 1890. In childhood and for much of their adult life, Lady Wood's two youngest daughters were close. Having flown back to the nest so swiftly, Anna was at Rivenhall as Katie grew up and they hunted as a pair, literally and metaphorically. Their companionship always had the edge of many sisterly relationships, with blood-ties and background and some characteristics in common but too many disparate traits to make them devoted friends. In common they had a lack of awareness of other people's reactions and a self-confident disregard for conventions, but Katie liked men, did not possess Anna's sharpness and was inclined to please.

The most famous of the Wood children in his day was Evelyn—Katie became notorious while Anna operated in a field which had less glamour for the Victorian general public. From the moment of Clarissa's death, Lady Wood centred her attention on Evelyn, entertaining boundless hopes for his future greatness and glory. These were not misplaced—the boy who was sent into the navy as a midshipman made the rare switch to the army, won the Victoria Cross in India before he was twenty-one, and went on to become Field Marshal Sir Evelyn Wood. Without his mother's devotion it is doubtful whether he would have survived to win his VC, because while serving as a very junior naval officer in the Crimean War he was stricken by the prevalent typhoid fever. Lady Wood insisted on making the trip to his bedside in Scutari, where she found Evelyn 'a living skeleton, with ulcers on his poor spine and hips, caused by lying so long on skin and bone'. His mother announced that she intended to take her son to England, where she would personally nurse him back to health, but she was told by many people that this was impossible, including the lady organising the hospital in Scutari. Florence Nightingale met her match, however, in Emma Wood. Both ladies came from upper-class backgrounds, both were equally determined and ruthless in their objectives, and Evelyn was escorted back to Rivenhall and health. He was a courageous soldier, a good tactician if lacking the mastery of the grand strategist, and an able administrator. In character he was more like his father than his beloved mother, he lacked her extra driving force, and in his private life he was amiable, not overorganised and later dominated by his wife Paulina.* Throughout much of his life, like his father, Evelyn was in financial difficulties, his army pay never stretching to meet the demands of Paulina and the children; and it was from their father that the Wood children inherited their attitude towards money. They grew up in an atmosphere in which finances were often straitened, in which their mother's personal needs were as Spartan as her general attitude towards life, but the idea that they should cut their cloth according to their ability to pay for it was not imparted to them. Money was a commodity which they needed in largish supply because it was essential to maintain a decent standard of living, and which they expected to turn up because it always had, somehow, when they were children.

It was in this household in which the conventions were not too strongly regarded—the Woods played little part in the general social life of the county, they made their own entertainments, invited their own guests and operated by their own rules—but in which their social status was nonetheless secure and in which self-confidence was taken for granted that Katharine matured. As she approached womanhood, physically she was small and plump, as early photographs show, and as they also show, she was neither conventionally pretty nor beautiful. Her face and features were heavy, but she had a profusion of thick curling hair which struck all observers as delightful, and a lovely English-rose complexion, even if it was the full-blown, height-of-season variety. What the photographs do not show is her vivacity and charm, qualities on which all observers again commented, nor do they show her character. Through her genes she had inherited more of her mother's than her father's traits, much as she adored the latter. She said her father was a fearless man and she acquired that trait from him as much as from her mother, and the general tolerance she so much admired in him was passed on. She was a member of the upper classes, daughter of a Baronet

---

* In a later novel, *Clove Pink,* Anna Steele has a character suspiciously like her brother Evelyn who when told by his sister-in-law 'You are a VC man, why won't you insist on your wishes being carried out?' replies with a smile, 'You ought to know how helpless the boldest man is in his own house.'

and a vicar, but there was no conscious religious or social superiority in her make-up and she was not an explicit snob or bigot. The gentleness and childlike acceptance of life which she described as being part of her father were not transmitted to her (it should be noted that Anna saw these traits in a more selfish light). Katharine was a volatile, restless, demanding person, possessed of the same headstrong determination Lady Wood had showed in her trip to rescue Evelyn from the Crimea, and it was from her mother that she inherited her capacity to love on a grand scale. Both her parents were affectionate but it was the intense, almost obsessive depth of feeling evinced by Lady Wood in her relationship with Evelyn which reappeared in Katharine.

She also matured in a household which was dominated by its females, and from her earliest days she had no sense of being a member of the second sex. Katie was not the material of which suffragettes were made. It never entered her mind to demand her right to vote or to have equal pay or equal opportunity, because she had a strong strain of coquettishness, an acceptance of the traditional female role as sexual playmate and helpmate which Lady Wood's lack of whole-hearted devotion and Sir John's doting companionship helped foster. Similarly, it never occurred to Katharine that she should, as Evelyn once advised her, 'Look lovely and keep your mouth shut.' Women in her world, while accepting their roles as wives and mothers, were not expected to keep their mouths or their minds shut in the process, or hide their talents, nor were they dissuaded from contributing to the family income if necessary. A friend of Lady Wood described Katharine in her young womanhood thus: 'I used to think—indeed still think—Kate a wonder of wonders. I admired her strength of character immensely. Shall I tell you what first of all made me discover that she was weak and mortal? She could not stand still to sing. She must fold her arms and walk about the room in and out among the furniture like a dreamer.' As she faced life as an adult, Katie was a strong-minded lady but she had weaknesses other than restlessness when singing. Life during childhood had perhaps been too kind to her, she expected it to continue to be an exciting, fulfilling, rewarding affair and on neither her emotions nor her expectations had an indulgent father or an unconventional family imposed discipline or cast doubts.

Chapter Two

Life in the early 1860s remained agreeable for Katharine, without stress or strain, with the delights of her awakening sexuality and power as an attractive young woman to make it more interesting. From the end of 1860 until the time of her marriage, an activity which evolved from the Belhus week-end parties engrossed much of her time and buttressed her self-confidence. Most members of the Wood family were emotional and possessed a strain of the dramatic; they also had an abundance of surplus energy, the females in particular. Emma Barrett Lennard composed music and wrote songs, Lady Wood painted, Anna Steele was an author, and they decided to put their combined talents and energies to use by organising their neighbours and fellow guests into amateur theatricals. The mounting and production of plays by amateurs was not then the middle-class English disease it later became, and if initially the plays presented were for home consumption at Belhus or Rivenhall, the family soon decided they had found an activity which satisfied and entertained them and might do the same for a wider audience. Throughout the 1860s the Belhus Dramatic Corps presented their plays, first near home, at Witham, Chelmsford or Colchester, or else in Brighton, then, as their fame spread, at various London theatres, the Westbourne Hall, the New Royalty Theatre, the St James's and St George's theatres.

In the metropolis they received rapturous notices from the leading papers of the day, including *The Times, The Globe,* the *Daily News* and the *Pall Mall Gazette.* This was in part due to their social status, in part to the novelty of the occasions, but the Woods took the whole business very seriously and made sure those friends engaged for the public performances were equally dedicated. They had themselves coached by Mrs Kendall and Marie Wilton (later Lady Bancroft), and they employed a professional to produce their plays, one John Clark, who was a popular favourite at the Strand Theatre. Generally they left little to chance; Charlie Wood's young children were organised into picking flowers which were made into bouquets to be thrown on stage at the end of the public performances, while distinguished audiences were invited—Anthony Trollope wrote to Anna Steele saying, 'Of course we will come. Will you get me 3 stalls for myself, wife and one of my boys? I send a guinea, hoping I don't intrude.'

The repertoire of the Belhus Dramatic Corps did not overtax its audiences' brains; it was mostly light-hearted stuff, including skits on *Romeo and Juliet* and *Kenilworth,* offerings such as *A Thumping Legacy, The Rosebud of Stinging Nettle Farm, The Fishwife, The Eton Boy* and *Beauty and the Brigands.* Among the repertoire was some original material written by Anna Steele, and her three-act play *Under False Colours* was a great success and became one of the company's standards. Katie's roles included Amy Robsart in *Kenilworth,* Violet Hope in *Orange Blossoms,* Lady Capulet in *Romeo and Juliet* and the Princess Badroulboudour in *Aladdin, or the Wonderful Scamp.* (Anna, who plumped for male roles when possible, was Aladdin in this play, which set the pattern for the traditional English Christmas pantomime, and which the Belhus Dramatic Corps was among the first to perform.) Katie said she was frequently nervous before she went on stage, but Lady Wood sat in the wings throughout all performances and gave her the courage to go on. The public performances were of course for charity, and the Belhus Dramatic Corps raised sufficient money to have a lifeboat built, which they placed at the disposal of the National Lifeboat Association. (Trollope further wrote to Anna, 'I don't care twopence about the life-boat. I wish you could take the money to buy hunters for yourself and the brother. Only Charley Wood mustn't ride home first when the fox is found.')

It was in 1862, as the Belhus Dramatic Corps gathered strength, that Katie remet William Henry O'Shea, who, following the current Christian name fashion, was always known as Willie. O'Shea was born in Dublin in 1840, but his father, Henry O'Shea, came from Limerick, and was described by Tim Healy (the Irish nationalist MP who became a bitter enemy of the O'Sheas) as 'a Limerick pawnbroker designated by an unsavoury Gaelic nickname.' With less venom and more accuracy, Henry O'Shea was a member of the impoverished Irish middle class and after childhood he spent little time in Limerick, although he retained some property there. When his father, Willie's grandfather, died, the family affairs were found to be in a hopeless tangle and, being the eldest son, Henry O'Shea took upon himself the task of sorting out the mess. In this endeavour he achieved better results than most eldest sons in a country approaching the Famine Years. Moving to Dublin, he trained as a solicitor and started to specialise in one of Ireland's particular problems, the legal intricacies involved in the salvaging or selling of bankrupt or near-bankrupt estates. In the process he became a wealthy man and married a Tipperary lady, Catherine Quinlan, who on account of her devoutness and services to the Catholic Church had been granted the title Countess of Rome.* They had two children, the elder the boy William Henry, the younger a daughter called Mary. Henry O'Shea, according to Katie Wood, was a hard-working, level-headed but generous, charming and witty man, of whom she was very fond (unfortunately he died before she married his son). Of the Countess O'Shea Katharine said she was 'a bundle of negations wrapped in a shawl', although always a very beautiful shawl. On only two matters, according to Katharine, did the Countess evince definite, affirmative characteristics; they were her devotion to the Roman Catholic Church and her profound sense of Katie Wood's undesirability as a daughter-in-law. Had she shown greater determination to prevent the marriage, Anglo-Irish history might have had a different shape, but she did not, and otherwise, again according to Katharine, the Countess acted as if she were an infirm, feeble nonagenarian instead of a woman on the verge of middle age.

From neither of his parents did Willie O'Shea inherit many characteristics. He lived and died within the Catholic religion, even if he did not marry in it, he was always worried about the good opinion of the Catholic hierarchy, but unlike his mother he could hardly be termed

---

* The practice of the Pope giving temporal titles for services rendered, as the Honours List in England, has more or less died out but it flourished into the twentieth century (cf. the most famous holder of a temporal title, the Irish singer Count John Mc-Cormack).

a devout member of the Church. Unlike his father he was far from a hard-working, level-headed professional gentleman. What he inherited from the latter was the charm and the wit, and perhaps what he inherited from his mother was an illusion of grandeur. She was a Countess of Rome, a being superior to ordinary mortals, but whereas her aspirations were spiritual, an honoured place in an exclusive Catholic heaven, her son's were temporal, an honoured place among the élite of the day. Willie seems to have been more like his Uncle Thaddeus O'Shea, who was always about to train the greatest race-horses Ireland had ever known to win every race in the Western calendar, who was permanently thwarted by fate, permanently insolvent, and permanently borrowing money from his brother Henry. But Thaddeus confined himself to horses whereas his nephew dreamed of influencing men and history and was thus more dangerous.

While Henry O'Shea toiled in his Dublin office, reaping his rewards from the confusion of English-imposed laws, he gave his children an expensive education. Following the tradition of the day—that the upper ranks of Irish society should be educated in England—in September 1850 Willie was sent to St Mary's College, Oscott, at Sutton Coldfield in Warwickshire. Oscott has since become one of the more famous Catholic seminaries in England, but in the 1850s and for many years thereafter it had a twofold purpose, the training of the pastoral clergy and the provision of a thoroughly Catholic education 'to ensure a lofty tone of morality among the pupils, and next, to furnish a liberal education as distinct from what would be described as commercial or professional.' The study of foreign languages held pride of place in this liberal education, but emphasis was also placed on the English language and elocution, an emphasis to which O'Shea responded by acquiring a plummy upper-class English accent which he retained for the rest of his life. Drawing and music were well represented at Oscott, also calisthenics, fencing, boxing, and there was a Chemistry Room considered ahead of its time. Katharine later said that her first husband had no natural taste for learning, but surviving mark books show that during his five years at Oscott O'Shea was well above average in scholastic ability, usually second in the monthly class placings, never less than fifth. During his years at Oscott, in July 1852 the first Provincial Synod of the New Hierarchy met there, and John Henry Newman preached his famous sermon 'The Second Spring'; among his contemporaries was Wilfrid Scawen Blunt, poet, Arabist, passionate campaigner for various causes, including the Irish nationalist one. Blunt later recorded in his diary, 'I was at school at Oscott with O'Shea and hated him as cordially as the Irish do today. He was older than me, a bit of a dandy, a bit of a bully.' Willie's education was filled out by travelling, as the O'Sheas had relations in France and an immediate kinship in Spain where Uncle John O'Shea had settled and founded a bank. He learned to speak French and Spanish fluently, and also acquired the easy, assured confidence of the well-travelled-when-young. On his return to Ireland he was entered for Trinity College, Dublin, which was acceptable to the English-oriented sections of the Irish community as a bastion of the Ascendancy, but his stay at Trinity was brief and in 1858 his father bought him a commission in the 18th Hussars, which was more to his taste. The rank of Cornet was purchased in this expensive, exclusive, sporting regiment, which was happy to welcome the confident, charming young Irishman whose outstanding talent was his skill as a horseman.

It was owing to his ability as a rider that Willie O'Shea was drawn into the Wood, or specifically into the Barrett Lennard, circle. Through the army he knew Frank Wood, later he met Evelyn, who introduced him to Sir Thomas Barrett Lennard, and as the latter shared O'Shea's passion for horses and was always eager to welcome a good horseman to Belhus, Willie became a frequent guest. When at a week-end party in 1862 Evelyn reintroduced Captain O'Shea to his youngest sister, it was with the information that he was 'the only man who sat properly over the fences at the Aldershot races.' Willie was already urbane and self-assured, convinced of his personal worth, certain he would make the world his oyster and discover the largest pearls. He was cynical, travel had opened his eyes and he knew that most people in most countries were fools; his wit was frequently barbed—if the fools could not take care of themselves, *tant pis*. His charm was superficial but he was gay and amusing, and he was good-looking—5 feet 10 inches tall, slim, with curling hair and a superior expression—and as Wilfrid Scawen Blunt noted, he cared about his appearance. When Katie remet him he was dressed in the height of 1860s fashion, a brown velvet coat, a sealskin waistcoat, black- and white-checked trousers and what she described as 'an enormous carbuncle and diamond pin in his curiously folded scarf.' Her comment then upon her future husband was that after being so much the companion of older men she enjoyed his youthful good looks and vivacity, but she was probably more smitten than her words implied.

After the reintroduction, Katie and Willie met quite frequently, as he was among those roped into the amateur theatricals (a young officer in a fashionable regiment in the peace-time British army of the day had as many idle hours to fill as his civilian friends). Willie did not participate in the public performances, perhaps because he could not guarantee to be free for the weeks of serious rehearsal or because his acting ability failed to measure up to the exacting Wood standards. Family history says that O'Shea was coached by a leading professional actor but, in the face of the overripe vowels acquired at Oscott, the task was abandoned as hopeless. However, he played Queen Elizabeth in a production of *Kenilworth* at Rivenhall, and on his first entrance some of his brother officers in the audience started to sing 'O *She* is a jolly good fellow', which did not please Willie, and picking up his skirts he stalked off the stage in high dudgeon. If he was noted for his ready wit, he did not possess a sense of humour, particularly when the joke was on him. Punning on the name O'Shea was not confined to his brother officers, and Katie related that at Belhus one night her sister Emma was organising people for dinner and when asked who should be Katie's escort replied, 'O *she* shall go in with *O'She*.'* At Belhus, Katie said the pun ruffled her sense of importance and it might indicate that the Wood family did not rate the gallant Captain too highly; Katie was the baby of the family and he was sufficiently amusing to be her dinner partner but no more. On the other hand, no attempt was made by the Woods to prevent a relationship maturing between the two young people, and they spent an increasing amount of time together. They were at Belhus for the best part of a summer, a perfect one according to Katie's memory, with sun-filled days and long golden evenings, and *she* going into dinner with *O'She* became the accepted pattern rather than a slightly contemptuous witticism.

Willie attended as many of the public performances of the Belhus Dramatic Corps as possible, his attention focussed on the youngest Miss Wood, whom he would afterwards present with beautiful bouquets over which hovered jewelled bees and butterflies, and as a family rhyme indicates, he became a welcome guest at Rivenhall, too— 'Anna prepared a sop in the pan, All to do honour to Katie's young man.' When they were parted he bombarded her with a profusion of poetic letters, and when about this time he had a serious accident when

---

* For those who believe the correct Irish pronunciation of the surname is *O'Shay*, it should be noted that Willie himself did not. He pronounced it *O'Shee* and considered anybody who did otherwise to be an abject ignoramus.

riding on the Downs outside Brighton (the 18th Hussars being currently stationed at Preston Barracks), Katie related how upset she was. As soon as he was fit to be moved from the barracks hospital, Willie was taken to the Barrett Lennards' Brighton house (as well as owning Belhus, they had a house in Brighton), and as he started to recuperate he was driven to Belhus, where Katie was among his first visitors. During his convalescence he presented her with a beautiful locket and slipped a ring onto her finger, and she was 'happy to know how much Willie cared for me.'

By 1864 O'Shea had become a regular guest at Belhus and Rivenhall, and in mid-Victorian days even unconventional families like the Woods did not encourage young men to hover persistently round their daughters without thoughts of marriage. However, being a flirtatious young lady, Katie had other admirers, she announced openly how many dozens of Valentines she received each year, and when a proprietorial Willie frightened off one young man by kissing her smack on the lips in public, she was not pleased, as she liked the gentleman in question. Whether Sir John saw Captain O'Shea as his favourite daughter's husband is difficult to ascertain—Lady Wood seems always to have had reservations—but there was one grave problem. The gentleman was a Roman Catholic. He was not a particularly ardent one, he did not trouble his hosts' sensibilities by raising the subject or going to mass over-frequently while staying at Belhus or Rivenhall. But nonetheless he was a Catholic and there was never any suggestion that he would recant the faith of his fathers, notably of his mother, while Katie came from a long line of English Protestants and was the daughter of an Anglican vicar. Probably O'Shea was regarded as Katie's young man, whom she might one day marry, and the difficulties the match would entail were not faced.

In the next twelve months, two deaths occurred which helped clarify or precipitate the relationship. First O'Shea's father died, then Katharine's. Willie had by this time, early in 1865, left the army, not because he had wanted to but because even his indulgent parent had finally refused to pay any more of his bills. When Henry O'Shea had first bought his son the commission in the 18th Hussars, he had unwisely given him the advice 'First become a smart officer; secondly, do what the other men do and send the bills in to me.' Willie had followed this advice to the hilt and thousands of pounds'-worth of mess bills and bills for uniforms and bills for the sporting life had poured in to Henry

O'Shea, who had duly paid them. When the cost started to become prohibitive, O'Shea senior called his son home and gave him a lecture about thrift and responsibility, but he then proceeded to buy him the higher commission, the rank of Captain, in the hope that the added responsibility would produce the desired effect. It did nothing of the sort. Willie continued to follow his father's initial advice and eventually he was called home again, and told that an allowance would be made but the regimental bills could no longer be met, otherwise his father would be bankrupt. A temporarily contrite Willie thereupon decided he would cut his cloth according to his allowance, leave the regiment with the rank of Captain and embark upon the task of becoming self-supporting. With his father's death he returned to Dublin and for some time saw little of Katie Wood.

Katharine's later account of her emotions at this period indicates that she was not unduly perturbed by the departure of the young man who had been her escort and companion over the last few years. She said that when she did meet Willie O'Shea again, at a small private ball in London, she felt a curious distaste towards him. This might have been because he had in the interim months grown a set of the fashionable mutton-chop whiskers, which she found most unattractive, or it could have been premarital aversion, or it could have been a retrospective adjustment of her emotions. Because, although she herself implied that she had never really loved Willie, Wood family history insists that at this juncture she was at the very least deeply infatuated, if not hopelessly in love. In the event, the two young people were not immediately re-thrust into each other's company, as Willie went to Spain while Katie returned to Rivenhall. Then, in the autumn of 1865, Sir John and Lady Wood, Anna and Katie went on a prolonged visit to Belhus, at the start of which Sir John travelled each Saturday to Cressing to take the Sunday service there, returning to Belhus on the Monday morning, but after Christmas he became too ill to undertake the cross-country journeys. By February 1866 his strength was ebbing and for the last fortnight of his life his beloved youngest daughter stayed with him constantly, sleeping on a sofa at the foot of the great bed in which he lay, the bed in which Queen Elizabeth was reputed to have laid her royal bones in 1588. Katharine was with him at the end, his hands tightly clasped in hers as they recited the Lord's Prayer together, then the grip relaxed and her father was dead.

The grief-stricken Katharine was given an immediate sedative, and when she awoke from her drugged sleep, the people on whom she set eyes were her sister Emma Barrett Lennard and Willie O'Shea. The family had telegraphed to him in Spain, which shows how large a place they considered he held in Katie's affections, even if they did not regard him as the automatic choice for her husband. (And if Katie's statement is accurate rather than romantically tinted, it must have been a strong sedative, as it took more than a few hours to travel from Madrid to Essex). To comfort the stricken Katharine, Willie brought with him a King Charles spaniel which proved to be the first in a long line of beloved dogs, but he had to return to Spain and she was left to face the chilling fact of her father's death, the first real sorrow she had known in her life. She was not alone, she had her family round her at Belhus, but she was without a particular male on whom she could lean, with whom she could share her sorrow, and despite her self-confidence she had grown up to trust and rely upon the male sex and she needed a man to fill the vacuum created by her father's death.

A more immediate problem was finance. Sir John's demise had left Lady Wood near-penniless, and Katharine related an illuminating anecdote from the many discussions which ensued at Belhus about her mother's future. Emma Barrett Lennard said, 'We must sell the cow, and, of course, the pig', which made everybody laugh but illustrated the Wood attitude towards adjusting to a reduced income. In the event, drastic reduction was not necessary for Lady Wood, as her sister Maria—Aunt Ben—settled a substantial yearly income on the bereaved lady. Having married the two Woods, uncle and nephew, and thus established an extra bond, Maria and Emma had remained close all their lives, but while John Page Wood lived until 1866, Benjamin Wood had died in 1845 and Aunt Ben had therefore already been a widow for twenty years. But she was an extremely wealthy widow, and she was childless, and on his death-bed Benjamin had instructed her, 'You will be kind to John and Emma, and the children—they will probably want assistance, and as far as you can I should wish you to give it.' Over the years John and Emma and the children had wanted assistance, which Aunt Ben had generously given, and the children in particular were already in the habit of looking towards her as their financial fairy godmother. However, Emma Wood did not sit back and calmly accept her sister's charity, immediately welcome as it was, but she decided she should do something about earning an income for herself. It was after Sir John's death, at the age of sixty-six, that she embarked upon a new career as a novelist. In the next twelve years she wrote (and had published) fourteen novels, all of them three-volumed affairs in the current fashion for weighty reading matter, apart from editing a book of poetry, *Leaves from the Poet's Laurels,* which included verses by her friend George Meredith, and translating Victor Hugo's *L'Homme qui rit* under the English title *By Order of the King.* One of Emma Wood's novels, *Sorrows on the Sea,* created a scandal on account of its subject matter, the evils of baby farming, and of the passionately indignant manner in which the author dealt with the callous treatment, too often leading to death, of the unwanted babies who were farmed out. William Page Wood, by then Baron Hatherley, was so appalled that his sister-in-law should have written a book on such an indelicate matter in such a forthright manner that he bought up every available copy and had them burned.

While her mother and sister adjusted to life at Rivenhall without Sir John, immersing themselves in their literary output, their immediate financial worries secured by Aunt Ben, Katie's future had a bleaker aspect. She did not possess her mother's or sister's talent or artistic drive (nor, in fact, did Anna have the same burning energy and concentration as Lady Wood; it was not until 1877 that she produced her next novel, *Condoned,* then there was a long gap before *Clove Pink* and *Lesbia* appeared in 1894 and 1896 respectively, though she did some journalism as well). Katharine's need and talent lay in making a man happy and successful, in being a partner in a rewarding relationship. To hand was a man who wanted to marry her, whom she found charming and attractive and who was filled with grandiose schemes for the rich, rewarding future she craved, he being Willie O'Shea.

It was later said by Tim Healy that it was Evelyn Wood who arranged the match with 'his subaltern', that the subaltern replied that he was too poor to marry but 'was assured Miss Wood possessed £30,-000' and thereupon promptly agreed to the wedding. This was nonsense, since O'Shea was not Evelyn's subaltern, and if Aunt Ben's will was known to be made out in favour of the Wood children she was a formidable lady and anything might cause her to alter her will, which indeed it did, with disastrous results. Willie O'Shea proposed to Katie Wood of his own volition and because he cared for her, although her membership of a distinguished, upper-class English family with a wealthy relation in the background was no handicap. She accepted him because she cared for him, although other factors influenced her and one of those was finance. On their marriages, Aunt Ben gave each of the Wood children £5,000, then a *very* good sum of money, the exception being Evelyn, who married an Irish Catholic lady, Paulina, a union of which Protestant Aunt Ben did not approve. Katie was intending to marry an Irish Catholic but she was not proposing to sanctify the union in a Catholic church, and the thought that she would acquire £5,000 on her marriage and thereby some financial security and independence probably influenced her decision to accept Captain O'Shea's proffered hand. When Katie told her family she intended to marry Willie O'Shea she ran into opposition from her mother, which again probably strengthened her decision because she was as headstrong as Lady Wood. Despite the fact that O'Shea had been a welcome guest over the years, when the moment came, Lady Wood objected partly on religious grounds, partly because she did not personally like him, partly because he had no secure income.

Katharine overcame her mother's objections and on 24 January 1867,* less than a week before her twenty-second birthday and in his twenty-eighth year, Katharine Wood and William Henry O'Shea were married in Brighton, at the parish church of St Nicholas, according to the rites and ceremonies of the Church of England. For the sake of Aunt Ben's £5,000 dowry, Willie O'Shea put his immortal soul in some jeopardy by marrying outside the faith and failing to take one of the four main sacraments of the Catholic Church, but in 1867 the English Catholic hierarchy did not insist that the faithful married within the Church, he would not have needed to have obtained a special dispensation, and as long as both parties were baptised the marriage was valid in Catholic eyes. It seems probable that Katie agreed to a compromise on the religious issue; they would marry in a Protestant church but any children of the union would be brought up as Catholics. Whether the Wood family knew about the compromise is doubtful, but as Katie did not immediately produce a child, by the time she did, the matter had become blurred. The devoutly Catholic Countess O'Shea and her daughter Mary naturally did not attend the wedding, but several members of the Wood family were present, with Anna Steele acting as her sister's witness and Emma Barrett Lennard providing the trousseau. At the

---

* In her memoirs, Katharine gives her wedding date as 25 January 1867, but a copy of the marriage certificate confirms that it was 24 January, and Willie got the date right in his divorce court evidence.

ceremony, Katharine was nearly married to the wrong man, as Willie and his best man, Robert Cunningham Grahame, were in incorrect positions, and the vicar actually asked Mr Cunningham Grahame if he would take this woman for his lawful wedded wife and was somewhat surprised when he replied, 'No, no, no.'

The marriage could be called a love match. Nobody had forced Katie and Willie into each other's arms, and she did not marry him for his money or his position, as he had comparatively little of either. The honeymoon was spent at Holbrook Hall, lent to the newly-weds by Sir Seymour Fitzgerald, but it was not the most rapturously happy of events. This does not appear to have been because the young couple found the sexual side of marriage difficult or unsatisfactory—not that Katharine overtly mentions sexual matters in her memoirs, no well-bred Victorian lady would. The reasons for the disenchantment were that Holbrook Hall was enormous and staffed by an army of servants, Katie found the ensuing ritual wearisome, the weather was foul and as she said, 'We were, or rather Willie was, too much in awe of convention to ask anyone to come and relieve our ennui.' Their boredom in each other's company without the distraction of fellow guests did not augur well for the future, although Katie made no comment on their early ennui. Once the boring honeymoon was finished, the couple returned to London but only for a brief visit. At the time of the marriage Willie was without an occupation but he was always filled with plans, he had at the moment some cash to hand, and there was a definite proposition in view. The sale of his army commission had brought in £4,000, although it is doubtful that he had the entire sum intact in 1867, as money and Willie parted company as soon as they met, but on his recent visit to Spain he had been in touch with his uncle John O'Shea, who had offered him a partnership in the Madrid bank of O'Shea and Company if he would invest £4,000 therein. This was too good an opportunity to miss, the bank was fairly prosperous, banking was a gentlemanly pursuit, Willie spoke fluent Spanish and Katie had her £5,000. Accordingly, Captain and Mrs O'Shea and the King Charles spaniel set forth for Spain, to start a new life which would bring them riches. Before they embarked, Katharine was honoured with a visit from the Countess O'Shea and her daughter Mary, the ladies having reluctantly accepted the marriage once it was a *fait accompli,* perhaps encouraged by the news that any children would be baptised and educated as Catholics. Katharine's feelings towards her mother-in-law have been suggested; she disliked her, finding

[25]

the Countess narrow, bigoted and devoid of humour. Her feelings towards Mary were less cold, she said she could have liked her sister-in-law had she been met half-way; but while the Countess was mainly negative, Mary was a positive, quick-tempered woman whose energies, according to Katharine, were directed to producing 'bad Catholics out of indifferent Protestants'. As Katie did not like being ordered about and had no intention of becoming a Catholic, their rapport was not high. The intense, devout, humourless O'Shea in-laws were not to have much influence on Katharine's life. After the London visit and a further encounter in Paris, where Mary had settled, she made sure that she saw little of the two ladies.

The young O'Sheas broke their journey in Paris to stay with Mary, and were then forced to break it in Biarritz because Katharine was taken ill with whooping-cough which developed into pneumonia. During her illness she was well cared for and showed two of her strongest characteristics, her abilities to inspire affection and to attract male attention. In Biarritz it was a young Basque chambermaid who became her slave, sitting by her bedside night after night during the worst phase of the pneumonia, and while she was convalescing, the elderly Duc de San Luca was a constant escort. During their prolonged sojourn in Biarritz, Wilfrid Scawen Blunt met up with the young couple, but when he came to record the incident, at a time when any information on the notorious O'Sheas had become of interest, he could only recall that Katharine was an attractive woman and that he still did not like Willie with his 'pretentious, affecting English ways'. When Katharine was fully recovered from her illness, the journey continued, and for one who had never before been out of her own country and whose knowledge of England was confined to the southern counties, everything was strange and wonderful. She was fascinated by the rugged grandeur of the coast round Biarritz, by the pine woods and rocky cliffs, by an exquisite sunset over Hendaye, the most beautiful she had ever seen, by the towering majesty of the Pyrenees, and as the train steamed south towards Madrid, by the acres of vineyards and the sense of space one does not find in the encapsuled prettiness of the southern English landscape.

Life in Madrid was enjoyable. Willie was popular with his Spanish-Irish relations and their friends, and Katie basked in the reflected admiration. There was a fair amount of social life, parties and the fashionable midnight promenades in the Prado, and the vivacious, attractive, self-confident young Englishwoman attracted her share of admiration. Katie's determined, unconventional streak was not as greatly appreciated; she was severely chided for appearing in the streets in the mornings and told of the Spanish proverb 'Only the English and the dogs go out in the day.' Such disapproval did not deter her, and she spent many happy daylight hours alone in the Prado Gallery, admiring the paintings, or walking through the Retiro Gardens.

The Madrid in which Willie and Katie O'Shea enjoyed the first months of their married life was in a state of ferment. For years there had been a series of short-lived ministries in Spain, within the last year there had been two uprisings, martial law had been declared and when the *cortes* was eventually resummoned in 1867 it merely voted away its rights, while the behaviour of Queen Isabella was growing steadily more outrageous, and the country was on the brink of civil war. Katie always denied that she was 'a political lady', but she had grown up in a household which was involved in the political scene, as a child she had trotted round with her father to election meetings, and while she was in Spain she evinced interest in its political affairs. She was fascinated that the merest mention of the government could lead to a brawl or that a quiet stroll in the Prado could be shattered by a volley of politically motivated bullets. While it is true to say that she was not 'a political lady' in that of her own volition she engaged herself in either English or Spanish politics, the interest in how countries were governed and how power was exercised was always present, and she did not require much encouragement once the opportunity for personal involvement was presented.

After nearly a year in Madrid, Willie O'Shea had a quarrel with his Uncle John which led him to withdraw his money from the bank, and shortly afterwards the young couple packed their bags and returned to England. O'Shea retained a financial interest in Spain, he had made many contacts during his year at the bank and he was to spend a considerable part of his life in the country, dabbling in its politics and constantly hoping to make his fortune there. Katie bade farewell to her Madrid relations with some regret, she said she found the admixture of Spanish and Irish blood most charming in its results, but on the whole she was not sorry to be going home. The Spanish sojourn had been a pleasant interlude which had opened her eyes to wider horizons, but her roots were in England and her future lay in her own country.

Chapter Three

On their return to England, the O'Sheas possessed a reasonable amount of money, and after much discussion they decided to invest it in a stud farm. Willie liked horses, he was an excellent rider, he considered himself knowledgeable about all facets of horsemanship, including the breeding of bloodstock, and again it was an occupation suitable for a gentleman. As Katharine also liked horses, she gave the idea her full blessing, and after some searching Willie found a property which seemed admirably suited to their personal and business requirements. It was called Benington Park and lay deep in rural Hertfordshire, some three miles from Stevenage and eight miles from the county town of Hertford. Benington Park, which lies just outside the village, is a late-Georgian house, not as large as Rivenhall Place but very pleasant, with extensive grounds, kitchen gardens, rose bowers, and lawns and wooded parkland at the rear. What attracted the O'Sheas to the house, apart from its comfortable proportions, were its riding facilities and associations. Benington Races were in their day famous, George IV was reputed to have stayed at the house and to have galloped along the ride, and the estate included stables, loose boxes and several paddocks, with cottages for the grooms.

When the O'Sheas arrived to take up residence in the spring of 1868, the parkland was carpeted with snowdrops, which delighted

Katie, and in considerable style they settled themselves in. She had two personal servants, a French maid called Caroline who had been with her in Madrid, and her old nurse from Rivenhall, Lucy or 'Loolee', as she was known to the Wood children. In addition there was the household staff—butler, cook and maids—and the gardening staff, while Willie employed a stud groom and twenty 'lads'. He also invested heavily in good breeding mares, and from the start the expense of running Benington Park was high. That their capital was limited, that it would take time to build up a successful stud, that it might be advisable to begin in less lavish fashion did not occur to either Willie or Katie. They also entertained a good deal; dinner parties were, as Katharine said, 'the chief form of social intercourse in the county' (for her stratum of society, that was) and the urbane Captain and his charming wife were soon in demand and expected to return the hospitality. Katharine said she found most such dinner parties excruciatingly boring and started to hide the invitations from Willie, who was eager to be in with the county. Katharine's own dinner parties were less boring, as she liked to mix together people who would not normally have met, and she gained considerable enjoyment from introducing the staid matrons and primly well-bred county girls to Willie's breezy, hail-fellow-well-met racing friends. She said she considered it one of her life's achievements that the young girls *actually enjoyed* themselves at her dinner parties.

After a short while at Bennington Park, the first tremors were registered in the fabric of the O'Shea marriage. Willie began to disappear for days on end, leaving Katie to cope with the running of the stud farm and to receive dinner guests by herself (not an accepted custom in Hertfordshire county circles). When he turned up he was full of charm and contrition and plausible excuses, but his absences grew more frequent, and his attention to the running of the business more erratic, and Katharine adapted to her growing responsibilities and to the solitude. It was during these solitary nights that she learned how to handle a gun, an accomplishment which years later surprised one of her few supporters. Willie was sufficiently thoughtful to insist that she had some sort of protection during his absences and at first it was a large dog, but when the animal half-killed a tramp he taught her how to use his gun. Thereafter, whenever she woke in the night she would fire it through the window, in case there was anybody lurking about, a habit which not surprisingly earned her the reputation of being a perfect terror with a gun. Left so much to her own devices, she proved to be an efficient lady, capable of taking decisions, and thereby the managerial side of her nature was strengthened, but Katie had her strongly feminine side, too, which wanted to be cosseted and to make a nest for its mate. Willie pampered her when he was present, but he was increasingly absent and she resented being left on her own to take the decisions. She wanted a man who would consult her in some ways and dictate to her in others, she wanted him to be there when she needed him, but most of all she wanted to be able to respect and admire him for his sterling masculine qualities. While her admiration for the witty, debonair, ex-cavalry officer she had married could be easily touched, her respect for Willie O'Shea was beginning to curl at the edges. She was discovering that he was not as capable or reliable as she was, and the discoveries did not please her. Willie in his turn did not understand words like 'responsibility' or 'reliability', he liked having an attractive wife whom others admired, but that his life-style should change now that he was married, that he should cease doing what he wanted, that he owed Katie a share in his life did not occur to him. He was only too delighted that she could shoulder such burdens as he found wearisome.

By the beginning of 1869 the problems of life at Benington Park were assuming an alarming aspect, as an overdraft mounted daily and the bills poured in. Apart from the expenses involved in living in style, entertaining in style and trying to raise blue-blooded mares, there was a further expense of stabling other people's horses. This was supposed to be a business proposition, but the horses thus lodged belonged to friends of Willie and he showed a singular reluctance in asking them to pay their bills so that he could meet some of his, and debt-collecting was not a chore Katharine considered adding to her responsibilities. Temporarily, in the middle of 1869, she had a respite from the increasing pressures of life at Benington Park, although it was not of a pleasant nature. Her eldest brother, Frank, was dying of consumption and Katharine returned to Rivenhall Place to help nurse him through his last distressing months. Frank was given large doses of morphine to deaden his pain, as a result of which he became a drug addict, an occurrence not unusual in Victorian times, with doctors unaware of the nature of addiction and the effect of drugs. Katie related how she sat with Frank in his bedroom at Rivenhall night after night, as he alternatively cried for release from his pain and fought with the shadows and terrors induced by the morphine. With Frank dead and this lacerating experience behind her, Katharine returned to Benington Park. By now she was pregnant.

Back home she found the scene only slightly more cheerful than it had been at Rivenhall, as in her absence Willie had indulged in a heavy betting spree in the hope that he would recuperate his fortunes. The hope had inevitably proved illusory, and the betting losses, added to the already existing bills, made it imperative that the O'Sheas sell their stock. As she watched the string of mares being led away to the station, en route for sale at Tattersalls, Katie cried bitterly while Willie stood miserably by her side. She cried even more bitterly and Willie looked even more miserable when the mares came back again, having failed to realise a single worthwhile bid. There was only one course left open to them, bankruptcy, but even in this catastrophe, brought on their own heads by themselves, there were more silver linings than most extravagant young couples would find.

The Woods rallied round the sunken ship, with Sir Thomas Barrett Lennard buying the majority of the mares for £500 (he then turned them loose in the park at Belhus), Aunt Ben assuming the role of fairy godmother, and Uncle William (Baron Hatherley, Lord Chancellor of England) producing a substantial cheque. The Barrett Lennard money enabled the O'Sheas to pay off their immediate debts, including the back wages to the servants, Aunt Ben's contribution was to rent a house in Brighton for her roofless, heavily pregnant niece, while Uncle William was approached not by the O'Sheas but by the enterprising young solicitor who was endeavouring to sort out Willie's bankruptcy. The solicitor suggested that the Captain be given a lucrative state appointment by the Lord Chancellor, but Uncle William, like Mr. Gladstone and other eminent gentlemen in years to come, considered there was no high office available suited to the talents of Willie O'Shea. However, he did produce the helpful cheque from his own personal account.

While her husband was trying to solve his financial problems, at the beginning of 1870, in the Brighton house rented by Aunt Ben, Katharine gave birth to her first child, a boy who was christened Gerard William Henry. It was a difficult birth, which the circumstances of having no fixed abode or income and the absence of her husband did not improve, and Katie was ill for some months after the accouchement, but she had her sister Emma close at hand (Aunt Ben had rented the house in Brighton because the Barrett Lennards were currently in residence in the town), and she had her two devoted servants and her mother, who came down from Rivenhall. Later in the summer of 1870, Aunt Ben rented a cottage for Katharine and the baby at Patcham, then a charming village to the north of Brighton, and there she was able to have her pony. (He had been salvaged from the bankruptcy proceedings at Benington, as he was old and of little value to anybody except Katie, and a Hertfordshire neighbour had kept him until such time as she again had space for him.) Life at Patcham was healthy and pleasant, Katharine enjoyed walking and riding and she was able to indulge both pursuits across the Sussex Downs, but it was also dull and lonely. Willie appeared infrequently, spending most of his time in London, doing what precisely Katharine did not specify other than a vague mention of business affairs, and it was at this time that Lady Wood made her feelings clear about her youngest daughter's husband when she wrote, 'Kate did not pay me the compliment of leaving O'Shea. He only gets there once a week.' Would that Kate had left her husband in the early 1870s, but while it was an action Lady Wood in similar circumstances might have taken, and one that her daughter Anna had taken, it was not a step Katie was likely to have considered seriously. Apart from needing a man more than either her mother or her sister did, she retained an affection for her errant husband. Nonetheless, the situation was not pleasant; in the reduced financial circumstances Katharine could not enjoy the life-style she had managed at Benington, and there was the nagging worry of where the money to enjoy any sort of life was to come from. Aunt Ben had always been generous but at this point she was a personally unknown quantity, and there was no guarantee that she would continue to pay her niece's expenses.

During the Patcham days, on her lonely walks across the Downs, Katie became friendly with a woman older than herself, a sad, quiet, contained person who hinted at past tragedy. Eventually she learned that her new friend had figured in a notorious divorce scandal, and the next time she met the woman Katie told her how disgracefully she considered society had treated her, whereupon the woman replied in language which would not have disgraced a penny romance (that is if one accepts Katharine's reportage as accurate), 'Little fool, I have gambled in love and have won, and those who win must pay as well as those who lose. Never gamble, you very young thing, if you can help it; but if you do, be sure that the stake is the only thing in the world to you, for only that will make it worth the winning and paying.' At this juncture of her existence, Katharine probably had no thoughts of gambling all for love. She was dissatisfied with life, which was failing to measure up to her youthful expectations, but how it could be turned into a stimulating, rewarding experience she did not know. However, after a few more months of Sussex seclusion, with Willie's visits growing more infrequent, she took some remedial action and said that if his business necessitated his spending so much time in London she would join him there. Finances at this time in 1871 were still limited, whatever Willie's business in London was, it was not being successful, and the O'Sheas had to settle for a small, dingy house on the Harrow Road, not far from Kensal Green cemetery. After the spaciousness and comfort of Rivenhall Place and Benington Park, compared even to the rented house in Brighton and the cottage in Patcham, it was a depressing residence, and shortly after they settled in, Willie was taken seriously ill. He developed some sort of lump on his neck and an emergency operation was performed by the doctor, with Katie efficiently acting as surgeon's assistant. Also about this time, her son became ill and Lady Wood wrote, 'Gerardie is in great danger—Kate's baby—and Kate is half mad with terror.' (Gerard, too, suffered from the fashion for 'ie' endings, in his case most unfortunately.) In these days, Katie learned some of the harsher facts of life, what it was like to have a small child to look after as well as a sick man (although she still had the faithful Caroline and Lucy to help her), what it was like to be at one's wit's end for money and to be personally dunned for it. Her charm managed to stave off the demands of a Jewish money-lender to whom Willie owed considerable sums, and she mentioned that he was Jewish because his behaviour seemed kinder and more considerate than many Christians she knew, and while Jews were supposed to be sharp about money, Christians were allegedly not.

Once again, a silver lining was just around the corner. Suddenly in 1872 Willie's prospects improved, due to what set of circumstances Katharine did not specify, and for this particular period of their lives one has to rely mainly upon her narrative, as the O'Sheas were then of interest to few people and when they became of riveting interest nobody bothered to sift through these years in detail. Whatever caused the improvement in the financial situation, a considerable amount of money was involved because the O'Sheas moved into a house in Beaufort Gardens in Chelsea, where they immediately engaged a large staff, including a butler and several maids, and started to entertain again on a lavish scale. It was at this juncture that Anna reappeared in Katie's life. Since their father's death she had lived at Rivenhall with Lady Wood, and Rivenhall was to remain her base until she could no longer

[33]

afford to keep it up, but Anna had become a figure in the literary world, she was earning a good income and she decided she needed a London house. Consequently, she rented a house in Buckingham Gate, a fashionable area lying just to the south of Green Park, not too far from Beaufort Gardens. Thus the two sisters were able to see a good deal of each other. According to Katie's hints, Anna also saw a fair amount of Willie O'Shea, whom she included in her short list of bearable males, and he began to regard the inquisitive Anna, who could be comforting when she chose, as his confidante, especially when he was having problems with her sister.

In 1872 and for a couple of years thereafter, there were few overt signs of problems with Katharine, mainly because there was again sufficient money to oil the creaking joints of the relationship. But however much Katie kept a front to the outside world and refused to pay her mother the compliment of leaving O'Shea, in the recesses of her soul she was not happy. She said it was at this time that she first began to drift away from her husband, metaphorically speaking, and literally to indulge in the habit of long solitary walks through the London parks. She was no more contented with the social whirl than she had been in the rural seclusion of Patcham or in the middle-class dinginess of the Harrow Road. She said she hated 'society' as such, the formal dinner parties, the dressing up, the irksome conventions which had to be observed, and viewing the ease with which she later settled into a life bereft of 'society', her statement can be accepted as accurate. For most Victorian females of the middle or upper classes who wanted to participate in a life other than child-bearing and house-minding, the outlet had to be through a male, and her husband was not providing the outlets she desired. He was thoughtless and irresponsible as far as his family was concerned, but these deficiencies might have been overlooked had he proved efficient in creating a position for himself. Unfortunately, he had not done so, and although he remained convinced that there was a pot of gold at the end of the rainbow, Katie was beginning to have doubts. However, she and her husband retained a mutual affection and they remained sexually intimate, for it was at Beaufort Gardens that two further children were born, both girls, Mary Norah Kathleen (known as Norah) in January 1873, and Anna Maria del Carmen (known as Carmen) in August 1874.

In the period leading up to the births of Norah and Carmen, Katharine's dissatisfaction with life led her towards the Catholic

Church. Could it provide her with the answers which would bring peace of mind and contentment of spirit? She had long enjoyed the ornate beauty of Catholic churches, she enjoyed sitting in the calm of the Brompton Oratory and for a time she received instruction in the faith, but it failed to provide the answers. She ascribed part of the failure to the examples of Willie, his mother and his sister Mary. Her husband, as she had learned, was a distinctly careless Catholic who went to mass occasionally but otherwise did little to follow the precepts of his faith. The Countess O'Shea and Mary proclaimed their devoutness from the roof-tops but for Katharine what this meant in practise was a stifling narrowness of outlook and a singular lack of compassion or humanity. Against these examples, the Fathers who tried to instruct her fought a losing battle. Katharine had not the temperament to become a Catholic convert; authoritarianism was not her line, she was not in need of the shelter of a clearly defined, orderly doctrine. Nonconformity, with its emphasis on the individual using his talents in the service of God, might have suited her better, except that she would have found its creed as narrow as and its chapels considerably less decorative than the Catholic. Indeed, her flirtation with religion ended, as she herself wrote, 'in an abrupt revolt against all forms and creeds.' By the time her second daughter, Carmen, was christened at the Brompton Oratory, she had become so disenchanted with religion in general, and the Catholic Church in particular, that during the service she stayed outside in the porch.

After Carmen's birth, Katharine's health was again poor and, as she wrote, 'our pecuniary affairs were again causing us considerable anxiety.' What this statement presumably meant was that her husband had spent the money which had mysteriously appeared in 1872 on living and entertaining in lavish style, instead of putting it to use in earning more money so that he could live in the style which he desired. Once again Aunt Ben came to the rescue and presented Captain O'Shea with a cheque so that he could take Katie away on a recuperative holiday. As it was now early winter and the end of 1874 was bitterly cold, it was decided that the Isle of Wight with its mild climate would be the most suitable place for the recuperation, and the O'Sheas departed for the island. After dutifully staying with his family for a week or two, Willie established them in a boarding house in Ventnor and himself returned to the more enticing delights of London. Left by herself again, with only the company (and pressures) of three young children—and Gerard

[35]

was, to use Katie's own adjective, a 'gusty' child given to displays of high temper and tantrums—surrounded mainly by elderly invalids who were hoping to regain their health in the relaxing air, Katharine's own health did not improve. She found herself unable to sleep and took to using sleeping draughts until the local doctor, into whose care she had been put, discovered the habit and immediately ordered her onto meat extract, which he said would do her more good. Apparently it did, and Katharine remained a believer in the beneficial powers of meat extract for the rest of her life, but otherwise the Isle of Wight was not noticeably repairing her health or revivifying her spirits. Accordingly, she moved with the children to Hastings. Whenever she was in an unsettled state mentally, Katharine's instinct was to move physically—the only periods of her life when she enjoyed staying put at all were her childhood days at Rivenhall and the later years in Eltham and Brighton. Once the family was settled, temporarily anyway, in Hastings, Captain O'Shea was informed of their whereabouts and duly came down to see them.

By the end of 1874, the O'Sheas had reached, not exactly a crisis in their relationship—the process and dénouement were too gradual and imprecise to call it that—but a turning point. After seven years of marriage, Willie had shown himself to be a strictly part-time husband. When he was in financial difficulties, as he was at the moment, he did not want to know about his family, he was content to let somebody else pay for their existence and to visit them from time to time. When he was in funds he liked having an attractive, capable wife who could act as his hostess, and he liked romping with his children occasionally. At all times he cherished the *idea* of being a family man and always viewed himself as a devoted husband and father because, in theory, he cared for Katie and the children, but in practise he found the notion of providing a secure income, being home at regular times, abandoning his own pleasures untenable. From her angle, Katharine had reached the point of acknowledging, if only to herself, that the marriage was not a success, as she had hoped marriage would be. There was no mutually rewarding partnership, there was no house filled with interesting visitors in informal fashion, there was nothing to stimulate her, and there was certainly no financial stability. But Willie was her husband, she did not hate him, she found him charming in small measures, and a divorce or a legal separation would achieve nothing. Obtaining money from him as his wife was difficult enough; as his estranged wife it would be impossible. What was required was a solution whereby the appearance of marriage could be retained without either of them having to practise too frequently the actual business of being married. But the essential in-gredient for an informal, unacknowledged semi-separation which would enable them to lead their own lives and make them both happy was money, and neither she nor Willie could provide that.

There were no rich O'Shea relations to whom the couple could turn, but there was an extremely wealthy Wood relative—Aunt Ben. It was she who was already providing the money for Katharine and the children to stay in Hastings, and while they were there her niece, some-times accompanied by her husband, started to visit the old lady at her home in Eltham. These visits were Katie's introduction to her aunt as an adult—despite the various gifts of much-needed money she had not actually seen Aunt Ben since she was a small child. What prompted these visits is difficult to assess; it could have been gratitude, the desire to thank her aunt in person, but the suspicion that Katharine hoped rich Aunt Ben might provide the solution to her financial and marital diffi-culties cannot be dismissed. But if she entertained the hope, it was at the back of her mind, she was not an openly grasping, mercenary character, sniffing blood-hound fashion after her aunt's fortune.

Aunt Ben—Anna Maria Wood, née Michell—was already eighty-two years old in 1874, and was a formidable character. She lived alone, that is personally alone, she had servants, of course, and had done so since her husband's death thirty years previously, in the most beautiful of houses, Eltham Lodge, surrounded by acres of equally beautiful countryside. The land had been Crown property for centuries—in the Domesday Book, Odo of Bayeux is recorded as holding it—but in 1663 Sir John Shaw, banker to Charles II, obtained the lease of some hundred acres in return for services rendered. He proceeded to have the Lodge built, the architect being Hugh May, the result one of the finest ex-amples of what became known as 'the Wren style' of English domestic architecture. The building is in mellow red brick, not large as country houses went but exquisitely proportioned, with a spacious entrance hall, a magnificent carved-oak staircase, a series of elegant, light-filled rooms, with an archetypally English view from the rear window over an ex-panse of gently rolling country, green and soft and wooded.

Since her husband's death in 1845, Aunt Ben had rarely left Eltham, and she left the house only for an hour each day to take a drive in the grounds or in the immediate vicinity of the estate. These drives were in the nature of a ceremonial occasion; Aunt Ben would descend the steps of the house backwards because she said a forward descent made her feel giddy, backwards she would be lifted into her ancient carriage by the servants, in the carriage she would sit bolt upright, glancing neither to right nor left, as it proceeded on its hour's journey. There was much that was regal, not to say imperial, about Aunt Ben, and she shared some characteristics with that other lady who had become a semi-recluse on the death of her husband, but Aunt Ben had a better brain than Queen Victoria, with a genuine love of learning. She read and spoke French fluently and delighted in the works of Racine, Corneille and Molière; she was a good Latin scholar and an excellent Greek one; she admired the works of Alexander Pope, Jonathan Swift, John Stuart Mill, John Locke and Goethe, and when the *Edinburgh Review* criticised the latter by saying, 'He not only strips himself stark naked but turns his pockets out into the bargain', she wrote to a friend saying it was a process of which she thoroughly approved; for what else did the artist and thinker exist but to communicate with the world with liberality and plenitude? She further wrote, 'No one with whom I associate cares about a passage in Homer or in a Greek tragedy, and the interest I feel in puzzling over them and reading them is so unparticipated, so unassisted and so unknown that it must be genuine, and believing it to be so satisfies my conscience when it would reproach me with the inutility of my occupations.'

It was partly in search of a person who could break her intellectual isolation that Aunt Ben employed George Meredith, paying him £150 per annum to spend one day a week talking and reading to her.* The post was arranged by Meredith's friend Lady Wood, and when it was suggested in 1868, he wrote to her, 'I am of all the intelligent gentlemen of my acquaintance the poorest just now, and perhaps I might be acceptable. I would propose another if I knew one. The task seems to me a privilege.' It proved to be a pleasurable and rewarding association for both Meredith and Aunt Ben, and each Thursday he came up to London from his Surrey home, delivered his copy of his weekly article for the *Ipswich Journal* and then travelled to the Lodge to spend the rest of the day with his 'Lady of Eltham'. The routine continued for many years, until in the 1880s the visits finally became too much for the aged Mrs Wood. Even in the early years, while accepted as

---

* Katharine said her aunt paid Meredith £300 a year, Lady Wood said £150, Meredith himself kept quiet on the subject, but £150 per annum seems the more likely sum.

a distinguished poet and novelist, Meredith was not allowed to read his own works, and according to Katharine, each Thursday more or less the same dialogue ensued on his arrival:

'Now, my dear lady, I will read you something of my own.'
'Indeed, my dear Mr Meredith, I cannot comprehend your works.'
'I will explain my meaning, dear Mrs Wood.'
'You are prodigiously kind, dear Mr Meredith, but I should prefer Molière today.'

The stories about Aunt Ben's behaviour and attitudes abounded. When her cook, Sarah, hanged herself from the splendid front staircase, her maid, wishing to spare Madame the sight, asked if she would go down to breakfast by the back stairs. Aunt Ben demanded to know why she should comply with this extraordinary request, was told, and replied, 'Why should I go down by the back stairs because my cook has committed a crime? Go and cut poor Sarah down.' When on another occasion a bold visitor, worried by her off-hand attitude towards religion, asked if she did not wish to go to heaven, she replied, 'Not if it is inconveniently crowded.' When the Duke of Connaught was about to be married, a deputation was sent to Eltham Lodge to ask if Aunt Ben would terminate her lease so that the royal Duke and his bride could take up residence. It was explained that the Lodge was perhaps rather large for one lady, perhaps in her advancing years she might care for a smaller place, as it was close to London it would make an ideal royal residence. Aunt Ben listened in silence to the request and the explanations and then said regally, 'Gentlemen, it seems to me that you shelter yourselves behind the fact that you are a corporation and therefore have neither a body to be kicked nor a soul to be damned. Good morning.' When in 1866 the railway was coming to Eltham, she behaved in similarly regal manner and frightened the company's directors into building the line away from her estate, so that for years Eltham remained without an immediate station and the inhabitants had to rely upon Mottingham. She had a horror of noise and untidiness; everybody had to tiptoe around the house, and as she enjoyed seeing the parquet flooring, only a few rugs were permitted, and therefore visitors, including George Meredith, had to leap-frog from rug to rug so that no squeaks should be heard and no dirty footprints implanted. One of her great-nieces recorded how, visiting Eltham as a child, she was on departure offered an apple or an orange, and was then ordered to take the apple as she might discard the orange peel and make the front drive untidy. If Aunt Ben considered religion an unnecessary bromide for herself, in the Anglican Protestant version she thought it beneficial for others, and each Sunday evening the staff was summoned to her upstairs sitting-room and forced to repeat the verses of scripture she had given each to learn the previous week.

It was this intelligent, astringent, autocratic and extremely rich old lady—Benjamin Wood had left a fortune in the region of £150,000 —that Katharine, sometimes accompanied by her husband, started to visit towards the end of 1874. They never stayed overnight because Aunt Ben disliked having gentlemen sleeping in the house, although she enjoyed Willie's company during the day since he was able to converse with her in fluent French. More than Willie's company, she found herself warming to Katie's vivacious personality, and in her old age she was beginning to feel in need of more permanent companionship than that provided by George Meredith. She later described how she was looking, or perhaps feeling, in a letter to Anna Steele thus: 'Do you remember, in one of Scott's novels, this motto to one of its chapters—"Age sits ghastly by the hearth; wrinkled, tattered, vile, dim-eyed, discoloured, torpid."? Take away the second and third epithet and you have a picture of me.' Shortly after the first O'Shea visit to Eltham Lodge, an agreement was entered into which satisfied the needs of Katie and Willie and Aunt Ben. The arrangement was made by Mrs Wood, but the idea may have been implanted by Katharine, who could have explained how much Willie was away (on business), how lonely she became, how difficult it was for her and the children to manage while her husband was trying to succeed in business; or it may have been subtly effected by Lady Wood, who was on the closest terms with her sister and was well aware of Katie's marital difficulties. Whoever shaped the agreement, it was that Aunt Ben would buy a house for Katharine, give her a regular allowance and pay for the O'Shea children's education in return for her niece's companionship in her declining years. Eltham Lodge was more than large enough for Katharine and her family to have moved into a section, but apart from disliking noise and untidiness, Aunt Ben had little love for children. When Katharine first started visiting the Lodge, Carmen was still a baby, and after being introduced to the child Aunt Ben wrote to Lady Wood, 'Dear Swan* seemed to expect me to kiss the infant; so I

---

* 'Swan' was Aunt Ben's pet name for Katharine.

did, but had to go upstairs afterwards and rinse out my mouth and
nostrils, as I like not the odour of milk.' The arrangement suited
Katharine, her own residence was more desirable than an apartment, and
a legal document was drawn up settling the house and income on her
and covering the children's education. Whether the matter of the companionship was legally noted is uncertain, but Katharine carried out her
side of the bargain with affectionate diligence, although the number of
years it was to last was immeasurably longer than anyone could have
foreseen.

Chapter Four

Eltham in the 1870s was a quiet, small Kent town, only eight miles from central London but enjoying its rural seclusion. The High Street with its cottages and almshouses, its public house, larger residential houses and few discreet shops was the main thoroughfare, and between the High Street and the northern boundaries of Aunt Ben's estate lay a tree-lined road called North Park. In the 1860s detached houses had been built in North Park and it was one of these, named Wonersh Lodge, which Aunt Ben bought for her niece. Compared to Eltham Lodge it had no architectural beauty, it was solid, middle-class Victorian, the front garden was small, and the houses, although detached, were not secluded, as they did not possess sufficient land, but there was a good-sized rear garden and there were stables. Aunt Ben had a gate made in the northern wall of her estate to give Katie easier access to the Lodge, but it was a good ten minutes' walk from North Park through the grounds of the house.

Early in 1875, Katie, the three children, Gerard, Norah and Carmen, the dogs and the servants moved into Wonersh Lodge and embarked upon a new phase of their lives, but it should be emphasised that there was no suggestion of a formal separation between the O'Sheas. Willie was expected to appear at Wonersh Lodge, even to live there occasionally, but the first clear incision had been made in the marriage because he had shed his responsibilities and his wife was now financially independent of him. O'Shea himself considered that he was acting nobly in allowing his wife to go as a companion to her aged aunt, and neither Katie nor anybody else seems to have spelled out the situation for him; namely, that his family was living in Eltham because he had failed to provide a roof or income for them, that Victorian middle- or upper-middle-class husbands did not allow their families to be subsidised by other people and did not absent themselves for months at a time (not unless they were consolidating the Empire or engaged in a remunerative occupation). Or if anybody tried to tell Captain O'Shea that he was in fact a rotten husband, he failed so completely to comprehend their meaning that they gave up their attempts and allowed him to nurse his delusions. In 1875 it did not greatly matter that Captain O'Shea led a semi-bachelor existence while believing himself to be the ideal Victorian husband, or that his wife, secure in the folds of Aunt Ben's patronage, fostered his belief.

When his family first moved to Wonersh Lodge, Willie spent more time than usual with them, but he was soon drifting away to London and for once he was engaged in a project which led to concrete results. He had decided there was a great future in developing a sulphur mine in Spain, he drew up a prospectus for it and managed to persuade several of his business friends to invest their money in the enterprise. Among those whom Katharine named as being particularly interested was an old friend from the days of the Belhus Dramatic Corps, a gentleman from a well-known family, Christopher Weguelin. It was later suggested that Christopher Weguelin's interest was prompted by the fact that he and Katharine were having an affair. Tim Healy said that among the hundreds of personal letters O'Shea presented to his solicitors at the time of the divorce case in 1890, there was one in which Katharine had written, 'You did not object to Christopher', to which he had replied, 'Christopher is dead. Parnell is not.' These particular letters were not produced in evidence and have not proved traceable, the accusation that Katharine was unfaithful to her husband before she met Charles Stewart Parnell was not widely made, and Tim Healy was not the most unbiased or reliable of sources in any circumstances, certainly not in connection with the O'Sheas. Wilfrid Scawen Blunt, who also levelled the accusation, is again not to be trusted implicitly, not because his insights were warped or his observations lacked depth, but because he was so careless about factual information. In the same paragraph in which he stated that

Katharine was a woman 'who had other affairs before that with Parnell' he also asserted 'the house at Eltham was really Parnell's.' When in the second volume of his diaries he had the grace to admit that this latter information had been inaccurate, he compounded the initial error by making more, saying the house Parnell and Katharine lived in at Eltham was Eltham Lodge, which belonged to the Wood family, and that his mistake had been pointed out to him by Mrs Anna Steele who was the *niece* of Mrs O'Shea.

Nonetheless, the accusations of Katharine's previous infidelities were made, so have they any validity? Frankly, it is impossible to say with any degree of certainty; one can only guess from not too many straws in the wind. Without doubt Katie liked men and they liked her, she admitted her first quarrel with Willie was on account of an admirer, and there are constant amused references in the early chapters of her memoirs to the males who tried to court her, before and after her marriage. She also asserted that her husband encouraged her to be friendly with and to flatter such of his men friends as he thought could be useful in his various business projects, and she said he would not have cared if the flattery had extended to sexual involvement, as long as it was temporary and discreet. Few women in Victorian times lightly indulged in extramarital activities, the penalties were too high, which is not to say that none of them did or that Katharine could not have done so. Her husband was frequently absent, on his own admissions as much as hers, so she had the time and the opportunity, and according to her she would have had his encouragement. But that she was a sexually promiscuous lady as opposed to a naturally flirtatious one seems doubtful, and that she would have risked incurring Aunt Ben's wrath in 1875 so soon after having obtained her secure income, on account of a passing affair with Christopher Weguelin, would also seem doubtful, although it cannot be disproven.

What Willie was doing sexually in these years is again a question open to doubt. More people than mentioned Katie's infidelities dropped hints about his extramarital activities, and in 1890 Katharine herself dropped more than hints, she drew up a list of his alleged affairs, but as this list was never put to the test it cannot be accepted as fact. It would seem probable that the dashing Captain, so frequently away from his wife, had his amours, but masculine straying from the path of monogamy, if not openly approved or admitted, was of course accepted. From 1875 onwards there was the definite, if unacknowledged, separation in the lives of the O'Sheas; thus both of them had ample opportunity to stray if they wished.

Whatever prompted Christopher Weguelin's interest in the Spanish sulphur mine, and Katie freely admitted that he was interested—in the mine—he and other businessmen put up sufficient capital to make the enterprise viable. Later, towards the end of 1876, Willie was offered the job of manager at an excellent salary, and accordingly took off for Spain, where he stayed for the next eighteen months. During this long period Katharine remained at Wonersh Lodge and her husband did not once return to England, even for a holiday. Had it entered his head to query his prolonged absence, he would have attributed it to the pressures of his job. Life for his wife was well-filled, too; she had three small children to cope with, Gerard remained an extremely 'gusty' child, with a frightful temper and an absolute determination to have his own way, which a doting mother and the absence of paternal authority did not improve. Baby Carmen was also showing signs of self-willed temper, and the only placid member of the trio was Norah. During her husband's absence Katharine had to deal with an outbreak of diphtheria, caused by the defective drains at Wonersh Lodge, which a horrified Aunt Ben promptly had ripped out and re-laid by the best experts she could find, but not before Carmen and Katie herself had succumbed to the dread disease. Like Lady Wood, Katie was an affectionate mother and lavished as much time as possible on her children, but she employed nurses and governesses. This was partly because several hours of each day had to be devoted to Aunt Ben and Katie trekked across the park in all weathers to read and talk to the old lady and to accompany her on rides in the ancient carriage (Katie said it swayed like a galleon in a heavy sea but its effects, unlike the forward descent of the steps, did not apparently make Aunt Ben dizzy). The nurses and governesses were also necessary because Katharine involved herself in her husband's Spanish affairs. The O'Sheas might be separated literally at this period, apart from the more tacit arrangement of Wonersh Lodge, but they retained contact. Katie, as much as Willie, enjoyed letter-writing, and he used his wife as his London link, a position to which she had no objection. She thus spent a fair amount of time in the capital, chasing up supplies for the mine, wining and dining with various directors, and in the role of helpful, not to say managerial, wife she enjoyed herself, and her appetite for negotiation and for being part of an interesting operation was sharpened.

[45]

By the beginning of 1878 the mine was failing to show a profit, the directors in London refused to put up more capital and later in the year Willie came home, once again jobless and penniless. He stayed at Wonersh Lodge for a while because he had nowhere else to go and insufficient money to find a place of his own, but he and Katie had been separated for eighteen months and she had grown accustomed to his absence. She remained willing to help her husband in his career, whatever that might next prove to be, she responded to his charm but she was no longer prepared to live with him permanently. In her own words, 'Our totally dissimilar temperaments began to make us feel that close companionship was impossible, and we mutually agreed that he should have rooms in London, visiting Eltham to see myself and the children at week-ends.' Without much doubt the O'Sheas came to an agreement of this kind in 1878, but as with the initial move to Wonersh Lodge it was wrapped in a comforting tissue of evasions which enabled Willie to believe that he was going to London for business reasons, that Katie had persuaded Aunt Ben to pay his expenses for the same reasons, and that he remained the responsible head of the O'Shea household. It was from this time that the precise nature of the relationship between Captain O'Shea and his wife began to assume importance because her fateful encounter with Charles Stewart Parnell was becoming nearer. Whether she and her husband were living together in a happily married state affected Parnell's position as a home-wrecker and the nature of his and Katie's love for each other. Katharine's version was that she and her husband had ceased to live together in any regular sense of marriage virtually since 1875, certainly since 1878, when by mutual agreement and at Aunt Ben's expense he took rooms in Charles Street. Apart from Willie's prolonged absences and his total financial irresponsibility, which hardly fit the concept of a Victorian marriage, there is a physical factor which seems to support her version. From 1874 until after Parnell had appeared in her life she bore no children, nor did she have any miscarriages. She was not sterile, she had six children in all and appeared to conceive easily enough when she so desired, and if she and her Catholic husband had been living together in the devoted manner he later depicted, it seems likely that during eight years she would have had another child. In all probability the O'Sheas continued to have sexual intercourse occasionally, events in 1881 suggest that they did, but it was only occasionally and Katharine's claim that they had found a *modus vivendi* which had little connection with the accepted standards of marriage seems valid.

When O'Shea took up residence in Charles Street in 1878, he was thirty-eight years old and what thus far had he done with his life? For all his undoubted ability in setting up business deals he had not, naturally through circumstances beyond his control, succeeded in that sphere. Perhaps it was the wrong sphere, might not his talents be better suited to another one? His thoughts began to turn towards the world of politics in which he already had many friends, notable among whom were the O'Gorman Mahon and Frank Hugh O'Donnell. The former was a splendidly idiosyncratic character, then approaching his eightieth year, who had lived mainly on his wits and had an inexhaustible fund of stories about the duels he had fought, the ladies he had conquered and his escapades in general; he was also an MP and from the inception of the Home Rule movement had been one of its more ardent supporters. Frank Hugh O'Donnell was almost as eccentric a character as the O'Gorman Mahon but not in the same outrageously theatrical mould. Known as *Crank* Hugh O'Donnell to his fellow Irish nationalists, he had a good brain capable of formulating political strategy and tactics, and himself claimed that all the early Home Rule tactics were his brain-child, although he did not become an MP until 1877. But O'Donnell could not leave a point alone, he had to hammer it to death, in the process contradicting an originally good argument and irritating others beyond measure. His besetting weaknesses were conceit and lack of self-awareness, like his good friend Willie O'Shea, but his sense of humour was even weaker than O'Shea's and he was more obsessed with his standing as an Irish Catholic gentleman. O'Donnell's view of O'Shea, one of the few not to change as events matured, was that he was 'gay, an amusing rattle, a bright talker, an incorrigible diner-out . . . a thoroughly good fellow, of exceptional tact and ability when he took the trouble.' This description was not inaccurate, except it depended on one's viewpoint how thoroughly a good fellow one considered Willie to be, and the proviso 'when he took the trouble' was a key to one of his weaknesses. O'Donnell also met Katie about this time, introduced by her husband, and he recorded, 'I was struck by her clever conversation, while a little bored with her persistent questioning. She wanted to know everything about everything. She seemed to know everybody, but there was an infinitude of things, apparently, which she wanted to know, or to know about more thoroughly.'

To say that Katie knew everybody who was anybody in London was an exaggeration, but from childhood she had known a number of influential people, among her contemporaries were those who had become so, and in the last two years of acting as her husband's London-Spanish agent she had made further contacts, so when he suggested that he enter the political arena he had no difficulty in persuading his wife to use her contacts and act as his hostess; the venue chosen for their dinner parties was Thomas's Hotel in Berkeley Square, where Katie was well-known from her childhood days. O'Shea was an Irishman and a Catholic, so it was his duty to find a seat in Catholic Ireland, whose political scene, as he saw it, was peopled by clodhoppers, and required men of his calibre. If Ireland's problems were to be solved, again as he saw it, men were needed who possessed finesse, who were skilled in the difficult art of negotiation, who were accustomed to dealing with Englishmen of stature and who appreciated England's problems, too; in short, men like himself. When in March 1880 Disraeli (by then Lord Beaconsfield) unwisely dissolved Parliament, O'Shea managed to get himself adopted for County Clare in harness with his friend the O'Gorman Mahon. Both men stood as Home Rule candidates, and if O'Shea's position was vague, he was not alone in having ambiguous aims in the confusions of the 1880 election. For him politics was the sphere in which people's lives were shaped and history was made but to what ends and for what purpose was not the important matter. It was the shaping which was exciting, and if one gained personal glory and accrued some money in the process, so much the better. By entering the political arena Willie O'Shea indeed helped make history, although not perhaps in the way he had hoped or would have wished.

After the election, in which O'Shea and the O'Gorman Mahon were both returned for County Clare, immediate money was again a problem, as MPs were not then paid for their services, nor had the Home Rule League a wealthy party organisation. Katharine told of an evening she spent with the two men after their return from their successful campaigning in Ireland. It was a pleasant evening, enlivened by the O'Gorman Mahon's powers as a raconteur, but towards the end O'Shea fell into a deep gloom. Finally, the O'Gorman Mahon explained the reasons for his friend's malaise—kind, generous Willie had guaranteed to pay both their election expenses which had of necessity been rather high, £2,000 in fact. Now his friend was worried because it appeared he did not possess £2,000, and could Mrs O'Shea think of a solution to their difficulties? Katharine could, as her husband well knew, in the shape of the bottomless purse of Aunt Ben, and she persuaded her aunt to pay his (and the O'Gorman Mahon's) election expenses and to subsidise his political career, as O'Shea himself later privately admitted.

Before her husband embarked on his new career, Katharine suffered a loss which she surprisingly fails to mention in her memoirs, the loss being the death of her mother and the surprise being that, having dealt with her father's death and that of her devoted nurse, Lucy, she ignored her mother's. Emma Wood died at Belhus in December 1879. Her fortitude stayed with her to the end, and on the night of her death she said, 'Put away my paint-box and brushes, I shall not want them again.' On hearing the news of his old friend's death, George Meredith wrote to Aunt Ben: 'Lady Wood is a loss to me also, though I shall never lose the spirit of the image of that slender vitality which was beaten down but to rise, and seemed unconquerable, as the heroism animating her was in truth, and the ardour for all things brave and beautiful in our world. She was one of those who enrich the feelings for human life in me.'

Generally, by the spring of 1880 life had assumed a more satisfactory hue for Katharine. She had her secure base at Eltham, she had earned Aunt Ben's gratitude and the old lady had already altered her will, leaving a larger share to Katharine than to the other Wood children in recognition of her niece's devotion, so her future, too, looked secure. She had three attractive children, if two of them were headstrong and spoiled and Gerard had had to be sent away to school early because no governess could control him. She had come to an arrangement with her erratic, irresponsible but charming husband, they were 'good friends', and his new career promised to make life more interesting. Nonetheless, there was a good deal missing and it was of this time that Katharine recorded the most revealing of her personal statements. One day, feeling restless and dissatisfied, on an impulse—and she was an impulsive lady—she decided she must go down to the sea, so she left Wonersh Lodge early in the morning and caught the train to Brighton. Once in the train she felt in no mood to meet her Barrett Lennard relations who were currently at their Brighton house, and consequently detrained at the stop before the town, hired a cab and drove to Patcham to view her old haunts. At Patcham she decided she wanted to be absolutely alone, dismissed the cab and started to walk across the Downs. It was a bright sunny day, and as she climbed up the bridle path towards the Devil's Dyke, with the sweep of the Downs around her, the chalky brown-white ploughed fields, the green of the switchback hills and the clumps of trees on one side, the roof-tops of Brighton and the sea way below on the other, she felt an exhilaration of spirits such as she had not known for years. Then the wind changed, rushing through the grass and whipping up the distant waves, the sun disappeared behind dark clouds, a storm seemed imminent and her spirits dropped. She considered going into Brighton, to the warmth and comfort of her sister Emma's house, but the Barrett Lennards would only ask how Willie and the children were, so she dismissed the idea and instead asked herself: 'Why should I be supposed to have no other interests than Willie and my children? Willie was not, as a matter of fact, at all interesting to me. As to my children, I loved them dearly, but they were not old enough, or young enough, to engross my whole mind. Then there was dear old Aunt Ben, who was so old that she would not tolerate any topic of conversation of more recent date than the marriage of Queen Victoria. What a curiously narrow life was mine, I thought, narrow, narrow, narrow, and so deadly dull.'

It was the *cri de coeur* of many women before and since Katharine O'Shea, women who have found the vaunted delights of wifehood and motherhood insufficient, but who have failed to find or make a compensating outlet. Katharine's cry has a certain novelettish ring, it would not be called an intellectual analysis of the female condition, but it was nonetheless genuine and heartfelt. What she longed for was Sir Galahad to come riding by, sweep her up on his charger and lead her forth to the stimulating land of Camelot where she would find physical and mental satisfaction. For Katharine, as for few other women, Sir Galahad actually appeared. In fact, he had already made his entrance, which may have accounted for her sudden sense of exhilaration on the Sussex Downs, for when she stood above the sea at Patcham she had met Charles Stewart Parnell.

Within the previous two years, Parnell's rise to prominence had been meteoric, but he had been a sluggish starter. He was born on 27 June 1846, at Avondale, County Wicklow, the seventh of the eleven children of John Henry and Delia Tudor Parnell, and his ancestry, like that of his future mistress and wife, was distinguished. The Parnells were members of the Anglo-Irish, Protestant landlord class—the original settler had come from Congleton in Cheshire and had been given the land in County Wicklow in return for his support of Cromwell. Since the seventeenth century the family had acquired a more nationalistic outlook, and included among Parnell's ancestors was a forbear who had voted against the Act of Union in 1800, and another who had been a supporter of Daniel O'Connell. In addition to their intermittent nationalism, the Parnells had had their literary associations with Dean Swift and Tom Moore, and the family had a history of eccentricity, indeed of insanity—and that Parnell himself must be partly mad became (and has stayed) a popular theme. Of his parents the key figure was his mother; his father was a kindly but vague personality, of whom Parnell appears to have been fond but who died in 1859.

His mother was an American, the daughter of Commodore Stewart who had fought successfully against the British in the war of 1812 and had earned the nickname 'Old Ironsides'. Charles was said to be like his American grandfather whose 'control over his passions was truly surprising. . . . In the moment of greatest stress and anger he was as cool and quick in judgement as he was utterly ignorant of fear.' Delia Parnell was also fearless and one could say unconventional, although to be the latter there should be some regard for the conventions, and she had none. She was a strong-minded, egocentric lady who existed in her own world, acting on her own feelings, beliefs and prejudices with a sublime disregard for other people's. She allowed her many children to interfere in her life as little as possible, adored travelling and hated the English. She did not believe in demonstrations of personal emotion, and when she was briefly at Avondale she neither encouraged her children to show nor gave them affection, so the young Parnell, unlike Katie Wood with her secure, stable background, grew up in an environment which would now be described as emotionally deprived, seeing little of his mother, his father dead by the time he was thirteen. As a child he displayed sudden, startling temper tantrums, but the outbursts were discouraged and his education furthered the process of disciplining the emotions. Delia Parnell was a snob—she said to another of her sons about the Home Rule party, 'Your brother is the only gentleman in the whole set. . . . Hear all the Billingsgate of some of the others.'—and thus, despite her Anglophobia, she acquiesced in the tradition of an English education for her children (and her daughters were presented at court). The young Parnell went through the rigours of various nineteenth-century English boarding schools, none of great renown, finishing up at Cambridge University, and in this process, like Willie O'Shea, he acquired an upper-class English accent which he never altered, and he learned to control his feelings. After a couple of years at Cambridge he was rusticated for a term and did not return to take his degree but stayed in Ireland, following the life of a country gentleman, hunting, shooting and playing cricket.

As he stepped into manhood Parnell was very English in looks, manner and speech. The exterior was cold and aloof, the emotions apparently absent, and to an extent the interior was aloof, too. He had inherited his mother's oblivious disregard for other people's *mores,* although he had good manners and when he hurt people's feelings it was by default rather than intent; he had an innate shyness and could be racked by nerves; and he had no interest in what made human beings, as individuals, function. What the interior was *not* was passionless. Parnell had a mass of emotions seething beneath the cool surface, a capacity for affection, an ability to feel rage and anger, but the dominant emotion was pride. It was not so much an arrogant, overweening sense of his own importance—although he was to be accused of this sort of pride—but a proper pride in his abilities, his judgement, his lineage and above all in himself as an Irishman. Along the road of his English education, Parnell had learned that the Irish were regarded as second-class citizens of the United Kingdom of Great Britain and Ireland, at best a quaintly maddening race, at worst lazy, untrustworthy rogues. There was nothing second-class about him, Charles Stewart Parnell, or his native country if it were given half a chance.

Avondale was not in his childhood a politically committed household, his mother's Anglophobia was persuasive but intermittent and undirected, and what precisely made the indolent young sprig of the Anglo-Irish Ascendancy decide that Ireland's destiny needed his helping hands is uncertain. It was later suggested that rejected love had been the driving force, because if the writers could imply that Parnell had been a libertine before he met Mrs O'Shea, it strengthened their case against his moral unsuitability to lead Ireland after his love for her had become public knowledge. The sole impetus Parnell himself acknowledged was the Fenian uprisings—he was the least introspective of men, hated letter-writing and left no private papers. The Fenian risings occurred in 1865 and 1867 and it was not until 1874 that he took the first step along the road of destiny (and for those favouring the rejected love theory he was in the United States in 1873, visiting his brother John, who was then farming in Alabama, and Katie confirmed that he had loved an American lady). But Parnell had an innately lazy streak, surprising in a man who proved himself capable of such intense concentration and activity, and until he was convinced that action was essential, he preferred to sit around doing nothing in particular. Between 1867 and 1874 it is possible that he was slowly, methodically surveying the ground, considering the factors which had led Ireland into her present position. It was often asserted that Parnell had no knowledge of Irish history, a grave weakness in an Irish politician, that he acted only for the present and the possible future without reference to the past circumstances that had shaped the present and must influence the future. But other colleagues, not necessarily kindly disposed towards him, said he had a fair knowledge of his country's troubled past and it seems reasonable to assume that some study of Irish history led him into politics.

In the late 1850s and early 1860s, after the trauma of the Famine Years, a new secret movement was born in Ireland which became known as the Irish Republican or Revolutionary Brotherhood. There was some argument about what the 'R' stood for, but less about the aims of the new movement, which were to throw off the yoke of English oppression. There was nothing particularly novel about this, but what was new was the means by which the IRB hoped to achieve its end. Constitutionally-based campaigns, operating within the framework of the law (English law), had failed to get back even a modicum of independence for Ireland. This was because England, as the IRB saw her, was a repressive country, increasingly imperialistic in outlook, and the only weapon she understood was force. The first evidence of the IRB conclusion that Ireland's independence must be won by force of arms were the Fenian uprisings of 1865 and 1867. They were botched, ill-organised affairs which the British Government had no difficulty in suppressing, but if their immediate effect was no greater than a stone being thrown into a pond and sinking to the bottom, the water was considerably disturbed by the ripples, which caused a great many people to do some thinking, or rethinking, among them Charles Stewart Parnell and a gentleman named Isaac Butt.

In 1870 Butt founded the movement which Parnell was to galvanise and lead so close to victory. Butt was an Ulster Protestant who had been an MP and barrister, a warm-hearted lion of gregarious manhood whose weaknesses were wine and women. He had no wish to sever the links with England, he considered Ireland could gain from England's greater wealth, power, industrial and scientific know-how, even from the Anglo-Saxon cultural heritage. But while the Fenian risings had convinced him that violence was not the answer, they had also made him certain that Ireland's current position as an integral but despised part of the United Kingdom was untenable, and that fresh proposals to reactivate a constitutional solution were essential. He therefore proposed, not a straightforward repeal of the Act of Union for which Daniel O'Connell and others had campaigned and which would give Ireland a legislative independence, but the formation of an Irish Parliament on the English model, responsible to an Irish executive for internal affairs without any veto from Westminster, but with Westminster retaining control over Imperial affairs and a number of Irish MPs continuing to sit at Westminster to make Ireland's voice heard on these wider issues. Butt's cherished solution of federalism—he suggested that Scotland and Wales similarly have their own Parliaments and be represented at Westminster—appealed to a fair number of people, if for various reasons, and it was consequently a strange assortment of bedfellows who attended the inaugural meeting of the Home Government Association in Dublin in 1870. By 1873 the Home Government Association had expanded considerably and changed its name to the Home Rule League and in the 1874 General Election it met with considerable success, fifty-nine members pledged (if verbally and vaguely) to supporting its aims on being returned to Westminster.

The movement which Charles Stewart Parnell joined in 1874 had quickened the Irish political pulse after a period of inertia, but it remained a disorganised body, with too many disparate horses pulling on the reins and no firm hand to control them. Butt had his vision and was stout-hearted, but he lacked real powers of leadership and the disarray of his private life carried into his political one. In any case, he did not see the Home Rule League as a political party, with rules and discipline, acting in unison to obtain its aims, he saw it as a pressure group which would slowly influence the British Government and British public opinion as a whole. There were those who considered that gentle persuasion would get Ireland nowhere, with most Englishmen viewing Home Rule as at best nonsense, at worst a canker that must be quickly cut from the Imperial bosom, and that any British Government, whether Tory or Liberal, would have to feel the pressure of Ireland's justified demands before it would act. Notable among this group of militants were Willie O'Shea's friends, Frank Hugh O'Donnell and the O'Gorman Mahon, and Joseph Biggar. Like Isaac Butt, Biggar was an Ulster

Protestant, a short, squat man (almost a hunchback) who delighted in calling a spade a spade in his rasping, metallic Belfast accent. From the start, Biggar's actions influenced Parnell, and later he was to the forefront in the first major contretemps caused by the Willie/Katie O'Shea/Parnell triangle.

When Parnell announced that he wished to join the Home Rule League he was welcomed with open arms; a candidate who was rich enough to pay his election expenses and had a historic name in Ireland was not to be ignored, even if he had 'a fatal, obtrusive, ultra English accent', could hardly string three consecutive sentences together, broke down during his election speeches and was stiff as a ramrod on the platform. Parnell's first attempt to become an MP in 1874 was, unsurprisingly in view of his performance, not successful but in an 1875 by-election the electorate of Meath gave him a majority, and as the new member took his seat in the House of Commons, Joseph Biggar staggered into the chamber carrying a pile of Blue Books which he proceeded to read *in toto,* including the vital words 'Printed for Her Majesty's stationery office by Eyre and Spottiswoode, printers to her Queen's Most Excellent Majesty'. The policy of obstruction, of slowing down the business of the Commons by utilising the customs of the House against itself, was not new. British members had on occasion used it to further a particular cause or spike a Bill, but the use had been limited and the motive had not been deliberately to hamper British business and thereby focus attention on Ireland. Biggar's obstruction was heavy-handed, and it was left to Parnell to raise the tactic to a fine art and a formidable Irish weapon, which he did initially in a slow, methodical way by keeping quiet and learning every rule and custom of the House of Commons. When, towards the end of 1876, he was selected to go to the United States to present the Irish nationalist congratulations to President Grant on the hundredth anniversary of America's independence, the selection was made not because he had impressed the House of Commons or the Home Rule League but because he had a historic name and a famous American grandfather.

By 1877 Parnell was beginning to make his mark. The shy, reserved young man who had entered political life was not noticeably less aloof, but a fear of crowds and the halting speech had been conquered. He never grew to love public meetings—he told Katie he always had to steel himself to address one—and he was never a great orator, but he disciplined his thin voice into the most laconic and succinct of instruments, and it made a change to have an Irish politician who was not enchanted by the flow of his own rhetoric but who said what he had to say, no more, no less, and then kept quiet. If nature had been miserly with the vocal chords, it had been lavish with good looks and Parnell had on his side commanding height, a slim well-proportioned figure, a fine head and features. It was his eyes on which everybody commented, on their strange, uncanny, magnetic, mesmeric power; Frank Harris said they were 'the finest eyes I have ever seen in a human head, except those of Richard Burton'. Parnell looked like a leader, or most people's idea of what a leader should look like, which was no handicap, but the qualities which led him to the forefront were his fearlessness, his pride, his coolness and a quite remarkable ability to pick out and concentrate on the essential factors, to realise how far he could push and when to retrench. Parnell was a master tactician who knew how to utilise others' strategy and keep the long-term aim clearly in view.

By 1877 Parnell had been elected chairman of the Home Rule Confederation of Great Britain (a better-organised, stronger body than the Irish parent league), and another vital sector of the Irish political scene cast its eyes over the Master of Avondale. This sector was the Irish-Americans, who were beginning to assume importance because there were by now so many of them, because some of them had prospered in the United States and could therefore lay their hands on money (a commodity badly lacking in native Irish nationalist circles), because many of them were dedicated to rousing the potentially enormous strength of American public opinion in favour of Irish independence. By 1877 the Clan na Gael had emerged as the dominant body in the turbulence of the Irish-American scene, with John Devoy as its leading figure, and he became convinced that the various strands of Irish nationalism must be drawn together, as their internecine warfare was wasteful and only a united front would achieve the desired end. But the problem was to find some common ground on which the two main-streams—the constitutionalists and the Fenians—could meet, and a leader whom both sides would accept. For a period it seemed an insurmountable problem, but early in 1878 the Clan na Gael made contact with Parnell, which encouraged them to believe he was a constitutionalist who did not discount the use of violence (another of Parnell's outstanding qualities was his ability to convey the impression his listeners wanted to hear without actually committing himself). Towards the end of the year, John Devoy made a concrete move in what became known as the 'New Departure' when he publicly promised American Fenian aid to Parnell, on certain conditions which nevertheless left Parnell plenty of room for constitutional manoeuvre. The only snag to Devoy's dramatic action was that Parnell was not the leader of the Home Rule movement, Isaac Butt retained that position, if precariously, and the common ground in which the two sides might bury their differences was still lacking.

Devoy's selection of Parnell as the possible leader of a Fenian–Home Rule joint front indicated what strides Parnell had made in establishing himself in recent months, and in 1879 when the common ground was found, it proved to be the issue that could ignite the masses. In fact, it had been there all the time, various people had stressed its vital nature over the years, but it took the combination of appalling weather, terrible harvests and one man's passionate involvement to make it the obvious key. The issue was the Irish land question and the man was Michael Davitt. By mid-1879 he had founded the Land League of Mayo, dedicated to the immediate task of forcing the British Government to amend the land laws radically, and by the autumn he had convinced Parnell that a National Irish Land League was a necessity. Parnell in his turn calculated that he could channel the newly-roused fighting spirit into the battle for Home Rule.

In the next six months the momentum gathered force, Michael Davitt devoted his energies to furthering the organisation of the National Land League, John Devoy threw his weight behind it, while Parnell as its President went on a fund-raising tour of the United States, covering 11,000 miles and sixty-two towns and cities in two months. The peak of Parnell's American visit was the exceptional invitation to address the House of Representatives, and he took full advantage of the occasion to remind his audience of England's past and present misdemeanours in Ireland. The tour was a success, despite the surprise invoked by this Irish nationalist leader's English accent and his reserved off-stage manner, but it had to be cut short when Disraeli dissolved Parliament in March 1880. Parnell returned to Ireland to fight the General Election on a land-reform-cum-Home-Rule platform, covering fewer miles but as many meetings in a whirlwind campaign through his native land, and the descriptions of him were glowing—'He was a glorious creature in those days,' said one colleague; 'He was an exquisite of some sort,' said another, while he reminded a reporter of 'a Greek god come to take part in a festival organised by his votaries.' He met with a more resounding success than on his American tour, over sixty candidates being returned to Westminster on a Home Rule ticket, although by no means all of them were Parnell votaries or supporters of the Land League. It was widely acknowledged that the greater part of the success of the Home Rule candidates was due to the outstanding qualities of leadership and personality shown by the Master of Avondale, and in May 1880 Parnell was elected chairman of the Irish Parliamentary Party. It was also widely acknowledged, if in many quarters without enthusiasm, that Ireland had found a new leader, one who had the nucleus of a genuine political party, as opposed to the gentlemanly association Isaac Butt had led into the House of Commons, one who had the backing of the peasants, the Irish-Americans, much of the Fenian impulse, increasingly (if with reservations) of the Catholic hierarchy and clergy: a formidable combination in the hands of a formidable man.

Among those who voted Parnell into the leadership of the Parliamentary Party there was, T. P. O'Connor, the Irish nationalist MP and journalist, noted, 'one man whom I saw then for the first time, and whose demeanour particularly attracted my attention. Slightly over-dressed, laughing, with the indescribable air of a man whom life had made somewhat cynical, he was in sharp contrast with the ragged, plainly-dressed, serious figures around him.' The man was Willie O'Shea, whose vote surprised everybody, including perhaps himself, because he was the type of anglicised Irishman alien to the new spirit of the Home Rule movement. What prompted O'Shea to vote for Parnell, the embodiment of this new, implacable, determined Irish spirit, remains uncertain. It was perhaps his gambler's instinct to back a winner, or perhaps like so many others he was temporarily mesmerised by Parnell's personality, but he had reservations about his choice. After he had voted, he telegraphed to Katie informing her of the fact but added that he feared Mr Parnell might prove too advanced and extremist in his views and tactics. Despite the reservations, he was eager to be on better terms with the new leader and he urged his wife to invite Mr Parnell to one of their London dinner parties. She did not need much urging because Parnell, apart from being a fast-rising star, was also something of a mystery man. While in London he lived alone in lodgings in Bloomsbury (not then a fashionable area), he did not socialise, he had few friends, and to get him to attend a dinner party would be a feather in her cap.

Chapter Five

Urged on by Willie and by her own curiosity, Katharine plied Mr
Parnell with invitations to O'Shea dinner parties at Thomas's Hotel,
most of which he typically ignored, then when he accepted one he failed
to turn up, another typical action. At one particular dinner, with a seat
left vacant for the elusive Parnell, another guest regarded the empty
chair and defied Katie to fill it, a challenge she acknowledged with the
words, 'The Uncrowned King of Ireland* shall sit in that chair at the
next dinner party I give.' Accepting the challenge was one matter,
actually getting Parnell to attend was another, and it required more than
routine channels of polite, impersonal invitation. Katharine decided on
the bold approach; she would beard the lion in his den by going to the
House of Commons and asking to speak to him, but as this was an
unconventional act for a well-bred lady to perform alone, she persuaded
her sister Anna to accompany her. One summer afternoon in 1880,
Katie O'Shea and Anna Steele had their carriage driven into Palace
Yard, from where they sent a note across to the House of Commons,
asking Parnell to come and speak to them. Normally he disregarded
demands on or for his social presence, but boldness won the day and he

---

* It was Tim Healy who first called Parnell 'the Uncrowned King of Ireland', at
Montreal during their recent North American tour. It was then a premature description
but soon became apt.

emerged, the ladies introduced themselves, Katharine asked why he had ignored her previous invitations and what she could do to induce him to attend her next dinner party. Parnell said he had not opened his letters for days, another typical action—various people commented on his habit of leaving his mail untouched, sometimes for weeks, then striding into the House, collecting the letters and disappearing into the library, where he would remain until the mountain was dealt with. He promised he would accept Mrs O'Shea's next invitation if at all possible, and the meeting came to an end.

Katharine recorded her impression of the first fatal encounter thus: 'He looked straight at me smiling, and his curiously burning eyes looked into mine with a wonderful intentness that threw into my brain the sudden thought: "This man is wonderful—and different".' Her effect on Parnell, who never himself recorded his impressions, was apparently just as startling and he later told her that from the first moment he had looked into her eyes he had known that she was his destiny. As the two sisters were leaving Palace Yard, Katharine leant out of the carriage to say goodbye and the rose which was fastened to her bodice fell off. Parnell picked it up, kissed it lightly and put it in his button-hole, and when the rose had withered he did not throw it away but carefully placed it in an envelope on which he inscribed Katharine's name and the date, and within a short while he was writing to her, he who so rarely put pen to paper. The first letter, written from the House of Commons, was dated 17 July 1880 and mentioned the pressures which had prevented him from wandering 'further from here than a radius of about one hundred *paces allons*. And this not withstanding the powerful attractions which have been tending to seduce me from my duty towards my country in the direction of Thomas's Hotel', and said he hoped to have an opportunity of seeing her as soon as he returned from Paris.

The political pressures were indeed immense. The General Election had returned Gladstone and the Liberals to power with a large majority and Gladstone had remembered that his mission was to pacify Ireland, a country currently in need of a great deal of pacification. The eviction notices were, in his own vivid words, falling like snowflakes, the Land League had consequently become increasingly militant and was being successful in its militancy, and some measure which would allevi-ate the Irish tenant farmers' lot seemed essential. On 18 June, Gladstone introduced a Compensation for Disturbance Bill; it was a moderate Bill but it met with fierce opposition in the House of Commons, partly because it struck at the rights of the propertied classes, partly because it seemed to some to be bowing to the lawlessness of the Land League. When Parnell met Katie O'Shea at the beginning of July 1880, the Bill had just had its stormy second reading and he was engaged in keeping in check as disharmonious a team as Isaac Butt had tried to lead, on the one hand fighting for the Bill because it was needed and to keep the moderates happy, on the other hand being intransigent to prove to the Fenian element that he was aware of its limitations and that he intended to press the British Government relentlessly. When Parnell managed to take up Mrs O'Shea's invitation—probably on 30 July, although the letter assuring her he would attend is simply dated 'Friday'—the Compensation for Disturbance Bill had passed through the Commons but what the Lords would do with it remained doubtful.

After the dinner, a small one attended by Anna Steele, Justin McCarthy, the novelist and Irish Home Rule MP, and a couple of other people, the party went on to the theatre, as Mrs O'Shea thought the entertainment would be a welcome change for Mr Parnell after his recent parliamentary exertions. During dinner she said Parnell spoke mostly to Anna, but at the theatre he and she 'seemed to fall naturally into places in the dark corner of the box . . . while my sister and the others sat in the front.' They also seemed to have spent most of the time engaged in whispered conversation rather than attending to what was happening on the Gaiety stage, and it was during the course of this evening that their mutual attraction was acknowledged. Immediately thereafter the political scene became even more tense; on 3 August the Lords threw out the Compensation for Disturbance Bill by an overwhelming majority and the nationalist reaction was predictably and justifiably one of immense anger. Parnell's reaction was the coolest; he stepped up the obstruction tactics, forcing the House of Commons into several all-night sittings, otherwise keeping ominously quiet, but several of his colleagues launched into bitter anti-British attacks, while the situation in Ireland itself was explosive, with the power of the Land League increasing and that of English law decreasing daily. Yet during this tense period Parnell found time to take Katharine into the country on several occasions, to have tea and lunch and to dine privately with her at the Cannon Street Hotel, and when she missed her train back to Eltham one afternoon to hire a cab and drive her home. She said they discussed Willie's career during their country jaunts, politics at the

Cannon Street Hotel, and that she would not let Parnell stay when he accompanied her back to Eltham. By inference he already wanted to stay at Wonersh Lodge, and without doubt their rapport and desire for each other were almost from the first moment overwhelming. Frank Harris, who claimed to have met them both at a dinner party in the early days, said that while Mrs O'Shea talked vivaciously, 'the dour, silent, handsome man opposite devoured her with his flaming eyes' and soon 'everybody knew that they were lovers and lost in a mutual passion.' As Harris also claimed that Mrs O'Shea 'exaggerated her Irish brogue with some artistry' when she wanted to emphasise a point, his observations have to be regarded with suspicion because why an English lady who had never set foot in Ireland in her life should have an Irish brogue is beyond comprehension, except, of course, that she was called Katharine O'Shea and Harris never bothered to check his facts or his imagination.

Mutual passion was something of which Harris thoroughly approved, but for many later critics the fact that Katharine and Parnell allowed their passion to develop was objected to partly because of their ages when they met. It was felt that she at thirty-five and he at thirty-four should not only have known better but should not have had such strong feelings at all, as if physical passion were the prerogative of the very young. And Katie retained above-average nineteenth-century youthfulness; Frank Hugh O'Donnell said, 'She was very handsome, about thirty-five it seemed to me, but with the delicacy of feature and softness of charm which often reach their prime when more material types have already begun to pay their debt to time'; and another observer said that she had 'a most vivacious and winning manner . . . and, with her hair thick and short and curling over her merry eyes, she suggested despite her age, a high-spirited and romping girl.' It would seem probable that when they first met both she and Parnell were suffering from sexual frustration or denial; whether or not she had affairs or was in cohabitation with her husband, it can only have been infrequently, while Parnell's energies had long been directed into politics and his sexual life seems to have been fairly blank. There was the story circulated by Tim Healy that he had had a recent casual affair with a barmaid in Manchester, but it rests on Healy's word and it does not seem very likely, as Parnell and a Manchester barmaid—whom Healy coyly designated 'Lizzie from Blankshire'—would not seem to mix. Certainly, apart from his love for the American lady, Parnell had enjoyed no deep relationship with a woman. He had been deprived of maternal love, he had for years

[62]

disciplined his inner feelings, and the shy, reserved side of his nature meant that he suffered doubly from the occupational disease of Irish parliamentarians—loneliness—cut off from their homes and roots as they were for at least half the year. Now here was a woman he found devastatingly attractive, a woman of his own class, well-bred and well-mannered, one who was sufficiently confident to meet his innate shyness more than half-way, one who was bored and dissatisfied with her own life. That she was a married lady, that her husband was one of his Home Rule colleagues, did not enter into Parnell's calculations. He was enchanted, enraptured, overripe for love, and that was all that mattered.

It never entered Parnell's mind that by falling so passionately in love with a married woman who was the wife of a colleague he was automatically sailing into dangerous waters, and little in Katharine's character made her consider the reality of the potential dangers. She had grown up to believe that life should be a rewarding affair—and here, without doubt, finally, was the reward she craved, the love of an extraordinary man—and the last five years she had spent as the companion of her formidable aunt had done nothing to persuade her that one could not always have one's own way. Initially, the strength of their mutual fascination drove them irresistibly along, without thought of social implications or moral niceties or possible dangers, although there was an alarm clock ticking at the back of Katie's mind which rang three interconnecting bells—Willie, Aunt Ben's money and some observance of the conventions. But they were muffled bells, and they could doubtless be dealt with as thus far she had managed to sort out the other complications of her life. For her, as for Parnell, all that mattered was that they wanted each other with a rare, passionate intensity, and no impediment could be admitted to a marriage of true minds and bodies.

When Parliament was prorogued on 7 September 1880, Parnell crossed to Ireland, leaving everybody on the political front wondering what he intended to do when he got there. Would he continue to act constitutionally, however near the limit he had already reached? To co-operate with Mr Gladstone's Liberal administration in any way? Or would he bow to the militant, Fenian clamour and launch an all-out land war in Ireland which could lead anywhere, including revolution? Could he at this stage control the tough, determined Irish spirit which he had helped create, with its constant threat, if not yet fully implemented use, of violence? Did he in any case want to control it? With such questions left skilfully dangling in mid-air, Parnell's first action on arrival in Dublin was to write to Katie telling her that the prospect of ten days away from London in the valleys and hills of Wicklow was nowhere near as attractive as it had been, and could she suggest a reason? Two days later he was writing to her from Avondale: 'I am still in the land of the living, notwithstanding the difficulty of either living or being, which every moment becomes more evident, in the absence of a certain kind and fair face.'

On 19 September Parnell was in Ennis, where he made his first speech since the prorogation of Parliament, and it proved to be a historic one, but his personal attention was focussed on Katie O'Shea and on 27 September he wrote, 'I cannot keep myself away from you any longer, so shall leave tonight for London. Please wire . . . if I may hope to see you tomorrow, and where.' In the event he was unable to see the woman who was engrossing his mind and body, as Lucy, the old nurse who had spent her later years partly at Rivenhall with Lady Wood but mainly with her beloved Miss Katie, had had a stroke and was dying at Wonersh Lodge. In the circumstances, to her credit, Katharine felt she could not leave Eltham, even to spend a few hours with the man who was the pivot of her thoughts. She stayed with the dying Lucy to the end—although it was Willie O'Shea who accompanied the body to Cressing for the funeral—and consequently she did not see Parnell. He had to return almost immediately to Ireland, where he was due to address further Land League meetings, but he bombarded Katharine with letters, explaining how he had come to London 'on purpose for you, and had no other business', how he had chased round the capital trying to find her, then sympathising with her bereavement, again saying how much he wished he could have seen her if only for a few minutes. On 2 October he informed her 'something from you seems a necessary part of my daily existence, and if I have to go a day or two without even a telegram it seems dreadful', and that he was coming to London next week and of course it was especially to see her. Unfortunately, Katharine did not print any of her replies to Parnell's letters—as he cherished the rose from her bodice until his dying day, he almost certainly kept her letters, too, but somewhere along the line they were lost. The impression gained from the one-sided correspondence as published is that at this stage the initiative and impetus were Parnell's, although there was no discouragement on Katharine's side, and he was able to say, 'I received your two letters quite safely, and you may write me even nicer ones with perfect confidence.'

Parnell's arrival in London was delayed by gales in the Irish Sea but by 7 October he was there and it was on this visit, one assumes, that they became lovers (if they had not already committed themselves). In her book Katie obliquely pin-pointed the time by carefully inserting among her selection of Parnell's letters the one dated 5 October from Dublin, saying he would meet her in London anywhere she wanted, followed by one dated 17 October, also from Dublin, which begins pointedly 'My own love' rather than 'My Dear Mrs O'Shea'. The consummation they both devoutly desired presumably occurred at Wonersh Lodge, where from an early date Parnell was given the bedroom at the top of the stairs which conveniently interconnected with Katharine's bedroom via her dressing-room. Katharine made few comments about her sexual life with Parnell, but from her hints one gathers that he was passionate—she spoke of his fiery kisses—and masterful, on one notable occasion throwing her over his shoulder and carrying her into the bedroom. To such approaches the coquettish, submissively feminine side of her nature presumably responded enthusiastically. From early October 1880 Parnell became a semipermanent resident at Wonersh Lodge—Katharine herself briefly stated that from this time he came to stay with her at Eltham, only crossing to Dublin as occasion required.

Occasion required Parnell's presence in Ireland a great deal in the late autumn and early winter months of 1880, and the constant crossing backwards and forwards to snatch a week-end or a few days with Katie can have done his health no good. Despite his splendid physique, Parnell had always had a weak constitution, he had several serious illnesses in his childhood which left him liable to throat and chest infections and rheumatic attacks, and his exertions over the past few years, not to mention the extra exertions of the past few months, had already taken a serious toll of his health. Since the Act of Union general good health and a strong constitution had been essentials for any Irish politician who took his job seriously, for he had to travel frequently between Westminster and his constituency, an arduous journey which entailed taking the boat train from Euston station to Holyhead in Anglesey, followed by the frequently stormy sea journey from Holyhead to Kingstown (now Dun Laoghaire), another train to whichever part of Ireland he was visiting and then the return trip. Fortunately Parnell was a good sailor—he was one of the few people standing upright after the Atlantic crossing on his recent American journey, one of the worst on record—so at least he did not suffer from the agonies of sea-sickness, but his bodily health as opposed to his mental and physical satisfaction would have been improved had he not been driven to undertake the frequent journeys from Dublin to Eltham.

The speech Parnell made at Ennis in the middle of September assumed historic proportions because it was shortly afterwards, following guide-lines enunciated by him, that the practice of 'boycotting' was inaugurated. In the process of dealing with the internal problem which had long plagued Irish agrarian movements and which even the Land League had not fully solved, namely the question of land-grabbers—i.e. families who moved into a holding from which the tenants had just been evicted, thereby continually strengthening the landlords' hands—Parnell gave certain instructions. In the cold, precise, simple language of which in the absence of native rhetoric he had made himself such a master, he urged his audience to shun the land-grabber, to leave him severely alone, to put him into a moral convent as if he were the leper of old. By a peculiar set of circumstances the person thus isolated like the leper of old was not an Irish land-grabber but an English land-agent, Charles Cunningham Boycott, who had farmed in and around County Mayo for some thirty years and made himself thoroughly unpopular in the process. Within a few weeks Captain Boycott's situation had become headline news, Irish loyalists organised a relief expedition to assist the beleaguered gentleman, Gladstone's administration was forced into a position where it had to provide the expedition with an escort, some thousand troops eventually being poured into the area of Boycott's farm. The spectacle of crack troops of Her Majesty's Hussars guarding the expedition while it dug up Captain Boycott's turnips in foul November weather caused great amusement and earned world-wide headlines. The result of the episode was that the Irish had forged a new weapon, an unpleasant but non-violent and virtually unbeatable one, for if all the tenant farmers of Ireland combined to isolate land-agents and landlords there was little the British Government could do about it. Parnell, the man who was credited with having conceived the idea, reached a new peak of popularity.

Further governmental action taken at the end of 1880 served only to increase Parnell's popularity, in nationalist Ireland, that was. With much the same reluctance as it had supplied troops for 'the invasion of Mayo', Gladstone's administration finally decided that it must take some action to reimpose Westminster's authority in Ireland. Gladstone moved reluctantly because personally he believed that the Irish had some justification for their current campaign of disobedience and was convinced that the radical Land Act for which the Land League was fighting—and on which he was already working—was essential. As the Prime Minister of the United Kingdom he also felt he must curb the power of Parnell and the Land League, not only to still the clamour of his right and centre wings, which were fulminating against the breakdown of law and order, but because the law should be respected and order had to be maintained in any civilised state. Consequently, he allowed the prosecutions against Parnell and other Land League leaders to be instituted, on the charge of conspiracy to prevent the payment of rents. The prosecution took place in Dublin and it reminded one reporter more of an opera house on a gala night than a state trial, with Dublin society ladies throwing flowers at Parnell, while in the streets outside crowds chanted Land League songs and poems, particularly 'Hold the Harvest', which had been written by their beloved leader's sister Fanny Parnell. The defence lawyers also seized the opportunity to remind the watching world of England's past cruel treatment of Ireland, and when the trial ground to its conclusion on 24 January 1881, the jury (as Gladstone had also feared) failed to agree, the defendants were triumphantly acquitted, and Parnell reached an even higher peak of popular idolatry.

Throughout this period when Parnell was solidifying his mass appeal and thereby placing himself in a position from which he could impose his will on the inner political scene, his personal life was centred on Katie and he was returning to Eltham at every possible opportunity. In mid-November he told her 'how very much you have changed my life, and what a small interest I take in what is going on about me, and how I detest everything which has happened during the last few days to keep me away from you—I think of you always, and you must never believe there is to be any "fading".' Indeed, there was to be no 'fading', Parnell's love and need for Katharine remained intense until the moment of his death, and from the earliest days she won his trust and confidence. During those autumnal months of 1880, vital political papers were removed from Avondale and his London lodgings and hidden at Wonersh Lodge, while two extremely important documents were secreted in the hollow of a bracelet which Parnell had made for Katie, and which she said she did not take off her arm until three years later when they were no longer vital and were destroyed. In November she actually hid Parnell in her dressing-room at Wonersh Lodge for a full fortnight. She said that he spent most of the time reading *Alice in Wonderland,* which he regarded with the utmost seriousness, that the rest did him a great deal of good, and that the servants commented on the amount of food she was consuming. This particular escapade was prompted by political considerations, as Parnell knew the subpoena for the Land League trials was imminent and thought it would be a good idea to go to ground temporarily.

However, from the start of the relationship, both of them practised a more general deception. To a degree this was necessary and inevitable, even for two people with as little regard for the conventions as they, that was, if he wanted to stay in public life, which he did and Katie wanted even more. With his disregard for other people's social, religious or moral convictions, his belief that what he did personally had no connection with his public life, as long as he remained true to himself and his standards of honour, Parnell might have been willing to take the risk of facing public outrage by openly setting up house with Katie. (According to his standards of honour, he was justified in embarking on his liaison because Mrs O'Shea was a free woman, by which he meant she had long ceased to live with her husband in wifely fashion. His definition of marital freedom in Western society would cause some eyebrows to be raised in the more permissive atmosphere of the 1970s; in 1880 it was outrageous.) If Parnell were willing to take the risk of declaring his love to the world, Katie was not. More clearly than he, she realised that an open liaison could destroy him, as he stood poised to take Ireland forward and perhaps become the first Prime Minister of a semi-autonomous state, and there was also Aunt Ben's money to be safeguarded. This was a paramount factor in preserving a façade, in Katharine's mind as important as protecting her lover's political position. In her early life with Willie she had known the miseries of financial instability, in the Harrow Road she had endured something akin to poverty, she had no wish to be in that situation again, or to put her children into it, and their education, indeed their whole future as members of the upper-middle class, a membership to which Gerard and Carmen and to a lesser degree Norah had grown accustomed, was tied to Aunt Ben. Without her money they would have nothing, and Aunt Ben might not take kindly to the news that her beloved 'Swan' was breaking her marriage vows. Katie dared not risk an unfavourable reaction, and there was also the factor that her aunt was now dependent on her, which made her anxious to avoid giving distress because she genuinely cared for the old

[68]

lady. Apart from wanting money for herself, her children and her husband, Katharine soon grew to realise that financial matters meant nothing to Parnell. More than she, he had grown up in an atmosphere where money was something that was always around, which one dealt with as if it were a personally reprintable bit of paper, and she related an illuminating anecdote about Parnell's financial naïveté. One day in later years, when they were living in Eastbourne, he sent one of the young servants into the town to buy some small article with a £50 note, and was immensely surprised when the boy returned under police escort, neither the shopkeeper nor the constable being willing to believe that anybody would send a working-class lad on such a small errand with such a vast amount of cash. In fact Parnell was not rich, Avondale was already mortgaged and he was in financial difficulties; there was therefore a further impetus for Katharine to preserve the *status quo* and safeguard the present income and future fortune from Aunt Ben.

In the autumn of 1880, therefore, Mr Parnell officially came to stay at Wonersh Lodge for a temporary visit, in order that Mrs O'Shea might help restore his fragile health, and he retained his lodgings in Keppel Street. Katie later insisted that her husband urged her to invite the Irish leader so that she could further his (Willie's) career and that he had no objection to her taking the process to the bedroom, as long as she was discreet and obtained the desired objective. Initially, keeping up a respectable façade was not difficult, as Wonersh Lodge was by no means an ideal love nest—it housed three chattering children, the nearly eleven-year-old Gerard, the seven-year-old Norah and the six-year-old Carmen, in addition to the servants. Some eyebrows were raised at the arrangement whereby an attractive unmarried man regularly visited the house of an attractive married lady, particularly by those who knew the Captain lived in London and spent little time at Eltham, but it could be attributed to O'Shea's known ambition and wish to be of service to the Irish leader. However, from the beginning, Katharine went to some lengths to hide the true nature of her love from her husband, and so at her bidding did Parnell. Her motives were compounded of the fact that not telling her husband the truth was the way the marriage had survived thus far, her conviction that she could manage him as long as the supply of Aunt Ben's money continued to flow and his ambitions were fostered, and her partial realisation that he must not have his self-esteem too overtly punctured. After they had become lovers, while in one letter Parnell would address her as 'My Dearest Wifie', in another he would

[69]

start 'My Dear Mrs O'Shea' because she might need to show this one to her husband. In her memoirs she makes unexplained comments such as 'This letter was really written in London but sent to Dublin to be posted', which again presumably was to deceive O'Shea about Parnell's whereabouts (the sole defender of Katharine's reputation to date suggested that the comments were not written by her but by the O'Shea editors of the book, a point we shall examine later). She—and probably not an O'Shea editor in this case—supplied the information that Parnell's cryptic query: Was it all right? meant: Had Willie left England for Madrid so that they could meet in safety at Eltham? While Parnell himself warned her about telegrams he was on the point of despatching to her and Captain O'Shea 'which are by no means strictly accurate.'

Thus the relationship which meant so much to Katharine and to Parnell, and brought both of them so much personal happiness, started in a quietly deceptive way. Unfortunately, from the moment the indefinable spark flared between them in Palace Yard, Westminster, and they slid into their deeply intimate life at Eltham, it was not only their personal future that was engaged, it was that of Ireland and Anglo-Irish relations. For increasingly Ireland's future was dominated, and Anglo-Irish relations were therefore shaped, by the force of Parnell's personality.

Chapter Six

Parnell managed to spend the Christmas of 1880 with Katie at Wonersh Lodge, but he had to cross to Dublin for the opening of the Land League trials on 28 December. As he told her in a letter, 'So far as I can see there is no necessity for the presence of the Traversers [i.e. the defendants]; one of them, Gordon, who had broken his leg, has not appeared at all, and his absence has not been even mentioned or noticed.' Accordingly, he was back at Wonersh Lodge on 5 January, but there was a dual reason for his presence, as the new session of Parliament opened the next day. At this time Katharine was in a scratchy mood, and over Christmas she and Parnell had one of their few squabbles. Later she explained that the reason for their quarrel was Parnell's overwhelming sense of possession and his jealousy, a situation to which she soon responded but which, having been Willie O'Shea's wife for fourteen years, she initially found irritating. The evidence of Parnell's letters does not support her claim, for they suggest that it was she who needed the indications of his possessiveness and demanded constant reassurances of his love. Even for the unconventional Katharine, to have decided to live with a man who was not her husband was, in the England of the 1880s, to have taken a large step. She wanted to be certain that if, in the words of her divorcee friend on the Sussex Downs, she was gambling all for love, the stake was not only worth the world to her, it was worth the same to him. Parnell had given her such reassurances; he had already told her, in novelettish language similar to that of her Sussex friend, 'For good or ill, I am your husband, your lover, your children, your all. And I will give my life to Ireland, but to you I give my love, whether it be your heaven or your hell.' After her more recent visit to Sussex when she walked on the Downs above Patcham alone, on her return to Charing Cross Station, Parnell had been standing at the barriers, hopefully waiting for her. He had wrapped his coat round her wet, dishevelled figure and whispered, 'I love you, I love you. Oh, my dear how I love you.' But six months later, Katharine was having doubts, and when a paragraph appeared in the *Freeman's Journal* stating that a lady had accosted Parnell and handed him a note as he made his way to the trial, it was she who was angrily jealous and he who had to write begging her 'to believe in me while I am away, and never again to feel unhappiness from want of confidence.'

Early in January 1881 Katharine was not the only O'Shea experiencing a lack of confidence or in need of reassurance, for it was then that she and her legal husband had the first of their many contretemps on the subject of Charles Stewart Parnell, that is, according to her version of events. According to Willie's he remained in blissful ignorance until the July. Thus one embarks upon the murky waters of the triangular relationship which grow murkier with the passing of the years, in which one has to take on board Willie's account of what he knew, two accounts provided by Katharine, information furnished by outsiders, in addition to how Captain and Mrs O'Shea and Mr Parnell behaved. Willie's version was consistent and simple: he trusted his wife and Mr Parnell and he was deceived. While it will be contended, as it was by some people at the time and has since been by most historians or writers on the subject, that Captain O'Shea's unawareness was unbelievable or impossible, as we push our particular way through the confusions and contradictions, it should be borne in mind that O'Shea himself adhered to his position of duped innocence like a leech, and that no private papers have yet emerged which categorically reveal his knowledge of the affair, at least not in the early years.

Parnell's position was again consistent and simple, though unlike O'Shea he made no lengthy public or private statements, and only once briefly referred to his love for Katharine and her relationship with her husband; it was that he worshipped Katie and regarded her as his wife because she had ceased to live with Captain O'Shea long before their fateful encounter in Palace Yard, Westminster. Katie's versions of the affair are more complicated in that there are two of them, and that the first one, contained in her memoirs, was written with an impossible dual aim. Her memoirs are actually entitled *Charles Stewart Parnell, His Love Story and Political Life,* and the main purport is to tell of their great mutual love, but the book has a preface by Gerard O'Shea, her eldest child and only son, in which he states that his mother will refute all allegations that Captain O'Shea knew of or condoned her affair with Mr Parnell. This obviously puts the author in a difficult position because if she was devoted to Parnell from the moment they met in 1880, it is hard to explain what sort of relationship she had with her supposedly equally devoted but deceived husband, and the result is ambiguous and ambivalent to say the least. However, after Parnell's death, Katharine had long conversations with Henry Harrison, one of his youngest and most devoted adherents. Years later Harrison published what she had then told him, and her statements to him were more forthcoming and categorical on the subject of what O'Shea knew than any she permitted herself in her memoirs (or the O'Shea editors permitted her, for it was Henry Harrison who considered the book had been tampered with, mainly by Gerard O'Shea).

In January 1881 the situation was that Willie O'Shea had invited Mr Parnell to stay as his guest at Wonersh Lodge in the early autumn of the previous year, since which time Parnell had been as permanent a resident as his political duties permitted and Captain O'Shea had been conspicuous by his absence, in part actually out of England, attending to his ever-hopeful business ventures in Spain. According to Katharine, she and her husband had long since reached an agreement that he would not descend on Wonersh Lodge without prior warning, but one night early in January he arrived unannounced and in a furious temper. What ensued between them, in the opaque fashion of her memoirs, she did not reveal other than hinting that rumours about her relationship with Parnell had reached her husband's ears and stating that they had a blazing row. It does not seem surprising that rumours were circulating, for Parnell and Katie had known each other six months, in the early days they were seen frequently in each other's company in London, and since October he had used Wonersh Lodge as his English base. It was not an isolated estate, servants and neighbours had eyes and tongues, and Parnell was a striking figure, with a face well-known through the columns of the illustrated papers.

[73]

The clue to Willie's reaction is that the rumours had swelled sufficiently to have become public property in the circles in which he moved. He was a gentleman, an ex-cavalry officer, and there was a code of conduct by which he lived. It enveloped male affairs but it did not countenance women cohabiting outside the marriage bed unless they were *very* discreet, and it certainly did not encompass real passion. If, as rumour suggested, his wife and Parnell were genuinely in love, then apart from the moral issues he was being made to look a fool, and he had to act to suppress the whispers. Parnell was not present the night O'Shea descended (that is according to Katharine's version) but his portmanteau was, and after some hours of bitter argument, Willie stormed out of Wonersh Lodge, taking with him the portmanteau, which he flung out of the train at Charing Cross Station. He also announced that he intended to challenge Parnell to a duel, on the grounds presumably—though nobody ever actually stated the grounds—that the Irish leader had seduced his wife. To substantiate her version, Katharine published a letter of Parnell's written on 7 January 1881, in which he plaintively requested, 'My dear Mrs O'Shea, Will you kindly ask Captain O'Shea where he left my luggage? I inquired at both parcel office, cloak-room, and this hotel at Charing Cross today, and they were not to be found.'

In Willie's version it was not until the month of July that he heard rumours about his wife's relationship with Mr Parnell, but then the basic story-line is much the same. He had been away in Spain, he returned home to Eltham to find that Mr Parnell had been staying there without his permission, and he and his wife had a violent quarrel. This lasted most of the night and ended with Willie storming out of the house and walking eight miles to London, and the person to whom he turned in his anguish was his wife's sister Anna Steele, on the door of whose London house he pounded in the early hours of the morning. Undoubtedly, Anna and Willie O'Shea were very good friends at this period, as his thundering on her door indicates, and Justin McCarthy wrote to Anna: 'Your brother-in-law, my colleague, Captain O'Shea, talked of you to me yesterday, and promised me the chance of meeting you again some time.' How intimate the relationship was, whether Anna and Willie were, as Katie later stated, having an affair, remains unknown, but Anna was told of Captain O'Shea's suspicions—of which she assuredly had an inkling, as she was then also friendly with her sister—and started to act as mediator, a fact confirmed by Katie although the time span is longer in her version. According to Willie's version, Anna then interviewed Parnell in London and obtained from him assurances that there was no truth in the allegations, but in the meantime Captain O'Shea issued his challenge to the duel, to be held in France, sending the O'Gorman Mahon to attend on Parnell as his second. While the matter of the duel was hanging fire, Anna persuaded O'Shea to meet his wife at Wonersh Lodge, and there another stormy scene ensued, with Katharine also denying the allegations, and Willie saying he would leave her but eventually agreeing 'that their relations should be resumed as before' (a somewhat ambiguous statement, in view of what they were). Anna and Willie then returned to London together and it was at this point, according to his evidence, that is *after* he had accepted his wife's first-hand assurances and Mr Parnell's second-hand that no improper conduct had occurred between them, that he threw the portmanteau out at Charing Cross Station. Katharine confirmed that the affair of the duel reached its climax in the week of 20 July 1881, by printing a series of letters from Parnell which she said were in cipher 'bearing on the matter of the threatened duel', but as she did not reveal the cipher they are not very helpful.

If Katharine's version that the contretemps dragged on from January to July is accepted, substantiated as it is by the January portmanteau letter from Parnell, what she told Willie in January that successfully, if temporarily, stilled his suspicions or made him decide to turn a blind eye is not clear. The position in July, if not translucent, can be interpreted in a clearer light because between January and July a great deal happened, both politically and domestically. On 6 January the new session of Parliament opened and the Queen's Speech contained two items of outstanding Irish significance, namely that the Government intended to apply for 'special powers' to deal with Ireland and that an Irish Land Bill would be introduced. The decision to enforce coercive measures in Ireland, including the suspension of Habeas Corpus, had not been reached easily by the Liberal Cabinet but it had been decided upon, and Parnell had to fight it with every means at his disposal. Supported by a good half of the sixty-strong Irish Party, he immediately launched into the obstruction tactics, succeeding in prolonging merely the debate on the address in reply to the Queen's Speech for eleven nights. When on 24 January Mr Forster, the Chief Secretary for Ireland, sought leave to introduce the Protection of Persons and Property (Ireland) Bill, obstruction was brought to its peak as a method of wrecking

Parliament's ability to function, with a twenty-two-hour sitting on January 25/26, and a forty-one-hour sitting which started on 31 January. But this was the all-time record for obstruction because in the early hours of Wednesday morning, 2 February, the Speaker intervened and introduced the *clôture* (or closure as it was later called in anglicised fashion) which gave control of the House to him if a majority of members voted that business was urgent. The closure was not only the death-knell of obstruction as an endlessly disruptive Irish weapon, it was the end of unlimited debate in the House of Commons, and some British parliamentarians never forgave Parnell for being the cause of the curtailment of debate.

With the continual night sittings, Parnell, encouraged by Katie, fell into the habit of driving down to Wonersh Lodge in the early hours of the morning, a habit which could only confirm the suspicions of those already interested in his relations with Mrs O'Shea. The manner in which he went about covering his tracks was not brilliant either. He travelled to Eltham by cab in order, in Katie's words, 'not to become well-known on the Eltham railway' (by 1881 Eltham had its own railway station, Aunt Ben having been unable to stave off the march of progress any longer). In his efforts to avoid travelling regularly on the railway, Parnell took one cab from Westminster to the Old Kent Road and changed there into another for Eltham, thus becoming a familiar figure among south London cab drivers and, as was later noted, 'he could not have adopted a better plan for betraying his secret.' On arrival at Wonersh Lodge, Parnell would enter by the conservatory. Sometimes Katie would be sitting up waiting for him, or if it was very late and she had gone to bed she would immediately come down. The fire would be kept blazing in the sitting-room, with Parnell's slippers warming in the hearth, and in this atmosphere of domestic bliss he would silently unwind, eat his supper and then start to talk to Katie of what had happened that night in the House of Commons, of his political hopes and plans, frequently until the dawn broke, when he would retire to bed. Parnell's early-morning arrivals at Wonersh Lodge did not pass unnoticed among the servants, though none of them felt it his or her business to make official comment. One of them, Phyllis, had replaced the dead Lucy as Katharine's devoted personal maid and never made any public comment, another was Irish and so overwhelmed at the thought of having 'the Chief' in the house that anything he and Mrs O'Shea did was all right by her, but when the time came in 1890 one witness was

[76]

forthcoming to tell of the nocturnal arrivals. Katharine later told Mr Gladstone that it took her a full two years to penetrate Mr Parnell's political reserve and suspicion of the Anglo-Saxon mind, but this would seem to have been a point made to emphasise her position as political confidante because in 1880 Parnell had entrusted her with the vital documents and she was hiding the two most secret in her bracelet. It is doubtful that he withheld much from her during their long discussions in the warmth of upper-middle-class comfort, with the firelight flickering and the curtains shut against the outside world. What it is perhaps true to say is that in the early days Katie was a political novice, she had not found her feet and she knew she had not. Like most English people she had taken little interest in Irish problems until forced to; in her case the forcing had occurred in the most delicious manner, and with her deep personal interest, her curiosity, what Frank Hugh O'Donnell termed her 'slightly aggressive intellectuality' she learned fast. In the early days she was content to absorb and accept Parnell's view of Ireland and Anglo-Irish relations and not to try to influence him.

It was also in January 1881, a fairly busy month in all directions, that Parnell's secret became known to some of his Irish nationalist colleagues, though in this instance the disclosure was made as much by his autocratic nature as a leader as by his ineptitude as a conspiratorial lover. His colleagues needed to get hold of him as an urgent decision was required, but Parnell had not left an emergency address and nobody knew where he was. After a solemn conclave, the inner group of Parnellites decided that a clue to their leader's whereabouts might be contained in his pile of waiting correspondence, so with great reluctance they opened his mail. It was as a result of this action that, Tim Healy claimed, they discovered an address in Holloway where the Manchester Barmaid, 'Lizzie from Blankshire', was living in a dismal garret, nursing a baby (Parnell's, of course), with a newspaper drawing of her seducer pinned to the counterpane of her bed, and, according to Healy, Joseph Biggar then saw to her financial needs and that was the end of that incident. Other Parnellites later confirmed that the necessity of the hour dictated the distasteful task of opening their leader's private correspondence but did not mention the barmaid in Holloway, though T. P. O'Connor and Michael Davitt said a letter from Mrs O'Shea was among the unopened pile, giving them the first indication of their leader's apparent liaison. Having discovered where the Chief was—because Katharine always wrote on headed notepaper—nobody had the temerity to do anything about it, and like Willie O'Shea they decided to let sleeping dogs lie.

On both his own and Katie's submissions, Willie stayed in somnolent mood for the next three months. This might have been because the political scene was so active that nobody had the time to bother about Parnell's private life, what he was or was not doing at Eltham, and the rumours consequently subsided. On the political front, immediately after the introduction of the closure, the news was given that Michael Davitt had been arrested, which produced more angry, Irish-initiated scenes in the House of Commons, culminating in the expulsion of Parnell and thirty-five of the Home Rulers. Parnell had done what he had been threatening to do, he had collided head-on with the British Government, proving that there was now an Irish party representing solely Irish interests in the effort to obtain justice for their country. Having got himself expelled, to the enthusiastic cheers of his grass-root supporters both Irish and Irish-American, various plans for more militant action were urged. There were those who wanted Parnell to set up an independent Parliament in Dublin, and there were those who advocated a more dispersed plan of campaign which would continue to combine the semi-revolutionary with the constitutional, by Parnell himself going to America to raise money and enthusiasm there, by the Land League battling against coercion in Ireland, and other Home Rulers staying at Westminster. The course Parnell chose to follow was to return with his party to Westminster and to fight where the battle could be legally won. The choice has since been viewed as proof that he was a constitutionalist rather than a revolutionary, and in the make-up of this son of the Anglo-Irish Protestant landlord class there was a strong streak of conservatism. He was also a political realist and he knew that England, faced by secession from Westminster, could pour troops across the Irish sea, and that the Catholic hierarchy would not support him on illegal secessionist ventures. There is another factor which has not been given much attention, namely that he was living with a lady who had absorbed the tenets of nineteenth-century English Liberalism, who had an inbred respect for Parliament, for the supremacy of the law and for negotiation by sweet reason, and whose admiration for Mr Gladstone was then, as Katie herself said, 'almost akin to a religion.' While it is not suggested that she made Parnell return to Westminster, her influence on his decision may have been stronger than has been allowed.

With the Home Rule party back at Westminster, the Coercion

Bill became law. The nationalists fought every clause of the Bill, but with the obstruction weapon gone they could not stop its passage. Gladstone then introduced his Land Bill, and if it was not the final solution of the Irish land problem, it was an enormous step forward. Getting the Bill through the House of Commons, against the virulent opposition, which said it undermined the sacred rights of property (which it did) and that in introducing it Mr Gladstone had submitted to the illegal, disgraceful pressures of the Land League, was one of the Grand Old Man's greatest achievements. In his efforts Gladstone was not entirely assisted by the man whom, on the Liberal face of it, he should have been, Mr Parnell. For, ironically, the introduction of this long-needed, recently-fought-for piece of radical legislation put Parnell into a difficult position. He knew this was the Land Bill Ireland wanted, that most of the peasants, the Catholic hierarchy and the moderate nationalists would gladly accept it, but boiling on his left flank was the Fenian element at home and particularly in America which regarded the Bill as a minor stepping-stone, forced out of the Liberal Government only by the semi-revolutionary activities of the last year. If the ultimate goals of full peasant land-ownership and Irish independence were to be achieved, the militants thought the pressures must be kept up, but Parnell recognised that there was a strict limit to the revolutionary fervour of his other flank. His position was further complicated when in May one of his ablest and most fiery lieutenants, John Dillon, was arrested. Earlier Parnell had stated that if any of the Irish leaders were arrested under the terms of the Coercion Act, he would immediately implement one of the militants' most favoured schemes, the No-Rent campaign. Parnell was not enthusiastic about this plan for all the tenant farmers to withhold their rents and thus cause economic chaos, because in practise he thought it impractical and unlikely to succeed. But he had to do something to keep his left wing in check, so he became intransigent in Parliament, urging the Home Rulers to vote against the second reading of the Land Bill on the grounds that it did not meet all the Irish demands. Many members of the party failed to heed their leader's injunctions, which made Parnell aware of the strength of moderate opinion, and he then worked hard on the committee stages.

While Parnell was performing his political high-wire balancing act, trying to keep all the strands of Irish nationalism, within and without the parliamentary party, in his grasp, he nonetheless found time to follow Katie down to her beloved Brighton. During May 1881 an old friend came to stay with Aunt Ben and Katharine thus felt free to take the children away on holiday, but she had only stepped off the train in Brighton when a man accosted her and for a moment, not expecting Parnell to join her, she did not recognise the beardless face. Thinking his presence in the well-known Sussex watering-place at the same moment as Mrs O'Shea's might cause comment, Parnell had snipped off his beard with a pair of pocket scissors in the train. In Brighton, presuming his beardless face would disguise him, he stayed for about ten days with Katie, a sojourn both of them regarded as their 'honeymoon', not without reason because it was in Brighton that Katie became pregnant with his child. By the next month Katie suspected that she might be pregnant and knew that the child would be Parnell's, and it was in this month of June that Willie O'Shea reappeared on the scene when he started to act as the Irish leader's secret intermediary with Mr Gladstone. Viewing the action retrospectively and objectively, it seems incredible that Parnell should have used his mistress's husband as his mediator, a man known to have little sympathy with the new Home Rule movement and therefore already politically distrusted by Parnell's supporters. Some men in his position might have made the choice out of sheer devilment—how deliciously reckless and unconventional to select the cuckold—but if Parnell had little regard for the conventions and could be reckless, he did not possess the Machiavellian malice essential for this manoeuvre. Outside of politics he was in many ways a simple man, but Katharine was not such a simple lady and her hand may be detected in the choice. She suspected that she was pregnant for the first time in eight years, the child was Parnell's, her husband (accepting the January portmanteau evidence) was already suspicious, Parnell was deep in his parliamentary battles and fighting to control his diverse cohorts— now was therefore not the moment to upset the *status quo*. One way of keeping her husband quiet would be to offer him the task of secret intermediary whereby he could submerge his suspicions to his ambitions. Would it not moreover be a practical arrangement? She and her husband retained contact, Willie was therefore available much of the time, and the delicate discussions could be confined to the intimacy of the family circle.

If Katie presented such arguments to Parnell they would win the day, because preserving the *status quo* and Willie's quiescence were domestic issues about which she knew so much more than he, and if she further intimated that he might be about to become a father he would have acceded to her slightest whim or wish. Certainly in June 1881 contact was made with Gladstone through the medium of Captain O'Shea to the effect that if the Liberal Cabinet would accept Mr Parnell's proposals for needed amendments to the Land Bill, then he would cease his opposition in the House of Commons and 'give the Bill an effectual support in Ireland, such support to be loyally afforded even if outwardly and for the moment prudently veiled.' Katharine's hand may also be detected in this early offer of co-operation with the Liberal Party, but in the event nothing concrete emerged from the offer. In the face of the continuing violence in Ireland and Parnell's far from prudently veiled opposition, Gladstone was in no mood to make a deal with him.

Assuming Katie convinced Parnell that her husband would accommodate her pregnancy in return for political advancement, the suspicion remains—a suspicion that does not place Katharine in a favourable light—that she took another course of action about which she did not tell her lover. This is that she clinched the matter of her husband's possible parental doubts by having sexual relations with him after she had guessed she was pregnant. Willie O'Shea never really claimed that the two children borne by his wife in 1883 and 1884 were his, or to be precise he infrequently and mutedly made the claim, but he seems to have believed that the child conceived in 1881 was—or at least could be—his. In her memoirs, while affirming that the child was Parnell's, Katharine emphasises her husband's belief that he was the father, whereas she makes no such statements about the two children born in 1883 and 1884. She does not go into the implications of her claim, i.e. that she must have been having sexual relations with both men, and Henry Harrison's interpretation was that by the time the book was published, Katharine was too infirm to realise the implication which had been inserted by the O'Shea editors. It is a possible interpretation, but ours is that Katharine knew what she was doing when she stated in print that Willie O'Shea thought he was the father of this child because she had in this instance panicked and deceived Parnell.

Thus one comes to July 1881, the month in which Willie O'Shea openly stated that his suspicions about his wife's relationship with Parnell were roused, and if it was in July that Katie informed her husband of her pregnancy, that piece of news could have been one of the reasons for their bitter quarrels. But if the thought that he was not the father of the child entered O'Shea's head, Katie presumably assured him that it was unjustified, and they returned to their former relationship, he living in London and she (and Parnell) staying at Wonersh Lodge. From the date of the bitter July quarrel, Katharine stated categorically, 'Parnell and I were one, without further scruple, without fear, without remorse', one of the few categorical statements in her memoirs and one which might intimate that up to this date she had not been exclusively Parnell's. Years later, in the course of her conversations with Henry Harrison, she said that of course Willie had known about her affair with Parnell, almost from the start, but the understanding had been implicit rather than explicit, suggesting that during their various quarrels everybody talked round in circles with nobody openly shouting the stark facts that she and Parnell adored each other and Willie was being cuckolded. Then again she told Harrison that she did once blurt out the truth to her husband, and it was to him she related the story of Willie's being at Wonersh Lodge one night and coming into her bedroom to talk to her, whereupon Parnell strode in, put her over his shoulder, marched into his bedroom, flung her on to his bed and shut the door, leaving her husband in no doubt about the relationship. According to Sir William Harcourt, then the Home Secretary, the triangle was clarified at this early date; he said that O'Shea threatened to divorce his wife in 1881 but was dissuaded by her counter-threats to reveal his easily proven adulteries.

Against these explicit statements O'Shea's constant, unwavering assertions of deceived unawareness have to be balanced, as has the fact that Katharine and Parnell kept up a measure of deception, albeit in inept fashion. One can fairly say that from the start Willie O'Shea's gullibility seems to have been beyond belief. He was no innocent country bumpkin, by his own and everybody's accounts he was a cynical, sophisticated man of the world, and it therefore seems incredible that having had his suspicions of adultery aroused, having quarrelled bitterly with his wife and threatened to leave her, having challenged Parnell to a duel—all this on his own admissions—he then calmly accepted that there was no truth in the allegations. What is not so difficult to believe is that in 1881 his wife managed to convince him either that the affair was at an end, or that if it should continue she would be extremely discreet. What is also easily believable is that Willie wanted to dismiss the knowledge from his mind, because there were many reasons why he should pretend he did not know. There were his pride and his sense of possession—and if compared to Parnell he had little, he had some; there were his income from Aunt Ben and his political ambitions, both of which would disappear if he were involved in a scandal with Parnell;

and there was the thought of the scandal itself, a situation which a conventionally-minded man, and a believing if lax Catholic, would abhor.

As the tension subsided domestically, it continued to mount politically. By the end of July, the Land Bill was safely through the House of Commons, so Parnell donned his revolutionary hat and at the beginning of August made an outrageous speech in the House for which he was suspended. He immediately crossed over to Ireland, where for the next two months, as he wrote to Katie, 'Her husband [i.e. himself] has been so busy he has not even had time to sleep, but he has never been too busy to think of her.' In Ireland he busied himself with the purchase of a newspaper to propagate the force of his leadership and his views on how Home Rule should be obtained. It was called *United Ireland*, was edited by the young Parnellite William O'Brien and was to play a vital part in the future struggle. A united Ireland was what Parnell wanted, under his leadership, but when the Land Bill received the royal assent towards the end of August, the militants urged him not to accept its terms but to continue to fight for full peasant proprietary, initially and immediately by implementing the No-Rent campaign. From his American supporters he received a cable advocating similar action: 'Unfurl the banner of No Rent. . . . Hold the Harvest. . . . If this is not done America will be disheartened.' If this were done he would lose the support of the moderates, including the Catholic hierarchy and clergy, and it required every ounce of Parnell's tactical finesse to hold the balance. In the process of trying to do this, he embarked upon a series of highly inflammatory speeches in Ireland, and on 7 October 1881 Mr Gladstone came to his rescue when he made one of his most famous speeches in the Cloth Hall at Leeds. Parnell's utterances had become too much for Gladstone to bear, and reading them with hindsight, one can see that he had justification for his anger. He had exerted every ounce of his energy and his vast parliamentary skill in getting the Land Bill passed, it was what Ireland had demanded, now here was the Irish leader apparently trying to frustrate its implementation. At Leeds, Gladstone surveyed the Irish scene, paying special attention to Daniel O'Connell and contrasting the present Irish leader unfavourably with him. Interestingly, Aunt Ben had already been introduced by Katie to Parnell as a new friend of the family, and had found him charming and an improvement on the last great Irish leader, Mr. O'Connell. Like Gladstone she was sufficiently old to have met 'the Liberator' and she told 'the Chief', 'I much prefer your voice, Mr. Parnell, for Daniel O'Connell's enunciations were startling to me.'

In the Cloth Hall at Leeds, Mr Gladstone was not impressed by anything about Mr Parnell. He said that whereas Mr O'Connell had been a true Irish patriot who believed that the essence of a civilised society was a respect for the law, for other people's rights and properties, Mr Parnell, who professed to be an Irish patriot, appeared to be bent on destroying everything that was of value by preaching a doctrine of public plunder. He warned Parnell, 'And if . . . it should then appear that there is still to be fought a final conflict in Ireland between the law on one side and sheer lawlessness on the other . . . then I say, gentlemen, without hesitation, the resources of civilisation are not yet exhausted.' Parnell duly took note of the warning, and two days later in Wexford he delivered his equally famous reply in which he said, 'It is a good sign that this masquerading knight-errant, this pretended champion of the liberties of every other nation except those of the Irish nation, should be obliged to throw off the mask today and to stand revealed as the man who, by his own utterances, is prepared to carry fire and sword into your homesteads unless you humble and abase yourselves before him and before the landlords of this country.' There were many observers who believed that in this speech Parnell deliberately courted arrest, and in the event Gladstone obliged him and on 13 October the Irish leader was arrested and lodged in Kilmainham gaol, alongside other prominent nationalists.

For Katharine this was a shattering, if not unexpected, blow. In her own euphemistic words, typical of the period, her health was then 'delicate', which meant she was having a bad pregnancy. She and Parnell had kept in constant touch but she had not seen him for two and a half months, and Katharine always liked to have her men around when she needed them. At this moment she needed Parnell desperately, to soothe and to sustain her, because perhaps for the first time in her life she was really frightened. Apart from the physical strain of the pregnancy she was suffering from great mental stress, bereft of her lover, fearful for his safety, pretending to her husband that the child she was carrying was his, on the surface playing the O'Shea version of happy families. Despite her ill-health, Katie had been acting on Parnell's behalf in London, trying to discover from her Liberal contacts whether the Government intended to arrest him, then when it seemed certain that they did, to ascertain the precise date so that she could warn Parnell and he could destroy secret or incriminating documents. Katie had at least one highly placed Liberal contact (whom she did not name), and after a hastily summoned Cabinet meeting on 12 October she was able to telegraph to Parnell in Dublin telling him that his arrest was imminent. The news plunged her into despair, she had to see Parnell once before he was arrested, and she sent him another wire begging him to meet her in Holyhead. The extent of her distress can be gauged from this telegram, because Katharine had previously shown—and thereafter showed—little inclination to travel far afield to meet her lover, it was Parnell who came to her. His reply dissuaded her from the journey, said he must suffer arrest for the sake of Ireland but assured her he would behave himself in Kilmainham so that his imprisonment would not be for long.

During the early hours of 13 October and throughout much of the day, gale-force winds swept across southern England. Katharine was unable to sleep, as much because of her fears for Parnell and her own distraught condition as because of the howling winds, and early in the morning she went for a walk through Aunt Ben's estate, battling against the strength of the wind, watching the autumn leaves spiralling into the air like geysers, the branches rip and the trees crash, and the wildness of the elements was attuned to the wildness of her fears. During the day she had to attend to Aunt Ben and she was grateful for the ordered stillness of Eltham Lodge, for the steady drone of her aunt's voice as she talked of the days of her youth and of events that had no connection with Parnell or Ireland. When she returned to Wonersh Lodge, hearing Parnell's voice in the raging wind telling her to be brave, Katharine was greeted by her legal husband. The visit was not unannounced, he had previously written to say he would like to come to dinner that evening, but he had hastened down earlier than expected to give his wife the news of Parnell's arrest. Katharine recorded a grisly dinner *à deux* during which her husband gloated over the news, and said the Irish leader fully deserved his imprisonment, while all the time watching her reactions. She managed to survive the ordeal with composure, and the next day she received the letter Parnell had written as he was being arrested at Morrison's Hotel in Dublin. In this he told Katie 'that she must be a brave little woman', saying that the only worry he had was that his imprisonment might upset her and the child but that she must not grieve because 'I can never have any other wife but you, and if anything happens to you I must die childless. Be good, and brave, dear

[85]

little Wifie, then, Your Own Husband.' He added a post-script which upholds the contention that he had deliberately courted arrest as the best way out of his present difficulties: 'Politically it is a fortunate thing for me that I have been arrested, as the movement is breaking fast, and all will be quiet in a few months, when I shall be released.' By being imprisoned Parnell automatically acquired in Ireland the martyr's halo accorded to a victim of British repression, but the resolution was not to be as simple or as speedy as he hoped.

Chapter Seven

From Kilmainham, Parnell quickly managed to establish contact with Katie, first with the help of an officially recognised prison visitor who smuggled their letters in and out, then, when this source was stopped, by means of a friendly warder and various kinds of invisible ink and special notepaper. There were frequent instructions from Parnell on their use. 'You had best test the No 1 solution by attempting to bring it out with No 2. If it does not come out well increase the strength of both solutions. Use unglazed rough paper', and 'In future you had best brush any letters I write to you at E[ltham] with No 2 solution' and 'You need not write so heavily or use so much ink, and it would be also better to have a softer paper, more like blotting paper' and 'The paper of the 6th, which reached me today, is exactly suited; but Wifie, in sending two sheets, one of them quite blank, makes a bad conspirator.' In truth, both he and Katharine were rotten conspirators but in the Kilmainham days they succeeded in covering their tracks. The reason they wished to do so was partially political, in that they did not want to harm Parnell's reputation, but it was more the desire to keep the personal *status quo*. Had any of the letters fallen into the hands of Parnell's opponents, they would not have learned much of what was going on in his mind politically but they would have been astounded by the emotional revelations. The figure Parnell presented to the world was capable of being charming, some even spoke of the sweetness of his sudden smile, but he was generally regarded as being aloof, cold and iron-willed, while in his letters to Katie there was revealed a man not only devoured by passionate love but one who expressed it in a whimsical, childish fashion. When Katharine made the letters public they were designated 'such as a kitchenmaid might receive from the underfootman', and this typically English class-conscious castigation is not without justification, as a selection from the letters will indicate.

Apart from the ones openly written and posted to 'My Dear Mrs O'Shea', the letters started 'My own dearest wife', 'My own darling Queenie', 'My own darling wifie', and were signed 'Your loving husband', 'Your own husband', 'Your own loving King', 'Always your king'. Most lovers, married or otherwise, have pet names, certainly at the start of a relationship, so there is nothing unusual about 'King' and 'Queenie', except perhaps as an indication of the eminent plane on which they regarded themselves and their love, but much of the phraseology is coy, doubly so in contrast to the sparse direct nature of Parnell's public utterances. Soon after his arrest he wrote to Katharine: 'If Wifie is very good and becomes strong and happy again I may let her come over and see me after a time . . . and now goodnight, my own dear little wifie. Promise your husband that you will sleep well and look as beautiful when we meet again as the last time I pressed your sweet lips.' A fortnight later he was writing: 'Queenie, then, will see that she also must try not to be so unhappy, especially as her husband's love is becoming stronger and more intense every hour and every day . . . I am going to ask Katie to put her proper initials upon the inner envelope of her next letter—thus, K.P. . . . with a thousand kisses to my own Wifie, and hoping soon to lay my head in its old place, Good night, my darling.' In December 1881 he wrote: 'I expect to be so fresh when I get out that even Wifie won't be able to hold me . . . although her bonds are very strong and pleasant.' There were constant references to the child she was bearing: 'Do beautiful Wife, take care of yourself and your King's child', 'Am rejoiced to learn that Wifie hopes our child will be strong—I think it ought to have a good constitution', 'Give my best love to our little child, and take good care of yourself and it for my sake', 'Queenie has been very good and very loving to her husband to give him this child, and to take such care of it during this long, sad interval.'

There were references to Queenie's legal husband: 'Has he left yet? It is frightful that you should be exposed to such daily torture' (this referred to Captain O'Shea's unwanted presence at Eltham and to Katharine's complaints of his thinly-veiled taunts); and again: 'I am trying to arrange that you may see me as soon as he is gone to Madrid.' But above all there were the reassurances Katie needed in the affirmation of how much she meant to him: 'My darling, you are and always will be everything to me, and every day you come more and more, if possible, more than everything to me', and 'How could I ever live without my own Katie?—and if you are in danger, my darling, I will come to you at once', and 'But my darling, you frighten me dreadfully when you tell me that I am "surely killing" you and our child. . . . Rather than that my beautiful Wifie should run any risk I will resign my seat, leave politics, and go away somewhere with my own Queenie, as soon as she wishes.' Apart from their sentimentality, the other striking feature of Parnell's letters is their humbleness—it was his darling Queenie who was doing him the favour by loving him—and their sublime indifference to reality. Theirs might be a marriage of true minds and bodies, a sanctified union in the sight of their personal God, but Katie was not his wife and he was not her husband.

By mid-December 1881, when she wrote to tell Parnell that his continued imprisonment was 'surely killing' her, Katharine was feeling desperate. Everything had become too much for her. She was seven months pregnant, she was not carrying well, she had the burden of running the house, attending to Aunt Ben and the older children, she had nobody in whom she could confide, the man she did not love was appearing at Eltham more frequently than he had ever done, and the man she wanted was wilfully keeping himself in prison. Apart from her own miseries, she was fearful of the effects of prolonged imprisonment on Parnell's always delicate health, and these fears were not soothed by frequent references in the Irish nationalist press to the poorness of the prison fare and the news that Mr Parnell was in the infirmary or that the doctor had been summoned to attend him. The nationalist papers were naturally eager to seize on any point which would emphasise the gross injustice of their leader's imprisonment and the oppressive nature of Gladstone's supposedly liberal Liberal Government, but a distraught Katharine took their every emphatic word to heart. Parnell spent a considerable amount of notepaper assuring her that the food was quite good, in fact he was not on prison fare, the reports about his health were alarmist, he was only staying in the infirmary because it was so pleasant, later that he had only caught a slight cold, he had put on weight, and really he had never felt better in his life. Katharine was not impressed. She knew—who better?—how fragile his constitution was, he needed her to look after him, and if he insisted on staying in prison he would end by killing himself physically and her mentally. Surely, if he cared for her as much as he professed, Parnell could make some deal with Mr Gladstone and get himself out?

In December, as his Queenie's desperate, accusing letters reached him, Parnell extended tentative feelers to the Prime Minister, but they were ignored. Much of British and Irish loyalist opinion was outraged by the mounting violence in Ireland, it did not view the situation as a direct result of the Irish leader's imprisonment, it saw it as the inevitable corollary of Parnell's recent campaigns with their threat of force, therefore he should stay in prison until the fully justified coercive measures proved effective and he had learned his lesson. Gladstone himself was no lover of repression and was far from convinced that coercion would do other than stiffen resistance, but he was the Prime Minister, it was his duty to maintain law and order, he had many voices reminding him of the fact, and for the time being he did not consider that Parnell's staying in gaol would harm him or worsen the situation. However desperately Katharine wanted Parnell out of Kilmainham, she was not prepared to accept his offer to abandon his political career—it was a splendid declaration of love but it was going too far. When it became apparent that Gladstone was not in the mood to release him, as the moment for her confinement drew near, she rallied her strength and there were long-distance discussions as to whether she should go to London or Brighton for the birth. In the event, the child—a girl—was born at Eltham on 16 February 1882, after a long labour and a difficult delivery. When her 'poor husband' received the news in Kilmainham on 14 February that his own darling Queenie had started labour he burst into tears, and could think of nothing but her until he received the further news on 17 February that mother and child were doing well. In fact, Parnell had expected to be released with the opening of the new session of Parliament in February but throughout March he remained in Kilmainham, now possessing an added incentive for freedom in the desire to see his child. The secret letters continued: 'I want Queenie when I see her to be an even younger little Wifie than when I gave her that last kiss. The idea of nursing our little daughter was too preposterous. Do, my own darling, think of yourself and take great, great care of your husband's own little Wifie.' Towards the end of March the child was ill and

Parnell wrote: 'I am very anxious about our little daughter. Is it dangerous?' but two days later he was relieved to hear that his daughter was better and begged for a snip of hair to put in the locket which already contained Katie's portrait and some strands of her hair. Katharine obliged and Parnell found the hair 'absolutely lovely' and was 'so glad it is more like Queenie's than mine.' But the baby's condition was deteriorating, by mid-April her mother was told that she could not long survive and the situation was heart-rending. In Eltham was Katharine, subject to the stress and strain, mental and physical, that many women experience after giving birth, with the knowledge that the baby was dying, while its father languished in prison unable to comfort her or perhaps ever see his child alive. Apart from being poignant, the situation had its gruesome side because her legal husband was on the spot, showing particular solicitude as the child's condition weakened. The strain of accepting Willie O'Shea's unwanted kindness must have been almost unbearable, and that the situation was largely of her own creation did not make it less so.

There was one ray of light. The situation in Ireland had deteriorated as fast as the baby's health, and by early April Gladstone was accepting that he would have to come to terms with the only man who could possibly control it, Parnell. When the Irish leader's nephew died in Paris, the Government was willing to take advantage of the sad opportunity and grant him parole to attend the funeral. Parnell, devoured by his love for Katie, wanting to be with her and the baby, was as willing to accept the offer which might lead to a compromise on both sides. In fact, prior to his temporary release he had started to sound the ground about a mutually acceptable deal with the Government, and on 8 April Willie O'Shea wrote to Mr Gladstone asking whether he had recently considered the compromises he had proposed last year (i.e. Parnell's proffered deal on the Land Act) in the light of possible present compromises. O'Shea said he wrote 'without any recent communication elsewhere', but though the role of sole begetter of secret Anglo-Irish initiatives was the one for which Willie had cast himself, it is doubtful that he wrote to Gladstone without Parnell's—or Katie's—knowledge. On 19 April Parnell was released on parole and made straight for Wonersh Lodge, where the baby still clung to life. She had already been christened in the Catholic faith, at Willie's insistence and with Katharine's consent—'Parnell and I had long ago agreed that it would be safer to have the child christened as a Catholic'—in the drawing-room

[91]

of Wonersh Lodge, before an altar of flowers constructed by her mother as the baby was too weak to be taken to the church. As he was officially *en route* to Paris to attend the funeral, Parnell was unable to stay more than a few hours in Eltham, but he managed to hold the sickly Claude Sophie in his arms and to have a political discussion with Captain O'Shea. (The child had been given the second name of Sophie on Parnell's suggestion 'as it was the name of one of my sisters whom I was said to be most like of the family'.)

In Paris Parnell remained for nearly ten days, partly to comfort his sister in her bereavement but mainly because he became ill with a fever and was forced to rest. In his absence but not without his knowledge Willie O'Shea was active, first writing a further enormously long letter to Mr Gladstone. In this he assured the Prime Minister that he had the Irish leader's permission to mediate since 'the person to whom Mr Parnell addresses himself in many cases (much as I differ from him in serious matters of politics and policy) is myself', and he revealed the startling information which surely nobody other than he could have believed that 'eighteen months ago Mr Parnell used every effort to induce me to take over the leadership of the party', this is a means of reassuring Mr Gladstone that he was not acting with 'fatuous officiousness'. Gladstone replied on 15 April, telling Captain O'Shea that he need not apologise for the length of his letter, or the freedom of its expression, and that he was sensible of the spirit in which it had been written. The door to negotiations was now firmly ajar, and on the same day as Gladstone replied to him, O'Shea made contact with Joseph Chamberlain, a leading Radical member of the Government. Whether he did this of his own initiative, or whether it was at Parnell's or Katie's urging, remains uncertain, but by writing to Chamberlain, on 15 April 1882, he drew that formidable and, as it proved, fatal figure firmly into the drama.

Chamberlain was forty-six in 1882, an elegant man with his slim build, dark hair and monocle, such as to delight O'Shea's dandified heart. Born into a prosperous middle-class background, Chamberlain had been a late-comer to the national political field, but he had earlier established himself as a national figure by his campaigns for free elementary education for the children of England and Wales, then by his work as the reforming Radical Mayor of Birmingham when he had embarked on council reorganisation and slum clearance schemes. With his capacity for hard work and ability to get things done—it was said that had it been possible for land-locked Birmingham to be linked with the sea, Chamberlain would have achieved it—he was by many regarded as the personification of the salutary new power of radical, middle-class, nonconformist England. In some quarters he was also regarded as the next leader of the Liberal party, and as Mr Gladstone was in his seventy-third year and had already semi-retired once, that prospect seemed imminent. Apart from his general qualities, the known ambitions matched by ability, Chamberlain had long shown an interest in Irish affairs, one that was sympathetic to the nationalist demands. However, he was a subscriber to the idea then very popular, that the Anglo-Saxon races (the English in particular) must inherit the earth by virtue of their superior intelligence, albeit by peaceful means. Long before Chamberlain became enmeshed in the concept of the grandeur of the British Empire, his public utterances made it clear that he would not tolerate the disintegration of even the less grand empire, but the warning reservations contained in his statements were ignored by the nationalists, and they then regarded Joseph Chamberlain as one of their more useful and forceful allies.

In his letter of 15 April O'Shea said he was taking the liberty of addressing Mr Chamberlain and enclosing a copy of the letter he had written to Mr Gladstone, because Mr Chamberlain appeared to be 'a Minister without political pedantry' who might persuade the Liberal Party that honourable compromise with the Irish nationalists was desirable. Chamberlain, who had no knowledge that Parnell had entered into any sort of negotiations with Gladstone, however tentative they then were, replied in guarded fashion, saying he was not in possession of all the facts, nor was he in a position to commit the Liberal party to a *détente*. However, he thought Captain O'Shea's proposals worthy of consideration, adding the warning that both sides would have to make concessions, and thus far the nationalists had done nothing to understand or appease British public opinion. O'Shea replied by return of post, asking if he might communicate the Minister's letter to Mr Parnell? Chamberlain said he could, and himself immediately wrote to the Prime Minister, stating his opinion that negotiations should be secretly opened with Parnell, who was assuredly tired of prison life. He pressed one further point for Mr Gladstone's consideration: 'Might not Mr Forster offer Mr Parnell, who seems to be suffering from indisposition, an extension of his parole under present conditions?' In the meantime, O'Shea had written another letter to Gladstone in which he said he had heard from Mr Parnell in Paris, and the latter agreed that the correspondence was worth pursuing and that the prospect for a compromise looked favourable. When Parnell returned to Wonersh Lodge, officially breaking his journey at a friend's house *en route* back to Kilmainham, the prospects had assumed a rosier hue politically, but personally they were heart-breaking.

During this week which had—as both Parnell and Gladstone had hoped when they negotiated the parole—opened the way to compromise, Katharine had been watching the life ebb from her baby, again without Parnell's presence to sustain or comfort her, with the putative father heavily engaged in negotiations of vital importance to the actual father's political future. On 21 April 1882 the triangular relationship reached a macabre peak. Early in the day Willie O'Shea had hurried down to Eltham, bearing the news that Mr Chamberlain had obtained from Mr Forster an extension of Parnell's parole if he so desired. But Parnell did not so desire; he was prepared to enter into a deal for Ireland and risk the Fenian backlash on that score, but he could not allow his personal release (which an extension of the parole would probably become) to precede a deal, for that would damn him in all nationalist eyes. Whether, in view of the dying Claude Sophie, he told Katharine that he could remain at liberty if he wished is unclear—she herself does not mention the extension of the parole—but during the day he managed to have some conversation of a political nature with her, and she impressed upon him her passionate wish that he should reach a compromise with Mr Gladstone, as much, she claimed, for the sake of his political future as to satisfy her personal desires.

It was in the evening of 21 April that the extraordinary, macabre scene ensued. Upstairs in the nursery the baby Claude Sophie was dying, watched over by her distraught mother, while downstairs in the sitting-room—the one in which Katie and Parnell had already spent so many blissfully domestic evenings—the two men who each believed himself to be the child's father hammered out the details of an agreement which would be acceptable to Ireland and the Liberal Government and which Captain O'Shea could transmit to Mr Gladstone. Throughout the night, as Katharine sat by the cot watching the baby die, the two men discussed and argued, and as the dawn broke, O'Shea retired to bed while Parnell stole into the nursery. He appears to have been present as Claude Sophie sighed the last breath of her brief, six-week life, but then by the terms of the original parole he had to return to prison in Dublin. The atmosphere at Wonersh Lodge on 22 April must have been incredible, with the baby dead, Parnell unable to show his grief too openly, and both men too involved with the political negotiations to spend much time with the distressed Katharine. She herself made little comment upon the situation—it was inherent in the stance they had all decided to adopt—and she had the hope that the compromise worked upon as her child lay dying would soon effect its father's permanent release. At this point in the proceedings, Katie was assuredly being what Parnell had urged her to be as he was arrested six months earlier, a good, brave little wife.

As Parnell returned to Kilmainham on 22 April, the Cabinet met and Chamberlain was authorised to negotiate with him, though he was warned that if he failed to conclude a mutually satisfactory deal and the news became public, he would be disowned by his colleagues. In the evening the accepted intermediary, Captain O'Shea, was summoned to Chamberlain's London house, where he transmitted the outline terms he and Parnell had thrashed out the previous awful evening at Wonersh Lodge. A few days later, with the knowledge that the Government was willing to release Parnell (and the other imprisoned Irish leaders) if he would guarantee his side of the bargain, O'Shea crossed to Dublin. Parnell had already drafted the final terms of what became known as 'the Kilmainham treaty' on 25 April from prison, the day Claude Sophie was buried in the Catholic cemetery at Chislehurst, and in the letter he wrote to his own darling Queenie keeping her abreast of events he said, 'It is too terrible to think that on this saddest day of all others—and, let us hope, the saddest day we *both* shall ever see again—my Wifie should have nobody with her.' (Willie O'Shea was present at the funeral but he did not count.) When O'Shea called on Mr Forster to acquaint him with the results of his several interviews with the imprisoned Irish leader, Forster was not enthusiastic, considering that Parnell had given insufficient guarantees and had failed to condemn violence. However, Parnell had written another letter, officially to Captain O'Shea, though it was for Gladstone's eyes, which the Prime Minister considered 'the most extraordinary I ever read.' Apart from the contents, it is the most extraordinary letter to regard, being written on the black-edged note-paper then popular, in bright purple ink, virtually illegible (Parnell had at the best of times a spidery hand distinguished by swooping loops), with sentences crawling up and round and down the edges of the main text. It is an example of Parnell's supreme confidence that he should despatch such a vital letter in such a slap-happy manner.

[95]

The letter was officially dated 28 April 1882, reiterated the terms that Parnell was prepared to accept regarding the Land Act and then said that a practical settlement of the land question would—and these were the vital historic words—'enable us to co-operate cordially for the future with the Liberal party in forwarding Liberal principles and measures of general reform.' When Gladstone read this astonishing offer of co-operation he considered it 'an *hors d'oeuvre* which we had no right to expect, and I rather think have no right at present to accept.' Whatever his feelings about the premature nature of accepting Irish nationalist co-operation, he decided Parnell had given sufficient guarantees to justify his release and on 2 May he was freed. Gladstone might have been interested to know that the historic letter was 'in substance' drafted by Katharine O'Shea and Parnell at Wonersh Lodge a week earlier than it was dated, and was finally handed to her husband on 28 April because, as Parnell told Katie, 'he would have been dreadfully mortified if he had nothing to show.' The nationalists would also have been interested to learn of Mrs O'Shea's role in the affair, for when the news of the 'treaty' was leaked it came as a bombshell to most of them. Inasmuch as the Fenian-constitutional merger of 1879 was generally approved as the 'New Departure', Parnell's Kilmainham deal was in many quarters disapproved of as his 'one man New Departure'.

Katharine's influence on Parnell during the Kilmainham negotiations and after has been the subject of some speculation, though not a great deal because most writers have concentrated on him, but his life was now inextricably linked with the O'Sheas' and Katie said she brought all her influence to bear in persuading Parnell to compromise and write the historic letter. She said it was because she dreaded the extremist forces which were threatening to plunge Ireland into disaster, she knew only he could subdue them, she was most anxious that he should reign constitutionally (the choice of verb is hers), and her personal wish for his speedy release was of secondary importance. If one accepts that her motives were political rather than personal (and she had been very political about Claude Sophie's death and had not demanded that Parnell stay with her), the question remains, how greatly did her English Liberal view of the world affect him? Katie was a headstrong, emotional woman, she had a good belief in her own intellectual abilities, and if she thought she was right she pursued her own way relentlessly. Gladstone was among those who considered that she had led Parnell onto the path of moderation, while Frank Hugh O'Donnell said that from this period, 'the highly gifted woman who was the Egeria of the member for Cork* was the predominating partner of his political ideas.'

As indicated, when O'Donnell got a bee in his bonnet it buzzed with insistent ferocity, and one of his bees was that it was he who had originally initiated the Kilmainham negotiations, which had gone wrong when his advice was ignored, but some of his insights and observations have validity. While the idea that Katie was the predominating political partner (before or after Kilmainham) can be dismissed, her influence was perhaps greater than has been allowed. Parnell himself recognised that the semi-revolutionary fervour of the Land League had brought him thus far and focussed attention on Ireland, but he also knew that the limit to daring had been reached, for the time being anyway, that the British Government would not be pushed too far by one section of one part of the United Kingdom and that it was in his interests to control the extremists. His own political judgement and character moved him towards the straighter constitutional path, but whether without Katie's pressures it would have been at that precise moment or in those precise terms is less certain.

When Parnell emerged from Kilmainham, he and Katie continued to view their private life as one matter, his public life as Irish nationalist leader as another, each separate and distinct. But the use of Willie O'Shea as Kilmainham negotiator had further battered down the domestic and political dividing line—a thin one from the outset—and it was not long after Parnell's release that several comments were made which cast an interesting light on Liberal knowledge of the entanglement. Gladstone's close personal friend and political colleague Lord Granville remarked to him that 'She [Katie] is said to be Parnell's mistress'; Edward Hamilton (Gladstone's Private Secretary) noted in his diary, 'She seems to be on very intimate terms with Parnell; some say his mistress'; while Sir Charles Dilke, a prominent Radical member of the Government, recorded in *his* diary comments made at a Cabinet meeting held on 17 May. Dilke wrote: 'At this cabinet Harcourt made himself specially disagreeable. He told the Cabinet that the Kilmainham treaty would not be popular when it was discovered that it had been negotiated "by Captain O'Shea, the husband of Parnell's mistress".' Dilke went on to record the allegations already referred to by writing:

---

* Parnell had been returned for Cork in the 1880 election.

'He [Harcourt] informed the cabinet that he knew that in 1881 O'Shea had threatened Parnell with divorce proceedings, and that it was only Mrs O'Shea's discovery of adulterous relations of her husband which put him in her power; that he had shut his eyes and made the best of it but after all this it would hardly do for the public to use O'Shea as negotiator.'

It has been pointed out that there was no official Cabinet meeting on 17 May 1882, but it did meet informally, and information in a recent book* suggests that Harcourt continued to make himself 'specially disagreeable' by stating that if the Cabinet did not agree to a renewal of the Coercion Act in Ireland, he would not only resign but would make public his knowledge of the Parnell–Mrs O'Shea liaison, a revelation which would harm the Liberal party as well as the Irish nationalists. (The idea of negotiation with the nationalists was in some quarters regarded as tantamount to treason, for at worst they were terrorists, at best they were citizens of the United Kingdom who should be glad to enjoy its benefits and cease to cause trouble.) As Home Secretary with direct responsibility for the police and secret security forces, Harcourt was in as good a position as anybody to know of Parnell's movements and activities (the Irish leader had been under surveillance for some time). Harcourt was also a rumbustious character who enjoyed making himself disagreeable and had no love for Parnell, so there seems little reason to doubt that he threatened the Cabinet with his information, which he believed to be accurate. Whether the Cabinet allowed itself to be influenced by Harcourt's threats is another matter, for the great difficulty about public revelation of the liaison was that O'Shea's co-operation was needed because if he denied that his wife was committing adultery with Mr Parnell the bold informant could be in legal trouble.

Apart from Harcourt's categorical statements about O'Shea's position as *mari complaisant* from an early date in the affair, there is a further piece of information which substantiates the claim. In the aftermath of Parnell's death, Henry Harrison had access to many O'Shea documents and letters which were not produced in court, and one in particular caught his attention, this being an agreement made in 1882 between Captain and Mrs O'Shea. In this letter, according to Mr Harrison, Katharine said she would pay her husband £600 per annum from

---

* *The Governing Passion* by A. B. Cooke and John Vincent.

the money she was then receiving from Aunt Ben on the understanding that he would not interfere with her life but would leave her free to pursue it in the manner she chose. Supporting the idea of a definite agreement, Parnell had written to Katie from Kilmainham after the birth of Claude Sophie: 'If my own can make an arrangement now for him to keep away, I think she ought to do so. It will be too intolerable having him about always. When I see Wifie again or am released, I can consider the situation, but until then, if you can you had best make some arrangement.' The agreement did not openly state that Katharine had chosen to live with the man she loved, but its terms were fairly explicit, and it seems reasonable to assume that O'Shea knew about the affair almost from the start, that there was the major contretemps in 1881 (when Katie may or may not have threatened her husband with retaliatory measures if he took action), that the matter simmered while Parnell was in Kilmainham and that on his release a typical O'Shea agreement was reached. It was that a financially remunerated Willie would hear nothing, see nothing, know nothing as long as his wife and Parnell were discreet and his political career flourished. Certainly O'Shea was not much in evidence at Eltham for the rest of 1882—one of his witnesses in the divorce court when asked if Captain O'Shea came down on Sundays replied, 'Sometimes, but not very often.' Also about this time O'Shea changed his London abode, with his wife's assistance, moving into 1 Albert Mansions, Victoria Street, a property belonging to Katie's nephew, Matthew Wood.

After Parnell had returned to Wonersh Lodge, the political scene demanded his attention and he was unable to enjoy his reunion with Katie for long. When Gladstone decided on the releases from Kilmainham, an outraged Mr Forster resigned, which meant that a new Chief Secretary for Ireland had to be appointed, and who was to undertake the job, which was currently almost as crucial as the Prime Minister's? One person who would have liked it and was convinced he was equipped to succeed in it was Joseph Chamberlain, and on 3 May Willie O'Shea, astonished but undaunted by his own audacity, wrote to Mr Gladstone to assure him that if Mr Chamberlain went to Ireland Mr Parnell would work for his success as heartily as for his own. This letter could have been penned on Willie's initiative because he was at this euphoric, post-Kilmainham moment enraptured by his 'insight into so many details of Irish affairs, political and personal', as he told Gladstone, but the appointment would then have had Parnell's backing. Gladstone had other ideas and he selected his nephew-by-marriage, Lord Frederick Cavendish, to be the new Irish Chief Secretary. As soon as the appointment was made public, Willie O'Shea switched allegiance and wrote to the Prime Minister saying he felt his responsibilities deeply but he was hopeful about the future and would therefore like to make the acquaintance of Lord Frederick, to which Gladstone's secretary appended the laconic summary, 'Wishes to make better acquaintance with Lord F.C. Is hopeful.'

Lord Frederick Cavendish was the bearer of a historic name, was much loved by the Prime Minister, was by no means a fool but seemingly lacked the personality or experience for a job such as Chief Secretary. Whether he would have developed into a good Secretary remains unknown, because on the evening of 6 May as he strolled in the park in the early summer evening sun, taking the air after his arrival in Dublin, he and his companion, the Permanent Under-Secretary, Thomas Burke, were brutally stabbed to death. The 'Phoenix Park Murders' had been committed. Katie allowed herself some musings on what the future would have held if Joseph Chamberlain had been offered and had accepted the post. As 'the Invincibles' who were later found to have been the perpetrators of the crime had not apparently intended to murder Lord Frederick, the hated Burke being their victim, would Chamberlain's known nationalist sympathies have saved him? If he had survived would he have become a supporter rather than an opponent of Home Rule? Would he have been the Chief Secretary to have earned the laurels of Irish peace? Or if he had been killed would Home Rule, without his leading opposition, have passed through Parliament? In her opinion, the fact that Chamberlain was not asked to become Irish Chief Secretary in 1882 was 'one of the most momentous in British politics'. As it was, the impact of the murders, brutal stabbings in a public park in the summer sun, was momentous enough. Everybody except 'the Invincibles' themselves and a few extremist nationalists was shattered by the news, not least Parnell.

On 6 May Parnell travelled to Dorset to greet Michael Davitt as, under the terms of the Kilmainham deal, he came out of Portland prison, returning to Eltham in the evening. Early the next morning Katie drove him to Blackheath station to catch the local train to London, where he was again meeting Davitt to discuss the political situation. While they were waiting for the train Parnell bought *The Observer,* and as he read the headlines telling of the Phoenix Park murders, his face became ashen, his body rigid, and when Katie rushed to discover what was the matter he grasped her hand so tightly that the rings cut into her flesh and bruised her fingers. She was not the only person who commented on his stricken reaction. Davitt himself said, 'His face was deadly pale, with a look of alarm in his eyes which I had never seen in any expression before or since.' Parnell was so horrified by the deed and the feeling that Ireland's cause was doomed that he wrote to Gladstone, naturally through the medium of Willie O'Shea, offering to resign his parliamentary seat. Gladstone refused the offer, officially deeply sensible of the honourable motives which had prompted it, privately convinced that if Parnell went, no restraining influence would remain and no British repressive measures could possibly control the outrages. Katie was also convinced that Parnell must remain in politics and she showed early symptoms of the headstrong defiance which buttressed her lover's stance during the divorce storm in 1890—her King was no coward, he must fight back and regain control of the situation.

Chapter Eight

In the aftermath of the Phoenix Park murders, Gladstone was one of the few Englishmen willing to grant Parnell, or any Irish nationalist, any sort of honourable motive. The House of Commons reflected the mood of Great Britain at large and was militantly anti-Irish, and on 15 May MPs demanded to know on what terms Mr Gladstone had agreed to release the imprisoned Irish leaders. Gladstone asserted that their release had not been promised or negotiated by his administration, which technically it had not been as Chamberlain had been told to act without official backing and Parnell's freedom was not mentioned in the correspondence. The Opposition continued to press the matter and eventually Parnell read to the House his letter of 28 April, but as soon as he sat down Mr Forster jumped up to enquire whether all the letter had been read. Parnell said it had, whereupon Forster produced his copy, which happened to contain some lines the honourable member for Cork had omitted, those being the ones about the future cordial Irish nationalist co-operation with the Liberal Party. There was then uproar in the House, and it was Captain O'Shea's turn to rise and produce an extraordinary, complicated explanation. It was he who had handed to Mr Parnell the copy he had just read with the vital lines omitted, although these lines had admittedly been in the original as drafted by Mr Parnell. Captain O'Shea had asked for them to be expunged when he had handed the letter over for Liberal consideration; he thought his request had been carried out and therefore the copy he had given to Mr Parnell was as he thought it had been delivered to Mr Gladstone. The answers far from satisfied the critics and left a nasty taste in many mouths about dubious Liberal–Home Rule deals, which were especially obnoxious in the light of Phoenix Park, and that Parnell should have forgotten within the space of a fortnight that he had agreed to co-operate with the Liberal Party is odd, or an indication of how little weight he attached to his offer. The incident also gives an early indication that O'Shea as an intermediary was liable to expunge or interpret intentions and is noteworthy for being the only occasion when Mr Parnell and Captain O'Shea publicly and amicably stood shoulder to shoulder, which would seem to underline the serenity of the domestic arrangements in mid-1882.

Throughout May and June, O'Shea continued to act as intermediary between Parnell and Gladstone. The Prime Minister had decided to press ahead with the Arrears Bill, which embodied the Irish amendments to the Land Act, and the secret bargaining lay in how many amendments Gladstone would try to force through the hostile, post-Phoenix-Park-murders Parliament in return for Parnell's limited opposition to an extension of the Coercion Act. By this time Katie had found her political feet, and it was her wish to help her King in every way she could. The concept of Home Rule for Ireland had flowed into her from Parnell like water into an empty pitcher; it was essential, it was just, it was inevitable, and like Parnell she did not trouble herself about the reasons, the motives or the passions of those opposed to the idea of a partial hiving-off of a section of the United Kingdom. The strategic aim was clear and immutable, but the question of tactics was fluid. For the moment Parnell thought a period of entrenchment was required in which he would investigate the possible fruits to be borne by co-operation with the Liberal Party. Of these tactics Katie thoroughly approved, and it occurred to her that she could supply a more direct, personal link with Mr Gladstone than that provided by her husband. Because of the hostility to the nationalists and the feeling that they were a temporary irritant rather than a serious political threat (as strong in the Liberal Party as in the Tory), any communication between Parnell and Gladstone was bound to be tentative and secret. Who better to provide a new secret link than she who had Parnell's absolute trust and confidence, and as the niece of Gladstone's former Lord Chancellor had high Liberal credentials?

Accordingly, at the end of May 1882 Katharine made contact with Mr Gladstone, in fact to ask if he would grant Mr Parnell a private interview. She stressed that she was writing in absolute confidence, begging Mr Gladstone not to reveal the request to *anyone,* 'not even to Captain O'Shea', and how soon Willie became aware that his wife was also acting as intermediary is unclear, though he later professed to have known of her activities. To this first letter Gladstone replied promptly but regretted that he could not agree to a private meeting, as he considered it might cause serious mischief and have the effect of injuring Mr Parnell's position and weakening his hand. So Katie wrote again, fearing she was one of 'the many examples of "Fools rushing in" ', and asked the Prime Minister to spare *her,* as Parnell's political confidante, a few minutes of his precious time. To this request Gladstone acceded, and on 2 June the Prime Minister and Mrs O'Shea met privately at her favourite hotel, Thomas's in Berkeley Square, and proceeded to discuss matters pertaining to Ireland and Mr Parnell. Katie said this was the first of many interviews with Mr Gladstone, initially at Thomas's Hotel, then at Downing Street, and she described his courtesy, his charm, his 'wonderful eagle eyes', his habit of taking her by the arm and pacing up and down while they talked, in the privacy of Downing Street, that was, not at Thomas's Hotel. (When Katie made this revelation in her memoirs Gladstone was dead, but his son Herbert was outraged and said the idea of his father cosily arm-in-arm with Mrs O'Shea was too ridiculous for words.)

Throughout June and July 1882 Katharine was in constant touch with Mr Gladstone, being fortunate to meet a Prime Minister who liked women and did not consider it ridiculous that his contact should be female. At the end of their first interview, according to Katharine, her position was clearly understood; she said that Gladstone 'allowed me to know that he knew, what I desired that he should know—that my personal interest in Parnell was my only interest in Irish politics.' As she later accused Gladstone of hypocritical perfidy about her relationship with Parnell, it would seem fair to say that he both knew and did not know she was the Irish leader's mistress. By the time of their first meeting the information had been bandied about, but it was the sort of information that Gladstone, in some ways as naïve as Parnell about the implications of his personal actions (cf. his habit of wandering through the streets of the West End trying to save prostitutes from their lives of sin), would tend to discount.

Within a short time Katharine was signing her letters to Gladstone 'Katie O'Shea' rather than 'K. O'Shea' and had become chattily confidential in a manner which might indicate that their personal meetings were as cosy as she suggested. Despite her general self-confidence, she suffered from the female habit of explaining her motives and actions, rarely starting the letters with the meat but first justifying her reasons for writing. There were no major initiatives or moves in this period—the shock of the Phoenix Park murders had dampened spirits—but the meat was political. Katharine transmitted Parnell's proposals for amendments to the Arrears Bill, and she told Gladstone that he was taking steps to ensure that no portion of the Paris Funds should henceforward be withdrawn without his consent. (These Paris Funds represented the surplus money that had flowed into the Land League, mainly from America, and they had been sent to Paris for safety when the Land League had been proscribed in 1881. Parnell's reasons for gaining control of them were not merely to assure Mr Gladstone that they would not in future be used for semi-revolutionary purposes but because they represented the main source of money for the Home Rule party.) She also told the Prime Minister that the Irish leader would facilitate the passage of the Coercion Bill and co-operate 'in those other measures of general reform for the benefit of both England and Ireland which now constitute the programme of the Liberal Party.'

The theme of moderation and conciliation runs through Katharine's 1882 letters to Gladstone, and in this context she wrote an interesting letter to him in October, the one in which she said it had taken her nearly two years to penetrate Parnell's 'habitual reserve and suspicion of the Saxon; sufficiently to induce him to make his views known at all and thus shake himself free of the set by which he was surrounded.' To prove that Parnell had now shaken himself free from the extremists she enclosed a telegram she had received from him from Dublin, which read as follows: 'You may rely that your wishes and advice will be strictly complied with and that I will not permit myself to be drawn or pushed beyond the limits of prudence. . . . Have completely foiled the other side and expect conference will support me. If it does not will not go with them an inch.' As already indicated, Gladstone was among those who considered that Mrs O'Shea had been influential in turning Parnell into the path of moderation and that she would continue to exercise her influence, for he imagined that Parnell 'prefers the wife to the husband as an organ.' There were members of the administration who did not share Parnell's preference or care for either of the O'Sheas, notably Lord Spencer, the new Lord Lieutenant of Ireland. While admitting the usefulness of the link to Parnell's private views, Spencer thought the Prime Minister was playing with 'edged tools', by which phrase he was probably referring to Mrs O'Shea's relationship with the Irish leader, to the danger of further Liberal–Home Rule co-operation and certainly to its becoming public property. He continued to emphasise his fears that the communications might leak out and to urge the Prime Minister to cease the correspondence, whereupon Gladstone agreed that he would not again meet Mrs O'Shea (he did), but said he could not control her correspondence, which in any case he thought useful.

As Katharine assumed her role as link-woman between the two leaders, there was an important development on the personal front, for in June 1882 she again became pregnant. Parnell wanted a child, not just a child, but Katie's and his—and he had already told her that if anything happened to her he would die childless. Katharine's love for Parnell was such that she could not contemplate the thought of this eventuality, thus she decided to embark again upon the seas of motherhood. This pregnancy seems to mark the crucial point in the relationship between Katharine and her husband. If one is defending O'Shea or giving him the benefit of the innocence he always claimed, up to this point one can say that he was suspicious but he trusted his wife and was deceived by her protestations of a purely platonic relationship with Parnell, allowing that Katie cohabited with him before the birth of Claude Sophie. Beyond this point one can only give him the benefit of the doubt by accepting that she deceived Parnell as much as her husband by continuing to have sexual intercourse with both men for a period of six years. The period is six years because after 1886 O'Shea himself admitted that he and his wife ceased to live together, but six years is a long time for a woman to deceive her husband and her lover when the basis of the relationship with the lover is the ringing claim that theirs was a true affinity of mind and body, producing one of the consuming passions of history. Katharine's continuing to cohabit with her legal husband when necessary is the only way in which Willie O'Shea's assertion of deceived unawareness can hold true from 1880 to 1886. If he was truly deceived, then she was a liar and a cheat and the justification for an affair whose results were catastrophic slips from the realms of genuine love into something sordid and squalid, at least on her part. Parnell himself always believed that she was his and his alone, that she adored him as much as he adored her; was he right, not in a political or moral sense, but by his own standards, in giving his whole love to Katie O'Shea and in his profound belief that she returned it? In the summer of 1881, when his beloved found she was pregnant for the first time in eight years so soon after meeting him, perhaps not. Perhaps as suggested she did then panic and take the only step which could help convince her legal husband that he was the father of Claude Sophie. To panic once, to deceive your true love once, while not particularly admirable is understandable. To do it twice more—at least, because Katharine could hardly have dashed up to London each time she found she was pregnant and then have nothing to do with her husband sexually until the next time— is sordid, particularly when you have declared you love, as Katie did, when she wrote that from July 1881 she and Parnell were one 'without further scruple, without fear, without remorse'.

It cannot be proved that when Willie O'Shea allowed the paternity of the child conceived in 1882 to be registered in his name (Katie did the actual registering), he knew he was not the father for the good reason that he and his wife had not cohabited since, at the very latest, July 1881. Apart from Katharine's insistence that her love for Parnell was true, there are several factors which go towards substantiating the assertions that she and her husband finally separated sexually in 1881, that the child conceived in 1882 was not therefore his and that from this date (if not before) O'Shea knew about the adultery and condoned it. There are the straws in the wind, such as the few paternal claims he made about this child (and the one born in 1884), but there is also the evidence, or lack of evidence, which resides in the pages of Katharine's memoirs. The three children of her union with Captain O'Shea— Gerard, Carmen and Norah—are frequently mentioned, at least in the early pre-Parnell chapters, and baby Claude Sophie's brief life and sad death are recorded, but neither the child born in 1883 nor the one born the following year existed according to their mother's memoirs. Henry Harrison's interpretation was again that Claude Sophie only appeared because of O'Shea editorial interference and because in 1914, when the book was published, Katharine was too unbalanced to realise what the editors had done.

Why did the other two children not similarly appear? One has to assume that even the O'Shea editors could not bring themselves to blacken Katharine's character to the extent of making her a six-year deceiver of both husband and lover. If one accepts that Katharine had sufficient *nous* in 1914 to realise the implications of the Claude Sophie admission, a further inference can be drawn. She had agreed to help clear the late Captain O'Shea's name from the charges of connivance which by 1914 had adhered to it, she was willing to cast herself in a black light over the birth of Claude Sophie because in this instance she had deceived Parnell, because she needed to let the world know that she had borne him a child and this was the only way she could do it and at the same time salvage Willie O'Shea's reputation, but she neither could nor would admit that he might have been mistaken about his paternity of the two later children, because there was no possibility of their having been anybody's but Parnell's, and thus they had to be ignored. There is another piece of information relating to these two children, whose source is O'Shea's counsel, Sir Edward Clarke. In his memoirs, when discussing the Irish leader's intention to leave the country with Mrs O'Shea in 1890, Clarke spoke of Parnell's taking with him 'the two girls, born in 1883 and 1884, who were unquestionably his.' Having dropped this bombshell, Sir Edward then refrained from producing the evidence which had convinced him that the girls were 'unquestionably' Parnell's but that such an outright statement, unhedged by words like 'suspicion' or 'belief', should come from Willie O'Shea's own counsel, the man most closely involved with his side of the divorce, one with a sharp clear legal mind well aware of its implications, would seem damning to Captain O'Shea and his protestations of deceived innocence.

Returning to 1882, if one accepts that Katharine was being faithful to Parnell and the child in her womb was 'unquestionably' his and therefore O'Shea equally unquestionably became the complaisant husband, it is not to say that the triangular relationship was clarified. On the contrary, in many ways it grows murkier, with all three participants retaining contact, at times close, at times harmonious, at times not, with Katie and Parnell continuing to practise their inept measures of deception, and with nobody openly voicing the truth. How Katharine conveyed the news to her legal husband that she was pregnant with Parnell's child or if she ever did directly, are unanswerable questions. But O'Shea's overall state of mind in the summer of 1882 was euphoric, he was the man who had acted as negotiator in the Kilmainham Treaty, whom Mr Gladstone and Mr Chamberlain trusted, who would shape the course of Anglo-Irish relations because he was the *éminence grise* of

Irish politics. The strength of O'Shea's belief in this role can be gauged from some of the letters he wrote in these months. To Gladstone he wrote: 'I can now assure you that the Bill is safe from obstruction, and, further, that I have already induced Mr Parnell to listen to my suggestions.' When it quickly became apparent that the extended Coercion Bill was not safe from obstruction he wrote to Chamberlain, 'Parnell is frequently in a "moony" drifting state of mind nowadays, with which it is difficult to keep one's temper', consequently he had been forced to speak to him 'in the very strongest terms', while to Parnell himself he wrote of the exasperation his behaviour was causing, telling him that unless he pulled himself together the consequences would be deplorable, and even he (O'Shea) would not be able to rectify them. When O'Shea learned that his wife was again pregnant, he had, as he saw matters, an unbounded political future before him; during this period there were no particular rumours circulating about Parnell and his wife; even he then realised that his future as much as his wife's was tied up with the Irish leader, though he considered that Parnell owed him as much, if not more, than the other way round. Thus, in addition to the old motives of Aunt Ben's money and the horror of a scandal, O'Shea had the incentive of a bright personal future to keep him an unquestioning, condoning figure.

By the autumn—when he must presumably have known about her condition—Katie was doing her best to brighten his political future and keep him unquestioning. She wrote to Mr Gladstone about the possibility of her husband being appointed to the post of Under-Secretary for Ireland to replace the temporary successor to the murdered Burke. Willie himself had already intimated that he would like the post, an application which drew the following comment from Lord Spencer: 'I cannot for a moment conceive it possible to entertain the idea of O'Shea being fitted to succeed Hamilton [as Under-Secretary]. The post is one which requires the highest administrative qualities of an experienced official, and if I were to judge of Captain O'Shea from the volumes of letters which he pours into the Chief Secretary and myself on every conceivable subject, I can hardly think of a man more unfitted for the place.'* With this view, if less vehemently and acidly, Mr Gladstone

---

* Edward Hamilton, Gladstone's secretary and no relation to the temporary Irish Under-Secretary, gave an interesting early assessment of O'Shea in his diary (November 1882), thus: 'There never was a man who played a difficult part more awkwardly, and who unconsciously so discredited those he intended (as I believe) to assist, but to assist with motives of self-advancement.' He also referred to Katie as 'that bothersome woman.'

concurred, though he sugared the pill by circulating an internal memo-randum informing his colleagues 'who had any considerable amount of civil patronage at their disposal' that they might think of spreading some of it in Captain O'Shea's direction in recognition of his services during 'the very embarrassing predicament in which we found ourselves last spring' (i.e. Parnell's release from Kilmainham). Katharine was not aware of the influential Liberal view of her husband's capabilities and limitations and she continued to press the point, sending Gladstone a letter she had received from Willie which said frankly, in reply to a direct question of hers, 'Yes, I would like to be Under-Secretary very much and I think I might make a useful one . . . I believe we should be more likely than most people to conciliate influential members of all parties.' At the end of October she returned to the attack, saying her husband was most anxious to know whether there was any hope regard-ing his appointment, reiterating that he was sure he could be useful in the post. Gladstone appended a query to the bottom of her letter, 'What have I told her before?' to which his secretary replied, 'That you would refer her application to the Viceroy.' The Viceroy, Lord Spencer, had made his views clear, and that was the end of Captain O'Shea's hopes.

The mind tends to boggle at the thought of Willie O'Shea as Under-Secretary, not only because one accepts Lord Spencer's view that he was singularly unfitted for the post, not because the majority of the Home Rulers already mistrusted him and would not have given their vital support, but because there, in a crucial Anglo-Irish position, would have been the husband of the Irish leader's mistress. It is not surprising that O'Shea thought he was the ideal candidate. He always had his illusions of grandeur and after Kilmainham he had some justification for his high opinion of himself; it was only in the innermost recesses of his mind that he accepted that his wife was Parnell's mistress. It is doubtful whether Parnell thought the Liberals would be stupid enough to accept O'Shea, but he was aware that Katie was pushing her hus-band's case. He did not discourage her, and that they were both so oblivious of the implications of the appointment emphasises their personal insulation and how blurred Parnell allowed his political vision to become when Katie and her husband were involved.

For the first few months of 1883, as during much of 1882, O'Shea continued to be conspicuous by his absence from Wonersh Lodge. Katie was entering the last phase of her pregnancy but this time she had Parnell 'at home' for much of the trying period, though he was still travelling frequently to Ireland and officially he retained his lodgings in Keppel Street. On 4 March 1883 his and Katie's happiness was increased when she was safely delivered of a child at Wonersh Lodge. The baby was another girl, which may have been a slight disappointment to them, though Parnell had said of Claude Sophie, 'I shall love her very much better than if it had been a son.' She was christened Clare Gabrielle Antoinette Marcia and was duly registered to the paternity of William Henry O'Shea, Member of Parliament for County Clare, Ireland. Information on the life of Clare is hard to come by, as according to her mother she never existed, and while her putative father briefly admitted her existence in the divorce court—'in the early part of 1883 my daughter Clare was born'—otherwise he made little comment about her. One of the few people who came into contact with Clare and later recorded his impressions was Henry Harrison, and he said that physically she was very like Parnell, with his colouring and eyes, a vivacious, clever, generous child. Norah O'Shea, who in later years helped her mother bring up young Clare, also confirmed that physically she was like Parnell and that she had an attractive personality.

Clare's putative father was in Ireland when she was born, but only ten days after the birth Katharine exerted herself on her legal husband's behalf by writing to Mr Gladstone, which as she had not been in contact with the Prime Minister for three months might indicate the renewed desire to placate Captain O'Shea. What she did was to send Gladstone a long rambling effusion she had received from Willie in which he stated his views on Ireland and on a subject then troubling the Irish scene, one he could have solved had the Chief Secretary or Lord Spencer consulted him, in which he attacked Spencer, eulogised Joseph Chamberlain and stated that 'Parnell, with all his talents, is about the worst judge of character I have met', and if, urged on by the extremists and smarting under the insults of Lord Spencer and company, he chose to stump the United States, then even Willie would have no power to control him, this despite the fact that 'Mr Gladstone knows what my influence has done, Parnell's judgement in my case being lucid.' What Mr Gladstone made of the effusion remains unknown, and exactly why Katie thought her husband's letter would improve his chance of advancement likewise, but her reason for writing was to try to persuade Gladstone that O'Shea deserved and was worthy of an Irish post. Gladstone failed to rise to her pleas and made the comment at the bottom of the effusion, 'It was I think arranged that she should address herself to Ld. R. Grosvenor [Richard Grosvenor, the Liberal Chief Whip].' Temporarily, the political scene was dormant and Katie as the direct link-woman to Parnell was put into cold storage. But snubs did not prevent her from continuing to write to Gladstone directly, conveying Mr Parnell's opinions on various matters. In June, when writing to ask Mr Gladstone if he would grant her a further personal interview (he then declined), she made it clear that she had accepted one fact, that her husband was not in line for political promotion by the Liberals, when she said, 'I hope you will not refer me to anyone else. I can assure you I do not desire to ask for the Viceroyalty! or any favour but that of a few minutes conversation with you.'

By this time, in mid-1883, Katie and Parnell had established a happy domestic routine, and apart from the fact that they were living in the blackest sin, their home life was such to have delighted the heart of Queen Victoria. Again apart from the unfortunate fact that she was a married lady, Parnell could not have selected a more suitable mate. Katie was domestically minded and had a strong maternal instinct which provided the secure nest Parnell needed, yet she was intelligent, with an equally strong interest in politics and power which provided the mental companionship he required. She was capable and efficient, as the way she ran her home, looked after Aunt Ben, acted as secretary and link-woman and kept Willie O'Shea happy for so many years showed, and Parnell in his private life was indolent and needed organising. She had inherited her mother's energy, which counter-balanced her lover's fragile constitution, she had the confidence to override his shyness and the passion to respond to his hidden fires. She was also highly emotional, headstrong and self-willed, but had she not possessed these characteristics it is doubtful that she would have become his mistress in the first place.

At an early date in their blissful unmarried life, Katie cured Parnell of the habit of sleep-walking and of the nightmares from which he had suffered for years, by the methods of holding him in her arms when he awoke in a panic and by putting him on a strict diet (perhaps including the meat extract to which she had been introduced on the Isle of Wight). In their free time they often wandered or rode through the countryside which then surrounded Eltham, with Katie vainly trying to teach Parnell the names of the wild flowers as her father had taught her. Their rides took them to Chislehurst, and though Parnell had a horror of death or anything pertaining to it, they would stop at the Catholic cemetery and place wild flowers on the grave of Claude Sophie, for, as

Parnell told Katie, she was not dead, she was only sleeping. Kent is a hop-growing country and not infrequently Parnell would be recognised by the hop-pickers, many of whom were Irish, and they would swarm round him, chanting, 'The Chief, the Chief.' (Katharine made the comment that the Irish hop-pickers were popular among the Kent farmers because they did not complain so loudly as their English counterparts at their 'scandalously inefficient accommodation.')

If Parnell was no expert on wild flowers he loved the cultivated rose, white being his favourite colour, and Katie sent to Worcester for a special breed which she then kept blooming in the conservatory all the year round so that he should have a button-hole available whenever he made a speech in the House of Commons or on other important occasions. Apart from sporting a flower in his button-hole Parnell, unlike her legal husband, had no interest in his general appearance, and Katie fought a losing battle in the matter of clothes. When he became engrossed in one of his hobbies, it took her all her time to get him out of his old cardigan and into his frock-coat to attend the House of Commons, and persuading him to buy a new coat was not worth the effort involved (a parliamentary correspondent commented on Parnell appearing in the House looking like 'a cross between Mr Oscar Wilde and a scarecrow'). When Parnell was actually speaking in the Commons, Katie would frequently travel to the Ladies Gallery to hear him, as she had in the early days of their acquaintance. They did not travel together, deeming it inexpedient to be seen arriving in harness. Sometimes her duties to Aunt Ben made her late, sometimes she came without warning but whenever she arrived in the House Parnell apparently knew. Katharine said there was a form of telepathy between them, and he would immediately acknowledge her often unseen entrance by lifting his head towards her and touching the white rose in his button-hole. Sometimes, if it was known that there would be a late sitting, Katie would go up to London in the early evening to ensure that Parnell had a good, well-balanced dinner, as he hated dining in the House (not noted for the standards of its catering, anyway), and tended to forget about eating unless she was present. Her maternal instinct was in evidence in the way she fussed over Parnell's health, not without reason because he was always catching what he termed 'slight colds', but she had to move with tact and discretion as he had as great a horror of illness as of death, and would never admit to bodily ailments other than those 'slight colds'. Frequently, Parnell would ask her to meet him after a session in the

House so that he could talk to her on the otherwise lonely drive to Eltham, and as nobody could guarantee exactly when a sitting would finish she spent a good deal of time waiting in an agreed place, usually a railway station. Such rendezvous were adopted to preserve the secret of their relationship, on the premise that a public place would cause less comment than a private one, though whether it did is open to speculation. Waterloo Station was a favourite rendezvous because it stayed open all night and was south of the river and therefore nearer to Eltham, and Katie admitted that she *thought* the railway officials knew who Parnell was, and as she spent many hours waiting, as she had a free travelling pass given to her by him and he often wired to her at the station from the House of Commons (albeit in the name of Preston), it would seem probable that they did.

Sometimes as they drove back to Eltham in the early hours of the morning they would stop at an all-night coffee stall for a warming drink, and Katie said how much Parnell enjoyed talking to the workmen, and how well he got on with the English 'common man' as opposed to his intense dislike of the English middle and upper classes, herself excepted. On one occasion Parnell had to catch the early mail train to Ireland after a sitting which threatened to be long, and Katie went to the St Pancras Hotel where he had booked a room for the night. It was not until the dawn had broken that her lover finally arrived at the hotel, and she spent the night waiting and watching for his arrival. The sights she saw and the sounds she heard through the window in that dismal area of north London horrified her sufficiently for her to comment on them in her memoirs. It is not particularly surprising that she had lived for nearly forty years without recognising the gulf that separated the rich from the poor, without realising the squalor and degradation and poverty in which so many people existed in the richest city in the world. The scenes impressed themselves so forcibly on Katharine's mind that she was impelled to mention them in her book, as similarly the plight of the hop-pickers slightly stirred her social conscience.

When Parnell returned from one of his visits to Ireland it quickly became a ritual that Katharine would turn out the pockets of his clothes. It was not a chore he was interested in, items collected in his pockets could stay there as far as he was concerned, but 'Wifie' discovering what her King had amassed during a particular trip became a pleasurable occasion for both of them, with Parnell sitting in the armchair smoking while Katie delved into the deepest recesses of the various pockets and placed the booty on show. Much of it was gifts from devoted admirers, countless images of saints, bits of rope that had hanged an Irish martyr, bullets which were believed by their donors to have acquired supernatural powers from passing through a body, and innumerable green handkerchiefs with shamrocks embroidered by adoring fingers. But Parnell was intensely superstitious, an odd trait in a man whose political brain worked so clearly, concisely and rationally, and he loathed the colour green as much as he hated the month of October and believed in the combination of 'lucky' numbers. The green handkerchiefs were withdrawn from sight, but Katie held on to many of the souvenirs and they were to comfort her in later years.

Parnell's hobbies were varied and well catered for by his efficient, devoted Queenie. He was interested in astronomy, architecture, assaying, and he enjoyed riding, shooting and playing cricket. His telescope was brought over from Avondale and duly set up with Katie's help, while his architectural books and assaying instruments littered her sitting-room, at least until 1885. He indulged his considerable ability as a marksman by shooting at the candles in the sitting-room, with an air gun, and when this habit became tiresome he was moved to a dried-up pond on Aunt Ben's estate where a target was installed so that he could practise his prowess with a revolver; as Katie was no mean shot with a revolver, perhaps she participated in the target practise. Parnell's enthusiasm for cricket she fostered by having a full-sized pitch laid out in a nearby field which she rented for the purpose. It was the practical side of his various hobbies which interested him, how buildings were constructed, how he could extract gold from quartz gathered in the stream at Avondale, how the telescope worked, and he later abandoned his interest in astronomy because it was a pursuit in which the method and the end product were swallowed by the infinity of the universe.

About Parnell the father there is scant information, other than that he wanted children and Katie said he was fond of them in general. What sort of relationship he had with the ready-made O'Shea family he inherited at Wonersh Lodge is mainly shrouded in silence, but Carmen and Norah were educated at home by governesses and though Gerard was away at boarding schools he had long holidays, so Parnell must have met the three of them frequently. A witness later said that Parnell often played cricket with the O'Shea and other neighbouring children, including herself, and made them all roar with laughter by such jokes as bowling an egg which smashed to pieces on impact with the bat. As Gerard grew old enough to appreciate the nature of his mother's liaison with the Irish leader, one knows that he did not care for Parnell, but whether he always resented this other father-figure is an unanswerable question. Katie told Henry Harrison that her O'Shea children got on well with Parnell and she also told him that her legal husband could not have failed to have known that Parnell was living at Wonersh Lodge because the children chattered about his constant presence on the rare occasions when they saw their father. In the ambivalence of her memoirs there is one reference to the O'Shea children and Parnell which suggests that their relationship was amicable. One day the children came dashing past her, saying they were going down to the cellars to look for cobwebs for Parnell. Intrigued as to why he should want a supply of cobwebs, she discovered that he required them to wrap round his bleeding finger, a wholly beneficial cure for open wounds he had learned from the peasants at Avondale, one which both horrified and amused Katie. (She was of the opinion that much of Parnell's superstition stemmed from the fact that as a child he had been neglected by his mother and had spent so much time in the care of kindly but ignorant Irish peasant nurses.)

However happy Katie and Parnell's private life was, it was an extremely insulated and self-contained one. This arose partly because of the nature of their relationship, the wish to keep it as secret as possible and the need to retain Willie O'Shea in quiescent mood, but it was also occasioned by their characters and their love for each other. Parnell had never liked socialising and had not come from a close-knit family—Tim Healy had earlier commented of the Parnells: 'One set of them doesn't seem to know where the other set is, or is living—or to care.' Katie had come from an affectionate family and had played her part in the social whirl, but she had always insisted that she found it tiresome and she slipped without demur into an isolated existence with Parnell. She did not lose touch with her family, Anna Steele was strongly in evidence for some time after Katie met Parnell—he wrote to Anna when he was in Kilmainham—but increasingly after 1882, when it would seem that an agreement was reached between Katie and her husband and she and Parnell settled into their own life, it was Willie O'Shea rather than his wife who turned to Mrs Steele for advice and comfort. Charlie Wood kept in touch with his sister, as he paid visits to Eltham to see Aunt Ben, and being a good classical scholar who could exchange quotations in Greek and play word games in Latin with the old lady, he was a welcome guest. Evelyn Wood was not greatly in evidence at this period, for the good reason that he was out of the country, soldiering with Sir Garnet Wolseley in Egypt, but Evelyn retained contact with his aunt, since he handled her yearly charitable bequests (and earned a suitably Aunt Ben-ish rebuke for wasting part of her money on a Home for Incurables who 'do but cumber the earth and are useless'). Evelyn was not averse to accepting Mrs Wood's charity for himself, and one letter he wrote to her on his return from South Africa in 1882 was considered by Willie O'Shea to be 'unequalled in my experience of begging letters' (and he had a fair amount of experience). The offending letter started by thanking Evelyn's dear aunt for her very acceptable loan and then came the part which outraged Willie, thus: 'Paulina put on a very old and thread-bare waterproof when driving with Her Majesty, who, examining it with interest, said, "I suppose you wore that all through Zululand?". "Yes," said Paulina—she might have added "and for several years previously".' There was more in similar vein about it starting to rain and Paulina—Evelyn's wife—being obliged to open her umbrella in front of Queen Victoria, revealing the many holes in it. The letter could be said to indicate that Evelyn's financial position was parlous and further offerings from Aunt Ben would be gratefully received, though in Wood family circles the story was related as a joke—how awful that Evelyn and Paulina were invited to stay with the Queen immediately on their return from South Africa and had not had time to renew their shabby wardrobe.

By 1883 Evelyn and Charlie Wood, one at close quarters, the other at a distance, were beginning to worry about their aunt and their sister. They knew that the old lady's will had already been altered once in Katie's favour, and they realised how dependent she now was on her 'dear Swan'. Like Katharine, neither of them was an openly grabbing, mercenary character, but each had a family, each needed to live up to an accepted social standard—Evelyn as an increasingly high-ranking officer, already knighted by the Queen, Charlie as a gentleman-farmer—each lacked sufficient money to satisfy these needs, and each was looking forward to the long-awaited fortune which would become his when Aunt Ben finally left the storms of this life for the calm of the next. Nagging worries about their sister's influence on the aged Mrs Wood were not improved by her behaviour—if she could do what she apparently was doing with Mr Parnell, what could she not do? It was not a matter which could in the circumstances be discussed—she might *not* be doing what she appeared to be doing with Mr Parnell, and her husband did not seem to be worried—and in the early 1880s sleeping dogs continued to litter the area of the Woods, the O'Sheas and Mr Parnell.

Chapter Nine

The Anglo-Irish scene was quiet in 1883. Ireland was far from peaceful and coercion remained in force, but the Land Act and the subsequent Arrears Act had temporarily satisfied the demands of many tenant farmers and the shock waves of the Phoenix Park murders continued to surge. In this quiet period, Parnell solidified his leadership of the Home Rule movement and started to create a coherent, disciplined party. At the end of 1882 the National League was formed and it was a very different body from the defunct Land League, with the obtaining of Home Rule the main plank of its platform and land reform relegated to second place. Apart from the reversal of aims, there was as significant a change of control, the National League being dominated by the parliamentary party in a manner its predecessor had not been. One of the principal functions of the National League was to prepare the machinery for an efficient parliamentary party capable of wresting Home Rule from a reluctant British government, by encouraging sustained activity at constituency level, by organising county conventions to select prospective candidates and by close co-operation with the constituencies and conventions thus organised. Later, in 1884, the final nail was driven into this efficient structure when the pledge was introduced whereby Home Rule MPs committed themselves to sit, act and vote in unison, and to resign if they failed to obey the party line without cogent reason. In this side of

Parnell's political life Katharine took little interest, other than being pleased that he was clamping down on the extremists and acting constitutionally. It was the grand sweep of the conception of Home Rule that appealed to her, the fascination of the subjective business of personal negotiation, not the minutiae of how Parnell controlled his party or how a political machine was formed. When one says that Parnell started to create this viable, disciplined party, it does not mean that he dashed all over Ireland himself; much of the donkey work was left to his lieutenants and local enthusiasts, but few within the Home Rule movement were in doubt that his was the personality and the iron will which kept everybody together.

At the beginning of 1883 Parnell's position as the leader of Irish nationalism (as opposed to his control of the parliamentary party) was not as secure as it seemed to those opposed to him. Ironically, his position was helped by the action of his opponents, notably Mr Forster, who in February launched a bitter personal attack in the House of Commons when he openly accused Parnell of having connived at and condoned the murders and outrages in Ireland, by implication the Phoenix Park murders, too. In Ireland the effect of such attacks was for all the nationalists to close ranks behind Parnell. The Fenian element had been angered by the recent lack of militant action, but the minute Parnell was attacked by English sources they rallied behind him, as did other sections who for various reasons were wavering about his leadership.

Further British action again helped the position of the man it hoped to undermine. In March 'A National Tribute to Mr Parnell' was launched by the *Freeman's Journal,* with the support of the majority of the Irish Catholic hierarchy, officially in recognition of his public services to Ireland, specifically to save him from threatened bankruptcy. At this time the Invincibles responsible for the Phoenix Park murders were being tried, and the public revelations of their activities did not produce an atmosphere in which people were eager to subscribe to the testimonial and it consequently languished. Then in May a Papal Rescript was addressed to the Irish bishops from the Holy See, which condemned the fund outright, and within a month subscriptions leapt from £7,000 to £20,000. The reason for this was partly because the Irish felt that Rome had no business interfering in their internal affairs—as one nationalist said, 'The Pope is the head of the Catholic Church, Mr Parnell is head of Ireland. They move in wholly different orbits and have no relation the one with the other'—but it was also because information was leaked that the British Government had had a hand in the Rescript. Directly, Gladstone's administration had not been involved, the moving spirit was an Irish Catholic MP representing the Catholic anti-Parnellite faction which thought censure from Rome would weaken, if not destroy, his position. Indirectly, the MP had received backing from the Liberal Government which also thought a move to provide some check on Parnell's ascendancy would be a good idea. Eventually, the Testimonial Fund reached the sum of £38,000 and a cheque was presented to Parnell by the Lord Mayor of Dublin at a banquet at the Rotunda. To the resounding cheers of a thousand guests, Parnell pocketed the cheque and then proceeded to speak for half an hour on the current sins of the Liberal Government without one word of thanks for the money. Everybody was astounded and uncertain whether the action represented appalling bad manners, absent-mindedness or a single-minded attention to political rather than personal matters. In the current atmosphere of devotion to Parnell, the last explanation was the one widely and charitably accepted. Fortunately, most members of the audience and the many thousands of Irish men and women who had contributed to the Fund were not aware that in the month it was launched Katharine O'Shea bore their leader a daughter, nor that in the month he received his cheque he was spending as much time as possible with her in Brighton.

It was after Clare's birth that Katie rented a house in Brighton, and the visit could have been in the nature of a recuperation because her previous accouchements had been difficult and her fifth child's may have followed the same pattern. Even when she was happy Katie was not the woman to stay permanently put, and however secure she now was about Parnell's love, the pressures of the situation, the need for secrecy must have overwhelmed her occasionally, so the trip to Brighton may have been an attempt to relieve the tensions. Unfortunately, Katie and Parnell took their duplicity with them to the Sussex coast, and at the Brighton house rented in April 1883—39 Bedford Square—Parnell was known to the staff, with massive originality, as 'Mr Smith', but it was a further visit to Brighton towards the end of the year which helped shatter his reputation in the divorce court. In the November the family took a house in Medina Terrace, at the Hove end of the town, and Willie O'Shea was more in evidence than he had been for some considerable time, the house actually being rented by Captain and Mrs O'Shea. He acknowledged that Mr Parnell came to stay at his invitation, as they had political matters to discuss, but then said he had to go to Ireland and was completely unaware that Mr Parnell visited Medina Terrace in his absence. The star witness in the divorce court was a maid employed at Medina Terrace and she claimed (among other things) that Parnell was known to the staff there as 'Mr Stewart', though why he should have been known as Mr Stewart when he had already been staying at Captain O'Shea's invitation was not clarified. Parnell used at least one alias in Brighton in 1883 (and he was to continue to use even more unfortunate ones), but they seem to have been adopted in the effort to stave off publicity rather than to deceive Willie O'Shea. There was no attempt to pretend to the staff at Wonersh Lodge that Parnell was other than who he was, and it was at Eltham that he spent most time during the liaison, perhaps because in Katie's own burrow they both felt safe from prying eyes. It was only when they issued forth to other areas that they deemed it necessary to cover their tracks, though as Sir Edward Clarke said, 'the expedients for securing secrecy were quite childish in their futility.'

In fact, Katie did not spend all that much time at Medina Terrace, as she was regularly travelling up and down to Eltham to attend to Aunt Ben. On Christmas Eve 1883 she made such a journey, but as her aunt disliked foolish Christmas junketings, she was able to leave her comfortably installed in bed and spend the rest of the evening with her King, who had also travelled from Brighton to Eltham, although not to be with Aunt Ben. It was a bitterly cold winter and the snow already lay thick, and Parnell and Katie went for a long walk in the moonlit grounds of the Lodge, looking across the silvery expanse of Eltham Chase, listening to the church bells ringing across the still, frosty air. As the occasional dark cloud crossed the moon and cast shadows on the snow, Katie thought of the days when Eltham had been a royal chase and pictured the ghosts of long-dead huntsmen, and Parnell, who had little imagination, was fascinated by her mental images. As the midnight bells tolled, celebrating the birth of Christ, he spoke of his personal belief in destiny and fate, of the uselessness of mortals contending against them, of his conviction that after death the soul started a fresh life on the planet under whose influence it had been born into this world. It was a curious doctrine for a man who had been brought up in the Protestant ethic of self-help and who acted as if Ireland should help herself, and if he was convinced there was a destiny which shaped men's ends it did not prevent him from rough-hewing them to the utmost of his mortal ability.

By the end of 1883 Katharine said her health was poor, that she was suffering from agonising neuralgia and that only her concern about Parnell's health prevented her from succumbing to a breakdown. It is not surprising that even her energy was running low, if one considers that in 1883 in addition to her normal burdens of running a house, acting as Parnell's go-between, keeping up the façade with Willie, caring for her three older children, attending to Aunt Ben, she had given birth and travelled backwards and forwards between Eltham and Brighton for several months. Throughout 1883 she had the extra worry of fear for Parnell's safety, as opposed to his health. In the aftermath of Kilmainham and Phoenix Park he received many letters threatening his life, mainly from those who considered that he had sold Ireland down the river. Katharine said that one night, as she and Parnell were driving back from a late sitting of the House of Commons, on a lonely, unlit stretch of common near Lee an attempt was made on his life, but the cab driver saw the gunman as he took aim, galloped the horses furiously, and the shot missed. She also said that at this time the Government offered Parnell police protection, but both of them regarded it as a manoeuvre to place him under *official* surveillance and the offer was declined. Unofficially, as they both knew, Parnell had been under surveillance for a long time; Howard Vincent, the head of the recently created Criminal Investigation Department, related how the Irish leader challenged an inefficient detective in Covent Garden in February 1881, after which incident conspicuous tailing was dropped. Throughout 1883 Parnell carried a loaded revolver with him; so did Katie on the night drives and she said her nerves were 'jarred and tense with daily fear for him'. Interestingly, when the discussions about Parnell's being given police protection took place, it was she who interviewed Howard Vincent on her lover's behalf. Despite the attempts to cover their tracks, she openly acted as Parnell's mouthpiece on a variety of occasions, and the officials she thus met, from Gladstone to Mr Vincent, were expected to know that she was Parnell's mistress (which to varying degrees they did) while pretending that she was merely his trusted friend.

It was as well that Katharine did not succumb to a breakdown because by February 1884 she was again pregnant. She had given Parnell a healthy daughter but they both wanted a boy who might one day, perhaps, be able to assume the family name and carry on the Parnell tradition, and as she was now thirty-eight years old it was inadvisable to wait too long. On his own evidence, Willie O'Shea went to Spain early in the March—Katie said he went in February, so if her pregnancy ran its full course he had hardly had time to be the father—and in the Iberian Peninsula he remained for the next three months. During these three months of untrammelled freedom, before the pregnancy became too trying, she and Parnell escaped on what she called one of their 'runaway visits'. Over the years they indulged in several such trips to various south coast resorts from Bournemouth to Herne Bay, when Katharine managed to organise Aunt Ben and her family into safe hands, and for a few days they forgot about politics and fortunes and husbands. This particular trip in the spring of 1884 was to Hastings, where they stayed at the Queen's Hotel and where Parnell found some notepaper in a stationer's with the embossd monogram 'K.P.' and proceeded to buy countless boxes for his own dear Wifie, Katharine Parnell. Whenever she had other days free from attending her Aunt Ben, the two of them would take the train down to Brighton and search for the ideal house in which they could live happily ever after the fact that she was married to somebody else had magically sorted itself out. For the other sad fact was that the only non-magic solution to their problems was Willie O'Shea's death, and apart from his gout and being overweight—by 1883 he was 14 stones 7 pounds—he was in reasonable health and but forty-four years old.

By the end of May Willie was back in England, though he later implied that he did not return until nearly the end of July. There is evidence that he crossed to Ireland in the last few days of May, staying as Parnell's guest at Avondale, a visit which emphasises how busily engaged both men were in preserving the façade. It was a visit which does not help Willie's protestations of innocence, as he said it was immediately on his return from Spain that he heard rumours to the effect that Mr Parnell had been a constant visitor to Wonersh Lodge during his absence, and that he again became suspicious about the true nature of his wife's relationship with the Irish leader and taxed her on the subject. On 24 July Katie replied to his suspicious enquiries in a letter which began 'Knowing what I do, it is very difficult for me to reply to your letters with patience. I don't in the least know what you mean or what "thing has to be done"—but this I do know—that I have put up with a great deal for a long time and I do not mean to any longer.' She continued in aggressive mood: 'I hope the children's position will never be hurt by you more than it has been', but then dropped into her ambivalent strain, dealing with 'the hints' Willie had heard, saying he had no business to allow people to hint things about her, and she would be obliged if he would send her 'a list of the people and what it exactly is that is "hinted" by your friends to you.'

It is unlikely that Willie obliged with a list, as he and his wife were continuing to perform their skating act which left no clear traces on the ice, but by the beginning of August he was really agitated. Also by the beginning of August Katharine was entering the sixth month of her pregnancy, and if one accepts that her legal husband was not in cohabitation with her, the two events could be not unconnected. Victorian garments tended towards the concealment of pregnancy so that at the end of May Willie O'Shea (and outsiders) could have been unaware of Mrs O'Shea's condition, but it must have been apparent by the beginning of August. While Willie had almost certainly agreed not to interfere with Katie's life and to shut his eyes to a discreet affair, her being pregnant *again,* flaunting her love before his eyes, was understandably perhaps more than he could bear. If one assumes that the 'hints' this time extended beyond the fact of adultery to the doubts about paternity—Mr Parnell was in permanent residence at Wonersh Lodge and Captain O'Shea had been out of the country for a long time— O'Shea had to do something in a situation which menaced his honourable standing.

On 4 August, from the House of Commons library he wrote to Parnell, a letter which began 'You have behaved very badly to me', went on to say that he had always welcomed Mr Parnell to stay at Eltham while he was there but had begged him not to do so in his absence, as a scandal must ensue. Then came the statement which showed O'Shea's genuine perturbation because it said he was taking his family to live abroad and would consequently apply for the Chiltern Hundreds to enable him to resign his parliamentary seat. Katharine had no intention of going to live abroad with her legal husband but that Willie made the statement, more importantly the offer to resign his seat, shows how deeply troubled he was. In reply he received a letter from Parnell and one from his wife, neither of which said anything about the crux of the matter, their adultery. Parnell's letter said briefly that he did not know of any scandal or any grounds for one, and then turned to the practical matter of O'Shea's applying for the Chiltern Hundreds. If this was the Captain's intention, he thought it would be helpful if he did so before the end of the session so that the writ could be moved and the election held during the recess. Katie's letter said she was surprised Willie should have waited for her at Albert Mansions because after the conversation they had had on Tuesday he surely could not have expected her to turn up, in any case the weather was hideously hot, she was not well and for her children's sake she did not think it would be a good idea if she died because they would thus lose all chance of Aunt Ben's money, and whatever good job Willie might get, they could scarcely have too much money, and nobody was more entitled to Aunt Ben's fortune than she was. However, she would be in London tomorrow, she could see Willie then but *not* to continue the conversation they had on Tuesday, and she signed herself formally, 'K. O'Shea'.

What manner of conversation Katie and Willie had when they eventually met in London is, alas, a blank, but we must believe that Captain O'Shea, having had his suspicions aroused to the extent of challenging Mr Parnell to a duel in 1881 and further aroused to the extent of threatening to take his family out of the country three years later, again calmly accepted his wife's protestations of innocence. Why Willie once again let the matter be closed so easily is more comprehensible. He still regarded himself as the *éminence grise* of Anglo-Irish politics (and his heyday as a negotiator lay some months ahead), no problems about Aunt Ben's money had yet arisen, and Katie was obtaining an increasingly large supply of it for him. For the sake of ambition and money he was willing to forgo his self-esteem and honour, and face his friends as a man who had talked things over with his wife (yet again) and had learned that there was no truth in the malicious, doubtless politically-motivated gossip, in the process convincing himself of the veracity of his stand.

Katie's position and actions were hardly more commendable than her husband's—Parnell can be ignored, as he had become an extra passenger on the O'Shea see-saw. One can only wish that Katharine had remained in aggressive mood and had clearly stated—as she told Henry Harrison she once did—that she loved Parnell, and that it was a situation her husband could accept or reject by positive action. But positive action would have meant a legal separation or a divorce and that was to be avoided, politically and personally, and in any case Katie was not the lady for the head-on, honest approach. Temperamentally she preferred the tangential method, she had her conviction that she was an expert manager of people and events, which to an extent she was, and she thought that what was not spoken could be happily ignored (a common failing of her generation). As the July letters suggest, she grew irritated when Willie broke the rules of knowing but pretending not to, and she could not appreciate the increasingly invidious position in which she was placing her husband. Was he not obtaining a great deal of money through her? Was she not still friendly with him when he behaved himself? Had not Parnell advanced his political career? What more could he want?

To prove how friendly she could be, in the early autumn of 1884 Katharine again exerted herself on her husband's behalf by writing to Mr Gladstone. After a lapse of eighteen months, Willie himself had written to the Prime Minister in the September, a lengthy epistle which started with a request for a Civil List pension for a Mr O'Hart who was 'the author of several laborious works on Irish geneal-ogy', but who nonetheless deserved his pension. It went on to castigate Lord Spencer for ignoring Mr Parnell, who was most tenacious in his resentment and never forgave slights, and rambled through interminable complications about Limerick, where Captain O'Shea had family connec-tions and where his choice for Resident Magistrate had been ignored. Gladstone's comment was 'tone of the letter impertinent', one of the first indications that O'Shea as a negotiator was beginning to be re-garded askance, and among people who had previously regarded him favourably. The request for the pension for Mr O'Hart was turned down, whereupon Willie asked Katie to write to Mr Gladstone because the matter was important to him. He earned his reputation and part of his shaky income by his contact with influential people, his ability to arrange pensions, obtain titles and generally be Mr Fix-it. Katharine, too, received a snub for her pains and Willie's reputation in another quarter was not enhanced.

Throughout the autumn of 1884 Katharine continued to be unwell, a fact she admitted in her memoirs, although the reason for her ill-health—her sixth pregnancy and accouchement—was not men-tioned. The child was born at Wonersh Lodge on 27 November 1884, and it was another girl, who was christened Frances Katie Flavia but who was always known as Katie. As with Claude Sophie and Clare, the birth was registered to the paternity of William Henry O'Shea, Member of Parliament for County Clare. This was the last child Katharine, now in her fortieth year, bore, and if it was a disappointment that their final child was a girl, she had given Parnell two healthy daughters and their happiness was deep. It would seem that after baby Katie's birth her mother was ill and had to go away to a nursing home. One has to say 'it would seem' because Katharine's own account of this period is so sketchy—it had to be since the child's birth was so totally ignored—but she published several letters Parnell wrote to her from Eltham at the end of 1884. In one letter he said: 'I came down here last night and was immensely relieved to hear that you are better'; in another: 'I am going to London now, and hope to return reasonably early, as the debate is not likely to be long. . . . There ought to be no difficulty in my seeing you tomorrow, and I will manage it. I do not like your having a headache, and you must really take care of yourself and not get up too soon. Phyllis is looking after me first rate' (Phyllis being Katharine's devoted personal maid at Wonersh Lodge). She related how, soon after she returned home, Parnell came back to Eltham in broad daylight in a hansom cab, bringing with him an invalid's couch, which was carried into the house. He then proceeded to arrange the couch in the sitting-room, and when it was organised to his satisfaction he carried Katharine downstairs and placed her carefully among the cushions. She recorded the incident to demonstrate how thoughtful and kind Parnell was to her, but it—and his staying at Wonersh Lodge in her absence—also show how unconcerned they both were about Willie O'Shea's reactions, and that her husband's agitated behaviour in August had not produced any alteration in the situation which had existed for the last four years, with Katie and Parnell at Eltham and Willie in London.

Indeed, soon after the birth of baby Katie, her mother took a fairly decisive domestic step, and it was one which might indicate that Katharine considered her husband had shot his last troublesome bolt, that if he had accepted this baby's birth he would accept anything and that the triangular relationship had now entered calmer waters. The decision was to have an extra room built onto Wonersh Lodge, specifically to serve as Parnell's workshop and study in which he could pursue his architectural, assaying and astronomical interests and work on his political plans. The room was built onto Katie's downstairs sitting-room and Parnell took great practical interest in its construction, making sure the concrete was laid sufficiently thick, sending to Avondale for wood for the panelling, the doors and the mantelpiece. When it was finished, to celebrate the occasion, Katie took his photograph, sitting in his favourite armchair, surrounded by his assaying instruments and holding his pestle and mortar. From the spring of 1885 Parnell finally gave up his lodgings in Keppel Street and moved into Wonersh Lodge; it was also in February 1885 that he had shipped over from Ireland his horses *Dictator* and *President,* soon to be followed by *Home Rule* (and the quip that *Home Rule* was an old crock earned loud laughter in the divorce court). All this activity, which was common knowledge in the North Park area of Eltham, was of course unknown to Captain O'Shea, and in her book Katharine printed a curious pair of letters. In one of them Parnell informed his own Queenie that he was sending over the horses permanently, while in the other he asked 'My dear Mrs O'Shea' if she could stable the animals for a few days. Her comment was that the second letter was written in case Captain O'Shea should chance to hear about them, substantiating the divorce court evidence about his unawareness of the horses' arrival. What sort of a marriage it was when the arrival of the horses might chance to reach her husband's ears was a factor then overlooked by her (and the divorce court). But the letters do prove that Katie and Parnell were practising a modicum of deception towards Willie as late as 1885, however ridiculous it was, when Parnell had moved himself and his livestock (some dogs followed) into Wonersh Lodge.

As the room was being constructed, O'Shea continued to write chatty letters to his wife. In January he was feeling in a low state and the doctor said his heart was affected, so he wondered if Katie could get up to Albert Mansions and possibly bring the little girls with her? In March he had the momentous news that Joseph Chamberlain had promised him, not the Irish Under-Secretary's job, but the top post of Chief Secretary 'on the formation of the Government after the election', and this would be 'an enormous thing, giving you and the Chicks a very great position.' In May he returned to the theme, if in less dogmatic tones, assuring Katie that 'if Chamberlain has power, which I think he will in the next Parliament, he will offer me the Chief Secretaryship.' One's first reaction to this information is that it is not credible because Chamberlain had no idea whether a Liberal Government would be returned at the General Election (it was not), he did not know what position he would hold even if the Liberals were returned and therefore he could not possibly offer Willie O'Shea the post of Chief Secretary. The information would seem one of O'Shea's delusions of grandeur. However, Henry Labouchere, a leading member of the Liberal party though not in the Government, later told Gladstone that Chamberlain had promised that 'O'Shea should figure in the Cabinet as Irish Secretary', so perhaps Chamberlain let his aspirations suggest a post he could not in any way be certain of implementing and O'Shea had some grounds for his belief.

Willie's letters to his wife have led one of Parnell's more recent biographers, Jules Abels in *The Parnell Tragedy,* to suggest that, contrary to generally held opinion, O'Shea remained in ignorance of his wife's adulterous relationship with Parnell throughout most of the ten years from 1880 to 1890. Mr Abels based his belief on the premise that no man who knew his wife was committing adultery could possibly have continued to write her such friendly letters. (And he gets round the matter which seems important, the births of the two daughters in 1883 and 1884, by following Katie's example and omitting to deal with them.) Admittedly, if one reads the letters on their own, without reference to what anybody else was writing or doing, to what was known to be happening politically and personally, it seems incredible that O'Shea *could* have been aware of the adultery, as otherwise it seems that he *could not* have been. They were friendly, intimate letters such as a devoted husband would write to his beloved wife, frequently addressed to his dear 'Dick' from her 'Boysie', but the O'Shea marriage had for years been a marriage by correspondence so it is perhaps not surprising that he should continue to write to her. It is the letters printed in Katharine's book on which Mr Abels bases his opinion, but since the book was published with the stated aim of defending O'Shea's reputation, presumably only those she (and/or the O'Shea editors) thought would not harm it were inserted, though some of them do not stand up well when placed against other people's statements and proven events. There is something pathetic about the way O'Shea wrote of the Chief Secretaryship and what an enormous thing it would be for Katie and the chicks, but another matter which cropped up in his letters early in 1885 is less pathetic, and that was his reliance on Aunt Ben's money. From Madrid, where he was in April, bringing his powers as a negotiator to bear on Spanish/Cuban affairs, he wrote: 'If Aunt accuses me of extravagance you can truthfully tell her that my sister's illness was an immense expense to me. This hotel is simply ruinous, and I never have anything but 1s 6d wine. I must have a sitting-room to transact business.' With regard to Aunt Ben and her money, Katharine later told Henry Harrison that news of her affair with Parnell did reach the aged Mrs Wood's ears but she refused to believe the rumours, not because Katie denied them or she could not think ill of her 'dear Swan' but because she was constantly asking for so much money for O'Shea that her aunt reasoned that she must care for him and could not therefore be involved with Parnell.

Politically the year of 1884 was again quiet, with coercive

measures still in force in Ireland and Parnell taking little active part in affairs either there or in the House of Commons. Katharine wrote a few letters to Mr Gladstone on his behalf, receiving only brief acknowledgements and not directly from Gladstone, but one letter she sent in May was of the utmost importance, not because of what she said but because of the document therein enclosed, this being no less than 'A Proposed Constitution for Ireland', Parnell's draft for Home Rule. It proposed a Chamber of three hundred members, two hundred and six to be elected, the remainder to be nominated under the Act constituting the Chamber (i.e. an upper and lower House on the British model), with proportional representation guaranteeing the rights of the Protestant minority; that the Chamber be re-elected and the upper members renominated every three years; that the Chamber have jurisdiction over all Ireland's domestic affairs and the power to enact internal laws, subject to the assent of the Crown; that the right of the Crown to levy taxes be abolished, with the Irish contributing one million pounds sterling to the Imperial exchequer in lieu of these taxes; that the right of the Crown to appoint officers be abolished; that the right of the Imperial Parliament to interfere in Irish domestic and internal affairs be held in suspense, only to be exercised for weighty and urgent cause; that the Crown maintain naval and military forces in Ireland as it thought requisite; that no Volunteer Force be raised without the consent of the Crown or the enactment of the Imperial Parliament; that Irish MPs might or might not be retained at Westminster. It was the basis of the first Home Rule Bill, soon presented to Parliament, and of the two Bills which followed thereafter, and with some alterations it was the constitution obtained by the six counties of Northern Ireland after 1922. When this momentous document was presented to Mr Gladstone in May 1884, he showed little overt interest, and all Katharine received was a brief reply from Lord Richard Grosvenor (Chief Whip for the Liberals) thanking her for her 'memo' and saying that it would receive careful consideration, but that at the moment it was impossible to make definite comment.

One piece of legislation enacted by Parliament at the end of 1884 was of significance, this being the Franchise Act which gave the vote to males of sound mind with household qualifications who lived in the British counties and to those in the boroughs and counties in Ireland (the British town workers with the right qualifications had been enfranchised in 1867). The extension of the franchise meant that, come the next election, Parnell and the Irish nationalists would have not only wider voting strength in Ireland but increased power in Britain, where some of the newly enfranchised workers were Irish. Katie said that as soon as the Bill became law at the end of the year, Parnell leapt into action because he recognised that he might hold a balance after the next election and that he could be in a position to force a British Government to introduce a Home Rule Bill. With the groundwork laid by the National League, the introduction of the pledge guaranteeing a disciplined Home Rule party, he now had a solid base from which to work. Parnell was not the only person aware that the Franchise Act could widen the nationalists' scope, and Joseph Chamberlain decided it was time to take a new initiative. He had a sympathy with the nationalists—if it had not been much in evidence in the last couple of years—but he was more influenced in his actions by a desire to get himself into a strong position in the British context. For at this period there were plots in the higher ranks of Liberalism to dethrone the aged and apparently failing Gladstone, and whoever effected a satisfactory Irish settlement would be in an admirable position to exert his will in a new-style Liberal administration. The scheme Chamberlain evolved was for a complete reform of local government in Ireland, with the creation of an Irish Central Board controlling such matters as education, communication and land. The Central Boards Scheme, as it became known, was in effect a modified form of Home Rule which Chamberlain hoped might satisfy the Irish demands, though he was not at this point opposed to a further devolution of power into Irish hands. By the end of 1884, for a variety of reasons, not least including the recent lack of sympathy, the nationalists had turned against their former ally, so that having evolved his scheme Chamberlain had to proceed cautiously, and the person to whom he turned to present his feelers to Parnell and other Irish interests was Willie O'Shea.

In the Kilmainham period O'Shea had proved a reliable, skilful negotiator as far as Chamberlain was concerned, and he was an Irishman with a foot in many camps; he was a member of the Home Rule party, and he had good contacts with the Catholic hierarchy in England and Ireland, notably in England through Cardinal Manning. Indeed, as he embarked upon his mission as Chamberlain's envoy, Willie was deeply involved in the intrigues and struggles to elect a new Archbishop of Dublin. In this case he was on the side of the nationalist angels, and the man whom he regarded as *his* candidate, Dr Walsh, the ablest and most nationalistically-minded of the Irish hierarchy, eventually secured the appointment in the face of strenuous opposition in Rome, Ireland and England. Willie later told Cardinal Manning that 'Doctor Walsh could not have been appointed to his position had it not been for my action at the time', a statement which underlines his vanity and self-esteem. Nevertheless, at this period in 1885 he had reason to regard himself as a figure of some importance on the Anglo-Irish scene, and Chamberlain had reason to use him as his envoy.

What Chamberlain did not fully appreciate was that in the years since Kilmainham there had been shifts of emphasis and relationship. In 1882 Willie O'Shea was accepted at Wonersh Lodge, he and Parnell could hammer out the details of the treaty face to face in Katie's sitting-room, but from the beginning of 1885, however chatty his letters to his wife might be, he was rarely seen at Eltham and he and Parnell met irregularly and in non-intimate fashion. O'Shea had emerged on the scene as Parnell's man (which was why Gladstone and Chamberlain had taken note of him in the first place), and to an extent, because of Parnell and Katie's desire to keep him happy, he still held that position, but its shape had changed. It had altered as much because of the shift in relationship between Chamberlain and O'Shea as between him and Parnell. Chamberlain enjoyed Willie's company and over the last two years Willie had wined and dined at Highbury (Chamberlain's Birmingham house), and the two of them had talked man to man. It was to Chamberlain's star that O'Shea had now hitched himself, it was Chamberlain who now received the self-reflecting veneration, because it was Chamberlain who fully appreciated his worth, not Parnell. An Irish nationalist said, 'Listen to him then, with "Chamberlain and I"', adding, 'And will ye tell me how much is "Chamberlain" and how much "I" in that cabal?'

By the beginning of 1885 Parnell regarded O'Shea as Chamberlain's man, which he was, but was willing to deal through him when he needed the Radical leader; O'Shea regarded himself as nobody's man but primarily as Chamberlain's valued associate and secondarily as Parnell's political mentor; while Chamberlain knew he had O'Shea in his pocket but overestimated his Irish influence and stature because Willie told him what he, as an Englishman, wanted to believe about nationalist Ireland. What Chamberlain wanted to believe then was that the nationalists would accept his Central Boards Scheme, and after complex negotiations and hard bargaining between Cardinal Manning, the Irish Catholic hierarchy, various nationalists and Parnell, by the spring of the year it seemed that his chosen intermediary, Captain O'Shea, had gained the approval of the interested parties. (It was, of course, this apparent success which convinced O'Shea that he would be the next Irish Chief Secretary.) The Irish hierarchy and Manning were in favour; Manning was an old friend of Gladstone's (and the friendship had survived his conversion from Gladstone's beloved Anglicanism to Roman Catholicism), he loved power and intrigue and as the head of the Catholic Church in England saw himself in an admirable position to help settle Anglo-Irish problems. In many ways a radical, he was also— as Sir Charles Dilke noted—'a ferocious Jingo'. He was therefore opposed to Home Rule, and the Central Boards Scheme seemed to him the ideal compromise; he used his power and influence to persuade the Irish bishops that this modified version would be to their advantage too (notably they would gain control of education and Mr Chamberlain's non-sectarian ideas would be firmly scotched). What Manning as an English Catholic failed to appreciate was that although the Irish hierarchy had immense moral and spiritual power over its flock, it was not matched by political power; if it had been, the Protestant, semi-revolutionary figure of Charles Stewart Parnell would never have emerged in the first place. Thus, in practical terms, the Irish hierarchy's enthusiasm meant little unless it was backed by Parnell, and Parnell had not given his blessing or at least not in the manner Cardinal Manning, the Irish bishops and Chamberlain, particularly Chamberlain, thought he had.

The person responsible for the failure of clear communication was the chosen intermediary Willie O'Shea. Parnell had stated his position with crystal clarity in two letters written to O'Shea in January 1885. In these he said that Captain O'Shea must emphasise to Mr Chamberlain that 'we *do not* propose this Local Self-Government plank as a substitute for the restitution of our Irish Parliament, but solely as an improvement for the present system of Local Government in Ireland', and 'the two questions of the reform of Local Government and the restitution of an Irish Parliament must, as I explained to you from first to last, be kept absolutely separate.' But from first to last O'Shea had been explaining to Joseph Chamberlain that Mr Parnell was prepared to accept this modified form of Home Rule as the solution to Ireland's problems. Moreover, over the last two years he had presented himself to his good friend Chamberlain not as the Irish leader's message carrier but as the man Parnell trusted and turned to for advice. How could he lower himself in Chamberlain's estimation by revealing that his information was inaccu-

[134]

rate and his position as trusted adviser suspect? The answer was that he could not. There was only one solution for Willie, which was to conceal the two vital letters, and trust that either his undoubted influence over Parnell would win or that things would sort themselves out once the Central Boards Scheme was implemented.

At the same time as O'Shea was suppressing the clear views of Parnell and assuring Chamberlain that he would settle for limited local government, the Irish leader delivered one of his most famous speeches. In Cork on 21 January 1885 Parnell stated: 'We cannot under the British Constitution ask for more than the restitution of Grattan's Parliament. But no man has the right to fix the boundary on the march of a nation. No man has a right to say "Thus far shalt thou go and no further", and we have never attempted to fix the *ne plus ultra* to the progress of Ireland's nationhood and we never shall.' The astute Chamberlain might have taken more note of this speech than he apparently did, particularly as he kept a copy of the speech in his private papers, and on exactly the same date he wrote a long letter to O'Shea in which he showed considerable ire over his friend's ability and reliability as an intermediary. The letter started: 'My Dear O'Shea, Speaking frankly, as a friend should do, I must say that you have the most damnable habit of letter-writing. To the present case: you come to me for a chat and I talk to you, and according to my wont, fully and openly—perhaps even indiscreetly—about Irish affairs *et omnibus aliis*. If you thought the conversation of sufficient interest to justify you in transmitting your general impression of it to any third person, I have no right to complain (tho' suggest "oral intercourse" better). But you go much further. You send me a detailed precis of this interview according to your recollection of it . . . as to which I will only say that it resembles the late Lord Brougham's nose in its most important characteristics, namely, that it is all on one side. I cannot of course control your private correspondence, only you must please not make me responsible for it . . . etc. etc.' Again on the same day, Chamberlain wrote to his friend John Morley, revealing more about O'Shea's version of the conversation and of his doubts: 'Referring to my recent conversation with you on Irish affairs, I am beginning to be a little uneasy on the subject of Captain O'Shea's volunteered communications. I believe him to be perfectly honourable and sincere but he has a perfect mania for diplomacy. Yesterday, I received from O'Shea in the shape of a letter from him to Parnell, a somewhat cynical account of a conversation distorted to suit his own views.' In

1888 this letter of Willie's assumed great importance and in that year Chamberlain came to the conclusion that if O'Shea had been capable of such misinterpretation on his side, he might similarly have misinterpreted Parnell, but in 1885 the thought did not strike him, or rather he did not let it strike him because he wanted to believe that Parnell and he could work together on his terms, whereas in 1888 he knew they could not.

In May the Liberal Cabinet, which had been considering the Central Boards Scheme, finally turned it down and also announced its intentions to apply for a renewal of coercion in Ireland. Chamberlain resigned. However, he remained convinced that his Central Boards Scheme was a viable proposition and, still accepting O'Shea's assurances, thought Parnell and the nationalists did too. In June, together with Sir Charles Dilke, he proposed to visit Ireland to sound the ground further, but in the meantime fresh prospects had materialised for the Irish, and first Cardinal Manning refused to give introductions, then the Irish nationalist papers launched bitter attacks on the visit and finally Archbishop Walsh expressed his disapproval (and Chamberlain had supported Walsh's election for Dublin). As he was successively slapped down, Chamberlain became more and more convinced that his scheme was the only practical, realisable solution, that radical reform of local government was the substance, Home Rule the shadow. He also began to focus his resentment on Parnell, the man who had apparently encouraged his scheme, who owned the newspaper making the most bitter attacks on him, *United Ireland,* and was capable of influencing the rank and file reaction, and the bishops if he wished. Even after his bitter rejections Chamberlain remained anxious to co-operate with the nationalists, anxious to assure them (via Willie O'Shea) that he was not totally opposed to a more complete version of Home Rule, and it was not until August, when Parnell published a letter in *The Times* stating that he had never regarded the Central Boards Scheme in the light Mr Chamberlain was now suggesting—i.e. as rather more than less a substitute for Home Rule—that Chamberlain started to become outraged. While it was not true, as he believed, that Parnell had deceived him, it was true that the Irish leader treated him in cavalier fashion, dropping him with less attention than a cold potato. Various political reasons have been suggested for Parnell's abrupt dismissal of Chamberlain, but even so he could have softened the blow or continued to keep a line open, as he did all the time via Katie with Gladstone, for he was not the only person who possessed pride and was most tenacious in his resentments.

In these Central Boards negotiations Katie took no part, neither Chamberlain nor Cardinal Manning being gentlemen to deal through a female intermediary, but her husband played a disastrous role, and had Parnell not loved her and bent to her demands for a preservation of the *status quo,* it is extremely doubtful that O'Shea would have been asked to negotiate or have had any fingers in the 1885 pie. As the pie continued to rise with startling rapidity O'Shea's tricky fingers were less involved, and in the first half of the year Katharine did not take much part either. Apart from her normal chores she had baby Katie to occupy her and her links were with and her inclinations towards the Liberals, while from May onwards Parnell was paying increasing attention to the Tories.

On 8 June Gladstone's administration was defeated, not on an Irish issue but on a British domestic one, by the combined votes of the Tories and the Parnellites. For some people this was as astounding an alliance as had been the Manning-Chamberlain association, for had not the Tories always been opposed to Parnell and had he not promised to co-operate cordially with the Liberals? But Parnell had also made it clear in many speeches that he would align himself with either British party as circumstance presented itself, and currently since the Liberals had made no recent Irish moves (and had rejected the one made by Chamberlain), and since certain members of the Tory party had made encouraging noises, circumstance suggested to Parnell that he see what the other sector of political power had to offer. The Tory making the most encouraging noises was Lord Randolph Churchill, and there is the theory that he was acting from much the same motives as Joseph Chamberlain (if not in tacit alliance with him), in that he wanted to shake up the Tory party as much as the latter wanted to re-shape the Liberal, and that for both of them Ireland was a tool. Whatever the underlying motives, on the surface the Tories were showing an interest in Parnell and they were the party in power, Lord Salisbury having formed a caretaker government until the General Election at the end of the year.

At the scent of a possible Tory-nationalist alliance, Cardinal Manning immediately dropped Joseph Chamberlain and any further thought of his Central Boards Scheme. The Tories were the people to whom the English Catholics looked for support, there was a greater natural sympathy between them and the Irish hierarchy and thus the new alliance was to be snatched with both hands. There followed much secret negotiation, including a cloak-and-dagger meeting between Parnell and

Lord Carnarvon (the new Lord Lieutenant of Ireland), and the Tories proved their friendship by dropping coercion and passing a Land Act which implemented the purchase proposals Parnell had long been suggesting to Mr Gladstone through the medium of Katie. Parnell responded by making noises intimating that he might give the Tories the Irish vote in Britain, while remaining quite as suspicious of Lord Salisbury's good Irish intentions as he had ever been of Mr Gladstone's. For if the motives of the leading British politicians in both parties were complex and had more to do with Britain than with Ireland, Parnell's were simple and wholly connected with his own country. He aimed to get himself into such a strong position that he could force one of the British parties into granting not some modified version of Home Rule but the version he wanted. In the middle of 1885, with the Tories for the first time showing an interest in him and the votes he carried, the prospects looked good.

Chapter Ten

At the beginning of July 1885 Gladstone responded to the pressure of Parnell's current dalliance with the Tories by dropping a memorandum to Lord Richard Grosvenor suggesting that he reopen contact with Mrs O'Shea. This Lord Richard duly did by writing to ask Katie if the document she had sent him some time ago 'written by a typewriting machine, containing Mr Parnell's views on local government in Ireland' still held good. A week later Katie replied in non-committal fashion saying she would write when she had ascertained Mr Parnell's views, that was, if Lord Richard would care to hear from her again. He replied immediately saying he would be delighted to hear from her, and after a few days he wrote again begging her to communicate Mr Parnell's views, but she failed to respond and on 4 August Gladstone himself wrote. (There was now no nonsense about Mrs O'Shea being a doubtful intermediary.) To Gladstone's letter Katie replied without delay, giving as an excuse for her previous silence the fact that she had been in Folkestone and had not had her mail forwarded, but the prompt response to the Liberal leader's personal letter indicates that Parnell did not wish to overantagonise him, for on balance he thought the Liberals more likely than the Tories to introduce a Home Rule Bill.

In this letter Katie said that people interested in the Irish question were now convinced that it would be putting the cart before the

horse to reorganise local government without granting legislative autonomy. What such people had in mind, having regard to the altered
circumstances, was an Irish constitution similar to that of one of the
larger colonies, with due guarantees for the authority of the Crown, for
equitable treatment of the landlords and for the rights of the Protestant
minority. If Mr Gladstone felt inclined to consider this proposition, Mr
Parnell would be pleased to send him a draft or she would be glad to
meet him personally to explain the details. Further, she would be grateful if Mr Gladstone would not mention her proposals to anybody
(particularly not to Mr Chamberlain) and she said that she was convinced that he—Gladstone—was the only man capable of carrying such
proposals to a practical conclusion.

In his reply Gladstone said her letter was 'too interesting,
almost, to be addressed to a person of my age and weakened sight, since
it substitutes for a limited prospect a field almost without bounds.' It
did not in fact do so, as Gladstone already had in his possession Parnell's much earlier draft for a Home Rule Bill, but it certainly widened
the recent field of revised local government. Gladstone continued by
saying that Mrs O'Shea had not explained the nature of the change
which had occurred since Mr Parnell's own proposals for local government in Ireland, but went on to make it clear that even a person of his
advanced age and weakened sight knew what she meant by referring to
'the altered attitude of the Tory party, and I presume its heightened
bidding.' He made it equally clear that he for one would not enter into
any counter-bidding, and indeed such naked bargaining as Parnell was
suggesting—the Liberals can have my support in return for an outright
commitment to Home Rule, otherwise I continue to parley with the
Tories and probably dish the Liberals in the General Election—contravened his principles. Gladstone finished by saying that he was still in the
dark as to exactly what Mr Parnell wanted and that he would therefore
be grateful to receive a detailed document such as Mrs O'Shea had
suggested, did not accept her invitation to a personal meeting, and
announced that he was off on a yachting holiday.

For the next three months Parnell continued to try to get Gladstone to commit the Liberals to open support for the *principle* of Home
Rule, but he foundered on a variety of rocks, the most jutting of which
was that Gladstone as much as any major politician was playing the Irish
situation by ear. Isaac Butt had first propounded Home Rule in the early
1870s, Parnell had been fighting for it for the last decade, the Franchise

Act had pointed towards his present strong electoral bargaining position, but in a curious way everything was now happening too quickly, even Parnell had to play his cards faster than was perhaps desirable, while the British politicians kept theirs as close to their chests as was possible.

As the General Election approached (voting was due to start at the end of November), as the hour for the crucial decision neared—behind which British party should Parnell throw the Irish weight to gain most advantage?—he was involved in yet another personal problem concerning his beloved Queenie's husband. O'Shea wanted a seat in the next Parliament, and his old constituency of County Clare had refused to renominate him as the Home Rule candidate. Way back in 1883 Parnell had told Katie that her husband's position in Clare was 'irretrievable' and in her memoirs she explained some of the reasons why he was so disliked by the Irish nationalists and many of his constituents. From the moment he took his seat in the House in 1880 O'Shea refused to sit with the main body of the Home Rule party and from his isolated seat kept up a steady flow of witty asides on the accents, manners and dress of his compatriots, for, as he told Katie, he could 'rejoice in, but could not sit with, unvarnished genius.' Such behaviour, typical of the Anglo-Irish Ascendancy at its worst, except that O'Shea was not a member of the Ascendancy, obviously did not endear him to the nationalists. Apart from this, there was his close alliance with Joseph Chamberlain, which by 1885 rendered him highly suspect in nationalist circles, and there was an apparently insuperable barrier to his being selected as a Home Rule candidate for Clare or any seat—he flatly refused to take the party pledge. In one way it can be said that O'Shea was showing signs of principle in refusing to take the pledge which committed him to sit, vote and act in accordance with the party line because he was not convinced that internal self-government was the sole solution to his native country's problems. In another way it can be said that he was being incredibly stupid, for why should he expect to stand for a party whose main aim he did not support in contravention of a solemn pledge agreed to by all members and prospective candidates of that party?

As Willie O'Shea was not a stupid man, one must ask what other reason he might have had for expecting to be returned as a Home Rule candidate without supporting the principle of Home Rule and conforming to party discipline. The obvious answer is that he knew his wife was the Irish leader's mistress, that she had been living with him

[141]

for the past five years and that he could threaten a nasty exposure unless his parliamentary wishes were granted. However, his explanation for expecting to stand for a nationalist constituency without being a *bona fide* nationalist was that he had Ireland's interests at heart, implicitly that he was too valuable and experienced a negotiator for the party to discard and explicitly that Parnell owed him a seat. This was not only on account of his past services but because Parnell had betrayed him, not personally with regard to his wife but as a *political* mentor and colleague. The root of the betrayal was the failure of the Central Boards Scheme, for in O'Shea's opinion Parnell had wantonly reneged on this deal and in the process had made him look a fool and robbed him of the Chief Secretaryship. He underlined his theme of perfidious political betrayal by telling Chamberlain that he had played second fiddle to Parnell 'for the benefit of the Irish people' and that his influence 'apart from the Kilmainham Treaty was a more potent factor throughout the Parliament than the speeches and antics of those who now take to themselves the credit of everything that has been obtained.' For some time prior to 1885, O'Shea had had a curious relationship with several Fenians, curious because nobody could accuse him of being a proponent of total Irish independence to be obtained by violent means, and it may have been his buried *personal* hatred of Parnell which led him into Fenian circles in the first place, as no avowed Fenian loved Parnell the constitutionalist dedicated to obtaining Home Rule by peaceful means. But it was from mid-1885, after the collapse of the Central Boards Scheme, that O'Shea became actively involved in Fenian manoeuvres to oust Parnell, which came to half-light at the time of the Special Commission in 1888, and that he openly began to express his *political* distrust of and resentment against the Irish leader.

Such political animosity, whether entangled with personal resentment or not, posed dangers for Katie and Parnell. During the last five years there had been several crises in the triangular relationship but they had been averted by ministering to O'Shea's pecuniary needs and political ambitions. But suddenly he felt that he had been thwarted politically, and unless these feelings were soothed—by Parnell exerting his influence to get him a safe nationalist seat—he might cease to be so domestically compliant. Katie seems to have been aware of the dangers; she devoted a fair amount of space in her memoirs to the efforts to obtain her husband a seat in 1885 (if in more confused fashion than usual, rendering the narrative difficult to follow). Her explanation for

[142]

her exertions on her husband's behalf followed the normal ambivalent line that Willie was the deceived husband, that he loved politics, that they kept him busy and he thus had little time to bother her at Eltham. But he had failed to trouble her overmuch from the time she moved into Wonersh Lodge in 1875, long before he became involved in politics, so why should she think him likely to return to the nest (and discover Parnell in it) if he lost his parliamentary seat? The extent of her exertions, which revealed what a formidable lady she could be when she put her whole mind to a task, suggest that she scented real danger from a conniving but by now bitterly resentful husband. None knew better than she the depths of Willie's vanity, and from his recent letters she was aware how badly scarred it had been by the Central Boards collapse and that he was in a mood of bitter self-pity (for when things went wrong it was never his fault and somebody must be made to pay). She had to act, to pull every available wire, in order to prevent her husband's resentment and sense of betrayal swelling to bursting point.

On 21 October 1885 O'Shea crossed to Ireland in Parnell's company, although not at his invitation—'When I arrived at Euston I found him on the platform' wrote Parnell to Katie—still hoping to be accepted for a nationalist seat. In Ireland he was finally and categorically told by several members of the Home Rule party that no power on earth (including Parnell) could run him for a nationalist constituency unless he took the party pledge, and this he stubbornly refused to do. Willie remained convinced that Parnell could run him, pledge or no pledge, and it was with ill-grace that he accepted the proposition that he should stand as a Liberal for an Ulster constituency which the nationalists were not contesting. This proposition had been pre-cooked by Katie, who had surely emphasised to Parnell the necessity of finding her husband a seat at Westminster. The idea of shifting O'Shea to the Liberal benches, away from direct contact with the nationalist scene, was a good one, but apart from requiring her husband's consent it also needed Liberal co-operation, as Parnell had no direct control over Ulster constituencies, which were mainly loyalist upholders of the Union. To obtain the Liberal co-operation Katie swung into action with a relentless, single-minded ruthlessness which showed how much political power her Parnell connection had given her and how much she was prepared to do to keep her husband happy.

The saga of the search for a parliamentary seat for Captain O'Shea officially opened on 23 October, when Katie wrote separate but similar letters to Lord Richard Grosvenor and Mr Gladstone. The core of these letters was a package deal she had persuaded Parnell to accept in the hope of getting the Liberals to adopt her husband as a candidate. One feels that at this period Katie's influence on Parnell was at its strongest, for keeping O'Shea quiescent was her province, and if the only way to keep him quiet was to use political tools, then they had to be employed. Katie told both Gladstone and Grosvenor that she was sorry to trouble them on a personal matter but her husband was most anxious to be returned to Parliament (where it might be remembered he had performed valuable services in the Anglo-Irish sphere). Unfortunately there was so much opposition to him in County Clare that she did not feel justified in asking Mr Parnell to support his candidacy there. However, the Irish leader was willing to support her husband in other directions and she plunged into the proposed deal thus:

> *Mr Parnell promises that if Mr O'Shea is adopted as the Liberal candidate for mid-Armagh, where the Catholic votes are within 600 of the Episcopalians and Presbyterians combined, Mr Parnell will get him the whole of the former vote and will moreover give his votes from East Down, North Antrim, North Armagh and North Derry for the Liberal candidates. He will also secure the Irish vote in Wolverhampton to Mr H. Fowler who seems despondent about the effects of its being cast against him.*

This deal, Katie continued, would guarantee the Liberals three seats, East Down, North Derry and mid-Armagh, where the Tories could be defeated by a combined Parnellite-Liberal vote, with a good possibility of success in North Antrim, North Armagh and Wolverhampton. She finished her letter by saying that of course Mr Parnell's proposition was dependent on Liberal co-operation and she would therefore be grateful if both Lord Richard, as Chief Whip, and Mr Gladstone, as the Liberal leader, would intervene *immediately* with the leaders of the Liberal Party in Ulster on Mr O'Shea's behalf.

At this early point in the saga, but not for the last time, Katie and Willie O'Shea showed poor liaison. For on exactly the same date as she wrote her two letters Willie also wrote to Mr Gladstone, which prompted the latter to comment in a note to Lord Richard Grosvenor: 'I inclose two letters from O'Sheas *he* and *she* . . . the subject matter of the letters is very curious.' It was indeed. Katie's estimates of the Ulster seats likely to fall into Gladstone's hands if Parnell instructed their

Catholic electorate to vote Liberal might be overoptimistic, but it was nevertheless an interesting proposition, as it was not the sort of deal by then common in British politics. Willie O'Shea himself later complained that Parnell had imported into the British political arena the worst features of the American scene, and while it was hardly true to say that the former had been free from bribery, corruption and chicanery, the Corrupt Practices Act of 1883 had stopped the worst offences and the inter-party pledging of votes such as Parnell was proposing for O'Shea was no longer general practice. It should also be remembered that at the end of October nobody knew which way Parnell would urge the floating Irish electorate to vote, although publicly he seemed to be leaning towards the Tories, and both they and some members of the Home Rule party would have been interested to learn that the Irish leader was willing to cast so many seats into the Liberal net; that it was for the sake of Mrs O'Shea's husband might not have surprised them, although it would have surprised the Parnellite voters in the constituencies thus named.

However curious Gladstone considered the subject matter of the O'Sheas' letters, neither he nor Lord Richard Grosvenor was averse to putting Mrs O'Shea's proposition to the Irish Liberals; the possibility of the Ulster seats was attractive, as was the more important question of Parnell's overall electoral co-operation. But the response from the Irish Liberals was not encouraging, although one of their leading members went to Belfast to sound the ground and push O'Shea's candidacy. After making enquiries in the area, he wrote to Lord Richard Grosvenor saying that Parnell's desire to help the Liberals seemed genuine (that was, if one could rely upon O'Shea's expression of Parnell's views) but O'Shea himself had been to Armagh and the Liberals there would not touch him as a candidate. The problem in other areas was that with O'Shea as the candidate the Protestant vote would certainly be lost, and O'Shea had not helped matters by being seen publicly in the company of a prominent Ulster Liberal with whom he was trying to arrange a personal 'deal', as it had suggested collusion between the Liberals and the Home Rulers. The best he could offer, therefore, was that O'Shea contest a seat which he could address as a Catholic, and the Liberals would help him secretly but they could do nothing for him openly. That was the end of Willie's hopes of being adopted for mid-Armagh or any Ulster constituency as a Liberal. He himself blamed the failure on Parnell, as he explained to Chamberlain: 'I went to Armagh yesterday.

. . . The Primate received me with the greatest cordiality—but Parnell's estimate of the Catholic vote—within 550 of the Episcopalians and Presbyterians combined—was altogether exaggerated', thus the Liberals could not be expected to back him (much as they really wanted him), and so he had not thrust himself forward. He gave a similar explanation when writing to thank Lord Richard Grosvenor for having troubled himself in the matter.

Having been rejected for mid-Armagh, O'Shea plunged into even deeper self-pity. He wrote to Katie: 'I wonder the little girls have not written to me: no one cares a bit for me except my poor old mother.' His sense of betrayal also deepened; he again wrote to Katie: 'All I know is that I am not going to lie in a ditch. I have been treated in blackguard fashion and I mean to hit back a stunner. I have everything ready; no drugs could make me sleep last night, and I packed my shell with dynamite. It cannot hurt my friend, and it will send a blackguard's reputation with his deluded countrymen into smithereens.' What the shell of dynamite was remains a mystery (although it was referred to again before the Special Commission in 1888), but as Willie mentioned it to Katie it cannot have been connected with their peculiar *ménage,* and as the friend referred to was Chamberlain it was presumably connected with the Central Boards negotiations, in which case it would have been dynamite to no one but him. However, it is letters such as this which lend weight to the contention that O'Shea cannot have been aware of his wife's relationship with the Irish leader, for how could he possibly write to her about blasting the blackguard's reputation if he knew they were lovers? The answer would seem to be that Willie O'Shea's powers of self-deception and ability to twist any situation to his design bordered on the pathological. What is evident in his letters, at least up to 1886, is his fondness for and reliance on Katie, especially his reliance on her political and financial power.

Once her husband's prospects in mid-Armagh had faded, Katie started to show her real mettle, and on 30 October she wrote to Gladstone again, saying, 'I am very anxious that Lord R.G. should find a seat for Captain O'Shea somewhere' (and by the way she enclosed a copy of Mr Parnell's proposed constitution for Ireland as promised in July), and she also wrote to Lord Richard Grosvenor entreating him to find her husband an English seat. When these letters produced nothing except expressions of regret that it had been impossible to find Captain O'Shea an Ulster seat, Katie went up to London to see Lord Richard personally, and from him she extracted an admission that it *might* be possible for her husband to stand as the Liberal candidate for the Exchange division of Liverpool. O'Shea himself was still in Ireland and was showing no interest in contesting an English constituency—he was an Irishman and he wanted a seat in Ireland and the perfidious rogue called Parnell should get him one for services rendered. To Chamberlain he elaborated on the manner in which he had dealt with the rogue: 'Parnell called on me yesterday afternoon to mumble something about sorrow that I had not seen my way to contest mid-Armagh and hope that an English seat might yet be found for me. I soon cut matters short by telling him . . . no man had ever behaved more shamefully to another than he had behaved to me, and that I wished to hold no further communication with him. He enquired whether I wished him to leave and I replied, most certainly. He then crossed the room and held out his hand. I informed him that I would not touch it on any account. . . . I never saw a man slink out of a room more like a cur kicked out of a butcher's shop.' What actually happened when Parnell called to see Captain O'Shea remains unknown, although one doubts whether it had much connection with the scene as depicted by the latter, but Parnell obviously felt a need to placate the gentleman, who did not adhere to his determination to hold no further communication.

Katie was both impressed and unimpressed by her husband's further displays of outraged self-pity, impressed because they foretold more danger, unimpressed because she knew how easily Willie could be made to turn full circle. She bombarded him with telegrams urging him to accept an English constituency; on 5 November he wired back, 'What seat? C[hamberlain] thought nothing left England except forlorn hopes'; and by the end of the first week in November he had accepted that an English seat was the only remaining possibility and reluctantly crossed to England, where he went to stay, not of course with his wife, but with Chamberlain at Highbury. At the Birmingham house he learned that another Liberal candidate had been adopted for the suggested Exchange division of Liverpool, information which he conveyed to Katie by telegram, whereupon she immediately stormed up to London to see Lord Richard Grosvenor, whom she recorded as being in an irritable mood. Katie admitted that as the Liberal Chief Whip in the run-up to a General Election he had problems on his mind other than Captain O'Shea's candidacy, but she had not, and she resorted to some quiet blackmail, approved by Parnell. For if her husband failed to return to his 'home' at Wonersh Lodge, despite the pressures of the election campaign her lover managed to fit in some flying visits, during one of which he agreed that if she failed to force the Liberal hand in Liverpool, she could announce that he personally would stand for the Exchange division, which, with its Irish vote, would put the cat among the pigeons.* With this news bruited in the right quarters, not surprisingly the next day Katie heard from Lord Richard that 'the fulfilment of my wishes was possible but complicated.' It was indeed complicated because a candidate had indeed been selected for the division, one T. E. Stephens, and it would require pressure from the very highest levels to persuade the Merseyside Liberals to drop Stephens and accept an ex–Home Rule Irishman unknown to them and to Liverpool.

Up in Liverpool, which he had finally condescended to visit, Captain O'Shea did not assist matters by promptly leaving and travelling back to London, where he informed Katie (by telegram again, naturally) that he would not return to contest the division unless he received the strongest personal recommendations from Mr Gladstone and Lord Richard Grosvenor. It was Katie's turn to show signs of irritation which, like Lord Richard's, were not without foundation. She was doing her utmost to secure her husband's adoption for the Exchange division, while he was being as unco-operative as possible. However, she sent another telegram to Gladstone asking if he could see his way to recommending her husband as the prospective candidate for the Exchange division, to which he replied saying not until he knew who the accepted but about to be rejected candidate was, and she would have to consult Lord Richard Grosvenor. Katie decided she had now reached the limit of personal appeals to Gladstone, but she had no such qualms about the Liberal Chief Whip, as she recorded thus: 'I grimly decided that I would make Lord Richard Grosvenor's life a burden to him until I landed Willie safely on the Liberal benches.' At a further interview she obtained Grosvenor's consent to her husband's candidature, but Gladstone's recommendation remained essential and she had to beard Lord Richard yet again before she received a promise that he would extract a similar approval from his leader. After this meeting Grosvenor told her, 'I am not at all sure that I approve of you in your political capacity; you

---

* Candidates could then stand for as many seats as they wished (or could afford to), and if they were returned for more than one, they made their choice and a by-election occurred in the rejected area.

are so terribly strenuous and determined.' Katie herself admitted that the highest Liberal endorsement was not obtained solely by her strenuous determination but was assisted by another Parnell deal worked out on a dash down to Eltham 'in case of too much difficulty in getting the G.O.M. and Lord Richard to act on Willie's behalf.' The deal offered this time was that if the Liberal Party adopted O'Shea as its candidate for the Exchange division, Parnell would secure the Irish vote for the Liberals in six other Liverpool divisions, but it also contained a threat, for if the Liberals did *not* adopt O'Shea, then Parnell and other leading nationalists would stand in four major Liverpool divisions.

Parnell had to put the threat into effect personally, and on 17 November it was announced in Liverpool that he had decided to contest the Exchange division. This was one week before the polling date for the Liverpool area (polling then extended over a period throughout the country), and taken in conjunction with the fact that on 17 November the original candidate, T. E. Stephens, issued his address to the electorate, it gives some idea how difficult and frantic were the efforts to obtain the nomination for O'Shea. One must again stress the amount of wheeling and dealing Parnell allowed himself to be involved in for the sake of Queenie's husband. What he allowed himself to do in Galway three months later has been well documented and commented upon, but his Liverpool efforts on O'Shea's behalf have been largely ignored. Viewed in the nationalist context they would seem almost as heinous as Parnell's behaviour in Galway, particularly as he finally instructed his followers to vote against the men who had coerced Ireland (i.e. the Liberals), but the Liverpool machinations have probably been ignored because they did not involve a direct confrontation with the Nationalist party, as they did in Galway.

Returning to the Liverpool saga—up to this moment Willie remained in London, refusing to budge until Katie received the highest Liberal endorsements for him, and in the meantime flexing his muscles in other directions. He had an acquaintance, the banker Samuel Montague, who was standing as a Liberal candidate in the East End of London, where there was a large Irish vote. Willie wanted to do Montague a favour so that his bank would be favourably disposed towards a Spanish loan he was trying to negotiate, and he asked his wife to get Parnell to commit the Irish vote to Montague. At this juncture Parnell was not at Wonersh Lodge, so Katie acted of her own initiative, told Montague he could have the Irish vote and then 'wired to a London agent of Parnell's (under a name as he would know the message emanated from him) to beat up the Irishmen for Montague; told Parnell that I had done so, and then set myself to attend to Willie's candidature.' (In the event Montague did not get the Irish vote on polling day as Parnell made only four exceptions, plus Captain O'Shea, to his 'Vote Tory' injunctions.)

O'Shea then suddenly decided that he did not want to stand for the Exchange division after all but would prefer the Scotland division of Liverpool. (This was a safe nationalist Home Rule seat, about the only one in England, held by T. P. O'Connor.) If consulted, O'Connor, who was also standing for what shortly became the notorious seat of Galway, did not play ball, and Katie rightly returned her attention to the problem of her husband's nomination for the Exchange division because progress there continued far from smooth. By 18 November O'Shea had consented to reappear in Liverpool; but his behaviour did nothing to facilitate his acceptance as the Liberal candidate. To Chamberlain he wrote 'Oh what a place! No wonder Schnadhorst loathed it', and complained of the boring meetings he had had with local party members, while Parnell was sufficiently worried by his manner to telegraph to Katie urging her 'Send W. a tip to be civil.' On the face of it, O'Shea's behaviour was incomprehensible. Every available wire had been pulled; Gladstone and Grosvenor had sent their personal recommendations; Chamberlain had been 'a brick' and had already sent his written approval; O'Shea was aware that Parnell was prepared to commit the Irish vote and would come to Liverpool in person to drum it up; he desperately wanted to be returned to Parliament; he had no objection to the Liberal party, of which his friend Chamberlain was a prominent member; and he could be charming to *hoi polloi* when he chose (the Fenians were not noted for their worldly sophistication or social standing). His incredible dog-in-the-manger attitude would seem to have stemmed partly from character—he was an Irish gentleman, a superior being, the negotiator of the Kilmainham Treaty and the Central Boards Scheme, therefore everybody should fall flat on their faces with gratitude at having him as a candidate—but partly from his resentment of Parnell. Apart from reducing the likelihood of his being adopted and returned for the Exchange division, all his actions made life more difficult for Parnell, and one wonders if subconsciously he wanted to be defeated in Liverpool so that he could force the Irish leader to get him a seat in the place where he undisputedly had control—nationalist Ireland.

By 20 November the desire to obtain Parnellite voting power had told on the Liberals and the weight of their hierarchy's wishes had worn down the Merseyside opposition, and the next day William Henry O'Shea's election address appeared. He told his Liverpudlian constituents that he was (now) a Liberal who would earnestly support Mr Gladstone's important measures of reform, and he informed his Irish-Liverpudlian constituents that he was sure they could not have failed to note the services he had rendered to Ireland, and as it had been in the past, so it would be in the future. At this juncture Mr Stephens had not withdrawn *his* electoral address and it was not until two days later, after a lengthy meeting of the local party, that the poor man finally issued a statement saying 'that in the interest of the party and at the request of those who were national leaders' he was withdrawing. In the meantime Parnell had appeared in Liverpool, and he spent two vital days attending to the matter of Captain O'Shea's candidature. At his first public meeting he told his enthusiastic Liverpool-Irish audience that he was still considering whether to contest the Exchange division himself, and in typically *insouciant* manner said he did not know if there would be any exceptions in Liverpool to his just-issued instructions for the Irish in Britain to vote for Tory candidates, but if there were, he would let them know by polling day.

The next day he again addressed a large enthusiastic crowd and then told them that he had decided not to contest the Exchange division because it would not be a good idea for the Irish leader to be defeated 'in a hopeless candidature', which latter information can hardly have cheered Captain O'Shea. He had considered the matter of exceptions to his 'Vote Tory' injunctions, and while there were only four out of the three hundred and fifty Liberal candidates who definitely passed the Irish test, it was true that Captain O'Shea had rendered services to Ireland and had a clear record in regard to coercion. Therefore, if the Irish electorate in that division wanted to vote for Captain O'Shea, as an Irishman and a Catholic, he could see no reason why they should not do so. Parnell's recommendation could hardly be termed enthusiastic, but in the virtually all-embracing Liberal veto he was making another exception, and for most of the Irish it was a royal command.

O'Shea had left himself little time to campaign but to the bitter end—and it was a bitter end—he continued to make himself as unpopular as possible. He told one public meeting that he had not come to Liverpool of his own initiative but solely on the instructions of leaders whom he had always obeyed, not a statement calculated to inspire his audience, and as he had sat in Parliament as a Home Rule member for the last five years, they may justifiably have wondered to which leaders he was referring. Then, having been explicitly instructed by Lord Richard Grosvenor and by Katie not to publish the private letter the former had written in favour of his candidature, he proceeded to do so. Lord Richard personally told O'Shea not to publish the letter because in order to pressure the Merseyside Liberals into accepting the unwanted candidate he had to travel to Liverpool. According to the editor of the *Liverpool Post,* in a private letter later written to Mr Gladstone, Lord Richard arrived in the town in the middle of the night and when asked why Parnell was supporting O'Shea as a Liberal candidate replied, 'Oh, he sleeps with O'Shea's wife.'* (It sounds the sort of remark the normally discreet Chief Whip might make in the middle of the night after a long, tiring journey.) Before the electorate went to the polls on 25 November, Mr Stephens announced the pleasure it had given him to make way for Captain O'Shea, but this noble, untruthful statement was to no avail, and when the results were announced, the Tory candidate had 2,964 votes and William Henry O'Shea had 2,909, with Stephens receiving thirty-six defiant Liberal votes (as he had been officially nominated, Stephens's name remained on the list).

There is one final comment to be made about O'Shea's unsuccessful Liverpool venture, or rather one final question to be asked. Might history have taken a different course had he been returned for the Exchange division? He would have been in Parliament as a Liberal, he could have followed the star of Joseph Chamberlain without crossing swords so disastrously with the Irish party, but the poison against Parnell was already in his veins and he wanted to reveal him to the world as a perfidious, treacherous villain, so perhaps he would still have acted as he did when he did.

---

* The editor further told Gladstone that personally, from his knowledge of O'Shea during the 1885 election campaign in Liverpool, he had little doubt that there had been 'prolonged and mercenary connivance' on O'Shea's side.

Chapter Eleven

How greatly Parnell's instructions to the Irish electorate to 'Vote Tory' influenced the swing against the Liberals is disputed; disapproval of Chamberlain's 'Unauthorised Programme' and a new mood of electoral independence are also credited with having had effect. It is not disputed that the result was interesting and put Parnell into a unique position, for the final count was more dramatic than a playwright would have dared envisage, with the Liberals having a majority of eighty-six over the Tories, but with eighty-six Home Rule members returned to Westminster, so Parnell had an exact balance of power to exercise as he saw fit. For the moment, without a clear majority for either British party, the Tories remained the Government, but Parnell immediately indicated where he was willing to place his support—with the Liberals—and from 10 December 1885 onwards the letters flew backwards and forwards between Mrs O'Shea and Mr Gladstone. Katie herself said that she was suffering from a nervous breakdown, occasioned by the exertions of the last few months and the bitter disappointment over Willie's Liverpool failure, and that Parnell returned to Wonersh Lodge to nurse and soothe her with the utmost love and tenderness. It is not surprising that she should have been on the verge of collapse, as the strain had been immense; in addition she had to perform her duties to Aunt Ben, give some attention to her children, and, however devoted her staff, organise the smooth running of the household. It was also approaching Christmas, a frantic time for the female head of the family in a household containing five children, and there was Willie O'Shea in the background re-demanding that Parnell find him a parliamentary seat, but somehow Katie managed to survive without overt signs that her nerves and energy were at breaking point.

On 10 December she wrote to Gladstone begging him to tell her in the strictest confidence whether he would now consider Mr P's Home Rule proposals, as Mr P was shortly to see Lord C. In reply Gladstone did not rise to her pleading but said he was glad to hear that Mr Parnell was seeing Lord C—Carnarvon, he assumed?—as he felt that the Tories were the party to get a Home Rule Bill passed, and he could not endorse any plan of Mr Parnell's for the simple reason that such a momentous step could only issue from the Government of the day. Katharine's next letter, which was an extremely involved, verbose affair, dealt mostly with how much she reproached *herself* for not having been more explicit in recent months, and said she hoped Mr Gladstone would give her some response which would simplify the issue of the future Irish vote. However, she enclosed a long letter Parnell had written to her (from her own house, on her own printed notepaper, which may have interested Mr Gladstone) in which he said that virtually all Ireland had voted in favour of Home Rule, therefore the question of the will of the Irish people had resolved itself and the remaining question was one of the details of the procedure to be adopted in obtaining the assent of Parliament. He emphasised the non-separatist aspects of his plan and said he was not proposing a repeal of the Act of Union but that new legislation be passed by Parliament which of itself could be repealed if it were abused. He said he could not bring forward his Home Rule proposals personally, they must be introduced by an English minister, but he would work to have them accepted as the final settlement of Ireland's grievances, which he believed they would be. He then went on to discuss how the Tories could be defeated by a nationalist-Liberal alliance, on a general vote of censure he thought, rather than a specifically Irish one, and with considerable cool, bearing in mind his recent 'Vote Tory' injunctions, he stated, 'I have always felt that Mr Gladstone is the only living statesman who has both the power and the will to carry a settlement it would be possible for me to accept and work out.' Finally, as much as Mr Gladstone professed to be in the dark about Home Rule, he was unclear how the Liberal leader's mind was working, so he would be grateful for enlightenment.

Before this letter of 14 December was delivered and Gladstone replied, the Liberal leader's mind was to an extent revealed, because on 17 December Herbert Gladstone gave an interview which became known as the 'Hawarden Kite' in which he said he thought his father's mind might be turning in the direction of Home Rule. It was a highly conditional statement, not made by Gladstone himself, but most people, knowing the character of Herbert and the Grand Old Man, were convinced that it must have had the latter's consent. Whether Gladstone in fact authorised his son's pronouncement is a moot point, he had been busy not committing himself to Katie for the last few weeks and there is a long apologia from Herbert in the Gladstone Papers in which he insists his father did not know of the 'Kite' in advance and that his own confidences had been wantonly betrayed. Gladstone had started to make notes on a possible Home Rule Bill in October 1885 and the 'Kite' was certainly viewed as the official indication of his views, but though the letters continued to travel backwards between him and Katie she obtained no further concrete assurances. He harped on his themes of not being the Government, of the Tories with their permanent majority in the House of Lords having the better chance of getting a Home Rule Bill passed, of the measure not being turned into a party issue, with persistent reminders of the difficulty of his position as the leader of a diverse party with many aims, unlike Mr Parnell who had a small band with one aim, namely Home Rule.

In one letter Katie told Gladstone: 'I have not, and have never had any desire to push myself forward as a means of communication. I have nothing to gain by it except the hope that some good may come of the interchange of ideas and views for the common good.' It can be said that she had acquired her position because Gladstone had no objection to a female intermediary, because he had not wanted to commit himself on Ireland and would not therefore initiate a more formal link, and because both he and Parnell recognised the value of an informal channel, but Katie nevertheless backed into her role with skill and enthusiasm. At the end of 1885 and during the first weeks of 1886, in the vital period leading up to Gladstone's declaration in favour of Home Rule, her role was crucial because she was the only real link between him and Parnell. In the same letter she said that Mr Parnell trusted and confided in her and her alone,* a statement which it can be said Gladstone accepted as

---

* Katie's insistence that she was Parnell's only true mouthpiece had considerable relevance, as there was an enormous amount of intrigue at this period and many people who professed to know what Parnell and/or the Irish nationalists wanted or would concede, notably Henry Labouchere and Tim Healy.

accurate, otherwise he would not have written to her so frequently and at such length. Katharine was feeling the strain of the position, and her domestic, maternal side was longing for peace and quiet, temporarily anyway, but she continued to shoulder her political burdens manfully.

By the beginning of 1886 Gladstone was wondering privately to Lord Richard Grosvenor whether they should persist in their policy 'of no spontaneous communication to Parnell', but a couple of days later when replying to another letter of Katie's he continued to be unspontaneous, saying he could not possibly tell her what Parnell should do, as for him to proffer advice would be tantamount to negotiation and as he was not the Prime Minister he could not negotiate. But matters were moving to a head. Publicly Gladstone clarified his position by intimating that he would consider introducing a Home Rule Bill should he be returned as Prime Minister, and on 23 January Katie wrote: 'I am authorised by Mr Parnell to tell you that he and the Irish members will be willing, since your speech on Thursday, to assist in ousting the Govt. if Mr Parnell could have a reasonable assurance that firstly, you will be sent for by the Queen, and secondly that you will form a ministry.' However, Katie continued, if the only result of ousting the Government were to be a Liberal ministry formed by Lord Hartington and Mr Chamberlain, the Irish party would prefer to support the Tories, and she also told him that Parnell had been approached by Chamberlain with regard to his support for such a combination. This information related to British political manoeuvrings on the lines of the previous year's attempts to oust Gladstone and to form a broad-based, moderate Liberal party, with Ireland as a useful political tool. But in the past twelve months Gladstone had bounded back from the verge of collapse, physically and politically, Lord Salisbury had taken a firm grip on the despondent Tory party and Ireland had become an issue on which leading British politicians were having to take a stand. Early in 1886 most of them were still wobbling hopefully, intent on jostling for internal power, and the idea of the new Liberal ministry led by Lord Hartington, but with Chamberlain as his most powerful lieutenant, was still being pursued. It has been suggested that if Hartington and Chamberlain had acted decisively early in 1886 they might have been able to carry a Home Rule Bill, but one objection to this thesis is that they would not have had Parnell's support. For if British politicians were in various minds about Ireland, Parnell was not; he knew what he wanted, and one of the things he did not want was to co-operate with Joseph

Chamberlain. (In the dislike which had always existed on Parnell's side and which was growing stronger each day on Chamberlain's, there was the element of *personal* animosity, more dangerous than political differences.)

Politically, Chamberlain was still willing to work with Parnell (on his own terms), and the approach mentioned by Katie was in the shape of a memorandum from him, delivered to her lover by her husband. In this Chamberlain said that the mood of the country was against Home Rule, that the Tories therefore wanted to be defeated to get themselves off the Irish hook, and the best tactics were to let them hang there until they had made themselves so unpopular in Ireland and Britain that the British mood would be ready for an Irish advance; and he reiterated his belief that the Central Boards Scheme was the answer because it would revolutionise Irish government without overantagonising the British. Much of what Chamberlain wrote was sense but the momentum was against him—there was no longer time to wait and see—and Parnell put his money on Gladstone rather than on a possible Hartington-Chamberlain joint front. Katie's letter announcing that Parnell would now be prepared to assist in ousting the Tories, as earlier suggested, on a British rather than an Irish issue, was written on 23 January. The next day Gladstone replied to Katie saying he was uncertain what to do about Jesse Collings—he being the champion of the newly enfranchised British rural workers who was raising an important motion in the House of Commons on 26 January, an ideal non-Irish issue such as Parnell had mentioned. By 26 January Gladstone had made up his mind, and Lord Salisbury's government was duly defeated on Collings's motion by combined Liberal-nationalist votes and then resigned. Now the momentum was fully released and something had to happen on Ireland.

What of course happened was Gladstone's final, official commitment to Home Rule, a conversion which at the time appeared to many people as the most dramatic since Christianity overtook Saul on the road to Damascus. The thesis has since been advanced (notably by J. L. Hammond in *Gladstone and the Irish Nation*) that the conversion was nowhere near as dramatic as it appeared; that Gladstone had always sought a fair settlement of Irish grievances; that increasingly over the years he had become aware that Irish unrest, if apparently intermittent, was a steady phenomenon, linked to dissatisfaction with English rule whether progressive or coercive; that he had more awareness of Parnell's

[157]

qualities than other major British politicians; and that in 1886 his genuine Christian sense of justice, and his grudging respect for Parnell as the man who could lead a semi-autonomous Ireland in statesmanlike fashion, made him come out in favour of Home Rule as a policy which was both just and necessary. More recently, another thesis has been extended (in *The Governing Passion* by A. B. Cooke and John Vincent), namely that Home Rule was a British political party game, played by professionals of the highest standing but nonetheless a game in which Ireland remained the chuck, with Lord Salisbury as much as Gladstone fighting to regain control of their individual parties and squeeze out the presumptuous heir presumptives, the Chamberlains and Hartingtons and Churchills. If it is admitted that Home Rule was, by British politicians, played in a British context (which does not seem surprising), whether from party political motives or a more genuine desire to try and settle the Irish question, it should also be acknowledged that it was Charles Stewart Parnell who had turned Ireland into the chuck with which Lord Salisbury, Mr Gladstone and other British contenders could play.

Gladstone himself used an analogy to explain his decision to the country at large, saying the Irish situation was like a ripened cornfield, ready for the successful harvest which, if delayed, could bring blight and disaster. This was picturesque and true, but unfortunately he had done nothing to organise the British hands to cut the ripened corn—the General Election had not been fought on the Home Rule issue. The Liberal leader's conversion therefore appeared like a thunderstorm on a clear summer's day and scattered the unprepared British public (including many Liberals) like the members of a picnic party sheltering from the downpour. As soon as he announced that his new administration was enquiring into the possibility of introducing a Home Rule Bill, the country started to polarise into pro– and anti–Home Rule camps. (If the contention is accepted that the whole battle was a Gladstone/Salisbury campaign to keep the two major parties intact, the polarisation was essential.) While the opposing factions were solidifying in the United Kingdom, Gladstone went ahead with the formation of his Cabinet, which Joseph Chamberlain joined, though Lord Hartington did not. As Chief Secretary for Ireland, the last man to hold that office should Home Rule be successfully accomplished, he made a surprise appointment, John Morley.

Morley was then in his late forties and had been a Member of

Parliament for only three years, though he had earlier established himself as a critic, biographer, journalist and leading exponent of philosophic radicalism. He had also been a long-time friend and political confidante of Chamberlain and was not at that juncture close to Gladstone. In some ways it was a good appointment, since Morley was intelligent, and on the whole supported the idea of Home Rule, and as he had only been in the direct political arena for a short while, trailed no unsavoury connections for the Irish. In other ways it was not such a happy appointment because he lacked political expertise, once he had committed himself to Gladstone his devotion increasingly tended towards the reverential and he had a melancholic strain which easily gave way to despair, but intellectually he was tough and he quickly learned how to clarify the Gladstonian circumlocutions. The appointment was interesting for Katie because she knew Morley from the days of the Belhus parties, when she was thrust into his company by her elders who found his 'oppressive intellectuality' kept them 'at too great a strain for pleasurable conversation.' After a short while her shyness and consciousness of his superior intellect vanished, she found him easy to talk to and as a result of the time spent in his company at Belhus she said all future fear of clever men evaporated. She and Morley do not appear to have maintained a close friendship, but in the crucial days of negotiating the long-awaited Home Rule Bill it was not unhelpful for Parnell to have a Chief Secretary whom Katie knew personally.

As Gladstone began to work on the draft of the Bill, Parnell was faced with a situation which led to the first open collapse of the dividing line between his personal and political life, and to the most discreditable episode of his career. More than ever Willie O'Shea wanted a seat in Parliament, but the English scene was exhausted, Katie knew she could not immediately bludgeon Gladstone for a Liberal vacancy and in any case her husband did not want an English seat and might behave just as badly as he had in Liverpool, which left nationalist Ireland. In Ireland, the only sure vacant seat—unfilled because T. P. O'Connor had duly been elected both for it and for the Scotland division of Liverpool and had chosen to continue sitting for the latter—was in Galway, a notoriously nationalist town, and O'Shea still flatly refused to take the party pledge. Katie said she had misgivings about her husband standing for a nationalist constituency, let alone Galway, because his unpledged nomination could not be effected without the strongest pressure from Parnell. If his influence was brought to bear, those opposed to his leadership would undoubtedly make public their 'foul insinuations', by which Katie meant their knowledge of the adultery. In fact, this had already been referred to publicly if obliquely by Phil Callan in a speech at Louth during the General Election. (Callan was an ex-Fenian, much involved in Irish nationalist intrigues, who knew O'Shea quite well and had no love for Parnell. At Louth Callan had asked why Captain O'Shea was being supported as a Liberal candidate by Mr Parnell in Liverpool whereas he, a devout nationalist, was not being accorded such support, and had further wondered what there was in the character and private history of Captain and Mrs O'Shea which made them superior to Phil Callan and his wife? In her memoirs, Katharine suggested that if Callan and his Fenian friends opened their mouths wider 'the foul insinuations' would 'necessarily be investigated by Willie', and when he thus suddenly became aware that his wife and Parnell had been committing adultery for the last five and a half years he might take action which could wreck the Home Rule Bill and, in Katie's ambiguous words, 'the silence of years made of none effect at the very time when this silence was to be rewarded by Ireland's freedom.' What action her husband might take is not clarified, nor is it too clear to whose silence she was referring. The whole Galway episode is given minimum space in her memoirs, which is understandable if their object was to defend Captain O'Shea's honour and, in this instance, Mr Parnell's. In her sketchy sequence of events and motives, Willie nagged and fumed about Parnell getting him the nomination, Parnell said he could not do so unless O'Shea took the party pledge, Willie went on nagging and fuming and saying that Parnell owed him the seat for his past services, and that Mr Chamberlain agreed. Katie continued to have her doubts, Parnell asked her to persuade her husband to take the pledge, he refused, and suddenly Parnell said, 'It is no matter, Queenie, I was thinking this afternoon that we are giving ourselves much trouble about what really does not concern us. I'll run him for Galway and I'll get him returned. I'll force him down their throats, and he can never again claim that I have promised and not performed. It will cost me the confidence of the party, but that much he shall have.' He then uttered more words about not worrying if there was a fuss, that if Ireland wanted Home Rule she would have it and what would be, would be. Then Katie abruptly finished the incident and the chapter with the sentence 'Captain O'Shea was returned for Galway.'

It makes an excellent chapter ending, but what went on before

Parnell forced O'Shea down his party's throat deserves larger attention than Katie gave it. Parnell's words, as quoted by her, have the ring of veracity: the insulated nature of their love which led to the extraordinary statement that O'Shea and Galway did not concern them; the fierce autocratic pride of Parnell the leader which made him decide to force O'Shea on his party; the Parnell honour which O'Shea touched by his insistence on past services and which would be finally and utterly redeemed; the fatalistic, *che sarà, sarà* side of Parnell's nature. The decision to run O'Shea for Galway was Parnell's and at the end probably influenced by such emotions as Katie described, but it does not explain why he felt he had to force through the nomination. Katie's reason, as explained and re-explained throughout the second volume of her memoirs, namely that O'Shea did not know about the adultery and had to be kept politically happy in order that he should stay away from Eltham, on her own admission collapses, for she admitted that she was frightened that if her husband went to Galway, the news of the adultery would be bruited and he could not fail to take note. (It was trumpeted and he failed to take note, but we shall be coming to that shortly.) Surely the only possible reason Katie and Parnell had for ramming her husband down the nationalists' choking throats, as in their efforts in Liverpool, was to keep him quiet *because* he knew of the adultery?

However, political reasons for Parnell's appalling action have also been advanced, and these concerned the figure of Joseph Chamberlain. At the end of December 1885, as it became necessary to decide who should fill the vacant seat in Galway, Gladstone had not committed himself to Home Rule but the 'Hawarden Kite' had been flown and it seemed probable that the Tories would soon be defeated and Gladstone would be returned to power and would introduce a Home Rule Bill. If this happened, every vote on the Irish side would be vital and the way Chamberlain cast his could influence more than a handful of Liberal members. There were Irish nationalists, notably Edmund Dwyer Gray, the owner of the influential *Freeman's Journal*, who considered that Chamberlain's fur should be smoothed, and Gray wrote to Parnell saying that from what he gathered Captain O'Shea had influence with Mr Chamberlain, and if Captain O'Shea's wish was gratified, namely nomination for Galway, he might exercise his influence and persuade Chamberlain to vote for Home Rule. Parnell replied saying he really felt he had done everything possible in respect of Captain O'Shea, that he had been unable to recommend him as an unpledged candidate during the General Election and he did not see that circumstances had materially changed. If Gray thought O'Shea really had influence with Chamberlain, and if Gray could persuade the members of the party to accept an unpledged candidate, then he would not oppose the nomination. Having thrown the ball into Gray's court, it was promptly thrown back: 'There is only one way of doing it in my opinion—for you openly to take responsibility. According to O'Shea the whole attitude of the radical leaders depends on him—get him a seat and all things are possible—don't get him a seat and nothing is possible.'

It was true that Chamberlain supported O'Shea's candidacy, but why he gave his support is one matter and how much it influenced Parnell's decision to force through the nomination is another. Katie herself has little to say about Chamberlain. The villain of her story is Gladstone, because she was a subjective emotional lady and she knew and dealt with the Grand Old Man, whereas she never met Chamberlain. A young lady whose powers of analysis and intellect were superior to Katharine's knew Chamberlain well at this period, she being Beatrice Webb. Herbert Spencer had earlier said to Beatrice Potter (as she then was) that Chamberlain was 'a man who may mean well, but who does and will do, an incalculable amount of mischief' (a view supported by Mr Gladstone). She was interested to discover why and recorded her contemporary impressions in an attempt to find the answer. She thought Chamberlain then was 'a curious and interesting character . . . with little self-control but any amount of purpose', that his desire to improve the lot of the masses was genuine but 'running alongside this genuine enthusiasm is a passionate desire to crunch the opposition to his will, a longing to feel his foot on the neck of others.' At the end of 1885 Chamberlain was trying to redefine his purpose and position, but he was not at all clear from which position he was likely to further his purpose, which was, sooner rather than later, to be Prime Minister. Currently the issue on which he had to take a stand was Home Rule, and personally he believed that Parnell had thwarted him over the Central Boards Scheme, personally he was keen to get his foot on the Irish leader's neck, but politically he was less certain what to do. Of Home Rule as opposed to some form of devolution he had never really approved, certainly not in Parnell's hands, but if he opposed it outright it would mean the break with Gladstone and he was not then ready for this step. Some Irish historians have seen Chamberlain's manoeuvres in the Galway period as the onset of his plot to destroy Parnell and thereby Home Rule, but issues other than Ireland were involved for Chamberlain and early in 1886 strategic and tactical uncertainty were the keynotes of his position. As events matured, his inability to weigh facts scientifically and his disruptive lack of self-control plunged him into an extraordinary position which proved fatal for Home Rule, but did not assist his career either.

If he was in a twilight zone, Chamberlain had no objection to creating trouble for Parnell, and one way of doing this was to back O'Shea's candidacy for Galway. Without doubt Chamberlain knew about the Parnell-O'Shea *ménage;* his biographer, J. L. Garvin, vehemently insisted that he did not (at least not until Captain O'Shea finally told him), but Sir Charles Dilke knew in 1882 and he was then Chamberlain's closest friend, and Henry Labouchere wrote to Chamberlain about O'Shea's nomination in 1885, saying the difficulty was the nationalists' knowledge of the love affair. In any case, to suggest that Chamberlain did not know lowers his standing as a highly political animal; the affair was part of the scene and any efficient, worldly-wise politician should have known. It seems reasonable that he pretended to be ignorant—all from Captain O'Shea to the Woods to Mr Gladstone to the Irish nationalists were acting as if they had no knowledge of the adultery, so why not Chamberlain? It would again seem reasonable that he did not discuss the subject with O'Shea; if a friend has a handicapped child or a nymphomaniac wife and seems unaware of these facts, one rarely says, 'Your child is retarded' or 'Your wife is having every man in sight.' On the one hand, Chamberlain realised the difficult position in which his advocacy of the unpledged husband of the Irish leader's mistress would place Parnell, with its trailing suggestions that satisfaction for his friend might induce his support for Home Rule. On the other hand, he had not then made up his mind to oppose Home Rule, he was willing to join Gladstone's ministry, his personal advocacy of O'Shea was not as strong as all that, so it is perhaps unwise to view Chamberlain's role in the Galway affair as the first signs of a Machiavellian plot to destroy Parnell.

The question remains how greatly Parnell was affected by Chamberlain's background intervention. By this time he knew O'Shea very well indeed and unlike Edmund Dwyer Gray, who was a friend of Willie's, he was not overimpressed by the assertion of the Captain's influence on Chamberlain. But he now needed Chamberlain's support for Home Rule as he had not needed it earlier in 1885, and he certainly put forward the necessity of placating the Radical leader as one of the reasons for O'Shea's nomination. Tim Healy considered it 'taradiddle', and while it cannot be dismissed quite so categorically, it seems true that Chamberlain's intervention was not the motivating factor but that it provided an excellent political cover for an action forced on Parnell by his love for Katie and her desire to preserve the *status quo* and placate her husband.

When, for whatever reason or mixture of reasons, Parnell came to the decision to force O'Shea down the nationalists' throats, one of the first people he informed was T. P. O'Connor, the man who had won the Galway seat at the General Election. He told Katie, 'You should have seen his face, my Queen; he looked as if I had dropped him into an ice-pit.' This was precisely how O'Connor felt—he said, 'My blood ran cold'—and his next reaction was to round up leading members of the party to oppose the nomination and thus convince Parnell that it was impossible. At the beginning of February, the opposing clan gathered in Dublin prior to travelling to Galway, and prominent among the opposition were Parnell's old friend Joseph Biggar, and Tim Healy. Born in Bantry in 1856, Healy was in some ways the English identikit of the Irishman, small of stature, witty of speech, a devout Catholic, an ardent nationalist and chauvinistic to a degree, but he also possessed formidable powers of concentration and a phenomenal capacity for work. Among Healy's failings were a too-volatile temper and an overwhelming desire to deliver the unkindest cut of all, which blurred his judgement and increasingly led him on a destructive path, but in 1886 he was a young man who had established himself as a leading nationalist.

What 'the Chief' was now proposing in Galway absolutely stuck in Healy's gullet, and one cannot blame him. However distasteful the liaison with Mrs O'Shea was to him and other good Catholic nationalists, it was Parnell's private life as *long as he kept it that way*. But to foist onto the party for no other reason (as Healy and his supporters saw it) than that he was the husband of Parnell's mistress a man who had shown nothing but contempt for the nationalists, who had recently stood as a Liberal in Liverpool, who refused to take the pledge, was monstrous. When O'Shea's election address appeared in the *Freeman's Journal* endorsed by Parnell, the majority of the leading nationalists felt they could not baulk their leader politically, whatever they might think of his action personally. A split in the ranks of the disciplined party Parnell had so skilfully built up over the last few years would be a

[164]

greater disaster than having Captain O'Shea on the Home Rule benches. T. P. O'Connor, who had started the rebellion, was among those who backed down when Parnell's support of the candidature appeared in print, but Biggar and Healy were made of sterner stuff, and they set off to Galway as planned to find out what the local nationalists thought about their new candidate.

In Galway they discovered that the local people were outraged and determined to nominate their own candidate, one Michael Lynch. Biggar and Healy decided to lend their support to Lynch's candidacy, and the telegrams started to fly backwards and forwards between Galway, Dublin and London. The majority of the leading nationalists continued to back Parnell and to beg Biggar and Healy not to split the party, but the two of them held firm, so Parnell wired a personal appeal to Biggar to withdraw his opposition for the sake of old times and present unity. In reply Biggar sent the telegram which acquired notoriety for its prescience: 'The O'Sheas will be your ruin.' (Healy said Biggar's original draft was simply 'Mrs O'Shea will be your ruin' but it was softened, on Healy's insistence, to the plural.) Willie O'Shea was by this time in Galway, preparing to canvass the constituency, and among the telegrams sent was one from him to Parnell which said: 'All hope gone unless you come at once. Things have gone so far that the presence of anyone except yourself would not save the situation.' What O'Shea meant by this was that the local nationalists, supported by the big guns of Biggar and Healy, had decided to go ahead with their nomination of Michael Lynch, which they duly did on 8 February.

Thus Parnell was forced to travel to Galway and dissipate his energy at a moment when he should have been conserving it for the imminent struggle for Home Rule, and he arrived in the town on 9 February to be greeted by an extremely hostile crowd to which he doffed his hat. Neither Healy nor Biggar had thought Parnell would dare to come to Galway in person, which was a reasonable assumption, except Parnell was not a reasonable man, he was streaked with genius, and his arrival in Galway showed his strengths and weaknesses in equal proportion. It was the supremely bold, decisive and logical act—if he was backing O'Shea he had to see the matter through as he would any other troublesome task—but it failed to take into account other people's moral or political beliefs. Once Parnell was in Galway, he proceeded to make the issue one of his leadership and of loyalty to Ireland: 'I have Home Rule in the hollow of my hand. The man who strikes at my hand strikes at the hopes of the Irish nation! If my candidate is defeated, the news will spread round the universe that a disaster has overwhelmed Ireland. The world will say, "Parnell is beaten. Ireland no longer has a leader".' Faced with Parnell's presence and this appeal, Healy decided the battle was lost, and a meeting was arranged between the local nationalists and the leading luminaries who had converged on Galway, to be chaired by Parnell. In the electric atmosphere of a crowded hall, Parnell reiterated the issue as he saw it, William O'Brien made an emotional speech in favour of 'the Chief', Michael Lynch then stepped forward and said he would withdraw and by an almost unanimous vote William Henry O'Shea was accepted as the nationalist candidate. Following that, as Katie said, her husband was returned for Galway.

The one exception to the voting in O'Shea's favour was Joseph Biggar, who climbed onto the platform and announced that he still favoured Lynch. Healy later said that he wished he had followed Biggar's example because he was right, Parnell was already rotten to the core, worm-eaten by the canker called Katharine O'Shea. While one does not support Healy's reasons—there was nothing rotten about Parnell's love for Katie—Biggar's instinct was right in that in Galway the boundary line between the private and the public was smashed, and Parnell's love could never again be a private matter. If Willie O'Shea's bluff had been called in 1886, if the leading nationalists had stood firm behind Healy and Biggar and said we cannot accept this man *politically,* the disaster might have been averted, O'Shea might have been so punctured that he would never have been capable of reinflation. Then again, he might have felt even more bitter and worked just as assiduously to dethrone his hated enemy, Parnell. But if the nationalists had made a stand in Galway the situation would have been clarified and Parnell and Katie made aware of the political dangers inherent in their relationship. Yet it was asking too much of the nationalists on the eve of Home Rule to baulk the man who had brought them thus far, who indeed seemed to hold in the hollow of his hand the goal for which they had striven, an Irish Parliament on College Green. If Biggar's instinct was right in one way, the majority nationalist one was right in the belief that Parnell was the only man who could hold the party together and wrench Home Rule from the reluctant English. In Galway, Parnell demonstrated the strength of his leadership but he paid a price, although perhaps more in moral than in practical terms. Nowadays, it is unfashionable to believe that politicians have moral standards but in 1886 it was not, and in Galway Parnell showed a failure of scruple which tarnished his leadership. This was not a failure in the narrow, sexual sense, his private life was his own and his love for Katie was genuine, but because he allowed this private relationship to interfere with his political judgement and because it led him to abuse his power.

It should be said that the question of Parnell's liaison with Katharine O'Shea, as the reason why he had foisted her husband on the constituency, was not officially raised. It was not discussed in the telegrams which flew backwards and forwards (apart from Biggar's) nor in the meetings with Parnell, and originally it was not the reason why the local nationalists rejected Captain O'Shea so fiercely. Their objections were because of his recent political record and his refusal to take the party pledge. If most members of the party hierarchy were too much in awe of Parnell's authority and aloofness to dream of mentioning their basic objections, either to him or in public, Joseph Biggar was not. He stumped round Galway, his Belfast accent rasping among the softer Connaught brogues, telling his audiences why he thought Parnell was forcing O'Shea upon the constituency, and emboldened by Biggar's insistence on calling a spade a spade, other nationalists raised their voices. By no means everybody in Galway learned about Katie and Parnell, but local knowledge was encapsuled in the statement 'The candidate's wife is Parnell's mistress and there is nothing more to be said.'

Willie O'Shea's own reaction to the news being bandied through Galway is not on record, although according to Tim Healy he heard the rumours because he went down on his bended knees and swore to the local Bishop that there was no truth in the allegations of his wife's adultery with Parnell. (Again according to Healy, O'Shea was well aware of the real situation because he told a local citizen that he was in a position to make Parnell run faster to his bidding than a young errand boy scurrying across the street on his master's orders.) O'Shea's explanations for his singular deafness in Galway, tendered years later, were either that he did vaguely hear the rumours but discounted them as malicious political gossip, or that he was not interested in stuff shrieked by such as William O'Brien, Tim Healy or Joseph Biggar, the last named a notorious evil-liver. (Biggar's sex life was active, he had several illegitimate children, was sued for breach of promise and admitted his sins openly.) One can only say, might it not have been a good idea if Captain O'Shea had not discounted the gossip but had forced himself to be interested in it?—because Healy and O'Brien were not notorious evil-livers, and that his wife was Parnell's mistress and his candidacy dependent on this fact was shrieked by a fair cross-section of the Galway population. But then, after his election, Willie felt able to write to Joseph Chamberlain: 'I am the most popular MP who has represented the borough for a quarter of a century,' and if he could believe that he could believe anything he chose.

Chapter Twelve

Parnell stayed in Galway one more day after securing Captain O'Shea's nomination, and on 10 February he addressed a meeting at which he assured his audience that he had been unaware of Michael Lynch's candidacy, and said it was only because he had thought there was no local candidate that, as leader of the Irish parliamentary party, he had suggested an outside man, Captain O'Shea being the best he knew. How large a proportion of his audience believed this equivocal statement is difficult to say, but his unawareness of Lynch's availability sounded feeble in the face of the man's actual nomination, and if Captain O'Shea, a recent Liberal contender, was the best candidate he knew, then the nationalist party was in a bad way. His statement can be regarded in the nature of a peace-offering to the citizens of Galway, as Parnell so rarely gave explanations for his actions. Soon after he had first met Katie, when she was worried about his failing to catch boat trains for important meetings in Ireland on her account, he told her, 'You do not learn the ethics of Kingship, Queenie. Never explain. Never apologise.'

The stench of the Galway affair wafted out of Connaught, and the Dublin *Evening Mail* (an anti-Parnellite newspaper) ran a short piece about the family friendship of the O'Sheas and Parnell, which might seem simple but in which, it suggested, there were more than political affinities. The item was a straw in the wind; no newspaper (however anti-Parnellite) was going to risk an outright statement, at least not *until Captain O'Shea moved*. After the Galway election the oblique references to the O'Shea-Parnell triangle started to appear in print, and one feels that the editors had justification for their innuendoes. If Parnell had chosen to bring the affair into the light by foisting his mistress's husband on Galway, on his own head the consequent newspaper interest. The items had no effect on Katie and Parnell (alas) or on his political standing, but their effect on Captain O'Shea was more cumulatively dangerous. When articles appeared in print speculating on the friendship and what the Irish leader was doing at Eltham and various places with Mrs O'Shea, Willie had to take note. He did not act as a result of the *Evening Mail's* innuendoes. It was not too influential a paper, in any case it was Irish and it was what was said about him in England that worried him, and in February 1886, having achieved his object and been elected for Galway, he was, despite his financial difficulties, reasonably happy. For Parnell it had been an unpleasant episode, one he would not have wished to have precipitated but which necessity had demanded. He had satisfied any possible claim Captain O'Shea might have on him, he had established his mastery over his party, the incident was settled and he could now return his whole attention to Home Rule. Accordingly he made his way from Galway to Wonersh Lodge, where Katharine was waiting to greet him.

On 13 March Gladstone presented his draft plans for Home Rule to the Cabinet, and they were in dual form, one section dealing with the setting-up of an Irish Parliament, the other with a land-purchase scheme. At this moment, the land-purchase scheme was in more detail than the Irish Parliament, but Chamberlain precipitated matters by saying that if Mr Gladstone had in mind an independent legislative body for Ireland he would resign. After a week in which some attempts were made to heal the threatened breach, Chamberlain and Gladstone finally collided in a Cabinet meeting marked by extreme bitterness on both sides, and Chamberlain officially resigned, declaring that he was not opposed to some form of Home Rule for Ireland but he could not support Mr Gladstone's present proposals. By this time what Gladstone proposed was known in limited circles, namely that Ireland should have two Houses of Parliament, each having a veto on the other's activities (though they were not to be entirely separate, like the Lords and Commons in England), which should have control of Irish affairs, with the Imperial Parliament retaining responsibility for foreign affairs, defence, war and coinage. Temporarily the Royal Irish Constabulary would remain in Imperial hands, the Irish Parliament would contribute one-fifteenth of the total expenditure of the Imperial budget but would otherwise raise and deal with its own finances, and Irish MPs were *not* to be retained at Westminster. It was this latter clause to which Chamberlain objected most strongly, believing that to cut the Irish MPs off from their links with and responsibilities to the Imperial Parliament, to leave them to their own devices in Dublin, was a sure way of hatching separatist eggs. When Chamberlain resigned it was still not clear how far he would take his opposition to the Bill and thereby sever his links with the main body of the Liberal Party; Lord Randolph Churchill probably summed up the situation accurately when he wrote: 'Joe is very anxious. . . . He is rather drawing his bow at a venture.'

However, it is the opinion of the authors of the recent book *The Governing Passion,* with their flood of new evidence and interpretations, that it was not Chamberlain who forced the issue by resigning but Gladstone who manoeuvred him into a position whereby he had to resign or submit tamely, in the process accomplishing a party purge of which any head of a totalitarian state would be proud, leaving himself as undisputed Liberal leader with his colours nailed to the mast of Home Rule, which he viewed as a tactical issue. After the resignation, the situation as it then appeared was that Gladstone by his precipitate endorsement of Home Rule had split the Liberal Party, with Lord Hartington and his supporters already standing against the Bill and Chamberlain having resigned on a matter of principle. The question was, could the Liberal breach be healed sufficiently to out-vote the Tories, already solid in their opposition? Apart from the Tory themes of the disintegration of the Empire and the obviously backward Irish needing England's guiding hand, Lord Randolph Churchill had produced another emotive opposition stand: 'I decided some time ago that if the G.O.M. went for Home Rule, the Orange card would be the one to play. Please God it may turn out the ace of trumps and not the two.' In 1886 it was not much higher than the two because Ulster was not given the time or the leadership to organise herself, but longer term it was the ace, and it was ironic that it should have been dealt by Lord Randolph Churchill, who had as genuine an understanding of nationalist Ireland as any British politician and who had earlier written of 'these abominable Ulster Tories . . . these foul Ulster Tories.' Churchill's production of 'the Orange Card' added fuel to the overall bitterness which was enveloping the Home Rule battle. Whatever the motives and feelings of those at the top, all who later wrote of this period from below the rarefied heights said it was impossible for those not then alive to appreciate how deep were the passions roused, how profound the bitterness. Gladstone and other Liberals were cut dead at social gatherings, and the Duke of Westminster went so far as to take down the Millais portrait of the Liberal leader which had adorned the walls of Eaton Hall. If not everybody in the United Kingdom was consumed by the question of Home Rule or took a stand for or against Mr Gladstone, the passion ran right through the social scale and split many old friendships and allegiances.*

Before Gladstone actually introduced his Bill to Parliament, whereby the general tensions and the internal Liberal manoeuvrings mounted, some curious events occurred in the O'Shea camp. Soon after Chamberlain's resignation Willie O'Shea sent Katie a letter written in the third person: 'Mr O'Shea refuses to believe that a compromise is even now impossible. Mr Chamberlain is known to be in favour of Home Rule and a settlement of the land question. Mr O'Shea can with some confidence express a belief that Mr Chamberlain is not wedded to mere words . . . etc.' Mr O'Shea himself was not known as a strong advocate of Home Rule, and the letter can be said to indicate that Willie still hopefully saw himself as an *éminence grise,* or that Chamberlain was continuing to use him as his message carrier. The former interpretation is the more likely because enclosed with the impersonal letter was one to his 'Dearest' (i.e. Katie) asking her to copy out the statement and forward it to Gladstone as quickly as possible. In the event, 'Dearest' did not specifically comply with the request but instead forwarded to Gladstone the statement in O'Shea's hand, together with his note to her which spoke of 'treachery flying about.' Shortly thereafter, there was evidence of treachery in the shape of somebody trying to precipitate a private meeting between Gladstone and Parnell. On 14 March Katie wrote to tell the former that she had received a message from a Mrs Rae, asking if Parnell would meet the Liberal leader that evening at a dinner

---

* On a personal note, my great-grandfather, a small mill-owner in a small Lancashire town, had been a staunch Liberal all his life and had a large photograph of Gladstone hanging on the wall of his front parlour. He could not accept Home Rule, and while he did not precisely follow the Duke of Westminster's example, the photograph was turned face to the wall, in which position it remained for the rest of his life. Any visitor unwary enough to glance at the blank cardboard was treated to a dialectic on Gladstone's betrayal.

party. Parnell had refused because neither he nor she had in their wildest dreams thought of Gladstone's 'compassing a nation at an evening party!' Gladstone replied saying he had no idea who Mrs Rae was, that the incident was 'strange and incomprehensible' and Mr Morley should be relied upon as an accurate and faithful means of communication. Then on 25 March Katie wrote a longish letter to Gladstone in which she said that at a recent meeting with John Morley he had intimated that Mr Gladstone might wish to see Mr Parnell privately, and while Mr Parnell thought he had conveyed all he had to say through the medium of her letters, he would be willing to meet the Prime Minister if he so desired. Personally she thought this would be an excellent idea, as she was sure it would do good and strengthen Mr Parnell, particularly since he was unable to consult much with his own party 'as they are nearly all connected with the press in some way.'

This letter dated 25 March was followed the next day by a telegram from Katie to Gladstone thus: 'I understand that a communication was sent to you yesterday from Albert Mansions in my name. I do not know anything about it and have not been in London for some time. Mrs O'Shea.' An interpretation of these two items (made by Cooke and Vincent in *The Governing Passion*) is that the letter of 25 March was the forgery—presumably done by Willie O'Shea, as his address was Albert Mansions—whose object was to trap the two leaders into an ill-judged *tête à tête*. The private meeting would then be revealed to the press as the Prime Minister introduced the Home Rule Bill, suggesting an underhand nationalist-Liberal deal on the lines of the Kilmainham Treaty, which would further poison the atmosphere. It seems that somebody apart from Katie was trying to set up a private meeting, but nevertheless the letter of 25 March appears genuine. It was written on Katie's North Park, Eltham, headed notepaper; she had long been in favour of a personal meeting between the two leaders (which would have been a very good idea if it could have been kept secret); in her earlier letters there were frequent references to Parnell not being able to confide in anybody (except her) and to people tittle-tattling to the newspapers; and if Willie O'Shea did write the letter, he was not only a brilliant forger but a first-class *pastiche* artist because the style as much as the handwriting is redolent of Katie. However, the telegram about the unauthorised communication from Albert Mansions shows that Willie O'Shea—and his mentor, Joseph Chamberlain?—was up to something, though exactly what would seem to remain unclear.

What is clear from the existing letters is that at this period, immediately after the Galway election, Willie and Katie O'Shea were still on speaking terms (and who told her so promptly that the un-authorised communication had been sent from Albert Mansions is an interesting point). A month later she wrote to Gladstone on her hus-band's behalf, perhaps the most astonishing letter penned during the ten years of her officially unrevealed liaison with Parnell. She started by apologising for yet again troubling the Prime Minister on a private matter but it was one that would brook no delay, then, as was her wont, she plunged into the deep end thus:

> My husband begs me to write and ask if you can and will give him the promise of some colonial appointment later on—the fact is that is is in very great *pecuniary difficulties*. . . . My Aunt, with whom I have been living for many years . . . will, she says, assist my husband out of his present difficulties, for my sake, if she can see any hope of his getting any lucrative occupation, but *if not, she will not help him, so you will understand how important your answer is to us in every way.*

Katie went on to say that she was bothering Mr Gladstone only because he had in the past promised to assist her husband with a suitable appointment (which was true of the Kilmainham days) and again begged him to help, as her husband was on the point of being made bankrupt.

A possibly sinister interpretation of this letter has been made (again by the authors of *The Governing Passion*), not on the lines that it was a forgery, but that it was O'Shea (prodded by Chamberlain?) who was trying to get Gladstone to commit himself to the Colonial Office appointment. Had Gladstone acceded to this request, his enemies could then have announced that he had silenced an opponent of Home Rule or had bowed to Parnell's demands and bought off an injured husband. The authors admit that the letter 'could have been innocent of all but purely financial implications', and from what one has learned of O'Shea's past financial dependence on Aunt Ben's money it would seem to be so. At this point in mid-April 1886, neither O'Shea nor his master Chamberlain had definitely come out against Home Rule—and O'Shea's opposition was hardly crucial—and for the Liberals to be damaged by the news that Gladstone had bought off an injured hus-band, somebody had to acquaint the public with the fact that O'Shea fitted the bill. From the personal angle, early in 1886, faced with the request not merely to pay Captain O'Shea's normal political expenses but to clear the whole of his debts, Aunt Ben probably decided that enough was enough and gave the ultimatum which prompted Katie's letter to Gladstone. How the situation was resolved *vis à vis* Aunt Ben is unclear, but presumably she paid the money without specific assurance that O'Shea had definite prospects, because he did not go bankrupt, he continued to obtain money from her via Katie and he did not make the final move against Parnell for three more years. Gladstone refused to be drawn, falling back on an old argument that he never interfered with his colleagues' departments (such as the Colonial Office). If Katie's letter was prompted by her husband's parlous financial situation, its timing is nonetheless extraordinary. Only shortly after the frenetic and bitter campaigns in Liverpool and Galway to get him back into the House of Commons, there she was writing to Mr Gladstone begging for an appointment which would take her husband away from Westminster—and inasmuch as she told Gladstone that her husband was willing to go *anywhere* the Colonial Office might send him, she was obviously willing to do *anything* to keep him quiet. However, the letter was written after Gladstone had introduced the Home Rule Bill but before O'Shea had decided how to vote, and if Katie could have got him the definite promise of a Colonial Office appointment in the near future it would have solved a lot of problems, including taking her husband out of the country for an indefinite period.

It was on 8 April that Gladstone actually introduced the Home Rule Bill to Parliament, and in her memoirs Katharine said that earlier in the day a messenger arrived at Wonersh Lodge from him, asking her to telegraph the one word 'Yes' if he were to introduce the Bill later that afternoon. Parnell had failed to give the Prime Minister assurances that the nationalists would support the Bill as it stood, since he was still trying to obtain further concessions. According to her, it had been arranged that she should stay at home waiting for Gladstone's message, and Parnell had told her that when it came she was to reply in the affirmative, for as he had said, 'This Bill will do as a beginning; they shall have more presently.' When Katharine's book appeared in 1914, Gladstone's son, Herbert, was even more outraged by the idea of Mrs O'Shea being the person who gave the signal for the introduction of the Home Rule Bill than he had been by her perambulating arm-in-arm with his father. He said he had never read such arrant rubbish in his life. Admittedly Katie's telegram saying 'Yes' is not among Gladstone's papers, but a further telegram sent in answer to another Gladstonian message on 8 May, which she also mentioned in her book, is; and Katharine's account of her part in the first Home Rule Bill is accurate when laid against the private correspondence in the Gladstone Papers (which papers were not available to the public in 1914 or for many years thereafter). On 8 May Gladstone sent Mrs O'Shea a letter by hand which read: 'Morley is most anxious to see Mr Parnell. Is anything known at Eltham of his whereabouts? This is really urgent. Morley has failed to find him here. I enclose a form of Government telegram on which please to write and despatch at once your reply. Yrs most faithfully W.E.G.' Katharine's reply read: 'Mr Parnell will call at Irish office this afternoon at four o'clock. Mrs O'Shea'; and in her memoirs she commented that it was apparently the most natural thing in the world to ask her where Parnell was, and by 1886 it was. It seems not unreasonable to assume that the earlier message was sent to Eltham and that it was Katharine O'Shea who, on behalf of Charles Stewart Parnell and the Irish nationalist party, gave the signal for the introduction of one of the most momentous Bills in British parliamentary history.

Increasingly, as the Home Rule struggle developed in the House of Commons, it became apparent that its fate lay in the hands of Joseph Chamberlain, whatever the reasons which had placed him in that position. The Tories opposed the Bill, Lord Hartington and his Whig/ Liberal faction now firmly opposed it, but Gladstone could still carry it with nationalist support if Chamberlain and those he influenced could be persuaded to vote in favour, or at least to abstain. For several weeks Chamberlain continued to intimate that he might support the Bill if the Irish MPS were retained at Westminster, but by 13 May Sir William Harcourt was writing to Gladstone: 'I am sure you will be deceived if you think Chamberlain is to be conciliated on *any terms*. He has no thought but war to the knife.' Further efforts were made to heal the breach but they came to nothing, and on 31 May Chamberlain called a meeting of his supporters, which with the coincidental irony life supplies as freely as fiction, was held in Committee Room 15 of the House of Commons, the room which was to be the setting of the last act in the Parnell/Home Rule drama. At the meeting Chamberlain read out a letter from John Bright which, as much as anything, swayed the assembled Liberals into outright opposition. John Bright was no longer an active figure in the party but he was as venerable as Gladstone, his influence remained strong and he said that he must on principle vote against the Bill. Bright was afterwards extremely upset that his letter had been read and had proved such a decisive instrument and there were those who accused Chamberlain of editing it to his own advantage, but he hardly needed to do so because the information that John Bright was voting against the Bill, rather than abstaining, was sufficient to convince the waverers.

Barring a miracle, from 31 May Home Rule was therefore a dead duck, but Gladstone continued to believe that he could obtain a small majority on the second reading, and the standard of speeches on all sides remained high, with Parnell and Gladstone producing some of the greatest oratory of their careers. But Parnell's request that it should be told 'for the admiration of all future generations, that England and her Parliament, in this nineteenth century, was wise enough, brave enough, and generous enough to close the strife of centuries and to give peace, prosperity, and happiness to suffering Ireland', and Gladstone's final plea, 'Think, I beseech you, think well, think wisely, think not for the moment, but for the years that are to come, before you reject this Bill', were to no avail. When the count was taken in the division lobbies shortly after 1 a.m. on the morning of 8 June 1886, the ayes numbered 311, the noes 341, of whom 96 were Liberals, many of them Harting-ton's supporters but some Joseph Chamberlain's.* In the heat of the moment Parnell expressed the current opinion when he pointed to Chamberlain and said, 'There goes the man who killed Home Rule.' On 26 June the shortest Parliament in Victorian times was dissolved and the country went to the polls, returning Lord Salisbury and the Tories to power.

For the time being, Home Rule became a dormant volcano. Had this first dramatic Bill ever a chance of becoming law? The answer is probably no, however much one feels that two giants such as Gladstone and Parnell should have been able to solve the Irish problem in a satisfactory manner. In the early stages Gladstone himself said that the odds were 49 to 1 against success, and this was true because the action was too dramatic and telescoped, the ground had not been patiently tilled in the British field (and it was Britain that mattered because she was the legislating power). It should be said that, having decided on the Bill, Gladstone fought for it tenaciously, if not with his full passionate

---

* Most writers, particularly contemporary ones, give the division figures as 343 to 313, but Hansard gives 341 to 311. The majority remains the same in either case.

energy, that he wanted to heal the breach in the Liberal Party (albeit on his terms) and get Home Rule through the Commons, even if he had no plans to deal with the Tory-dominated Lords, which would indubitably throw out the Bill. If this first attempt to obtain Home Rule can be viewed as a practise match played in the main stadium which nobody really expected to win, the concept had been established; henceforward the idea might be brushed aside but it could no longer be denied. What had also been established were the party political lines—the Liberals for the concept, the Tories and the new Liberal/Unionist party against—with the opponents unfortunately firmer in their beliefs than the proponents were in theirs (the nationalists obviously excepted).

William Henry O'Shea did not actually vote against Home Rule but he abstained, which was almost as heinous because he had been returned for nationalist Galway on a nationalist ticket, however unpledged he considered himself to be. In March, as we have seen, he was enclosing a letter to Katie in which he apparently favoured Home Rule, in April he was only too willing to abandon the whole business if his wife could get him a colonial appointment, but by May he was writing to tell Chamberlain that he would be murdered if he voted against the Bill (Katie also mentioned nationalist threats against her husband's life). From the moment he took his seat as the member for Galway, the nationalist bitterness and obloquy which surrounded him were something which probably even his thick skin could not ignore, and it was not only in Irish circles that obloquy was being heaped on O'Shea's head. Certain Liberals were doing their share, for it was in the middle of the final Home Rule battle that the *Pall Mall Gazette* saw fit to print a piece entitled *Mr Parnell's Suburban Retreat*. The *Pall Mall Gazette* was then under the editorship of W. T. Stead and was one of the most popular and influential Liberal papers of the day, pro-Gladstone and pro–Home Rule, and it used the excuse of Parnell's carriage having been in collision with a market gardener's cart at Eltham to say: 'During the sitting of Parliament the honourable member for Cork takes up residence at Eltham, a suburban village to the south-east of London. From here he can often be seen taking riding exercises round by Chislehurst and Sidcup.' It was not information which conveyed anything to the general public—so Parnell stayed at Eltham and went riding in Sidcup, so what?—but it conveyed something to those in the know and assuredly to Captain O'Shea.

Thus by May 1886 O'Shea was aware that his position in Irish na-

'*The Three Graces*': *from l. to r., Katie, Anna (Steele), and Emma (Barrett Lennard), sketched by their mother*

Captain and Mrs O'Shea at the time of their marriage in 1867

Mrs Anna Maria Wood—Aunt Ben

Parnell's favourite picture of Katie: he carried it in a locket wherever he went

Parnell in the sitting room at Wonersh Lodge (photograph taken by Katie)

Aunt Ben's house, The Lodge, Eltham

Avondale, County Wicklow, Parnell's ancestral home

The Phoenix Park murders: taking the dead to Steevens's Hospital

Leading members of the Home Rule party, 1887

JOSEPH G. BIGGAR.

ISAAC BUTT.

JAMES O'KELLY.

T. M. HEALY.

CHARLES STEWART PARNELL.

JUSTIN McCARTHY.

THOMAS SEXTON.

MICHAEL DAVITT.

T. P. O'CONNOR.

E. D. GRAY.

WILLIAM O'BRIEN.

TIMOTHY D. SULLIVAN.

TIMOTHY HARRINGTON.

JOHN DILLON.

Parnell reelected as the chairman of the Irish Parliamentary Party, 1890

Parnell in the witness box during the Special Commission, 1888

(Mansell Collection)

(Mansell Collection)

July 16<u>Th</u> 1886

Private   North Park,
                 Eltham, Kent.

Queens Hotel
Eastbourne

Dear Mr Gladstone,
      will you
kindly read the
Enclosed and
do as you
Consider best
with it —
      Yours Sincerely
            Katie O'Shea

308

(by courtesy of Mrs Christine Fitzgerald and The British Library)

William Ewart Gladstone in the 1880s

Facsimile of a letter from Katie to Prime Minister Gladstone, March 16, 1886

Parnell's funeral procession passing the Old Parliament House, College Green, Dublin

The houses where Katie lived: (ABOVE) *Rivenhall Place, Essex, where she grew up;* (BELOW) *Benington Park, Hertfordshire, the first (indeed only) married home of the O'Sheas (photograph taken by the author);* (OPPOSITE TOP) *Wonersh Lodge, North Park, Eltham, Kent, her home with Parnell;* (OPPOSITE BOTTOM) *and 39 East Ham Road, Littlehampton, Sussex, the terraced house where Katie died*

(OVERLEAF) *Katie's grave in Littlehampton Municipal Cemetery*

(by courtesy of Mr J. A. McMullin)

TO THE BELOVED MEMORY
OF
KATHARINE

WIDOW OF
CHARLES STEWART PARNELL
BORN 30TH JAN 1840
DIED 5TH FEB 1921
FIDE ET AMORE

A R□
ET
IN MEMORIAM
DILECTAE CARAE MATRIS FILIAE
NORAH CLARE O'SHEA
QUAE RITISS PANER CARRIS ET RECTAE MONITA
DE XXVIII DIE . . . CVI . . .
. . . .

tionalist circles was hopeless, through the *Pall Mall Gazette* that influential Liberal circles were aware of Mr Parnell's residence in Eltham (if officially O'Shea himself was not) and therefore his role as negotiator was probably at an end. By this time his friend and patron Chamberlain had decided to vote against Home Rule and thereby break with the Liberal Party, and if O'Shea had not the courage to do this he had sufficient to abstain, and then the sense to apply for the Chiltern Hundreds to enable him to resign his parliamentary seat. He wrote to Chamberlain saying: 'I look forward with equanimity to the approaching conclusion of my political career', but he was soon writing to his friend asking for a political appointment and later he suggested himself again for Parliament. As O'Shea crept temporarily into the shadows he further wrote to Chamberlain: 'Your right honourable friend your enemy is delivered into your hands'—though in precisely what manner O'Shea thought Parnell's head had been served up is not clear.

Away from the heat of the political battle, O'Shea continued to fight his rearguard action on the basis that he had no knowledge of his wife's adultery with Mr Parnell, while Katie similarly fought to preserve the *status quo* with vigour, not to say mendacity. As soon as the piece appeared in the *Pall Mall Gazette,* O'Shea wrote to her asking what the paragraph meant, and actually went in to see W. T. Stead to deny that there was any truth in the rumour of adultery, an action which would seem to be taking the role of innocent husband to the limit. Stead himself, according to T. P. O'Connor, had been considering for a long time whether he should 'ruin the Irish party by exposing the liaison between Parnell and Mrs O'Shea', though like everybody else who threatened such exposure he never put it into practise but contented himself with the occasional oblique paragraph in the pages of the *Pall Mall Gazette.* As for O'Shea, one can only say that it was extremely useful to him in the divorce court that his marriage had been conducted by correspondence for so many years and that he never bothered to go down to Eltham to discover whether Mr Parnell actually was living there.

By the beginning of July O'Shea had departed for Carlsbad to take the waters for his gout (a visit which underlines the fact that he had obtained money from somebody), and while he was there an American lady started to read a piece about him in one of the American papers, and then ground to a halt because the article was more emphatic than the *Pall Mall Gazette* on the subject of Mr Parnell's suburban retreat where he visited his Aspasia in the absence of her husband. Willie wrote to tell Katie about the incident in chatty fashion, saying he knew what it was about (really?) but had pretended to the American lady that he did not, intimating that it had been prompted 'by the worst features of American politics' being introduced into England 'by filthy swine like Parnell and his crew.' It was only when items were printed in the English papers that O'Shea was worried—in the autumn he again reacted strongly to a paragraph which appeared in the *Sussex Daily News* announcing that Mr Parnell was currently staying in Eastbourne with Mrs O'Shea.

It was in fact in May 1886 that Katharine first took the children down to Eastbourne. Initially they stayed at the Queen's Hotel, but she then rented a house in St John's Road and Parnell started visiting them. While the Home Rule battle was in progress he travelled from London as often as possible, but once the Bill had been defeated he took up residence in Eastbourne. Katharine had somehow organised Aunt Ben— she spoke of flying visits to Eltham to satisfy her aunt—and she had reason to place the demands of the aged Mrs Wood below those of her lover, because the fight for Home Rule had exhausted Parnell, and the first ominous signs of his constitution cracking under strain were evident. It was probably because of Katie's worries about her lover's health, because she thought the exhilarating, invigorating ozone would improve it (the Victorians were becoming great believers in the beneficial powers of ozone), that in August she rented another residence in Eastbourne, Moira House in Staveley Road, on a year's tenancy. Neither she nor Parnell lived there for the full next twelve months, they vacated Moira House as winter set in, but it was their presence in Eastbourne for prolonged periods in the summer and autumn of 1886 which prompted the paragraph in the *Sussex Daily News* which in its turn alarmed Willie O'Shea and caused Katie to write one of her more damaging letters. Because, in answer to her husband's demands to know what Mr Parnell was doing in Eastbourne, she lied flatly and said she had no knowledge of his whereabouts. Katie rarely lied in such outright fashion—on both sides the voluminous O'Shea correspondence was opaque and tangential—and one can only assume that, knowing her husband was in a more aggressive, resentful mood, she hoped a direct if untruthful statement would silence him. (Again, it never occurred to Captain O'Shea to visit his wife in Eastbourne and ascertain whether Mr Parnell was there.)

From Eastbourne Katie continued to write to Mr Gladstone, but as she herself said, the important period of her negotiations with the Liberal leader was at an end, because the party lines of battle had been drawn and when Gladstone and Parnell reconverged on the Home Rule issue, there was no need of a secret link. Katie's Eastbourne letters to Gladstone were of a more personal nature, although she sent enclosures from Parnell occasionally, and she told the Liberal leader that he had stemmed 'the terrible and unreasoning torrent of popular prejudice' against Ireland, that she was convinced that the prosperity of the two countries now depended on him, and in one letter she said chattily that she was in Eastbourne for 'a few days with my babies.' The few days extended to several months and, despite the worries about Parnell's health, they were among the pleasantest of Katie's years with him. Parnell loved swimming and sailing and he was able to indulge both pastimes from Eastbourne's shingle beach. Katie did not join him in either enterprise because she easily became sea-sick and she said her heart was not sufficiently strong to permit her to swim (three children in quick succession in her late thirties may have affected her heart slightly). But Parnell's horses were brought down to Eastbourne and they spent many happy hours riding through the flat countryside to the east of the town or driving further afield in the phaeton to the more spectacular scenery of Beachy Head and Birling Gap, where the chalk cliffs drop sheer to the sea. As in the Eltham area, Parnell was sometimes recognised and on one notable occasion, when he and Katie had driven to Pevensey, he was surrounded by a crowd pouring out of the railway station and the chant was taken up, 'Parnell, Parnell', as Katie said with the horrible incorrect English (and often Irish) emphasis on the 'nell'.

Apart from swimming and sailing, Parnell loved the sea itself and was enthralled by rough weather. When a storm looked as if it were brewing he would often drive Katie to Birling Gap, which was their favourite spot, and they would stand together watching the high-crested waves racing towards the shore and hurling against the cliffs, listening to the roar of the sea and the shrieks of the gale, holding tight to each other as the wind nearly lifted them from their feet. One warm evening Parnell persuaded Katie that, if she could not swim, going into the sea with her clothes on would do her no harm, and they waded out until the waves reached her shoulders. Katie must have been frozen because the sea off Eastbourne remains icy even in the hottest English summer, but she was apparently warmed by the passion of her wonderful lover's kisses and utterances as he carried her back to the shore. While this anecdote may illuminate the strength of their passionate love and their unconventional natures, it renders more ridiculous the deceptions and regard for the conventions they were practising in other areas, but if Aunt Ben's money and Parnell's political position could occasionally be forgotten, they kept looming in Katie's mind and prompting less untrammelled behaviour.

Within restricted circles the gossip about Mrs O'Shea's liaison with Mr Parnell continued unabated; England and Ireland at large had no knowledge of the affair, but with visits to Hastings and other south coast resorts, houses in Eastbourne and further sojourns at the old base in Eltham, the circles were widening. Throughout the second half of 1886 O'Shea was seriously worried about the rumours and was trying hard to establish a new relationship. First he suggested that he move back into Wonersh Lodge, an idea which was firmly vetoed by Katie. Then she suggested that she should live in Brighton or some place (such as nearby Eastbourne) and pay visits to Eltham, an idea which was vetoed by him 'as it would allow the scandal to continue unabated.' There were many references in his letters to the scandal and its injurious effects on Norah, Carmen and Gerard (significantly the two youngest girls, Clare and Katie, the ones who were 'unquestionably' Parnell's, were never mentioned) and what the scandal was if, as O'Shea insisted, there was no truth in the adultery, he did not explain. Increasingly there were the requests that Katie put the matter on a legal footing by consulting a solicitor and agreeing not to communicate directly or indirectly with Mr Parnell, and by the end of 1886 Katie herself admitted that her relations with her husband were 'violently strained.' In her memoirs she printed one letter which categorically (for the O'Sheas, that was) revealed the extent of the strain, thus: 'Dear Willie, I am perfectly disgusted with your letter. It is really too sickening after all I have done. The only person who has ever tarnished your honour has been yourself. I will call and hear what you wish to tell me, although I cannot see that any good can come of our meeting whilst you use such disgusting and ungrateful expressions about me. K. O'Shea.' All she had done for her husband referred mainly to the financial angle, and there was the strong financial undertow to the whole 1886 correspondence, with frequent references on Katie's side to Aunt Ben's money and her husband's debts.

In December 1886 the *Pall Mall Gazette* printed a further brief item, which said: 'Mr Parnell is at present paying a visit to Captain

O'Shea at Eltham'; this time O'Shea did not visit W. T. Stead personally but instead sent a letter denying that he had seen Mr Parnell since the previous May (which was correct) or that there was any truth in the statement (which was not). In February 1887 another newspaper joined the sniping, namely the *Saint Stephen's Gazette.* It used as its plank Parnell's complaints to the owners of a cab company about the behaviour of one of their drivers, mentioning the Irish leader's peculiar habit of changing cabs when he visited Captain O'Shea's house in Eltham. Again these were items which meant nothing to the public at large—so it was Captain O'Shea's house Mr. Parnell visited, so had not O'Shea been an Irish nationalist, if recently retired?—but they meant something to the gallant Captain. It was in this same month of February that Sir Charles Dilke (by now an ex-Liberal MP, having himself been involved in a divorce case which had wrecked his career) noted in his diary that he had been told by the Irish party's solicitor 'that O'Shea was going forward with his divorce action against Parnell, and that Parnell had no possible defence.'

By this time O'Shea was certainly aware of the adultery, if officially he continued to keep silent, because he later admitted to Chamberlain that it was at this period that he learned Mr Parnell was living with his wife at Eltham and had been doing so for some considerable time. From the admitted moment of truth (if only later and privately) a new note of determination crept into the correspondence between him and his wife. He continued to insist that she hold no further communication, direct or indirect, with Charles Stewart Parnell, and in the fresh negotiations Katie's brother Evelyn was involved. He had recently returned from Egypt, where he had further enhanced his military reputation during the relief of Khartoum, and from the end of 1886 onwards Major-General Sir Evelyn Wood was based in England, employing his administrative talents in the efforts to modernise the British army. Thus he was now directly involved in the Wood/O'Shea/Parnell manoeuvres. What attitude he then took towards his sister is unknown; in his memoirs he makes no mention of having a sister who became Katharine O'Shea, later Parnell, nor does his biographer touch on the noxious subject, but Katie went to him for advice on the urging of her husband, and one assumes that he told her she must take steps to arrest the spread of the scandal which was enveloping her name and that of Mr Parnell. Perhaps partly cajoled by her brother but more definitely threatened by her husband, in April 1887 Katie finally consulted Mr

Horatio Pym, who was Aunt Ben's solicitor. O'Shea's ability to threaten his wife had been strengthened by his son's entry into the fray, for it was in April 1887 that Gerard wrote to his father saying he had returned to Eltham to find 'that awful scoundrel Parnell there' and he thought he should let his father know so that he could give the bounder a good thrashing.

Gerard O'Shea's subsequent actions and career (or lack of) indicate that he was a chip off the paternal block, but in April 1887 he was seventeen and, being charitable, one assumes that he had only just become aware that there was something odd in his mother's relationship with Mr Parnell, because 'that awful scoundrel' had been much in evidence for the last seven years of Gerard's life, at Wonersh Lodge and on holidays in Brighton and Eastbourne and Hastings. Gerard's adoption of a pro-Willie, anti-Parnell stance placed his mother in an extremely difficult and painful situation because she loved him and had no desire to hurt him and there was another problem, inevitably financial. Gerard had been staying with his father at Albert Mansions, and Aunt Ben (who had obviously taken strongly against Captain O'Shea by this time) was extremely annoyed and said she would not pay further money for his education unless he returned to Wonersh Lodge forthwith. Katie therefore had to tread warily against the new combination of her son and her husband in her efforts to get Gerard back to Eltham to ensure the supply of Aunt Ben's money, while convincing him that she was not injuring his father by continuing to see Mr Parnell. Consequently she agreed to consult Mr Pym, but after her consultations and some acrimonious scenes with her husband—the O'Sheas did actually meet face to face at this period—in which he used the lever of Gerard's disaffection, Katharine still refused to give the assurance her husband wanted, namely 'that reports being wide and strong as to her relationship with Mr Parnell it would, for her children's sake, be expedient that she should declare renunciation of communications with him.'

If Katie then refused to commit herself to breaking off relations with Parnell, she allowed herself to be pressured into stating in writing that there was no truth in the allegations of adultery (not that anybody, least of all her husband, ever mentioned the word 'adultery', it was always the unspecified 'scandal'). This was a damaging admission for her husband to have gained after seven years of adultery and it was a trump card up his sleeve, but one of the probable reasons he failed to go ahead with his divorce proceedings early in 1887 was that Aunt Ben altered her will at this time, leaving a larger share to Katie and without the Woods taking action. Thus a financially straitened Willie had an extra inducement to keep quiet, for the old lady was ninety-five years old and surely could not live much longer. A further probable reason for holding his hand was that in March 1887 *The Times* launched its onslaught against Parnell, and as O'Shea had been involved in the murky manoeuvres which led to the paper's attack, he could hope that sufficiently damaging evidence would be produced to blast his enemy's reputation for good, without he himself having to take direct action. He might also have hoped that in the disintegration of Parnell's career Katie would desert him, or at least that the gossip about a wrecked leader would cease and he and his wife could resume their previous ambiguous relationship.

Chapter Thirteen

In the early months of 1887 it must have seemed to Katharine that the walls of the structure she had so skilfully built since 1880 were caving in, but, a tenacious fighter and a profound believer in her ability to have her cake and eat it, she kept her hands firmly to the tottering structure. Apart from her husband's new manoeuvres she had a further worry, the state of Parnell's health, which had shown signs of failing since the moment of the defeat of the Home Rule Bill. Initially his lassitude and tiredness may have seemed a natural reaction from the peak of concentration and hope to the valley of disappointment and inaction, but Parnell's lethargy grew worse. He had not the energy to put pen to paper or to read the newspapers, and Katie became so worried that she insisted he see a doctor. She took him to London in a closed carriage to Sir Henry Thompson, and Parnell was in such a nervous state that he refused to enter the consulting room unless Katie went in first and smoothed the way for him. She introduced him to Sir Henry as 'Mr Charles Stewart', and if Sir Henry recognised the famous face he pretended not to, but this alias was mainly political, as neither Katie nor Parnell wanted the news bruited that the Irish leader was suffering from serious ill-health (many people commented on how ill Parnell was looking in the latter months of 1886 and throughout much of 1887). Sir Henry's diagnosis was that 'Mr Stewart's' circulation was very bad and that this was the root cause of his digestive and other complaints. Henceforward Katie insisted that Parnell keep his feet warm. When he was at home she made him change his shoes and socks several times a day, and when he was away she provided a little black bag in which she placed spare shoes and socks.

It was also in the early months of 1887 that Katie persuaded Parnell to rent two houses. The first one was at 112 Tresillian Road, Brockley, on which a year's lease was taken in the January, and although Katie herself had little to say about this house it was almost certainly rented in an effort to soften the scandal and thereby placate her husband, for Brockley is in south London, not far from Eltham, and she and Parnell presumably decided that they could see each other without attracting the obvious attention of his presence at Wonersh Lodge. The manoeuvre did not work out the way they had hoped, far too many people were interested in the comings and goings of 'Mr Preston' (the alias under which the property was leased) and why the Irish leader should want a comparatively poky residence in an unfashionable suburb; the Brockley residence was consequently soon abandoned. Then in March another house was rented in York Terrace, Regents Park, and Katie said this lease was taken because of her continuing worries about her lover's health. She had finally decided that the long drives to Eltham, particularly after a night sitting of the House of Commons, were unnecessarily tiring and that it would be more sensible for Parnell to have a central London residence. He was not, in fact, appearing often in the House at this time, and pressure from O'Shea was mounting, but one accepts a basic concern for his health as the motivating factor. In any case he lived at York Terrace for about a month and then returned to Eltham. Katie said he could not bear being parted from her and the night of his return provided a further instance of the telepathy between them. On this particular night she found herself unable to sleep and started to stoke up the fire as she had on so many earlier occasions when awaiting his late return from the House of Commons. She dozed off in front of the blazing fire, then at three o'clock in the morning she heard the sound of a cab horse's hooves, and the jingle of the bells as the cab stopped at the top of North Park. She knew it was Parnell and opened the side door as she had so many times in the past, he came into the room, took her in his arms and whispered, 'Oh, my love, you must not leave me alone again.'

It is a touching story, but unfortunately the name under which

Parnell rented the house in York Terrace was the most disastrous alias he used: it was Mr Fox, and the allusions which could be made to the sly, rascally fox-figure were obviously endless. To make matters worse, when renting the York Terrace house, in the personal interview with the estate agents Parnell forgot whether he was Fox or Preston and had to invent a ridiculous story to cover his mistake. Early in 1887 Katie and he were paying the rent on three houses, the one in Eastbourne which had been taken on a year's tenancy from August 1886, the one in Brockley which had been taken on another year's tenancy, from January 1887, and the one in Regents Park, which had been taken on a two-year tenancy from March 1887. That was in addition to the upkeep of Wonersh Lodge, which was where they were living most of the time. Apart from the unnecessary expenditure, the leasing of the houses was a self-defeating action, that is if part of the motive was to dampen the scandal surrounding their liaison. For there were now four areas in which people could be curious about the relationship between Mr Parnell and Mrs O'Shea, and apart from personally paying the rent on the three leased houses, Katie appeared at all of them; while the use of the aliases was even more self-defeating, as after the Home Rule Bill Parnell's face was better known than ever, and every witness who appeared in the divorce court said, oh yes, they had known who Mr Smith/Stewart/Fox/Preston really was.

On the subject of Katharine's extravagant expenditure, Gerard O'Shea was later reported as saying that his mother was the most generous and hospitable of women, and it was true that her extravagance was not sheer self-indulgence. She was wildly, sometimes stupidly, generous to other people (in later years to her own disadvantage). For example, Gerard said that his mother gave £100 to a startled clergyman who came to the door of Wonersh Lodge begging for a small contribution to some charity, and with slightly more acerbity reported, 'No shop in Eltham was considered good enough for Mr Parnell's meals, and all the food used to be obtained from Bellamy's in Jermyn Street.' (If Katie was on the whole a good organiser, she did not pay her bills promptly and on one occasion, again according to Gerard, Bellamy's decided they had waited long enough for payment and sent the bill to Captain O'Shea at Albert Mansions. He obviously sent it straight on to his wife, but it was perhaps as well that he did not realise that the size of the bill was mainly due to the special food procured for Parnell.)

In June 1887 it was Gerard who was responsible for Katie's

most dishonest capitulation. Parnell's and her involvement in property having far from stilled the rumours about their relationship, O'Shea used his trump cards and blackmailed his wife into writing the two letters which were the most damaging of those produced in the divorce court. In these letters, addressed to her 'dearest Gerardie', Katie said that she was willing to meet her son's wishes with regard to Mr Parnell, that nobody who was in any way obnoxious to him should come to Wonersh Lodge and that she readily agreed 'there shall be no further communication, direct or indirect, with him' (i.e. Parnell). The next day she confirmed her decision and said she was giving up the lease of the stables (where Parnell's horses were kept), but added that she was not afraid of proceedings or any solicitor's clerks descending on Wonersh Lodge and would send the latter packing if they appeared. This was a reference to her husband's activities, and there is no doubt that Willie blackmailed Katie with threats of a divorce and, as woundingly, of Gerard's disappearance from her life if she did not consent to his terms. He admitted as much when he sent Joseph Chamberlain a copy of his wife's guarantee and said it had been obtained by his son, who had 'informed Mrs O'Shea that otherwise legal proceedings would be taken against her and that he would never see her again.' Katie's promise to have no further communication with Mr Parnell meant nothing, as her husband (if not her son) surely realised, but she had committed herself on paper to a flat lie and with two such damaging letters in his possession Willie O'Shea retired temporarily from the marital fray. He took no action whatsoever to ascertain whether his wife was implementing her promise—and in the divorce court the eighteen months between his acceptance that his wife had ceased to communicate with Mr Parnell and his initiation of the divorce proceedings were skated over at top speed.

If the domestic situation grew desperate in the early months of 1887 but seemed to have calmed down by the middle of the year, the political front contained increasingly explosive elements. It was the indirect scene which seemed to threaten Parnell rather than any direct action he took in 1887, for he was conspicuous by his lack of activity throughout the year, mainly because of his ill-health, and the new agrarian war being waged in Ireland was fought without his help or approval. The shortcomings of Gladstone's 1881 Land Act had finally revealed themselves, and it was left to three of Parnell's lieutenants— John Dillon, William O'Brien and Timothy Harrington—to evolve what became known as the Plan of Campaign, but they met tougher opposition in Lord Salisbury and his nephew and Irish Chief Secretary, Arthur Balfour, than they had in Mr Gladstone and Mr Forster. Ultimately, Salisbury's and Balfour's aim was to be constructive, to introduce land and other reforms, but initially the iron hand, not the velvet glove was revealed, on the premise that wild animals have first to be tamed.

It was as Balfour introduced a particularly fierce Irish Coercion Bill in March 1887 that *The Times* launched its onslaught against Parnell, with a series of inflammatory articles entitled 'Parnellism and Crime'. The object of the articles was tripartite: by revealing the extent of the Irish leader's links with terrorists and avowed murderers, of his dependence on American Fenian money backed by bullet and knife, *The Times* not only hoped to destroy his claims to constitutional leadership, it aimed to buttress the current Tory policy by torpedoing Gladstone's past policy—for what responsible English leader would have dreamed of allying himself with a man and a cause indebted to such dastardly, revolutionary blackguards? After the main body of the articles detailing Parnell's association with Irish and Irish-American terrorists came the *pièce de résistance,* which purported to be a secret letter written by Parnell immediately following the Phoenix Park murders, in which he said that he had to condemn the murders publicly, thereby implying that privately he approved of them. The letter itself was not in Parnell's handwriting, but *The Times* printed a facsimile and assured its readers that the signature was without doubt the Irish leader's.

Many letters poured into *The Times* offices congratulating the newspaper on its masterly exposé, on revealing the shameful truth behind the front of Parnellism, but neither the articles nor the letters elicited any response from Parnell or from the Liberals. Katie's account of her lover's reaction to the first article embodied his attitude. She knew what was in *The Times* that morning because somebody had cut out the first 'Parnellism and Crime' article and had pasted it to the gates of Wonersh Lodge (an action which proves the awareness of Parnell's residence in the Eltham area). At breakfast Katie watched while her lover buttered his toast and impassively read the onslaught on his methods and his creed, and when he had finished reading and eating, he calmly lit a cigar and said, 'Now for that assaying I didn't finish. Wouldn't you hide your head with shame if your King was so stupid as that, my Queen?' and proceeded to spend the next two hours working with his crucibles and fine-balancing machine, refusing to discuss anything *The Times* had to say about him. Indeed, Parnell thought the articles were beneath contempt; he spoke briefly in the House of Commons about the actual letter, saying the signature bore no resemblance to his, that both subject matter and phraseology were absurd and he would gladly have stood between the daggers of the Invincibles and the body of Lord Frederick Cavendish, for he had suffered more than any man from the terrible deed in Phoenix Park and the Irish had suffered more than any other nation. *The Times* continued to publish further articles and letters, saying Mr Parnell must reply in less off-hand fashion to the grave allegations levelled against him, as should the Liberal Party, which was guilty by association. Neither the Irish leader nor the Liberals bothered to refute the charges and the matter might have died a natural death, with some damage to both reputations, Parnell's in particular (at least in Britain), had not Willie O'Shea's old friend Frank Hugh O'Donnell suddenly intervened.

Before dealing with O'Donnell's intervention, which led to the setting up of the Parnell Special Commission, another strand of the tangled web surrounding Katie must be examined, because this one involves the Woods and Aunt Ben's money and seems of paramount importance. By the end of 1887 the Woods were deeply worried at the extent of their sister's influence on Aunt Ben—the old lady's will had already been altered twice, each time leaving a larger share to Katie. They were similarly worried about her liaison with Parnell, which she had patently not abandoned, whatever she might have promised Gerard. For the Woods, their youngest sister had become an untrustworthy, possibly sinister figure, changed by her relationship with Charles Stewart Parnell from the friendly Katie they had known, perhaps dominated by him and wanting Mrs Wood's fortune for his or Ireland's use, and one can sympathise with their fears to a degree, if not with the actions they took to overcome them. First, exhibiting a dismal lack of understanding of Aunt Ben's independent, autocratic nature, Evelyn and Charlie Wood and Anna Steele embarked on a campaign to persuade the old lady to change her will, at least back to its original form in which the surviving Wood children had equal shares. This they did by subtle attempts to blacken Katie's character, and while they were sufficiently clever to realise that outright attacks on their sister would achieve nothing, they were not clever enough to appreciate that any attempts to dictate to Mrs Wood could be disastrous. The result of their efforts was that an infuriated Aunt Ben indeed altered her will, by cutting the

Woods out of it altogther and leaving her entire fortune, which con-
sisted of nearly £150,000 personal estate and a considerable amount of
real estate, to her niece Katharine O'Shea (apart from a few minor
bequests).

The last will and testament of Anna Maria Wood, The Lodge,
Eltham, Kent, a person of sound mind, was witnessed on 8 March 1888,
and now the Woods had to take action. Evelyn and Charlie Wood,
Anna Steele and Maria (Polly) Chambers all considered themselves on
principle entitled to their fair share of their aunt's money. Evelyn and
Charlie needed their shares fairly desperately, Anna was not by this time
in the best of financial situations as she had not published a novel for
years, and while little is known about Polly's reactions she had never
been rich and she closed ranks with her siblings. (Emma Barrett
Lennard did not directly involve herself in the sordid affair, though she
and her husband gave moral support.) What action could the Woods
take to break the will? They could wait until Aunt Ben was dead and
contest it on the grounds that the old lady had been unduly influenced by
Katharine in drawing up the will, but there was a more immediate move
they could make. They could try to prove *now* that Aunt Ben was of
unsound mind, and if they could have her declared legally insane, then
the prospects of having the will invalidated, while not automatic, were
good.*

It was the immediate drastic move of trying to have Aunt Ben
certified insane that the Woods chose to make. In 1888 the procedure
under the existing Lunacy Acts was that any relative could present a
Petition to the Masters in Lunacy praying that they enquire into the
alleged lunacy of the said . . . This Petition was accompanied by
affidavits from the relatives and other witnesses convinced of the alleged
lunacy and also by medical evidence, and in the normal course of events
(most Petitions being served on people already in lunatic asylums as a
matter of legal clarification), the Masters in Lunacy then examined the
alleged lunatic, and if they were convinced of the insanity, an Inquisi-
tion document was issued stating such-and-such 'to be a person of
unsound mind so that he/she is not sufficient for the government of

---

* There had been a case in 1856 when relatives tried to invalidate the will of a person
declared insane, but they lost on the decision that the testator had been of lucid mind
when making it. Generally it was accepted that if a testator afterwards declared insane
had excluded from the will close relatives who were the natural objects of the testator's
bounty, then it would be invalidated.

himself/herself, his/her manors, messuages, lands, tenements, goods and chattels.' The person was then removed to a lunatic asylum (if not already there) where he/she stayed for the rest of his/her natural life, with the Lord Chancellor or the Masters in Lunacy administering the insane person's estate until death. However, the alleged lunatic had some protection, and once the initial Petition had been presented to the Masters in Lunacy, notification was served upon him or her so that he or she could contest the Petition in court, and if this initial Petition was upheld by the Masters in Lunacy, the alleged lunatic could then elect to be tried by jury.

The Woods—particularly Anna Steele—were not an unimaginative family and they may have discussed the effects on Aunt Ben of subjecting her to this procedure, but if they did, their combined fury, despair and outrage at the threatened loss of the fortune overrode their humanity and conscience. To prove the case for initial presentation, medical testimony was required, and how they introduced to the Lodge the doctor who testified to their aunt's disturbed condition is uncertain, but they acquired the necessary medical affidavit for their Petition, which Sir Evelyn Wood and Charles Page Wood Esq. duly presented to the Masters in Lunacy, praying for an Inquiry into the alleged lunacy of Anna Maria Wood.

When the notification of the Petition was served on Aunt Ben, Katie was appalled and horrified and her reaction was caused as much by fears for her aunt as by thoughts of the money. For if the Petition for an Inquiry were not fought, Aunt Ben could spend her remaining time on earth as a prisoner, and while the Woods (presumably) had in mind some private home rather than a grim Victorian lunatic asylum, to tear the old lady from the gracious house and place her in some alien institution was not a pleasant idea, and even if they envisaged leaving her at the Lodge, she would have been placed under strict supervision. Katie had little knowledge of the procedure of the Lunacy Acts, but after the initial shock and horror she swung into action with her usual determination, obtaining legal advice and filing objections to the Petition on Aunt Ben's behalf, which meant the case would have to go to court. As the petitioners were Major-General Sir Evelyn Wood, vc, and Charles Page Wood, Katie needed the strongest possible evidence on her side, so in her efforts to save Aunt Ben she appealed to Mr Gladstone for help, and he responded by arranging for her to see his personal physician, Sir Andrew Clark. At the first appointment Sir Andrew kept

Mrs O'Shea waiting for two hours and then said he was sorry but he could not see her, which cannot have pleased Katie, but she went up to London again and on 6 April 1888 she saw him and explained the situation, and Sir Andrew agreed to visit the Lodge the next day. At Eltham he spent two hours and then told Katie (in her words), 'It was a cruel thing for anyone to say my Aunt was insane. He thought her a most charming, cultivated woman, and although he had always managed to keep out of court all his life he would go through with it if necessary.' He also promised to send his report to Katie the minute he returned to London, and she hoped that with Sir Andrew's opinion in her possession the Woods would withdraw their Petition.

By 13 April Katie had still not received the report and she sent another frantic letter to Gladstone, accompanied by a note from Parnell in which he said he had never before addressed the Liberal leader on a personal matter but he did so 'on account of the magnitude of the interests involved, as I believe that in addition to those of pecuniary character, it has now become a matter of life and death. I am informed that your representation and your representation only can put the matter right, and that immediate action is of pressing importance.' It was indeed the sole occasion on which Parnell begged a favour, personal or political, from Mr Gladstone or any English leader, and his beloved Queenie was the only person who could have induced such a proud man to have done so. Katie's own letter stressed the life-and-death nature of the situation: 'My poor Aunt is suffering so cruelly from the suspense that I fear she cannot live much longer if it is continued . . . she has not slept more than ten minutes at a time since he [Sir Andrew Clark] came as she has been expecting me to show her his reports whenever the posts came . . . My Aunt's life cannot last very long in any case and it seems terrible that she should be made to suffer so cruelly in her last days.' Katharine had already organised George Meredith and other people who were willing to testify to Mrs Wood's sanity, but the medical evidence was essential, and she begged Gladstone 'to write or in some way urge Sir Andrew to give his report to you at once.' Thus urged by the Liberal leader, on 20 April Sir Andrew produced his report on 'Anna Maria Wood, a supposed person of unsound mind' in which he said he had visited Mrs Wood on Saturday, 7 April 1888, and spent about one and a half hours in her presence and that in the course of conversation he had found her to be 'attentive, capable of apprehension and reflection, to reply coherent and logical, free from illusions, delusions and hallucinations, full of old stories, able to quote largely from the French poets and sometimes seasoning her reminiscences with flashes of quaint humour.' The only defects he had noticed were 'very imperfect sight, an occasional forgetfulness of something previously said . . . and a slight tendency to repetition.'

Unfortunately, Sir Andrew's report did not produce the desired effect of persuading the Woods to withdraw their Petition, as they had their medical evidence and by now it was war to the knife. On 1 May Katie again wrote to Mr Gladstone, telling him that the petition 'brought by my brothers against my Aunt, will come on for hearing on Monday next, the 7th of May', and that Sir Charles Russell had been retained for her aunt. However, as the Attorney General had been briefed by her brothers, she was most anxious that Sir Charles should give the case his detailed attention and was therefore writing to ask if Mr Gladstone would either mention the matter personally to Sir Charles or give her a letter of introduction. She apologised for troubling him yet again but he had been so kind, and 'all the happiness my Aunt has in life depends on the favourable issue of this case.' To prove that she was not asking the Liberal leader to interest himself in a beaten cause she enclosed a copy of Sir Andrew Clark's report on her aunt's condition. Obviously Katie considered Gladstone the big gun in her fight, because Parnell could have given her an introduction to Sir Charles Russell, the famous Anglo-Irish barrister known for his nationalist sympathies. Once again Mr Gladstone obliged. In the event, Katie's guns fired loudest or right triumphed, and the Petition for an Inquiry into the alleged lunacy of Mrs Anna Maria Wood was dismissed.

The Wood position in the summer of 1888 was disastrous. While the old lady lived there was nothing further they could do and they had to swallow the knowledge that their sister stood to inherit the massive fortune, she who had been behaving so disgracefully in her private life for so many years. Once Aunt Ben died, the Woods could contest the will, but their position was not strong. The will was in Katie's favour and in addition she had the factors that she had devoted over fourteen years of her life to the old lady and that her brothers had been unsuccessful in their attempts to have Mrs Wood declared insane. When the Woods came to contest the will they would therefore need strong evidence that Katharine had been an undesirable influence on the old lady, and there was one area in which their sister was highly vulnerable, namely her adulterous, long-standing liaison with Charles Stewart

[195]

Parnell. If it could be proved that she was a person who had broken her sacred marriage vow, then it would be less difficult to convince a probate judge that she had exerted an evil influence on the old lady whose companion she had been for so many years.

It is not suggested that Sir Evelyn and Charlie Wood, Anna Steele and Polly Chambers sat down in solemn conclave in the summer of 1888 and hatched a long-term plan to destroy their sister's reputation by the method of persuading her husband to bring a divorce action. But the adultery was Katie's only too obvious Achilles' heel, and it is suggested that if their greed, fury and moral outrage had led the Woods to try and have Aunt Ben certified, they were capable of taking most actions to break the will. Towards the end of 1888 Willie O'Shea wrote to Chamberlain saying: 'Sir Evelyn Wood and the rest of Mrs O'Shea's relations would use any weapon to change her [Aunt Ben's] will.' Nothing further could be done until Aunt Ben was dead, the Woods could not themselves bring a divorce action against their sister, and the hinge of their possible future action was Willie O'Shea. In mid-1888 he was an unreliable hinge, for however strained his relations with his wife, she remained his main source of income via Aunt Ben, and if Katie inherited the entire fortune he could stand to obtain a great deal more money. However, in altering her will in March 1888 the old lady had so phrased it that the fortune was left entirely and personally to Katharine, outside the terms of the marriage settlement, so Willie would not be legally entitled to a share. But he could still hope to do very nicely by continuing to keep quiet about his knowledge of the adultery while using the same threats of divorce action or the withdrawal of Gerard's company as he had used the previous year. In the summer of 1888 he was not disposed to emerge from his cocoon because he thought it might continue to shelter him most comfortably, while Parnell would be destroyed by hands other than his.

By this time the Special Commission had been set up, with its roots in Frank Hugh O'Donnell's action in suing *The Times* for damages, for the libel against him in their 'Parnellism and Crime' articles. It is tempting to regard O'Donnell's friendship with Captain O'Shea as a possible motive for his action, and in this period any motive was possible on account of the passions Home Rule had aroused in some quarters and their desire to silence Parnell by any means. While it is possible that O'Shea influenced his old friend, it does not seem probable that he did, because O'Donnell was quite capable of acting on his own initiative and the reasons he gave for bringing his libel suit are fully in keeping with his character. O'Donnell's main reason was that he had been barely mentioned in the articles; *The Times* had insulted him by ignoring him, he who had been such an influential figure in the early days of the Home Rule struggle, and when it had briefly mentioned him it had got its facts wrong. The result of O'Donnell's suit, which finally came to court in June 1888, was that *The Times* had a field day, restating the accusations made in its articles and producing more secret letters, one of which was particularly damning. This letter, allegedly written by Parnell to Patrick Egan, the Land League treasurer, was dated 'Kilmainham Jan 9/1882' and ran thus:

Dear E,

What are these fellows waiting for? This inaction is inexcusable; our best men are in prison and nothing is being done.

Let there be an end to this hesitency [sic]. Prompt action is called for. You undertook to make it hot for old Forster and Co. Let us have some evidence of your power to do so.

My health is good, thanks.

Yours very truly, Charles Stewart Parnell.

The implication of this extraordinary note was that Parnell had not only approved of the Phoenix Park murders but had given the signal for their implementation by his call for prompt action (and Katie would have needed to hide her head in shame had her King been capable of writing such an incredible letter). However, as its contents were taken seriously by many sections of British opinion, even Parnell could not ignore this slander, and he requested a Select Committee to enquire into the authenticity of the letters produced during the O'Donnell suit. As an MP he was entitled to one, but Lord Salisbury was but one among thousands who believed Parnell could have written the letters and disbelieved that *The Times* would have produced them without conclusive proof of their authenticity. Lord Salisbury saw a splendid opportunity to destroy the nationalist party and Home Rule by open methods and demanded a Special Commission to enquire not merely into the authenticity of the letters but into the whole range of allegations made by *The Times* in its articles and during the course of the O'Donnell suit. A special Act of Parliament was needed to give statutory authority to this entirely novel Commission, but despite bitter opposition by Gladstone and the Liberals it received the royal assent.

Katharine said she consistently urged her lover to take action against *The Times* from the moment the first article appeared and he as consistently refused, and even after the legal apparatus for the Special Commission had been set up, when barristers and solicitors had to be briefed, witnesses gathered and evidence accumulated, she said, 'The case did not worry Parnell much—except that it took up so much of our all too little leisure time, which was so precious to us.' Their attitudes were characteristic; if Katie's methods were tangential, her instinct was to fight when attacked, irrespective of the cause, whereas Parnell fought only when necessary. Katie said she spent a great deal of time studying the facsimiles of the incriminating letters, deciding who could have forged Parnell's signature and passing on her conclusions to George Lewis who was one of the leading solicitors engaged for Parnell. She was much in evidence during the period when the nationalists were preparing their defence, and she recorded one occasion when she discussed Parnell's clothes with Mr Lewis. It had been agreed that Parnell must have a new frock-coat when he appeared before the Commission, and with some reluctance he had finally agreed to go to Poole's, a leading gentlemen's outfitters. The interesting thing about this anecdote is that Katie explained to George Lewis 'what a pleasure it was to me to be possessed of a man who was above clothes; not below them in slovenliness, but above them and unconscious of his coverings'. To him at least she apparently spoke with some frankness about her relationship with Parnell.

Whether in discussing the incriminating letters she was equally frank and mentioned Mr Parnell's suspicions that her legal husband might have written them, she did not record, but Willie himself admitted that Parnell's immediate reaction on the appearance of the letters in *The Times* was that he had forged them (and if the contention that O'Shea wrote the early 1886 letter trying to arrange a meeting between Gladstone and Parnell is accepted, he was already a dab hand at forgery). In the event it was proved that it was not Willie O'Shea but Richard Pigott who had forged the letters and Parnell's signature, and this fact was known in some Irish nationalist and Liberal circles months before it was finally revealed to the public. Pigott had been a nationalist in the early Isaac Butt days of Home Rule but in the intervening years had acquired a reputation as a blackmailer and pornographer, and it was basically for financial gain that he resorted to the forgeries, though it was the bitter anti-Parnell, anti–Home Rule atmosphere which produced the milieu in which a man such as he could flourish. In the period when the forged letters first began to circulate (and they were around for some considerable time and offered to several people before *The Times* finally bought them), Willie O'Shea was involved in murky activities which led him into the underworld of anti-Parnellite Fenianism, and he assuredly knew a great deal more than he admitted about the initial manoeuvres which led Pigott to hit on the idea of actually forging letters which would meet the requirements of certain sectors of the Parnell opposition. Soon after the Special Commission opened, Henry Labouchere wrote to tell Gladstone that Parnell thought one of the letters had been bought from an Invincible, that O'Shea was involved 'because O'Shea stated before the letters were published that compromising letters had been bought, and he was at that time on very intimate terms with an Invincible.' In this same letter Labouchere also told the Liberal leader about interviews he and Parnell and Sir Charles Russell had previously had with Pigott, mentioned the spelling of the word 'hesitency' which became the trap which ensnared Pigott in the witness box (though not till four months later) and reported, 'It was pretty clear therefore that Pigott was the forger. . . . He would not officially confess, and give us all the connecting links, but he admitted to us "in confidence" that he was the forger.' Three days later, on 30 October 1888, Labouchere again wrote to Gladstone, saying, 'I do not anticipate we shall get much more from Pigott until the last minute', which proved an accurate statement, but it is interesting to learn that as the Special Commission ground into operation, the Parnellite camp had a confidential confession from Pigott. It must have given them a great deal of heart in their endeavours and lent considerable irony to the opposition's long-winded attempts to discredit them.

Whether Willie O'Shea knew the letters were forgeries—as opposed to helping to find them and channel them to the right interested sources—is less certain, because he was not a stupid man and the inherent dangers of using them to destroy Parnell should have struck someone of his intelligence. Apart from O'Shea's involvement in circles panting to possess evidence which would wreck Parnell's career, there was another figure whom many Irishmen (before and since the event) believe to have been implicated in the setting-up of the trap, namely Joseph Chamberlain. The thesis is that Chamberlain used O'Shea and his Fenian contacts, was delighted to get the letters, possibly knew they were forgeries but did not care if they were and helped feed them into the credulous maws of *The Times*. The objection to the thesis is that Chamberlain was an even less stupid man than O'Shea, and one feels that if he had been involved he would have tested the authenticity of the letters more thoroughly. Admittedly *The Times* failed to check, but its managers were not of the same calibre as Chamberlain.

There is no doubt that once the letters had been widely accepted as genuine and Parnell had finally demanded a Select Committee, Chamberlain was to the forefront in pressing Lord Salisbury to appoint a Special Commission with virtually unlimited powers of reference, as he was unquestionably eager to expose Parnell in his vileness, for personal satisfaction and to solidify his new political stance. Before the first sitting of the Special Commission he had extra reason for wishing to destroy Parnell, because in July 1888 the mutual antagonism between him and the Irish leader came to a head in a bitter clash in the House of Commons. It was launched by Parnell and it might have remained a parliamentary matter, with blood drawn on both sides, had not Captain O'Shea rushed in with a letter to *The Times*. Chamberlain's biographer J. L. Garvin said that O'Shea 'blundered into print' without his master's knowledge, but he was not in fact dissuaded from widening the area of conflict by Chamberlain, who knew in advance about *The Times* letter. In this letter O'Shea upheld Mr Chamberlain's side of the parliamentary clash and specifically stated that the Central Boards Scheme of 1885 had been 'altogether Parnell's'. To this accusation Parnell bothered to reply, and in his letter to *The Times* he said it had been nothing of the sort and he had never accepted it as a substitute for Home Rule, whereupon Chamberlain wrote to *The Times* saying Parnell had thus accepted the scheme and he would produce the correspondence to back his claims. O'Shea and Chamberlain then got together, hoping to reveal Parnell in all his shady colours before the Special Commission delivered the *coup de grâce,* but O'Shea's suppression of the January 1885 letters came to light and Chamberlain suddenly remembered the letter his friend had written to Parnell purporting to give his views of the negotiations, a document which must still be in the Irish leader's possession. Chamberlain summed up the situation to his fiancée: 'What will happen if this letter is produced? In my own defence I must throw over O'Shea, and say what is the truth, that he grossly misrepresented me; but then if he misrepresented *me,* may he not also have misrepresented Parnell? And he is my chief witness against Parnell. Altogether a nice dilemma. Either he is a trustworthy witness, in which case my negotiations with him were of the most selfish and ignoble kind; or else he is untrustworthy, in which case I have no evidence to convict Parnell.' Chamberlain henceforward decided that O'Shea was untrustworthy, he again wrote to his fiancée saying that he now regarded the man as 'an indiscreet and therefore a dangerous person'. But the revelations and realisations meant he had to send a lame apology to *The Times,* agreeing that Mr Parnell had acted honourably in the Central Boards negotiations.

If this episode caused considerable chagrin to Chamberlain, who more than most men hated being placed in the wrong, it did not unduly upset Willie O'Shea and the two months between the establishment of the Special Commission and its first sitting were a euphoric period for him. With Chamberlain's assistance he entered into negotiations with *The Times,* the upshot of which was that he agreed to appear as one of their witnesses before the Special Commission, and thereby for the first time in several years he was at the center of the action, again being wooed by influential figures. It must surely have seemed to him that the objective he desired was within grasp: the blackguard Parnell's career would be judicially blasted without his having to take the drastic action of a divorce suit or of coming to blows with his wife over Aunt Ben's money.

Chapter Fourteen

Katharine herself, having checkmated her family and saved Aunt Ben from the horror of being certified insane, presumably felt pleased, and it is doubtful that she gave much thought to the obvious conclusion that if her siblings had been prepared to launch a Lunacy Petition they were not in future going to sit back and let her become an undisputed heiress. One has to presume and be doubtful because she makes no mention of any actions brought by her family against Aunt Ben, nor was she forthcoming on this subject to Henry Harrison. A certain sense of family loyalty, of *autres temps, autres moeurs* seems to have restrained her tongue and pen.

From September 1888 onwards, if it did not absorb their whole attention, the focus of Katie and Parnell's life, as of many other people's, was the hearings of the Special Commission. It was on Monday, 17 September 1888, that the initial sitting took place in Number One Probate Court of the Royal Courts of Justice, but the proceedings were then adjourned until near the end of October. Once they had begun in earnest, witnesses in their scores appeared to catalogue the crimes of the Land League, with the Attorney General appearing for *The Times* and the whole scene assuming the aspect of an English state trial of Irish nationalism. Some people were extremely interested in the crimes of Irish nationalism or in proving that the nationalist actions had been far from criminal and entirely justifiable, but for the majority of the citizens of the United Kingdom the crucial matter was whether Parnell had written the letters connecting him with the Phoenix Park murders (which the defence knew for certain that he had not). When it became apparent that the Attorney General intended to blast Parnell's reputation and that of the Home Rule movement by an accumulation of detail and a plethora of repetitive witnesses, interest in the Commission became intermittent and dependent on which witness was on the stand. One early witness who caused considerable interest was W. H. O'Shea.

Henry Labouchere told Gladstone that Parnell was 'in a somewhat excited frame of mind about O'Shea appearing as a witness, for there are reasons why it is difficult to reply to O'Shea. He says, however, that he will not spare him and if he holds to this, it can be proved that O'Shea was an actual thief in many matters.' Labouchere did not unfortunately specify in what proven matters O'Shea had been a thief, and they were not revealed in court because there were indeed difficulties facing Parnell's counsel in dealing with the Captain. O'Shea took the stand on 31 October, and a reporter said that normally he was 'a spruce, dandified man, filled with belief in himself and disbelief in others . . . the kind of gentlemanlike adventurer, cynically contemptuous under the guise of bonhomie', but that by 1888 he was showing signs of wear and in the witness box he looked 'shabby genteel.' He was first questioned by the Attorney General, who established that the witness had been a long-time friend of Parnell's, had acted as his political negotiator and knew his handwriting well. The Attorney General then produced the incriminating letters and asked O'Shea if he could identify the signatures as those of the Irish leader, O'Shea hesitated briefly and then said he believed the writing to be Mr Parnell's.

After the Attorney General had produced this admission from a man who had known Parnell intimately, it was Sir Charles Russell's turn to interrogate the witness on Parnell's behalf. Russell first objected, saying the witness had been sprung on him unannounced, but his objections were overruled on the basis that O'Shea had to attend to urgent business in Spain and might not return to the country for several months. Russell's aim was to negate the damaging evidence about the signatures by probing into the reasons O'Shea might have for wishing to discredit the nationalist leader, but he was of course handicapped by the well-known reason (i.e. to himself and other informed people) that Parnell lived with the Captain's wife. He tried to extract some political explanations as to why O'Shea had changed from friend and confidante to the position of believing Parnell capable of writing such letters by probing into his associations with Fenians, not to mention Richard Pigott. He tied O'Shea into several knots but on the whole Willie proved an astutely slippery witness—what he could not remember clearly was legion—and his own description of the interrogation to Chamberlain had some justification—'Once it came to fighting Russell, however, all was well and I had him down round after round.' If he did not have the eminent Anglo-Irish barrister panting on the floor, O'Shea undoubtedly kept on his own feet. The reason he had been perturbed *before* the contest with Sir Charles was, as he also explained to Chamberlain, that he went into the witness box 'under a very heavy load of anxiety owing to matters in themselves apart from charges and allegations.' This heavy load of anxiety was not connected with such suggestions as Henry Labouchere's that he could be proved to be a thief, but was there because he was worried that news of Katie and Parnell's affair might finally reach the press. Having given his evidence, O'Shea then departed for Spain, where he remained for the next six months, as he again wrote to Chamberlain, 'deep in Spanish politics.'

The Commission broke for the Christmas recess and it was not until mid-February 1889 that the matter of the forged letters was reached in any practical form. On 19 February John Cameron Macdonald of *The Times* appeared on the stand, and while admitting that the letters had obtained from Richard Pigott he said he personally had not ascertained how they had come into the gentleman's possession. The next day Edward Caulfield Houston (a well-known loyalist upholder of the Union) was the witness, and he agreed that he had originally bought the letters from Pigott in a series of cloak-and-dagger meetings in Paris, but had to admit that he had not bothered to check their authenticity. On 21 February Pigott himself took the stand and under merciless cross-examination by Sir Charles Russell failed to show Captain O'Shea's ability as a stone-walling witness. The pinnacle of the courtroom drama was reached when Russell asked Pigott to spell 'hesitancy', which he proceeded to spell 'hesitency', as in the letter supposedly written by Parnell to Egan in 1882, and as discussed by Russell, Labouchere and Parnell four months previously. (Parnell, incidentally, was noted for his meticulous spelling, another fact the opposition did not bother to check in its efforts to destroy him.) It was by now the weekend; on the Monday Pigott failed to appear in court to resume his evidence and Sir Charles Russell announced that he had fled the country, leaving behind a confession that he had forged the incriminating letters. The melodrama as a whole did not reach its peak until the following week, when the news came that Pigott had committed suicide in Madrid.

There were several people interested in the fact that Pigott chose to flee to Madrid, a city he had never previously visited, whereas he knew Paris well and might have been presumed to select the French capital. There was one well-known Irishman currently in Madrid, Captain William Henry O'Shea, and it was suggested that Pigott chose Madrid because he knew O'Shea was there and because he hoped the gentleman with whom he had had dealings in the early days of the forged letters might help him in his extremity. Obviously O'Shea himself denied such gross suggestions, but he took the trouble to write a long letter to Chamberlain explaining that he had observed a man in the Café Inglés in the Calle de Sevilla in Madrid, that he soon became convinced that the man was Pigott and that he mentioned the matter to his friend the President of the Chamber. (Willie had no friends of less than the highest social standing.) He also said he thought Pigott might have been 'got at' by Henry Labouchere—for it was Labouchere to whom he finally confessed in writing—and implied that the forged letters might in fact turn out to be genuine.

Few people in the United Kingdom shared O'Shea's opinion, and for the majority of its citizens the Pigott confessions and suicide meant the end of the Special Commission (in fact its hearings dragged on until November 1889 and its official findings, which more or less exonerated the Irish nationalists from the charges laid against them and totally exonerated Parnell from involvement in the Phoenix Park murders, were not published until early 1890). Parnell had been shown to be the victim of a sort of conspiracy; while nobody accused *The Times* of having commissioned the forged letters or having known them to be forged, it was widely felt that the newspaper (and the Tory Government) had wilfully, recklessly, blindly indulged their dislike of Parnell and Home Rule. The pendulum of British public opinion swung violently in the victim's favour and from February 1889 Parnell became the hero of the hour, given a standing ovation in the House of Commons, and the freedom of the city of Edinburgh, elected a life member of the National Liberal Club, invited to innumerable dinners and receptions and soirées and mass meetings (most of which he refused). Gladstone's daughter, Mary, kept most interesting diaries whose schoolgirl enthusiasm does not change with age (she was forty-two years old in 1889), and she described the ridiculous, dangerous swing of reaction in Parnell's favour. Immediately after the Pigott disclosures, Mary wrote with acumen, 'Parnell will be for a time as light an angel as he has been dark as a devil', but then recorded that her friend had met him at dinner and thought he had 'a beautiful face like a saint in a painted window, intensely quiet and reserved and utterly unselfconscious.' After she herself had watched Parnell in the Commission witness box in May 1889, Mary was carried to further raptures: 'He really exhibited all the fruits of the Spirit, love, peace, patience, gentleness, forbearance, long-suffering meekness. His personality takes hold of one, the refined, delicate face, illuminating smile, fire-darting eyes, slight tall figure.' Again seeing him in court she recorded: 'Loved Parnell's spiritual face, only one's heart ached over his awfully delicate frame and look.'

Katie, whose heart also ached for Parnell's delicate constitution (though she might not have recognised the long-suffering meekness), was not able to participate in the lionisation of her lover. Apart from the fact that he disliked the social life, his inability to take his beloved Queenie with him was a good reason why Parnell refused so many of the invitations. Another reason was that he was not over-impressed by the transports of British rapture, and he told Katie that the members of the House of Commons who had stood in ovation would be at his throat in a week if they could and that the upper classes and the common people were only applauding him because he had been found to be within the law and therefore their sense of justice was stirred. He elaborated this theme by saying, 'The English make a law and bow down and worship it till they find it obsolete—long after this is obvious to other nations—then they bravely make another, and start afresh in the opposite direction. That's why I am glad Ireland has a religion; there is so little hope for a nation that worships the law.' By this statement he revealed that he was indeed an Irishman, however English he might look or sound.

While Parnell was failing to be impressed by his new position of idolatry, Aunt Ben's strength was slowly ebbing away. In April 1889 she had an attack of bronchitis from which she never fully recovered, but even in the last weeks of her life she would not allow Katharine to sleep at the Lodge, as she said it would disorganise the household, so each evening Katie walked to the house to ensure that her aunt was comfortable. Frequently she stayed sitting on the bench underneath the bedroom window, watching and listening to the owls which nested in the great tree and which over the years had given Aunt Ben so much pleasure. Her aunt's maid told Katie that the mournful hooting was a sign that her dear mistress had not long to live, and when she pointed out that the owls had been hooting ever since Mr and Mrs Wood had moved into the Lodge some sixty years ago, the maid continued to believe in the evil omen. When Parnell was 'at home' he would accompany Katie on the walks from Wonersh Lodge, across North Park, through the private doorway into the Lodge grounds and up to the beautiful house, and sit waiting for her under the trees as she obtained the latest bulletin on the old lady's condition.

Early in the morning of 19 May 1889 Katie went up to the Lodge—as her aunt had been suffering from increasingly restless nights, she had fallen into the habit of early-morning as well as night visits. She found her aunt breathing with difficulty, and as Katie approached the bedside the old lady put out her hand and whispered, 'You do believe, do you not, my Swan?' to which Katie replied, 'Yes, Auntie, of course I do believe, most firmly.' Her aunt then said, 'I am glad. I wish you could come with me, my darling,' and Katie sobbed and wished that she could. She continued to sit by Aunt Ben's side, stroking the feeble, shrunken hands until the shallow breathing ceased. Katie said the death left an immense void in her life, and it must have done so; she had been Aunt Ben's constant companion for the best part of fifteen years, she had received not only money, position and security but the pleasure of an original personality, and there had been a genuine affection between the old lady and herself.

As a result of her aunt's death, Katharine stood to inherit the fortune, which she felt was hers by right. In 1884 she had told her husband that if she died they would lose Aunt Ben's money and nobody was more entitled to it than she was; since 1884 a great deal had happened. The Woods had launched their Lunacy Petition, she had saved the old lady from the fate of spending her last twelve months as a certified lunatic, she felt Aunt Ben had expressed her wishes clearly and had meant her to have the entire fortune, which undoubtedly the old lady had. This opinion was not shared by the Woods; Sir Evelyn and Charles, Anna Steele and Polly Chambers put in an application to the Probate Court to contest the will. This meant that from May 1889 onwards Katharine's source of income was gone and moreover she could not lay her hands on hard cash, for if in theory she was an heiress to a vast fortune, in practise nobody was going to lend her money until the probate action had been decided.

When Aunt Ben died, Willie O'Shea was in Spain, but he was back in England later in the summer, spending part of August in Llandrindod Wells, taking the water in the hope of relieving his gout. In the six months he had been out of the country the situation had altered radically. Far from receiving what O'Shea considered his due deserts at the hands of the Special Commission, Parnell had become the great British hero, a metamorphosis O'Shea found incredible and intolerable. The Woods consequently had fertile ground on which to work because the desire to wreck Parnell, to reveal him to the world in his horrible colours, was now as strong in O'Shea's mind as the financial considerations. Suddenly in the late summer of 1889—fifteen months after Aunt Ben's last will and testament had been made—O'Shea found that he had to intervene in the probate action between his wife and her family, as the terms of the will contravened his marriage settlement. He told Chamberlain that it was only because of his children's interests that he was forced to intervene (the theme of his children's welfare was one which he played with increasing vigour), and he also informed his friend of the esteem and affection being shown to him by members of Mrs O'Shea's family, saying, 'These feelings constantly find expression and last week at Belhus Park [Sir Thomas Barrett Lennard's] when almost the whole of Mrs O'Shea's family were assembled, these were very clearly exhibited before many persons belonging to the county and other strangers.'

What a good, old-fashioned snob Willie O'Shea was! Away from the gaze of people belonging to the county, the Wood family conferences were being held, with O'Shea firmly clasped in the comforting upper-class arms. At the nature of the conversations one can only guess, but it seems that the Woods were the instrument which pushed O'Shea into the final decision to bring the divorce action. Despite his high opinion of himself, O'Shea was not capable of taking decisive action on his own initiative; at his worst he was a mercenary, a not oversuccessful adventurer; at his best he was a go-between, a not unskilled negotiator; at all times he was a reactor to other people's needs and desires. It cannot have been difficult for the Woods to have played upon his vanity, his self-pity and his hatred of Parnell; in particular it cannot have been difficult for Anna Steele, who believed all men could be won by flattery and liqueurs and for whom O'Shea had long had an affection. His wife had been deceiving him for years, as O'Shea had finally discovered, poor man; she had been ruined by her lover's evil influence, but she had passed beyond the pale and there was nothing that could be done to save her; but there was something that could be done to rescue O'Shea from the hideous, dishonourable position in which Parnell had placed him; and if by taking divorce action to restore his position as a gentleman O'Shea assisted the probate action, then this was to the good, because his wife was no longer a fit person to be in control of a large fortune; and if he assisted in the probate action, having realised that Aunt Ben's will contravened the terms of his marriage settlement, then the Woods would ensure that he (or rather his children) received their due share of the fortune.

The Woods themselves had little direct interest in destroying Parnell. None of them was a highly political animal, and though it is doubtful that they favoured Home Rule and therefore would not be upset by the removal of the movement's leader, their motive was pecuniary. They had failed once with the Lunacy Petition, they could not afford to fail a second time, they had to be as certain as they possibly could be that they could break Aunt Ben's will. Whatever the result of the divorce action, their sister's reputation must be tarnished and their chances of proving her baleful influence on the old lady thus heightened. (The Woods may have had doubts whether O'Shea would win his suit, his condoning of the affair might be only too easily proved, but this did not matter to them, the stink of the divorce court would serve their purpose.) If the Woods' motive was pecuniary, a determination to obtain their share of Aunt Ben's fortune, they assuredly convinced themselves that they had moral justification for their action. Katharine had ceased to be a respectable woman, she had disgraced the family name, she had exerted pressure on their aged aunt whose faculties had been diminishing (even if she was not actually insane), and if she obtained the entire fortune it might be used for heaven knew what subversive measures in Ireland.

It is my contention that the Woods were the catalyst which made Willie O'Shea bring his divorce suit; their intervention explains the timing of his action, which has always been baffling, the reason why he acted in 1889 rather than in 1886 or 1887 or 1888 (and having failed with their Lunacy Petition, the Woods could not act until after Aunt Ben had died—in 1889). Having finally come to his decision, O'Shea naturally wrote to Joseph Chamberlain to justify it, and it was at this time that he told his friend that he had learned in 1887 that Mr Parnell was living at Eltham and had been doing so for some considerable period. He explained that he had not then felt able to take action because of his worries about his children's interests (that meant Aunt Ben's money) and his desire 'to avoid the injury certain to be inflicted on them by full publicity of a scandal gross in itself, but all the more re-echoing on account of the persons concerned.' He said he was still concerned about his children, particularly of 'putting my son (who is devoted to me) in the witness box against his mother', but 'owing to some recent circumstances' he felt the time had come for him to take strong action; what the 'recent circumstances' were he did not specify. Chamberlain replied in non-committal fashion, saying he never listened to any scandal about his friends, that he knew nothing beyond what O'Shea had told him, that he was in no position to express an opinion as he did not possess all the information, but he was glad his friend had the support of his wife's family since that would be a strong point in his favour. (O'Shea had emphasised the Wood sympathy and understanding of his predicament.)

Although I believe the Woods were the catalyst for the divorce action, it should be noted that many people believe it was politically motivated and the prime contender for political catalyst was Joseph Chamberlain. There is a strongly held opinion that Chamberlain, having failed to split the Irish party in Galway, having failed to destroy Parnell by means of the Pigott letters and the Special Commission, finally manipulated the only other means of destruction, and paid O'Shea's legal costs into the bargain. By 1889 Chamberlain had sound political reasons for wanting to remove Parnell from the scene (apart from any desire for personal vengeance), because he had not succeeded in his attempts at a rapprochement with the Liberal Party and he was still regarded askance by the Liberal-Unionists, but if he could break the nationalist party by discrediting the Irish leader he would prove his credentials to the Unionists and could hope to take over as their leader. There is no evidence that Chamberlain and O'Shea met in the months between the latter's return to England in the summer of 1889 and the moment when he finally decided to bring his action—October at the very latest, probably earlier, because strong rumours were already circulating in August that O'Shea would sue for divorce. On the financial side, the evidence of Chamberlain's providing money for the suit is again negative, and after the case was over O'Shea was in such a bad way financially that he had to beg his friend to lend him money. Finally, the way O'Shea instituted his divorce proceedings does not lend weight to the theory that Chamberlain was manipulating him. If one accepts that Chamberlain was sufficiently Machiavellian in his desire to destroy Parnell to use O'Shea as his instrument, then it should be allowed that he would ensure that the instrument employed more adroit tactics.

As O'Shea was unburdening himself to Joseph Chamberlain about his impending divorce action, he was also considering the subject of his immortal Catholic soul, and in the autumn he had several interviews and engaged in a long correspondence with Cardinal Manning. Only O'Shea's side of the story has been published, and Manning's surviving papers are fragmentary and do not unfortunately contain his negotiations in the vital months leading to the filing of the divorce petition. From what one can gather, initially O'Shea applied for a dispensation to enable him to initiate the civil divorce proceedings but met with little encouragement from His Eminence. Manning, who was well aware of the Katie-Parnell liaison (Sir Charles Dilke had noted, 'I was amused by finding how much he cared for general gossip and even scandal') and of the disastrous implications of a divorce action, queried the length of time it had taken O'Shea to consider instituting proceedings, his status as *mari complaisant* and his motives, and in reply O'Shea grew suitably outraged. Then suddenly he widened the whole area of his enquiries and was requesting information on the procedure to be adopted for an annulment of his marriage within the Catholic Church, to which enquiries Manning, as his spiritual adviser, had to respond. What possible grounds O'Shea thought he had for an annulment of his marriage by the Catholic Church is beyond comprehension, but he pursued the subject with vigour in the early days of December, talking about the case going to Rome. (He appears to have been confused, because either the case was dealt with by the diocesan tribunal which was empowered to annul the marriage if the evidence proved justified, or if the participants were well-known they could appeal direct to the Sacred Rota in Rome.) Whether O'Shea presented his annulment evidence to Manning is unclear, but if he did it would have been rejected, because straightforward infidelity (which was all O'Shea had to offer) is no ground for the annulment of a marriage in the Catholic Church; it has to be proven that there was actual exclusion of the obligation of fidelity at the time of the marriage, not an easy matter and a ground on which annulment is rarely granted. The attempts at annulment did not get far

[211]

because Katie knew nothing about them until years later, and she would have been fully informed of the evidence against her had it been presented to the tribunal. In reality, her husband had decided on the civil divorce proceedings, so it did not matter overmuch what Cardinal Manning said or did, it would merely have been comforting to O'Shea's Catholic conscience and sense of righteousness had His Eminence proved helpful. When Manning failed to co-operate, O'Shea came to the conclusion that he was trying to screen Parnell, and he went so far as to tell his counsel, Sir Edward Clarke, that it was Manning's perfidy which finally prompted him to sue for divorce. According to Willie, at one stage of the proceedings Manning asked for proof of Mrs O'Shea's infidelity, which he duly supplied in the shape of incriminating letters, but Manning promptly gave them to Sir Charles Russell and George Lewis (Parnell's barrister and solicitor) for their inspection, and it was this unpardonable action which led him to institute his divorce action. O'Shea's chameleon-like ability to colour his motives and actions according to the mood of the moment and the personality of his audience was never more in evidence than in the various reasons he gave for filing his divorce papers.

Before reaching the moment when Captain O'Shea finally produced his time bomb, we must return to Katie and Parnell, for a considerable amount happened in their lives in 1889, personally and politically. After Aunt Ben's death in May, Katie said Eltham had become intolerable to her. She consequently sold Wonersh Lodge (which had been hers since 1875, so there was no problem about probate) and rented a house in Mottingham, then a village a few miles from Eltham. As soon as she and Parnell vacated Wonersh Lodge, it was invaded by hordes of souvenir-hunters, anxious to obtain a memento from the house in which the Irish leader had lived. (The wide-spread knowledge about the suburban retreat could have been another reason for leaving Wonersh Lodge.) The Mottingham house proved damp and unsatisfactory, and in the summer of 1889 she and Parnell moved to Brighton, renting 10 Walsingham Terrace, the end house of a short terrace, a solid, spacious four-storey building, then situated on the western outskirts of the town, with open country stretching from it to Shoreham. It provided a reasonable degree of privacy—and they soon rented the adjoining house to give them more—while not being too inaccessible, as there was excellent train service between Brighton and London. In Walsingham Terrace she and Parnell settled with their horses and dogs, their devoted long-term servants, and Katie, Clare and Norah O'Shea. Where Gerard and Carmen were living at this time is unclear, but as they both sided with their father one presumes they did not make the move to Brighton.

Politically, 1889 marked the zenith of Parnell's career. From the moment of the Pigott debacle, Gladstone and he began to reconverge, but the impetus for a new look at the problem of Home Rule came from Gladstone, and Parnell was not over-hasty in his response, partly because the Tories were the party in power and he had no wish to alienate them entirely. In an interesting 'most private' letter Gladstone wrote to him at the end of August, the Liberal leader reiterated his belief that the Irish leader should accept from the Tories whatever they had to offer, and that the Irish party should keep itself independent of both British parties. He also warned Parnell not to count on his possessing the sort of influence over the Liberal Party which Parnell had with the nationalists, stressing that he presided over a large party with diverse aims and interests, whose backbone lay in the Nonconformists of England and Wales and the Presbyterians of Scotland, who were not always favourably disposed towards Catholic Ireland. This latter warning had prescience, as it was 'The Nonconformist conscience' which eighteen months later forced Gladstone's hand and was accused of breaking Parnell. Gladstone's injunctions about the Irish party holding itself aloof, while admirable in theory, were no longer viable in practice, and at the end of the letter he indicated that it was he, rather than the Tories, who was prepared to introduce a new Home Rule Bill.

Parnell continued not to rush his fences, and in October Gladstone again wrote asking if he could now suggest a definite date for a visit to Gladstone home at Hawarden, where the two leaders could discuss the concrete matters of changes in the 1886 Home Rule Bill. It was not until December that Parnell accepted the invitation, and Mary Gladstone nicely recorded the manner of his arrival—'at 6 on Wed. who shd arrive by telegram but Mr Parnell'—and she further noted: 'Much excitement in the atmosphere. . . . Was next to him at dinner. He never shows emotion, has a cool, indifferent manner, in sharp contrast to the piercing gaze of his eyes, which look bang through, not at, yours. . . . A most mysterious man of compelling power, and difficult to define where the latter lies. Voice low and weak. . . . Good nose . . . he is 43.' Mary also recorded: 'He looks more ill than any other I ever saw off a death-bed', and perhaps this was a feminine intuition, because male observers, including her father, were commenting that the Irish leader appeared in better health than he had for some years. In the memorandum Gladstone made after the meetings at Hawarden, he noted that nothing could have been more satisfactory than his conversations with Parnell, that the Irish leader was full of good sense and they both agreed that the greatest problem was the question of whether or not to retain the Irish MPs at Westminster, but it was one that they should play by ear. Parnell himself emerged from the confidential talks in high good humour and travelled to nearby Liverpool, where he made a speech in which he lauded Mr Gladstone and mentioned the great new battle for Home Rule which he and the Liberals would soon be fighting.

In mid-December 1889 it seemed to all those interested in Home Rule that victory was truly within grasp. Mr Gladstone and Mr Parnell had finally met in private conclave, the result of their face-to-face discussions had patently been satisfactory, there was every prospect of the Liberals being returned to power at the next General Election, and this time they would have a mandate from the country to carry Home Rule, for this time it would be a major issue. Throughout 1889, as publicly Parnell rose higher and higher in popular estimation, as each step was taken in the solidification of his political position, the seeds of his destruction followed a parallel growth rate. In August, as Gladstone wrote to him in such frank and friendly fashion, the news that Captain O'Shea was willing to institute divorce proceedings spread in anti-Parnellite circles; in October, as Gladstone pressed the invitation to a private meeting at Hawarden, O'Shea was tying up the loose ends of his impending action; in December, as Gladstone and Parnell met to put the seal on a Liberal-nationalist alliance in pursuit of Home Rule, O'Shea filed suit for divorce, citing Charles Stewart Parnell as co-respondent.

Chapter Fifteen

O'Shea filed his divorce petition on Christmas Eve 1889, and had anyone but he been the petitioner one might have suspected a sense of humour at work. The man to whom O'Shea went with his instructions was none other than Joseph Soames, the solicitor to *The Times* who had represented him in the Special Commission. One interpretation of O'Shea's choice of solicitor is that he was being manipulated by Chamberlain and/or *The Times,* but it seems too obvious a link (particularly for the astute Chamberlain). It seems more likely that O'Shea of his own volition went to somebody he knew—he had had dealings with Soames when preparing to give his evidence to the Special Commission—and he was not possessed of sensitive antennae which would have indicated the unsuitability of his choice. It struck other people, notably Sir Edward Clarke, who recorded, 'The impropriety, to say the least of it, of his acting in such a case at such a time, however, soon occurred to Mr Soames, or was suggested to him, and he advised the Captain to employ somebody else.' O'Shea next turned to Mr Day, the son of Mr Justice Day who had sat in judgement on Parnell for over a year at the Special Commission hearings, and as Sir Edward Clarke further noted, 'Mr Day . . . was the most unfit man, except for Mr Soames himself, who could possibly have been involved.' As we shall see, Mr Day was soon removed from the proceedings, but it was he who filed the petition on behalf of William Henry O'Shea of 124 Victoria Street, in the City of Westminster, Justice of the Peace for County Clare.

O'Shea's explanation for filing his petition, as given to the divorce court a year later and to Joseph Chamberlain at the time, was that he and Gerard went down to Brighton the week before Christmas, Gerard called unexpectedly at 10 Walsingham Terrace and to his intense surprise found 'a lot of Mr Parnell's things, some of which he chucked out of the window.' Gerard would have found a lot of Parnell's things whenever he had called at Walsingham Terrace but according to his father a dreadful scene ensued between Gerard and Katie, and the result was that 'on our return to London we went to the lawyers and settled that an action should be taken immediately.' After a decade of his wife's adultery, how simple O'Shea made the final decision sound; and how quickly Mr Soames must have discovered that he was an unfit person to act for the Captain and Mr Day must then have taken over. The immediate reaction to the news in Britain and Ireland was not pronounced. A London *Evening News* reporter went to interview Captain O'Shea, and when he asked, 'And Mr Charles Stewart Parnell is the co-respondent?' O'Shea replied with as intense surprise as his son had exhibited in Brighton, 'That is true, but how the deuce did you hear of it?' On 30 December Parnell granted the *Freeman's Journal* an interview in which he said Captain O'Shea had been threatening such action for years, ever since 1886, when he and O'Shea had separated politically, that O'Shea had known since 1880 of Parnell's residence at Wonersh Lodge, and that the action had been launched by *The Times* in a further attempt to discredit him as leader of the Home Rule party. Parnell's statement that O'Shea had known about his presence in Eltham for nearly ten years (in effect a charge of condonation) was not picked up by commentators, but the idea that the divorce was another *Times* manoeuvre became widely held by the general public in Ireland, and to a certain if lesser extent in England.

The newspapers in the United Kingdom were muted in their speculations about the divorce petition; on the Liberal side because they had no desire to upset the recently loaded Gladstone-Parnell apple-cart; on the Tory side because once bitten over the Pigott forgeries was twice shy about Captain O'Shea's suit; on the Irish side because they wanted to believe Parnell. The American papers had no such qualms, and on 29 December, the *New York Herald* ran a long piece headlined 'UN MARI COMPLAISANT, Captain O'Shea at Last Objects to Mr Parnell's Liaison with Mrs O'Shea'. The article started in reasonably calm if forthright manner, saying nobody on the inside of politics on either side of the Atlantic would be surprised by the news as Mr (or Captain) O'Shea had threatened legal proceedings on several previous occasions, but it then began to go awry with its facts and gave an extraordinary explanation for the initial friendship between Parnell and the O'Sheas. From what dubious source the *Herald* obtained the story remains its secret, but the explanation offered ran as follows: *circa* 1878, Parnell had fallen in love with O'Shea's younger sister (the devoutly Catholic Mary who lived in Paris); she responded to his advances and a date was set for the wedding; suddenly the young girl became ill and quickly died (she was still alive in 1885). On her death-bed, a heart-broken Parnell promised to befriend his sweetheart's brother, who about this time married Katie Wood, and thus it was because of his love for Mary O'Shea that Parnell had forwarded her brother's career and thereby met his wife.

Between its fact and its fiction, the *Herald* sandwiched its speculations. Would the suit be defended? If this seemed a curious question to ask about a divorce case, the truth was that the whole business was curious. Who was guilty and who was innocent? This was again a curious matter, but it seemed likely that some nationalists would speak their minds freely about O'Shea now that he had 'cast off his disguise and entered boldly upon the war path.' However much or little Mr Parnell might have sinned, nobody could accuse him of cold-blooded profligacy, as his friendship for Mrs O'Shea had been constant for years. Would the Irish party and people stand by him if it were proved that he had passed beyond the bounds of legitimate friendship with Mrs O'Shea? Nobody in London had been willing to answer this query, but the *Herald* suspected that the loyalty of devout Catholics such as William O'Brien would be sorely strained if damaging revelations were made in court. Finally, it predicted that there must be a smash of some sort when 'the great Eltham mystery' came to be unravelled.

O'Shea thought the article was atrocious, and he told Chamberlain that he intended to sue the *New York Herald* for libel, but he did not do so. As indicated, he was spared such speculative mixtures of fact and fiction in the United Kingdom, and while the newspaper silence at home is understandable, that of the leading Liberals and nationalists is more curious. Once the divorce petition had been filed, one might have thought somebody involved from each camp would have made some private approaches to Parnell to ascertain what he intended to do. For indubitably there would be a smash unless Parnell and Mrs O'Shea could provide a more than adequate defence, and what could be smashed would be not a private reputation but the new Liberal-nationalist alliance and the future of Home Rule. Admittedly, both Liberals and nationalists faced Parnell's aloof, proud, *noli me tangere* barrier and the insulation of his private life, but he appeared at the House of Commons from time to time and Brighton was not the North Pole. Admittedly again, the Victorians preferred to ignore circumstances which disturbed their vision of human behaviour, notably sexual irregularities, until forced to take note, but this particular irregularity threatened particular dangers. The Liberals were not simple-minded—nor were the leading nationalists, but they were on more difficult ground in tackling 'the Chief'—and one feels that somebody might have asked a few pertinent questions. As the early months of 1890 rolled by, nobody approached Parnell on the subject, both nationalists and Liberals relying upon rumour or inside information. On 3 February, for example, John Morley wrote to Sir William Harcourt to tell him that he had dined with George Lewis (Parnell's solicitor) and from what Lewis had told him about the affair he gathered that *The Times* would have its revenge and there would be a 'horrid exposure'. (At this precise moment in February 1890 the newspaper paid damages to Parnell for the libel contained in its original 'Parnellism and Crime' articles.) Another reason suggested for the Liberal detachment is that few leading members liked Parnell or Home Rule and had no greater objections than the Tories to his receiving his come-uppance or its being put into cold storage, but Gladstone had more or less committed the party to a new Home Rule Bill and there had been no internal revolt after the Hawarden meeting.

Katie's account of the eleven months between the filing of her husband's petition and the hearing of the suit, as contained in her memoirs, is even scantier than her reporting of the Galway election. She was more forthcoming to Henry Harrison, and fortunately there are other sources for her activities during these eleven months, notably her husband's letters to Joseph Chamberlain. (Chamberlain was out of the country for the first three months of 1890, travelling in Egypt—the current political joke concerned Joseph in Egypt—a physical absence which overrules his direct involvement in the early preparations of O'Shea's case.) Probably the petition came as a surprise to Katharine; she had managed her husband and kept the triangular raft afloat for nearly a decade, and she was not the lady to appreciate that people could be squeezed too hard. Having grasped the surprising fact that her husband was no longer prepared to be complaisant, at least not on the existing terms, Katie tried to effect new terms, and in these pourparlers Anna Steele was apparently involved. (Katharine told Henry Harrison that she was.) Anna's involvement is interesting because she had sided with her siblings in the Lunacy and Probate affairs, and one presumes that it was the Woods, rather than Willie O'Shea, who were then willing to do a deal with their sister—if she would agree to a fair split of Aunt Ben's money out of court, they might persuade Captain O'Shea to withdraw his petition—and they sent Anna along to sound the ground. If such was the content of the pourparlers—and one cannot think what else it could have been, because the Woods' interest was Aunt Ben's money, not Captain O'Shea's reputation—it foundered on Katie's determination to have the entire fortune, as decreed in the old lady's last will and testament.

The Wood-Katie contacts had presumably ceased by the beginning of February, because at this time Sir Edward Clarke was brought into the divorce proceedings on O'Shea's side. At the first consultation with Mr Day, Sir Edward was not impressed and it was he who quietly but firmly removed the young man from the case. Sir Edward then had his first meeting with Captain O'Shea, not a friendly one, as Willie stormed into his office in a furious temper because yet another solicitor had thrown him over. Sir Edward managed to calm his client down and to persuade him to engage a politically untainted solicitor. Thus from February onwards O'Shea's affairs were in the hands of an efficient firm of solicitors and of the Solicitor General, and Sir Edward gave instructions that 'no step should be taken in the case without my personal knowledge or advice.' Sources other than Sir Edward suggest that initially he refused to handle the case because he said the evidence pointed to O'Shea's knowledge of the adultery over a long period, but if he had such doubts (which he himself obviously does not directly admit) he managed to overcome them. In his memoirs he was not unfavourably disposed towards Parnell, which might suggest that he was as unimpressed with Captain O'Shea as he had been with Mr Day. It was Clarke, remember, who said that the two girls born in 1883 and 1884 were 'unquestionably' Parnell's, and in his chapter on the O'Shea divorce he makes frequent references to everybody having known about the liaison for years.

Having rejected the Wood feelers and learned that her husband was pursuing his action more firmly (and whether it occurred to Katie that the two moves were interconnected is doubtful), she herself continued to follow the tactic of trying to buy her husband off. In March Willie wrote to tell Joseph Chamberlain that Mrs O'Shea was bringing an action against him in the Irish Court of Chancery which appeared 'to be founded on a quibble in the text of the marriage settlement.' This was a sound move (accepting Katie's basic tactic), for if she could have the clause of Aunt Ben's will which left the fortune outside the scope of the marriage settlement upheld in a court of law, then Willie would be cut off from a legal supply of money, he would have no ground for intervening in the probate action and would be dependent on her bounty. The snag to this proposition was that Katie's bounty was Aunt Ben's fortune, and if her husband went ahead with the divorce suit she might not win the probate action, so she had to convince him that he would gain by supporting her, by withdrawing his petition or letting her divorce him because she could offer more financially than the Woods and the probate action. The idea that she might not be able to manipulate her husband this time had not occurred to Katie, because she took no steps to answer the charges made in his petition. And he further told Chamberlain that his wife was 'obstructing to the best of her artifices', including feigning illness, and Parnell was hoping to postpone the hearing until after the Long Vacation, which might mean December.

In mid-April, Willie informed Chamberlain that Parnell had filed his answer to the charges in the form of a simple denial of adultery but Mrs O'Shea had still done nothing in the matter. Now that Joseph had returned from Egypt, O'Shea bombarded him with letters and requests for advice. The two men definitely met at this period and assuredly Chamberlain extended the best possible anti-Parnell advice he could muster. According to O'Shea it was not until the end of July that his wife filed any particulars of her defence and counter-charges, though newspapers later said that she filed them in June. Her defence, like Parnell's, was that she had not been guilty of adultery, but Katie did not leave the matter there, she charged that her husband had both connived at and condoned the adultery, that he had neglected her and been cruel to her, that he himself had committed adultery and had delayed unreasonably in bringing the suit. (The distinction between connivance and condonation is that the former precedes while the latter postdates the adultery, so she did allege that O'Shea had encouraged her to have an affair with Parnell.) By this time, the idea that her husband might stick to his guns had presumably crossed Katie's mind, and her entering such a comprehensive list of counter-charges can be viewed as an attempt either to threaten him or, if she were to be forced into court, to have as solid a case as possible. Probably she hoped that tough measures, which could blacken her husband's character as much as he hoped to blacken hers, would cause him to collapse. If this was her hope it was not realised, and Sir Edward Clarke considered Katie's actions puzzling in the extreme. He made the obvious comment that by alleging condonation the adultery itself was admitted, and said he could not imagine who had advised her to take these steps. The answer was that Katie took nobody's advice; she dismissed one firm of solicitors in August and for several weeks thereafter remained without legal advice; and when George Lewis (who acted for her later) eventually handed her over to another solicitor he commented, 'I wish you joy of your client. I don't know how long you will keep her. She's a very charming lady but an impossible one. However, I hope you have better luck.'

Apart from the tacit admittance of the adultery (which could have been a good reason why Katie fell out with her solicitors in August), the most puzzling item in the counter-petition was among the list of Captain O'Shea's alleged adulteries, for Katie accused her sister Anna of having had an affair with him. One appreciates that if she could prove adultery between her sister and her husband it would negate the injurious effects of Parnell's having seduced his friend's wife, but unless she was certain she was going into court to fight hard (which she was not) it was an allegation of which she should have steered clear. The alleged affair between Anna and Willie was comparatively ancient history—Katie placed it in the year 1881—and the immediate effect of her charge was to close the Wood—Captain O'Shea ranks more tightly, while the longer-term effect was highly damaging. Willie O'Shea wrote to Chamberlain about the matter, saying, 'You can imagine the indignation of her brothers and sisters, low as she had sunk with them before', but he attributed the action to her lover's evil influence, saying that he had been astounded when he had heard 'of the depths to which Parnell has now dragged her.' If there was an element of sense in Katie's bringing her sister into the battle (providing she intended to contest the divorce strongly), one nevertheless feels that she involved Anna because she was particularly furious with her sister over the part she had played in the Lunacy Petition and the probate action and more recently in the pourparlers. The two sisters had been friends for many years and it is a human characteristic to turn most fiercely on those for whom one has cared.

In his letters to Chamberlain in August, Willie relayed the further information that he was being subjected to 'every kind of injury and persecution, gross extortion, attempts to corrupt witnesses of mine, unremitting shadowing', that his solicitors were being constantly plied with suggestions of compromise 'so as to avert a national calamity', and later in September that there was a conspiracy at work for the purpose of effecting his ruin which was being directed by Patrick Egan (the ex–Land League treasurer, then living in America) and Michael Davitt. From the moment O'Shea decided on his divorce action an extra strain of paranoia creeps into his correspondence with Chamberlain (it had always been there to an extent, with the illusions of grandeur, the sense of Parnell's betrayal and malicious hounding by the Irish nationalists). Without doubt, O'Shea was being subjected to pressure from various sources, though whether it extended to conspiracies is another matter, but the assertion that Michael Davitt was one of his persecutors is interesting because Davitt himself claimed that he was the first person to warn Parnell of the nature of O'Shea's case. Certainly he (and Egan) had been deeply involved in collecting information for the Special Commission hearings and both of them had proved good at it (it was Egan who initially put the finger on Richard Pigott as the forger), but if they were trying to amass the same sort of detailed information to smash O'Shea before he got into court, they received no co-operation or encouragement from Parnell or Katie, who were going their own ways. O'Shea also told Chamberlain of the pressure being exerted upon him by Cardinal Manning and Archbishop Walsh, but said he was being sustained by other members of the hierarchy who were seeking support from Rome. (The Pope had long shown a dislike for Mr Parnell so this would not be difficult to obtain.) Chamberlain made few replies to O'Shea's letters at this period, but he commented that the Irish bishops would have a splendid get-out in that Parnell was a Protestant and they were therefore not responsible for his morals.

On the practical course that matters were taking, also in August O'Shea told Chamberlain that his wife had applied for further time to prepare her affidavits and documents and the judge had allowed her fourteen days. He said Katie did not appear to have any idea of her legal obligations and seemed to regard court orders as something she could ignore. She almost certainly did, as her sense of the divine right of kings (and queens) was growing stronger as her ability to manage events weakened. In early September O'Shea told Chamberlain that 'it was only by serving Notice that application would be made to the Vacation Judge to commit her to jail for contempt of court' that his wife finally produced her affidavits and other documents. (It should be noted that Chamberlain was again not directly involved in O'Shea's divorce case, as he sailed for America at the beginning of August and the correspondence was consequently long-distance.) Once the required documents had been prised from a reluctant Katharine (and she did not file her final charges until 4 November), a date for the hearing could be set, and the case of O'Shea v. O'Shea and Parnell (Steele intervening) was scheduled for Saturday, 15 November 1890.

With the date for the hearing set, the Liberals decided they must contact Mr Parnell to ascertain what was likely to happen in court, and on 3 November John Morley wrote to Gladstone to say he had finally received a signal from Parnell who had suggested a meeting in Brighton the following week. Morley also relayed information which casts another shaft of light on Katie's manoeuvring, thus: 'I understand—this is for yourself exclusively—that O'Shea was formally asked recently whether, if no defence were made, he would still insist on casting mud at Parnell. He replied, No, but he must be guided by his counsel.' Morley commented that the counsel was Sir Edward Clarke, who he feared would do his best to get 'as many nasty things out as possible', and he also feared there were plenty of them to be unearthed. On 10 November the meeting between Morley and Parnell took place at the Hotel Metropole in Brighton, and the former noted the Irish leader's 'virtuous degree of punctuality' in arriving 'only two hours after the appointed time.' The two men spent the evening together—they had dinner and repaired to the lounge—informally discussing the Irish land question and various facets of a new Home Rule Bill. Eventually Morley got round to the raison d'être of the meeting, and as he told Gladstone, 'I was bold enough to ask him, with our apologies, whether there was any chance of certain legal proceedings resulting in his disappearance, temporary or otherwise, from the political stage.' To this apologetic query Parnell gave the reply which has been quoted over and over again, 'Oh no, nothing in the least leading to my disappearance will come out of the legal proceedings. The other side don't know what a broken-kneed horse they are riding.'

John Morley was not the only person to whom Parnell gave such categorical assurances. He also told Michael Davitt that he would emerge from the divorce court without the slightest stain on his name or reputation. Thus, only a few days before the hearing which wrecked his career and hopes of an Anglo-Irish settlement, Parnell told a highly influential Liberal and a similarly influential Irish nationalist that he and they had nothing to fear from the forthcoming suit. Despite the fact that both men had good knowledge of what O'Shea's case was likely to be (Morley from his inside information, Davitt from his own investigations), they accepted the assurances. Morley had reservations, since he was a more sophisticated, less passionate man than Davitt and less clouded by Parnell's Irish mystique, but in the face of such conviction, coming from a man not noted for the wildness or woolliness of his utterances, there seemed every reason for believing Parnell. Had he not recently turned the tables on *The Times* when the evidence had appeared overwhelming? Might he not do the same with O'Shea?

What led Parnell to give these uncharacteristically revealing assurances—and only a few days before the suit was due to be heard? The question of not defending the case had already been raised, and Parnell's only known move in the months preceding the hearing was to enquire whether there was a European country to which Mrs O'Shea could go with the two girls who were 'unquestionably' his and be safe even if an English court granted custody to her husband. Neither Katie nor he had left the country, and if the case was undefended the nastiest possible things could emerge, so what made Parnell so confidently optimistic? The answer appears to be that even in the last week Katie believed she could bribe her husband. She told Henry Harrison that if she could have laid her hands on £20,000 she could have bought off her husband at the eleventh-and-a-half hour. Sir Edward Clarke confirmed that O'Shea had been offered such a sum on the eve of the proceedings and O'Shea himself told Chamberlain that 'the last offer was made to me through my son the evening before the trial, and was equivalent to £60,000.' Thus Parnell felt able to give such categoric assurances to John Morley and Michael Davitt.

Katie's account of the day before Armageddon—as officially related in her memoirs—is detailed, at least in contrast to her skimpy treatment of the previous eleven months. If one places her muted version against other people's accounts, there emerges a sequence of events which makes sense and reinforces Parnell's optimism. On Friday,

14 November, he and Katie went up to London to see Frank Lockwood, the QC who had been retained for her, and she recorded Lockwood as begging her to persuade Parnell to let him fight the case on her behalf. She replied that she doubted her ability to do so, but the matter was not settled on 14 November, and Katie and Parnell returned to Brighton, leaving Lockwood with the promise that they would telegraph him by eight o'clock the next morning with instructions whether or not he was to defend the case for Mrs O'Shea. This gesture would seem to have been cutting matters to the bone (the hearing was scheduled to open at 10 a.m.), but if one accepts that Katie was still hoping to buy off her husband or, if she failed, was considering whether to defend, it makes sense. When she and Parnell left Lockwood's office, the final offer to O'Shea had only just been made and they were hopeful it would be accepted, in which case Lockwood's appearance in court would be a formality. If the offer was refused, Katie thought she might be able to persuade Parnell to let her defend the suit, in which case Lockwood would go into court with the accumulated evidence. The contention that Katie had not finally made up her mind about defending is upheld by a paragraph which appeared in the *Freeman's Journal* on the morning of the trial. The paragraph said the case was expected to last a week, Captain O'Shea was calling thirty witnesses, Mrs Steele was determined to clear her character and 'Mrs O'Shea was at the courts yesterday and has expressed herself in favour of the fullest investigations.'

After the visits to Lockwood and the court, Katie and Parnell returned to Brighton by train, in the Pullman car since they were unable to obtain a private compartment, and she said it was one of the more hideous journeys of her life. She must have been under barely endurable strain, not knowing whether her husband would capitulate, but the particular hideousness of the journey was because everybody in the carriage recognised Parnell. Normally Katie admitted to enjoying the moments of recognition and to basking in the reflected glory, but on this occasion she was suffering from a neuralgic headache, and seen through her mists of pain the passengers appeared like menacing animals, their eyes gleaming in anticipation of destruction. Parnell was oblivious of the eyes staring at him openly or from behind newspapers, and smiled cheerfully at the miserable Katie throughout the journey.

On their arrival at 10 Walsingham Terrace, Parnell immediately put Katie to bed and sat by her bedside feeding her morsels of food and making her sip a glass of sparkling Moselle, a wine which had been prescribed for her neuralgic attacks. After he had eaten his own dinner, he returned to the bedroom and again sat by Katie's side while they discussed the action they should take the next day. Presumably by this time they had learned that O'Shea had refused the final offer, lacking in concrete substance as it was, for Katie had been unable to find anybody who would lend her £20,000 (or £60,000, which sounds more O'Shea's price) on the prospect of her winning the probate action. A strong sense of anxiety, not to say fear, permeates her account of the final evening, but she asserted that she was prepared to fight and that it was Parnell who refused. Several writers on the nationalist side, including William O'Brien, Tim Healy and Wilfrid Scawen Blunt, were equally emphatic that it was Mrs O'Shea who persuaded the domestically pliant Parnell not to contest the divorce because it was she who wanted to marry him and become the uncrowned Queen of Ireland. But Katie's whole plan of campaign makes it clear that she intended to emerge victorious; she was convinced that she could buy her husband off, that if she delayed and counter-threatened he would collapse for the due financial consideration, and when the fact that he could not be bought this time (at least not by her) finally penetrated, she still wanted to defend the case. It is a moot point whether her basic premise, that she could in this instance silence her husband as she had silenced him for the past decade, was correct. O'Shea had endured years of humiliation—that he had accepted them was immaterial—and he wanted his revenge. He had Katie's upper-class family backing him—and among his paranoiac wails there was one gleam of light, for he retold Chamberlain of the affection and sympathy being lavished on him by the Woods. If he allowed himself to be bought this time, to withdraw his petition or let Katie divorce him, he would become a laughing-stock in the circles in which he moved, his honour would be tattered beyond repair, not to mention that he would incur the wrath of the Wood family and Parnell's political opponents, prominent among whom was his friend Joseph Chamberlain.

In the discussions by the bedside on the evening of 14 November, Katie quoted Parnell as saying, 'We have been longing for this freedom all these years, and now you are afraid!'—assuring her that she had been his salvation, that his private life belonged to her, and displaying his fatalism: 'If they turn from me, my Queen, it matters not at all in the end. What the ultimate government of Ireland will be is settled, and it will be so, and what my share in the work has been and is to be, also.' When she fell into an exhausted sleep, Katie said she was intending to travel to London in the morning, having not absolutely made up her mind whether or not to contest the suit. If only subconsciously, she must in fact have agreed with Parnell that if they wanted their freedom they must refrain from defence, because she did not take measures to have herself wakened on the Saturday morning as she would surely have done had she been genuinely undecided. When she eventually awoke on 15 November she found a cheerful Parnell sitting by her bedside, pouring a cup of tea and buttering toast for her, and as she shook herself into consciousness and asked what the hour was, he laughed and said, 'I've done you this time, Queenie: I sent the telegram long ago, and they must be enjoying themselves in Court by now.'

Chapter Sixteen

The hearing of O'Shea v. O'Shea and Parnell (Steele intervening) opened at 10 a.m. on 15 November 1890, in Number One Court of the Royal Courts of Justice. This was the chamber in which the Special Commission had sat, and one wonders if it was coincidence that the divorce suit was heard in the same court from which Parnell had recently emerged in triumph. The case was heard before Mr Justice Butt and a special jury,* and both press and public galleries were crammed to bursting point. The proceedings started with Captain O'Shea's solicitor saying that the petitioner sought a dissolution of his marriage on the grounds of his wife's adultery with Charles Stewart Parnell and emphatically denied the charges levelled against him in the respondent's counter-petition. Frank Lockwood then said he represented the respondent, Mrs O'Shea, but he would not be calling any witnesses, would not be cross-examining or taking part in the proceedings, and it was established that the co-respondent, Mr Parnell, was not represented at all. Sir Edward Clarke rose to open the case for Captain O'Shea and said he would not now need to call many witnesses, as it was practically unde-

---

* In an era when divorce was uncommon, divorce proceedings before a special jury (i.e. males who possessed extra property qualifications on the electoral register) were common and the petitioner then had the right to demand that his suit be heard before a jury.

fended. In lay terms the case was undefended, but the qualification was justified as Katie had entered her defence, which was read to the court, and it was her allegations that the petitioner had induced her to make the acquaintance of the co-respondent for his material gain and had connived at and condoned the adultery between 1880 and 1886 that allowed Sir Edward Clarke to introduce the most damaging evidence. Had the suit been entirely undefended (as it was on Parnell's side), Sir Edward would have been able only to produce evidence of adultery, but he further said it was his duty to remove from Captain O'Shea's character the gross imputations to which it had been subjected by the respondent's charges, and thereby the area of admissible evidence was widened.

How much Sir Edward Clarke enjoyed himself as he did his duty is a question only he could answer, but he can hardly have been in a delighted frame of mind until shortly before the proceedings opened (when Frank Lockwood informed him that he would not be defending). Until that moment Clarke must surely have had misgivings, because his client's case was as full of holes as a sieve; even laymen could note some of them and two laymen did, as we shall see. When Sir Edward rose to present the case he knew it would be unchallenged by expert counsel, and all he had to do was to convince the judge and jury that despite its holes it could be plugged to hold water. He gave a résumé of the O'Sheas' life from the time of their marriage in 1867 until the year 1880, noting that Katie was a lady of good family (who should have known better than to have behaved as she had done), saying that from the evidence of personal letters these years had been ones of unbroken domestic happiness, notwithstanding the fact that Captain O'Shea had experienced pecuniary difficulties over his 'racing stables' in Hertfordshire. It was established that three children were born in 1870, 1873 and 1874 (Gerard, Norah and Carmen) and that a further child was born in 1882 who had died shortly after birth (this was a good move, as 1881 and 1882 were tricky years evidentially). It was further established that Mrs O'Shea went to live at Wonersh Lodge in 1874 at the express desire of her aged aunt, to whom Mrs O'Shea acted as companion, that Captain O'Shea resided at Eltham during the years 1874–1880, except when business necessitated his presence in London, where he had chambers taken for him by Mrs Wood. In 1880 Captain O'Shea entered Parliament and thereby made the acquaintance of Charles Stewart Parnell, whom he invited to a dinner party at Thomas's

Hotel in Berkeley Square. Nothing happened to excite Captain O'Shea's suspicions about his wife's relations with the co-respondent until July 1881, when he returned from Spain to find that Mr Parnell had been staying at Wonersh Lodge without his knowledge or permission. Then came the evidence about the scenes with his wife, Anna Steele's intervention, the challenge to the duel, the throwing of Parnell's portmanteau onto Charing Cross station, all of which incidents, according to Sir Edward Clarke (and O'Shea's own testimony), occurred within a brief space in July. After these eruptions came peace and, again according to Sir Edward, 'the affectionate relations which had always existed between Captain O'Shea and his wife were resumed.'

Later in 1881 Captain O'Shea invited Mr Parnell to stay again at Eltham but this was at his wife's suggestion, since she said Mr Parnell's ceasing to visit might cause as adverse comment as his previous too-frequent sojourns. Captain O'Shea believed that Mr Parnell's visits to Wonersh Lodge were now rare, whereas in fact the co-respondent was spending a great deal of time there, arriving at all hours of night and day, by irregular means of transport, and sleeping in a bedroom which was interconnected with Mrs O'Shea's. These visits continued throughout 1882 with Captain O'Shea remaining in ignorance of them, despite his being engaged in delicate political negotiations on Mr Parnell's behalf. In March 1883 another child was born to Mrs O'Shea, a girl who was still alive, and shortly thereafter the family went down to Brighton, a fact of which Captain O'Shea was aware, as he occasionally visited them. In his absence another visitor called who was known to the staff as 'Mr Smith', and later in the same year a further house was rented in Brighton, where Mr Parnell was known to the staff as 'Mr Stewart' and where he usually called when Captain O'Shea was absent. In March 1884 Captain O'Shea had to go to Spain on business, and when he returned, some time in July, he heard fresh rumours about his wife's relationship with Mr Parnell and tackled her on the subject. The letters were then produced in which Willie said he would resign his parliamentary seat and take his wife and family out of the country, and Katie's and Parnell's replies which said nothing about the adultery, but according to Sir Edward Clarke both the respondent and co-respondent gave denials of their adultery and 'the matter was again closed.' By early 1885 Mrs O'Shea and Mr Parnell had so successfully lulled Captain O'Shea's suspicions that the co-respondent felt able to bring his horses over from Ireland and stable them at Wonersh Lodge and the respondent to build a room onto her house specifically for the co-respondent, one moreover which adjoined her downstairs sitting-room.

May 1886 saw the publication of the *Pall Mall Gazette* piece about Mr Parnell's suburban retreat and this did arouse Captain O'Shea's suspicions, but a letter of Katie's was read to the court in which she said she had no idea what her husband was going on about, and the *Pall Mall Gazette* article was surely meant to get a rise out of him. A telegram of Parnell's was also produced in which he said he was sorry if the article had caused Mrs O'Shea annoyance and he hoped to see her on Sunday. As was pointed out by Sir Edward Clarke, Mr Parnell was in permanent residence at Wonersh Lodge at the time he sent this telegram. There was further information about Katie and Parnell removing the offending horses from the stables 'lest Captain O'Shea should come down and find them there.' Extensive correspondence between Mrs O'Shea and her husband, covering the summer and autumn of 1886, was then read to the court, including the flat denial from Katie that she knew anything about Mr Parnell's whereabouts in Eastbourne, at a time when Sir Edward Clarke could prove that the two of them had been living in the town for a period of nineteen weeks. Evidence about the houses Parnell had rented in the early months of 1887 under the assumed names was given, with the implication that they had been rented in an attempt to deceive the by now somewhat suspicious Captain O'Shea. Sir Edward Clarke then produced the letter written by Katie's solicitor during the 1887 manoeuvrings in which she denied that her husband had grounds for his suspicions.

Next O'Shea was examined by junior counsel, and whether he enjoyed himself in his hour of triumph is again a question only he could answer. After the first day's hearing he wrote to Chamberlain saying nobody but he knew what a fight it had been to get the case into court, of 'the influences religious, social and pecuniary that were brought to bear in the hope of "squaring me" ', but he did not elaborate on his emotions as he actually stood up in court. The *Pall Mall Gazette* said he appeared in the witness box 'looking spick and span . . . very calm and composed', but unless paranoia had taken hold of O'Shea's brain, despite his calm exterior he must have given his evidence with some inward tremors because it was not the whole truth and nothing but the truth, even allowing that the two children born in 1883 and 1884 could have been his, that he did not know of the adultery until 1887, and that his acceptance of Aunt Ben's money was unconnected with his wife's

[231]

liaison. Generally O'Shea elaborated on the themes presented by Sir Edward Clarke, providing extra information about his deceived un-awareness and producing further damaging letters. To him was given the *pièce de résistance* in the shape of Katie's June 1887 letters to Gerard in which she had stated that there would be no further com-munication, direct or indirect, with Mr Parnell. O'Shea said his suspi-cions had then naturally been completely allayed and it was not until December 1889 that he received information that Mr Parnell was living with his wife in Brighton and thereafter consulted his solicitors and filed his divorce petition. Finally he was asked about the allegation that he had committed adultery with his wife's sister, Mrs Anna Steele, and he replied that there was not the slightest truth in it or indeed in any of his wife's counter-charges. He said his wife and Mrs Steele had been on most affectionate terms in 1881 when the adultery was supposed to have been committed, in fact the sisters had remained on affectionate terms until very recently. He was then asked by Anna Steele's counsel whether this particular charge had been made in July 1890 at a time when there was a great deal of ill-feeling between his wife and her sister 'owing to a pending probate suit.' O'Shea agreed that this was true, and the idea that Katharine had acted wantonly, after a family row over money, was firmly planted.

To prove the case and refute the counter-charges, substantive evidence other than the letters was required, and independent witnesses were successively called to the stand to be examined by Sir Edward Clarke. The first witness was Harriett Bull, who had been employed at 39 Bedford Square, Brighton, when Katie rented the house in the spring of 1883. She confirmed that Captain O'Shea visited the house 'some-times, but not often', that his visits did not coincide with those of Mr Parnell (whom she identified from a photograph), and that Katie and Parnell had been heard together in the bedroom, but she did not confirm that Parnell had been known to the staff there as 'Mr Smith'. It was the next witness, Caroline Pethers, employed as a cook at the Medina Terrace house in Brighton rented towards the end of 1883, who gave the most extraordinary and damaging evidence. She said that Mr Parnell first visited the house in the company of Captain O'Shea but then ap-peared later without him, and the court was asked to believe either that in O'Shea's company he was known by his real name but without him as 'Mr Stewart', or that he was known as Mr Stewart on both occasions, in which case there was nothing peculiar about the alias. (In the absence of cross-examination the evidence was suitably fuzzy and wholly damaging.) Mrs Pethers further testified that Mrs O'Shea and Mr Parnell 'were nearly always locked in a room together' and that Mr Parnell frequently slept at the house in Captain O'Shea's absence; and she then related that on one occasion Mr Parnell and Mrs O'Shea were in the drawing-room when Captain O'Shea rang the front door-bell, lo and behold ten minutes later who should ring the door-bell but Mr Parnell himself, requesting to see the Captain. When asked how she thought Mr Parnell had managed to make his dramatic appearance on the doorstep she said he could not have escaped by the stairs, but there were two rope fire-escapes from the upstairs drawing-room in question. Not content with presenting this single and singular picture of the Irish leader climbing down a rope fire-escape in full view of passers-by, Mrs Pethers said, 'This happened three or four times'; and what logic made Parnell ring the front door-bell on four occasions instead of quietly disappearing from the scene, was not explained. Why Mrs Pethers invented the story—because it really cannot have happened the way she described it—remains her secret, but if her motive was to hog the limelight, to be important for once in a dull life, she achieved her ambition. Why Sir Edward Clarke allowed her to prepare this evidence is another interesting question, because if the case had been defended, the testimony would surely have been attacked; but then, if it had been defended, Mrs Pethers's testimony might have been severely curtailed.

At this point Mr Justice Butt said he would be prepared to give his opinion to the jury if the Solicitor General would care to close his case, but Sir Edward Clarke had more witnesses to call and the intervenor, Mrs Steele, was not in court as she had not anticipated the lack of defence and consequent swiftness in the presentation of Captain O'Shea's case. Mr Justice Butt therefore agreed to a resumption of the hearing on the Monday morning, and on no more damaging note could Sir Edward have closed than on Caroline Pethers's story. The evening papers carried full reports, and the *Pall Mall Gazette* had line drawings of Mr Justice Butt, Mr Lockwood, Sir Edward Clarke, Mr Parnell and Captain O'Shea, but not one of Katie, which shows how secluded her life had been and how little she was known. The *Gazette*'s report was a mass of misinformation on minor detail—Katie's father was a noted surgeon, the first dinner party had been at the Hotel Bristol, and Wonersh Lodge was referred to as Warwickshire Lodge (the Eltham house came in for a variety of interesting spellings—the *Freeman's*

Journal called it One Ash, a nice translation of the oral evidence, or perhaps it was thinking of the late John Bright, whose Rochdale address had been One Ash). Despite the errors, the *Pall Mall Gazette* got the essentials correct, as did the other evening and Sunday papers, and by the end of the first day the essentials were sordid and sensational.·

When the hearing was resumed on Monday morning, 17 November, Sir Evelyn Wood and Gerard O'Shea were in court, as well as Anna Steele, and the *Pall Mall Gazette* said much attention was focussed on them (it described Gerard as 'a young man of sturdy build and dapper dress—the sort of youth whom any football captain would be proud to include in his team'). Mr Justice Butt reopened the proceedings by saying he did not approve of Mr Parnell being identified from photographs. Sir Edward Clarke said neither did he and in fact Mr Parnell had been subpoenaed to attend. It was then agreed that in this instance photographic identification would be sufficient and Sir Edward continued to roll out further witnesses. There was a lady who had been in Katie's employment at Wonersh Lodge in 1880 and 1882 who gave evidence about Parnell's late-night and early-morning arrivals, the situation of his bedroom in relation to Mrs O'Shea's and his constant residence between May and October 1882, and who said that Captain O'Shea appeared occasionally at week-ends 'but not very often' and that she had been instructed to tell anybody enquiring for Mr Parnell that the gentleman was not in the house. Next came a lady who had been employed by Katie between July and August 1885, and she testified that Parnell was then living at Wonersh Lodge, that a new room had been built for him, that he and Mrs O'Shea were out together every day, frequently returning after midnight. She was followed by Parnell's groom, who had moved to Eltham with him in 1885 and had stayed in his employment until 1888. He testified about Parnell's horses being stabled at Wonersh Lodge, to their being removed after the *Pall Mall Gazette* piece in 1886, and to taking one of the horses down to Eastbourne, where Parnell was staying with Mrs O'Shea in the summer of 1886. Then came three witnesses who testified to the sojourn in Eastbourne, including the house agent from whom Katie had rented the house and who identified Parnell as the man who had been with her. (The Eastbourne visit was important because the letter had been produced in which Katie had flatly denied knowledge of Parnell's whereabouts.) Finally, there were four witnesses who had been involved in the renting of the houses in Brockley and Regents Park in 1887, and the business of Parnell forgetting whether he was Mr Fox or Mr Preston was elaborated upon. On this note Sir Edward Clarke concluded his case.

Anna Steele was then called and briefly but absolutely denied that she had committed adultery with Captain O'Shea in 1881 or at any time. Before Mr Justice Butt could sum up, a bold juror rose and said he was interested in some of the charges in Mrs O'Shea's counter-petition which he did not think had been fully dealt with and he would therefore like the opportunity to cross-examine some of the witnesses. Mr Justice Butt admitted there were one or two matters which had troubled him, but unfortunately there was no counsel instructed for the respondent, therefore there was nobody who could cross-examine. Sir Edward Clarke said he would recall Captain O'Shea with pleasure, put a few extra questions to him and then, with his lordship's permission, any gentleman of the jury could ask further questions. O'Shea returned to the stand and Clarke re-established that he and his wife had been on most affectionate terms until he had finally learned of her unfaithfulness in 1889, that the arrangement whereby he lived in London and Mrs O'Shea at Eltham was one desired by her aunt, that he and his wife had been in constant communication, with him visiting Eltham on Sundays and his wife coming to London with the children, and that he had never been away from Mrs O'Shea for longer than a week without her consent.

Sir Edward's re-examination did not satisfy the juror and he asked whether Captain O'Shea had been responsible for his family's maintenance and had always cared for his children and their education, to which O'Shea replied 'Certainly.' The juror then asked how Captain O'Shea accounted for his constant absence from Wonersh Lodge when it was only an hour's journey from London, to which O'Shea replied that he was in fact at the house constantly, so the juror asked what he meant by constantly—he was not there every night, was he? O'Shea admitted that he was not but said nobody had accused him of lack of attention to his wife, and his diaries which had been put in evidence would show that he was a kind husband and father. The juror then changed tack and asked why Captain O'Shea had invited Mr Parnell to dinner after challenging him to a duel. O'Shea said he had not invited him to dinner after this incident, the juror said they had heard evidence about a further invitation, and Willie agreed that he had extended it but only because his suspicions had been allayed. The juror then wondered whether there were other letters from Mrs O'Shea which had not been produced in evidence. O'Shea said all his correspondence with his wife was in court (therefore available to the jury) even if it had not all been read. With the parting shot that Wonersh Lodge was only an hour's drive from London, this juror sat down, and an observant, pertinacious gentleman he was. The fact that Mr Parnell had been able to live with Mrs O'Shea at Wonersh Lodge and in Eastbourne, Hastings and Brighton for a period of ten years without Captain O'Shea's knowledge was the largest hole in his case, and if the matter of money had not been raised by Sir Edward Clarke, several of the letters produced against Katharine (particularly in the 1886 period) indicated that Captain O'Shea and his family had been living on Aunt Ben's money.

Another allegation in Katie's counter-petition—that her husband had delayed unreasonably in bringing his divorce action—struck a second juror as having validity. O'Shea had admitted in evidence that his suspicions had been strongly roused in 1886; what he had been doing between receiving his wife's assurance to her son early in 1887 and the moment when he filed his petition at the end of 1889 had been conspicuously ignored. This juror asked when Captain O'Shea had last lived with his wife, to which he replied it was in Brighton in the autumn of 1886 at the Hotel Bristol, he thought. The juror reiterated—was that the last time he had lived with his wife? O'Shea said yes, but he had seen her constantly since. Lacking legal expertise, both jurors abandoned their questioning, and Mr Justice Butt embarked on his summing-up. He stressed the difficulty of having heard only one side of the case but said the question of the adultery seemed to him to have been proved without any shadow of doubt; however, there was the question of the defence entered by the respondent. The allegation of neglect was a discretionary defence which would not prevent the granting of a divorce even if proven, and Mr Justice Butt instructed the jury to ignore this aspect of the counter-petition. The charges of connivance and collusion would most definitely prevent the granting of the petition and his lordship said the jury had to ask themselves this question: Ought the word of Captain O'Shea, who had sworn on oath that there was no truth in the allegations of collusion or connivance, to be believed, bearing in mind that no oral evidence had been presented to substantiate the respondent's written statements? Having put this question to the jury, Mr Justice Butt said that he had no doubt that Captain O'Shea should be believed; the persistent denials, the disguises adopted by Mr Parnell, the episode of the fire-escape, all pointed to the respondent and co-respondent's successful deception and to Captain O'Shea's innocence. Mr Justice Butt underlined the damage done to Parnell's reputation by Katie's counter-petition when he said:

> *If it had appeared that the husband was really a consenting party and accessory to his wife's guilt, Mr Parnell, although the issue of adultery might have been found against him, would still have stood in a better position than he does at present, because although it is an immoral, improper and reprehensible thing to indulge in intimacy of this kind with a married woman, whether her husband is a consenting party or not, nevertheless the man who stands in that position is to some extent not so guilty or blameworthy as the man who takes advantage of the hospitality offered him by the husband to debauch his wife.*

Interestingly, Willie O'Shea considered Butt a most partisan judge and said, 'If Clarke had not stuck to him like a bull terrier I should have been beaten throughout.' This might be taken as an example of his increasing paranoia, because nobody else considered his lordship to be pro-Parnell or pro-Katie, and on the whole Butt's handling of the case was impartial because he had to judge on what he heard in court—and if there were admittedly holes in the petitioner's case they *had* been plugged by the lack of defence and O'Shea's sworn testimony.

Having stated his opinion on the main points of the petition, Mr Justice Butt passed to the allegation of adultery between Mrs Steele and Captain O'Shea and said in his view it should never have been made. The jury were then asked to return their verdict, which they did without hesitation, finding the respondent, Katharine O'Shea, guilty of adultery with Charles Stewart Parnell, and that her husband had not connived at the adultery, and Mr Justice Butt pronounced a decree *nisi*. The matter of costs had to be dealt with, and his lordship awarded them against Mr Parnell but reserved judgement in respect of Mrs O'Shea until he had ascertained whether she had a separate estate. The long-silent Frank Lockwood then rose to beg his lordship similarly to reserve judgement in the matter of the custody of the younger children. Mr Justice Butt said usually custody was awarded to the innocent party, Sir Edward

Clarke claimed for the usual procedure to be followed in Captain O'Shea's case and his lordship duly ordered that it should be done. Thereby O'Shea obtained legal custody of Katie and Clare, which was an ace up his sleeve in any further battles with his wife, and the fact that the only intervention made by Katie's counsel was on behalf of young Katie and Clare seems to underline Parnell's unquestionable paternity.

Once the decree *nisi* had been pronounced, the newspapers were free to make comment and column after column in Great Britain and America, indeed in most countries of the world, was filled with reports of the O'Shea divorce and speculation about Parnell's and Ireland's future. In Britain the Tory, Unionist and generally anti-Parnellite papers followed *The Times*'s lead and enjoyed their moment of triumphant vindication to the full; they might have been wrong in principle in the Pigott affair but, by God, they had been proved right in theory. Parnell had been revealed for what he was, a base, treacherous, lying, deceitful rogue, and no reasonable person could fail to draw the connection between the private behaviour and the public cause. How could Home Rule be justified in the hands of such a man? To the anti-Parnellite sectors Captain O'Shea appeared as an honourable gentleman whose only fault had been 'trusting too easily the word of a treacherous friend, and of declining to believe vague rumours affecting the false wife'. The Liberal newspapers in Britain and the non-nationalist but always more pro-Irish than British newspapers in America were in a difficult position, and their columns recorded the view that the revelations had in no degree affected the soundness or worthiness of Home Rule as a legislative policy. With respect to the gallant Captain, the *New York Herald* stated: 'It is impossible to find a man of the world who does not believe that O'Shea was guilty of connivance'; and the *Liverpool Daily Post* commented: 'The way of life of Captain and Mrs O'Shea appears to have been undomestic.' The more rabid Irish and Irish-American nationalist papers adhered to the view that the case was the result of political machinations—the *Irish World* said it was 'part and parcel of the Pigott conspiracy, concocted by the same managers and carried out to serve the same ends'; while the more responsible nationalist papers followed the *Freeman's Journal* line on the question of changing leadership: 'We would not if we could. We could not if we would.' Outside Ireland and the ultra-nationalist papers in America, there was the belief that Parnell's leadership was now untenable, whether one approved of Home Rule or not, that he must resign, if only temporarily, but the matter was one which should be left for Ireland herself to decide, with the implication that as a devoutly Catholic country she would surely come to the right conclusion and demand Mr Parnell's resignation. With a few exceptions the newspaper attacks on Parnell were not immediately venomous, and Katie's role in the affair was then ignored. One of the exceptions was the *Sheffield Telegraph,* which wrote of 'a serpent which, when uncaged from Kilmainham, fastened its torturing fingers upon the very hand that had uncaged him, and left its slimy trail upon the domestic Eden into which he had crept.' This piece of purple prose and mixed metaphors earned the comment from *Vanity Fair* that 'provincial telegraphese is quite up to metropolitan standards.'

As far as the public was concerned, it was the fire-escape episode which caused the most damage, with the Mr Fox alias running a close second and the allegation of adultery against Anna Steele coming third. If one reads the divorce evidence carefully it is virtually impossible to resist the conclusion that O'Shea had condoned the affair (as the *New York Herald* said), but few people bother to read pages of densely packed evidence and those who might have been so inclined in 1890 were overwhelmed by the vision of 'Mr Fox flying down the fire-escape.' It was not only the newspaper columnists who enjoyed themselves; cartoonists had a field day, so did music-hall comedians and toy manufacturers, and models of the Brighton fire-escape, complete with miniature Parnell, were soon on sale. Both he and O'Shea were later alleged to have said that the house in question did not possess a fire-escape, rope or otherwise, and to anybody who knew the proud, fearless man the idea of his dodging Willie O'Shea in this manner was inconceivable, but it was obviously not to the public at large. Apart from the ridiculous aspect of the divorce court revelations, Mary Gladstone nicely summarised the revulsion of those who had recently put Parnell on a pedestal and of the contrast between the bold public man and the squalidly deceitful lover, thus: 'He has lived this life of lies all these years. A heartrending revelation. "Blot out his name" '; and thus: 'If only he had fought O'Shea and gone off with Mrs and owned it to everybody, I wd. not half mind.' Mary found one ray of light 'in his refusing publicly to perjure himself, as all our English gentlemen think it right and honourable to do in these matters', but she was almost alone in taking this view and most people saw the failure to defend the suit as a straight admission of guilt.

Another aspect which gained a considerable amount of column

space, particularly in the American newspapers, was the contrast with previous famous British adulterers. Nelson and Lady Hamilton topped everybody's list—and what harm had that liaison done to England's most renowned admiral?—with the Duke of Wellington and his amours, and Lord Melbourne and his involvement in a divorce case coming close behind. In refutation it was pointed out that neither Nelson nor Wellington had held the political future of a nation in his hands (the command of armies and navies was a different matter) and that Lord Melbourne had emerged unscathed from the divorce court (though quite as guilty as Parnell). In a letter written by Gladstone to John Morley a few days after the divorce, he noted: 'If I recollect, Southey's *Life of Nelson* was in my early days published and circulated by the Society for Promoting Christian Knowledge', and he wondered how future biographers of Parnell would treat 'the tender points'. The answer was that for years they ignored them almost as completely as had Robert Southey in his biography.

One man who kept well away from the centre of the storm and made only the briefest comment was Joseph Chamberlain. Whatever his involvement in the institution of the divorce proceedings, he wisely refrained from expressing an opinion on their resolution. In fact, he only returned from the United States as the decree *nisi* was granted and although besieged by reporters he refused to be drawn, other than making the comparison with the effects of Sir Charles Dilke's divorce which, as everybody knew, had been to ruin his career. As for the two people most closely involved in the affair, they were immured in 10 Walsingham Terrace, Brighton, with at least one O'Shea child, their own two children, Katie and Clare, their devoted servants and their animals. (O'Shea had been granted legal custody of Katie and Clare but he never tried to claim them. They remained a useful weapon in the probate action which still had to be fought.) The O'Shea child who stayed with her mother was Norah, but one assumes that Gerard was with his father and also Carmen, as she definitely moved in with him in the New Year of 1891. Walsingham Terrace was surrounded by reporters and sightseers—Katie wrote of the people who drove out from Brighton to view Parnell's house in normal times, and in these abnormal ones there was a constant flow of traffic. The reporters were trying to obtain interviews with Mr Parnell or Mrs O'Shea, but none of them was successful. Katie herself followed newspaper reports even if Parnell did not, as one of the letters produced in court contained the side-information that she subscribed to the Romeike press-cutting agency, a titbit which showed her interest in what was written about her and her lover. (She may also have been trying to keep one jump ahead of Captain O'Shea's reactions.) Less impervious to criticism than Parnell and more given to subjective moral outrage, she was perhaps somewhat shattered by the storm they had created, but her only comment on the days immediately following the hearing was that she and Parnell were particularly happy when the decree *nisi* was brought down to them in Brighton. He determined to have the document framed and was not amused by her suggestion that now she was almost free he might marry somebody else, and they spent the evening discussing where they should go and what they should do once the decree absolute had been granted, but not apparently in contemplating the Irish scene. There is evidence that Parnell was swiftly in a less happy frame of mind, that is, in respect of domestic not political affairs. A few days after the divorce hearing, he was in London, where he called in to Frank Lockwood's office and verbally attacked the distinguished counsel by saying that in failing to make an agreement about his children he had betrayed him and Mrs O'Shea. Lockwood said he had done nothing of the sort and nobody should speak to him in such a way, whereupon Parnell reputedly said, 'I see what you are going to do. You are bigger and stronger than I am, and you are thinking of throwing me out of the window.' Lockwood later commented that throughout the interview Parnell was so wild and peculiar in his manner as to show signs of insanity.

There was a hiatus for a few days following the granting of Captain O'Shea's petition, but unfortunately the adoption of clear stances by the three sectors most affected by the divorce—the nationalists, the Liberals and the Irish Catholic hierarchy—could not be delayed because the new session of Parliament opened on 25 November and the nationalists had to elect, or re-elect, their parliamentary leader, the man with whom the Liberal Party would have to negotiate, the man who, if the Liberals carried Home Rule after the General Election, would become the first Prime Minister of semi-autonomous Ireland.* The matter was precipitated by the fact that two meetings occurred on 20

---

* Some nationalist papers said the divorce hearing was deliberately timed for a few days before the opening of Parliament and the re-election of the Irish leader, but it was Katie who delayed proceedings, not O'Shea.

November, one of which was in the Leinster Hall, Dublin, in protest against the eviction of the tenant farmers, the other of which was the annual assembly of the National Liberal Federation in Sheffield. Both meetings had been scheduled weeks before the divorce suit, but at both the predominating topic became the burning question of Mr Parnell's leadership.

Chapter Seventeen

At the Leinster Hall meeting in Dublin, all those leading members of the nationalist movement currently in the United Kingdom were present. One of the difficulties which faced the nationalists was that six of their most prominent members—John Dillon, William O'Brien, T. P. O'Connor, T. P. Gill, Timothy Harrington and T. D. Sullivan—were in the United States at the time of the crisis, having sailed weeks earlier on a fund-raising mission for the Plan of Campaign. Thus at the moment when a first-hand assessment of the situation was essential, when the nationalists needed to meet in conclave, three thousand miles separated the movement's leaders and Dillon and Company had to rely upon second-hand news relayed by the American newspapers or hasty cables sent by their brethren in London and Dublin. Whatever their private doubts, their immediate public reaction was loyalty to Parnell, and a cable was sent to the Leinster Hall expressing unqualified support for him. (The exception was T. D. Sullivan, whose Catholic conscience forbade him to follow the leadership of a proven adulterer.) Those present at the Leinster Hall also voted overwhelmingly in favour of Parnell's continued leadership and it seemed as if his party would follow him to hell or Connaught. But in the most famous speech of the evening, that given by Tim Healy (and later held most fiercely against him) there was a warning note, for apart from making his stirring calls not to surrender to English opinion and not to speak to the man at the wheel, Healy also said: 'While we owe a duty to Mr Parnell, Mr Parnell owes a duty to us. We have stood by Mr Parnell. Mr Parnell must stand by us.' He could later contend (and thus excuse his disaffection) that Mr Parnell neither considered his duty to Ireland nor stood by the will of the parliamentary party.

The question of English opinion had already become important, for the rumblings of moral outrage, notably among the Nonconformists, made themselves heard from the moment of the divorce. At the Liberal assembly in Sheffield, the two leading members of the party present— John Morley and Sir William Harcourt—gave the flattest, most non-committal speeches possible in an effort not to heighten the temperature, but as Morley wrote to Gladstone, 'The feeling there was as strong as strong could be that Parnell's leadership is, for the time at least, intolerable. They declare they would vote for a Tory govt. rather than H.R. under Parnell.' Morley also wrote, saying: 'Stead has been to see me. He is going to raise the *fiercest whoops* against Parnell remaining in the post of leader—on the grounds that we can no longer have faith in anything that P. says.' By 1890 W. T. Stead was no longer editor of the *Pall Mall Gazette,* but he edited the annual *Review of Reviews* and he had already personally told Gladstone that 'unless Mr Parnell resigns his leadership of the Irish party I shall be—most unwillingly—com-pelled to undertake a vigorous campaign.' The idea of Stead unwillingly entering a moral campaign, particularly if it had to do with sex, is risible, and John Morley's assessment of his fierce whooping was more accurate, but as Stead also told Gladstone, 'I know my Nonconformists, and no power on earth will induce them to follow that man to the poll, or you either, if you are arm in arm with him.' Gladstone was hardly in need of the warnings from his high-ranking supporters because the letters and telegrams and postcards from the grass-roots were pouring in. Most of the correspondence was from Nonconformists; there was a letter sent on behalf of 40,000 Primitive Methodists in East Anglia, dozens from Methodist and Baptist ministers—one from a Baptist minister in Chatham expressed 'the passionate hope that yr. stainless life may be in no sense associated with Mr Parnell's character as revealed in the divorce court'—but there were also letters from 'Cross Benchers' and from the ladies of the Primrose League, stressing that the feeling against Parnell was widespread.

As was his custom, Gladstone jotted down *his* feelings on 'the

O'Shea suit', saying, 'It is no part of my duty as the leader of a party in Parliament, to form a personal judgement on the moral conduct of any other leader or fellow member.' However, it was his inevitable duty to form an estimation of the probable results of the suit, and the first question that arose was: 'What ought in such a case to be held to constitute knowledge? A line has to be drawn for practical purposes and in my opinion, knowledge on a subject of this kind, is cognisance of what has been judicially established. . . . All the matter then, which was put in proof of the O'Shea case, is to be taken as known.' As the judicial proof was so black, as early as this memorandum of 21 November, he adjudged 'with deep pain but without any doubt' that Parnell should retire temporarily from the leadership, and thought that while he had no right to express his views spontaneously he should give them if they were called upon 'from a quarter entitled to make the demands.'

For the time being, 'the quarter entitled to make the demands' (i.e. the Irish nationalists) was not issuing them; on the contrary it was tending to close ranks in the face of the upsurge of British moral outrage. When the Reverend Hugh Price Hughes, a Methodist minister, raised the standard high at a packed meeting at the St James's Hall in London, first using the phrase 'the Nonconformist conscience' and attacking Parnell as 'the most famous adulterer of the century', saying that if the Irish could accept such a man as a leader the British could not and if Ireland continued to accept him then she was morally unfit for self-government, there were some fiercely outraged whoops in Ireland. Virtually the sole exception to the initial nationalist solidarity was Michael Davitt, who as early as 20 November wrote in the *Labour World* (a paper he edited in England) that Parnell's retention of the leadership was untenable. He said it was untenable both on moral and on political grounds, and in a personal letter to Archbishop Walsh he emphasised these latter: 'I ask Parnell to note the tone of the British Home Rule press, and by studying the terrible import of neglecting British Nonconformist opinion to decide at once to efface himself for a few months.' Davitt's stance was partially occasioned by his anger at Parnell's having given him such categoric assurances of innocence only a few days before the debacle, but living and working in England as Davitt did, he was more immediately aware of the strength of Nonconformist opinion than were most Irish nationalists.

The Irish bishops' initial reaction (or lack of) was another matter which later earned much opprobrium, as like Tim Healy so many

[245]

of them (or their lower ranks) turned so viciously on Parnell. The hierarchy could obviously not approve of an adulterer or allow their flock to continue to do so, but they were aware that their flock had given loyalty to Parnell, that he had brought Ireland to the brink of the Home Rule they had recently supported, and they had no desire to raise the old Fenian spectre of priestly intervention in politics. Archbishop Walsh and the venerable Croke of Cashel were the most important bishops, with the highly political Walsh exerting the greatest influence. As did many people, Walsh hoped that Parnell would retire of his own volition, that if the hierarchy kept publicly quiet and privately made their views known, he would do so, then the Irish party would be intact, Home Rule would be saved and the bishops would be able to reassert their authority without having been seen to have intervened. English Catholic opinion also carried weight in the matter, particularly in the hands of Cardinal Manning, who, like Walsh, was worried that the Home Rule movement had fallen into the hands of laymen but, unlike Walsh, was unconcerned that the dethronement of Parnell might irrevocably split the Irish party, and he thought the divorce presented the Irish hierarchy with a splendid opportunity to regain control of the movement. Publicly he too kept quiet but privately he was extremely busy, urging Walsh to repudiate Parnell's leadership and telling Gladstone that the solution rested more with him than with any man.

Gladstone had no wish to be the man who cut this Gordian knot and he too remained hopeful that Parnell would tender his resignation. Had he not offered to apply for the Chiltern Hundreds after the Phoenix Park murders? Surely he would make the same honourable gesture now, and follow the sensible advice so succinctly cabled by Cecil Rhodes: 'Resign. Marry. Return.' As the general British pressure to remove Parnell mounted and he made no gesture, Gladstone decided he would have to do something spontaneous. On 23 November he wrote to Sir William Harcourt from Hawarden, saying he thought Justin McCarthy should be contacted—as Vice-Chairman of the Irish party—and asked whether the Liberals could expect a communication similar to the one they had received after the Phoenix Park murders. If they could not, he thought McCarthy should be informed that 'the continuance of Mr Parnell in the leadership of the Irish party at the present moment would be, notwithstanding his splendid services to his country, so as to act upon British sentiment as to produce the gravest mischief to the cause of Ireland; to place those who represent the Party in a position of irremediable difficulty; and to make the further maintenance of my own leadership for the purpose of that cause little better than a nullity.' The next day Gladstone returned to London and there was a meeting between him, John Morley, Arnold Morley (the Chief Whip) and Sir William Harcourt. Of the august Liberal quartet, Harcourt had never liked Parnell and was for delivering an ultimatum—either retire or we wash our hands of Home Rule—and while John Morley was not a devotee of Parnell's, he had confessed after the Brighton meeting, 'I liked him very much better than I usually do', and he and Gladstone were reluctant to exert too much pressure. After a conclave, the four Liberals agreed that Mr Gladstone should communicate the terms of his Harcourt letter to Justin McCarthy, who had been summoned to attend, and at a private interview between the two men it was presumed that Gladstone had done so.

McCarthy recorded that the interview was momentous, but whether he clearly grasped that Gladstone might retire from the leadership of the Liberal Party—and out of the window would go Home Rule—if Parnell himself did not resign is uncertain. Gladstone was a master of circumlocution in private conversation as much as public utterance and McCarthy did not know him sufficiently well to grasp instinctively his convoluted meaning. Gladstone could also be sensitive and what he had to tell McCarthy was a delicate matter, so the latter may have emerged from the interview realising that the Liberal leader thought the Irish one should retire temporarily, but without having absorbed the full impact of the conversation. (This was what he himself implied.) To emphasise his point, Gladstone also wrote a letter to McCarthy for him to hand to Parnell (though whether McCarthy received it is unclear), and then he wrote a further letter for John Morley to hand to Parnell. In the draft of this Morley letter he omitted the crucial phrase about *his* leadership being rendered a nullity if Parnell retained *his,* and when Morley and Harcourt persuaded him to reinsert the vital phrase, Gladstone said he thought it had been added as a postscript, a point which underlines his reluctance to force Parnell into resignation.

On the evening of 24 November and the morning of 25 November there were two men trying to reach Parnell with the same urgent message from Gladstone, but whether by intent or the intervention of others, he evaded them both. When he entered the doors of Committee Room 15 of the House of Commons on 25 November, it was without official knowledge of Gladstone's feelings. (Committee Room 15 was allotted to the Irish party to conduct their private business—the same room, with its mullioned windows overlooking Westminster Bridge and the Thames, in which Chamberlain had helped kill the Home Rule Bill in 1886.) Face to face with his party for the first time since August and the happy occasion of William O'Brien's wedding on this far from joyous day, Parnell offered its members no explanation for the disaster of the divorce court. He apparently told them that he would lift back the curtain—would that he had—but then proceeded to say merely that Captain O'Shea had never been his friend, that he had never betrayed his hospitality and that throughout the twenty-three years of his married life the gentleman in question had spent but forty nights at home. With that meagre information the nationalists had to be content, and Parnell continued by saying that he would never surrender and asking the party for its support. With reservations, for everybody knew of the swelling hostility to their leader and the implications for Home Rule, but also with loyalty and unaware of the content of Gladstone's letters, the Irish party proceeded to re-elect Parnell as Chairman.

John Morley then managed to find the re-elected leader and inform him of Mr Gladstone's views, but Parnell was not moved by them, or by Morley's pleas that his continued leadership could ruin the Liberal chances at the next Election and that he need only retire until the storm had subsided. A disheartened Morley went to tell Gladstone what had happened, and the latter exploded. Up to this moment Gladstone, forced to take hasty decisions like everybody else, had behaved with tact and consideration. He was aware of Parnell's pride, of the difficulty of any Irish leader seeming to bow to British demands, and for these reasons he refused to address the crucial letters direct to Parnell but had banked everything on McCarthy and Morley being able to persuade him privately that temporary retirement was the sensible course to follow. When he learned that his efforts had failed, that somehow despite the two letters and the verbal message his views had not reached Parnell, his temper erupted and he announced that the nullity letter must be made public forthwith so that the Irish would know exactly what his position was. For this decision Gladstone has been severely criticised, but he was human, a deep well of passion ran in his blood, and while it is true that he should have consulted the Irish party and let them have their say, his precipitate reaction is perhaps understandable. Private consultation with the Irish members might have saved the party's unity, and faced with a nearly unanimous demand for his resignation Parnell might have been forced to submit, but as it was, with Gladstone's nullity letter appearing in each edition of the *Pall Mall Gazette,* bursting on the nationalists as resoundingly and more surprisingly than the divorce, they divided like the Red Sea before Moses. A harassed Justin McCarthy wrote of 'Celtic devotion and Celtic emotion awakened on either side to the seething point of passion'.

The devotional and emotional sides proceeded to align themselves, and an emergency meeting was called at which a resolution was passed asking Parnell to reconsider his position at a full meeting of the party on the Friday. The next day Parnell said he had no intention of reconsidering his position, as he had been unanimously re-elected as the party Chairman and if the party wanted to remove him, it was up to them, not him. Speeches urging him to have regard for the Liberal alliance and Home Rule and resign until the storm had blown over were made on the one side, speeches urging him not to bow to Liberal dictation but to stand fast, on the other; then the meeting petered out and it was agreed to adjourn until the following Monday, 1 December.

Having made his stance clear, Parnell returned to Brighton, where he told Katie he thought he would have to fight and proceeded to turn the thought into action by composing his 'Manifesto to the People of Ireland', which was published on 29 November. The Manifesto, designated by Parnell as his answer to Gladstone's nullity letter, opened with a slamming attack on certain sectors of the Irish party 'who had been sapped and destroyed by the wire-pullers of the English Liberal party' and on the outright threat to independent Irish action contained in Mr Gladstone's letter, followed by an appeal to the Irish people not to throw him to the English wolves who were howling for his destruction. It continued by attacking Mr Gladstone's inadequate proposals for a new Home Rule Bill as outlined at the Hawarden talks in December 1889 and then attacked John Morley about matters discussed at their meeting in Brighton before the divorce. The Manifesto concluded on the theme of Irish independence of action—would it not be preferable to postpone Home Rule rather than to accept a castrated version under the Liberal alliance? There was no mention of the happenings in the divorce court and only the obliquest reference to the fact that Parnell's position as leader was in any way threatened or changed: 'I do not believe that any action of the Irish people in supporting me will endanger Home Rule or postpone the establishment of an Irish Parliament.'

If Gladstone made a grave error in publishing his 'nullity' letter without first consulting the Irish nationalists, it can be said that Parnell made an even graver one in publishing his Manifesto at all. In some respects it was an appalling document, and in every respect it was an extraordinary one. It was appalling because it broke faith and trust; the Hawarden talks, if official, had been secret, while the meeting with John Morley had been a discussion between the two men in which they had ranged over a number of topics, and unilaterally to reveal to the world what had occurred in private talks was abominable. All human relationships whether personal or political, whether those of a secret organisation or an official party, are based on trust and must collapse when that trust is betrayed. It was almost irrelevant that Parnell's version of what had occurred at Hawarden and in Brighton was distorted, if not downright untruthful. The Manifesto was an extraordinary document because of the sheer boldness of its tactics, and it could perhaps have come from no other man but Parnell. He attempted to dispel the stench of the divorce court by raising stinks in other directions, but the real boldness lay in the direct appeal to the Irish people over the heads of the Irish party (and of course of the Liberals). By this direct appeal, with the racial undertones of 'the English wolves' and the ancient call for Irish independence of action striking at national chauvinism and pride, Parnell by-passed normal channels of political behaviour (as he had done in the past) and staked everything on the strength of his record and personality. If the people responded to his call, then long-term he would win through because neither the Liberals nor his own party could continue to deny their will and their chosen leader.

Short-term the effects of the Manifesto were to diminish the hopes of the nationalist-Liberal alliance remaining in being under his leadership, and to polarise the split between the emotionalists and the devotionalists in the Irish ranks. What Parnell aimed at in the Manifesto was immediately clear to some people; Lord Randolph Churchill, himself a political maverick with a touch of genius, considered it a masterpiece; but many others were totally baffled (and appalled) by it and the feeling expressed by Frank Lockwood—that the Irish leader was showing signs of madness—gained ground. The fact that there was insanity in Parnell's family background was mentioned publicly and privately, and the idea that he had cracked under the strain of the liaison with Mrs O'Shea and was suffering from delusions of grandeur—Ireland, *c'est moi*—grew. It was an easy explanation for the failure to act sensibly or honourably, particularly in contrast to the Parnell of the predivorce year who had appeared in his moderate statesmanlike garb, but it overlooked the fact that he had not always worn such a garb, that he was a master tactician and that boldness and pride were two of his strongest characteristics.

It was with the knowledge of the immediate disastrous effects of the Manifesto on general Liberal opinion that the nationalists assembled in Committee Room 15 on the morning of 1 December 1890. In the preceding days frantic efforts had been made by both sides to canvass the support of the waverers, and shoals of cables had swum across the Atlantic to the Irish delegates there. The delegates had managed to coverge on Cincinnati and until they read the Manifesto they were willing (with reluctance on the part of T. D. Sullivan) to send a private cable urging Parnell to retire temporarily in favour of Justin McCarthy. Once they had read the Manifesto, five of them decided Parnell's leadership was now impossible (the exception was Timothy Harrington), and from Chicago they issued a statement explaining why they had come to their agonising decision. For them it was not Gladstone who had broken faith but Parnell, and as long as the Liberal Party held to the promises made in its Home Rule programme there was nothing subservient in the Irish party working with it to achieve the desired end. This public declaration by the five American delegates, all of whom were influential in the party, and two of whom—Dillon and O'Brien—ranked among the most respected and prestigious members, was a severe blow to Parnell and his hopes of retaining the leadership. When he re-entered Committee Room 15 on 1 December, however, it was by no means certain that all was lost for him, because there were flocks of telegrams from the branches of the Irish National League promising him undying support and the Catholic hierarchy had not thus far spoken against him.

Parnell's basic tactic during the momentous meetings in Committee Room 15 in the first week of December 1890 was to have and to hold by averting a vote on his leadership, with the secondary one of trying to put his opponents into the position of seeming subservient to the Liberals. Both tactics followed the lines of the Manifesto, and in pursuance of the first objective he proposed that the meetings be adjourned to Dublin. But the focal point of the Irish parliamentary party was of necessity London and he did not succeed with what Tim Healy rightly called his novel proposition. Parnell was more successful in utilising his powers as Chairman by wasting time on procedural matters and hair-splitting detail and by declaring out of order any motion which threatened to produce a vote on the leadership. The tone of the first three days of meetings was astonishingly restrained, considering that Celtic passion had already been roused, that it was Parnell's love life which had put the Irish party into the hideous position in which it now found itself, and that he himself was labouring under the strain of having to fight for his leadership and in the process to give some explanations. Tempers flared occasionally, particularly towards the end of the day when the oil lamps glowed and fog wreathed the winter waters of the Thames and the atmosphere became physically foreboding, but generally the tenor of the debate was high, every effort was made to keep the temperature political and to avoid personal or moral recrimination, and the restraint bears witness to the power and magnetism of Parnell's leadership and personality.

The lines of the split were already clearly defined and the two viewpoints were ably stated by John Redmond, who emerged as the leading Parnellite, and by Tim Healy who turned into the most bitter anti-Parnellite. Redmond eloquently reiterated the case that the issue was Irish independence of action and the leadership of the Irish race, not just in Ireland but throughout the world. Was any alliance worthwhile which threatened these, particularly the Liberal alliance which Mr Parnell had revealed as dictatorial and offering a newly castrated version of Home Rule? As eloquently, Tim Healy stated the case that the issue was Ireland and Home Rule, that since 1886 the keystone of Home Rule had become the Liberal alliance and that nothing had changed except the question of one man's suitability for continued leadership. On more detailed matters he rightly queried why, if the Hawarden talks had been as unsatisfactory as Parnell was now claiming, Parnell had not informed anybody at the time but had issued forth, as was *not* his wont, with public praise of Mr Gladstone?

Parnell countered the accusations with his customary adroitness, by saying he had not revealed his forebodings about the Hawarden talks because he had hoped to be able to obtain better terms and it was only when he realised that the Liberals were in a dictatorial mood that he felt he should tell the truth. He then swiftly passed to his own line of attack, namely the terrible dependence of the Irish on the Liberals, by saying he had sent Justin McCarthy to see Mr Gladstone with an offer of his resignation if the Liberal leader would agree to definite terms on Home Rule, an offer which had achieved nothing. A reluctant Justin McCarthy confirmed that he had seen Gladstone and other leading Liberals, who had not been as dismissive as Mr Parnell was suggesting but had said they could only negotiate with the leader of the Irish party.

On the Tuesday a vote was taken on a Parnellite amendment that the question of the leadership be shelved until Irish feeling as a whole had been sounded, and on a vocal count Chairman Parnell declared that the ayes had it, but when the names were called alphabetically the noes numbered forty-four and the ayes twenty-nine, which indicated the strength of the opposition. Both sides were still desperately trying to find a compromise which would save the party's unity without disgracing Parnell, and the next day the nationalists went into secret session and another resolution was proposed, namely that a deputation be sent to Gladstone, Morley and Harcourt, asking for fairly vague guarantees on Home Rule. If these were obtained, Parnell should then resign in the knowledge that the party had not sacrificed him for nothing. Parnell was not present when the hopeful resolution was proposed but came when summoned and asked for an adjournment to consider it, and on Wednesday evening, 3 December, this was granted. Several nationalists later said they then withdrew from the battlefield of Committee Room 15 believing that Parnell was prepared to accept the resolution, to allow the Liberals to fight the General Election unencumbered by his leadership, retiring as the man who had brought Ireland to within sight of the promised land and—who knew?—might yet be able to lead her once the storm had abated and she had crossed the Rubicon.

On the evening of 3 December Parnell, who had been staying in London thus far, returned to Brighton and Katie, and from this moment her involvement in the Anglo-Irish political scene and her influence on his actions (past and present) began to loom large. Several people were later adamant that it was Katie O'Shea who had been Parnell's evil genius for a long time, that it was she who intercepted Morley's letter from Gladstone and, most vitally, that it was she who changed the wish to retire into the decision to fight like a tiger to the bitter end. (Sir William Harcourt described Parnell as 'an expiring cat', a creature he said it was dangerous to approach, but even if he meant a wild cat the simile seems inappropriate for the passion and tenacity displayed.)

What effect did Katie have on Parnell's stance in those crucial three weeks after the divorce case? To back-track to the evening of 26 November when Parnell returned to Brighton after his re-election to the leadership and the publication of Gladstone's nullity letter, Katie maintained that he took her in his arms and said, 'I think we shall have to fight, Queenie. Can you bear it? I'm afraid it will be tough work.' She replied, 'Yes, if you can', and shortly thereafter he started work on his Manifesto and Katie watched in silence 'as the smoulder in his eyes grew deeper as he wrote.' There were those who insisted that the Manifesto must have been penned under Katie's influence and at her command, but this belief surely misinterprets Parnell's character and overestimates her political subtlety and comprehension of the Irish people, both of which factors were apparent in the Manifesto. Nothing in Katie's character suggests that she ever understood the Irish; she was an English lady brought up in the traditions of nineteenth-century English Liberalism who happened to have fallen in love with an Irish politician of genius and who accepted his views, but she had no particular sympathy with them outside the context of the man, and once Parnell was dead she displayed no further interest in Ireland. Despite her considerable political knowledge and her past position as intermediary, she did not possess the tactical finesse to have composed the Manifesto, even allowing that she had some insight into the Irish mind.

What Katie did possess was the inherent, headstrong will to have her own way, the certainty that somehow she could always obtain it—characteristics strengthened by the events of the past decade—the conviction that only cowards failed to fight when attacked, and her absolute belief in and love for Parnell which meant that her will and her way were totally directed towards him. While it seems doubtful that Katie made Parnell fight when he did not wish to do so, it is surely true that she urged him to battle and that had she wished she could have dissuaded him from so doing. She admitted that he would then have retired had she insisted, that she could then have persuaded him to live abroad—though there was the problem of young Katie and Clare, legally in the custody of Captain O'Shea. (Obviously Katie does not mention this problem in her memoirs, as the children do not exist therein.) In the days of Committee Room 15 she quoted Parnell as saying, 'I shall never give in unless you make me, and I want you to promise that you will never make me less than the man you have known', and she asserted that she thus solemnly promised. The correct assessment therefore seems that the basic will to fight was Parnell's, that faced with the direct challenge to the position and the cause for which he had striven for years, fatalism was thrown to the stars whence it came. It was Parnell rather than Katie who refused to defend the divorce suit. He must have realised that Captain O'Shea's unopposed case would cause some adverse comment and pose some threat to his continued leadership, and having made the one decision, the second decision to fight if the threat became real followed more or less automatically. When the clamour for his retirement proved greater and stronger than he had perhaps foreseen, had he not been living with a lady such as Katie, buttressing his will to the hilt, convinced that head-on assault was the only path to victory—her English Liberal belief in compromise thrown to the winds—his judgement might have convinced him that temporary retirement was the sensible course to follow. But then, had he not loved and lived with Katie, the disastrous situation would never have arisen, and it was expecting too much of either of them suddenly to change their characters, to become moderate, reasonable, conventional people when their very genuine love became such damaging public property. For both of them, the belief that their private life had nothing to do with Parnell's position as the leader of the Irish nationalists was the one they continued to hold.

When Parnell returned to London and Committee Room 15 after his visit home to Katie, his resolve to retain the leadership of the party was absolute, and if he entertained ideas of retirement when he left for Brighton, which is doubtful, she certainly disabused him of them. Parnell returned to the battle saying he would retire but only if the nationalist deputation to the Liberals obtained two concrete guarantees on Home Rule, with respect of the police and the land question. This was another brilliant tactical move, for Gladstone had already said he could only negotiate with the leader of the Irish party (and therefore until they had decided who their leader was he could not negotiate), so it was virtually certain that the Liberals would not commit themselves. If by any chance they accepted Parnell's demands, then he could retire as the man who had decisively shaped Home Rule and even in eclipse had demonstrated his power, and on the much likelier chance that the Liberals would refuse any commitment until the nationalists had sorted themselves out, then Parnell could say that the agreed conditions for his retirement had vanished, rendered invisible by Mr Gladstone's refusal to negotiate. By this time tempers were beginning to rise, and Tim Healy made the first personal remark when he said that Parnell's policy had 'perished in the stench of the divorce court'; later when Parnell said he would stand or fall by his new conditions for Home Rule, Healy shouted back, 'Then you will fall, Mr Parnell.' (Sir William Harcourt, temporarily addicted to feline similes, wrote to his wife saying, 'The Irishmen are upstairs fighting like Kilkenny cats, coming out at intervals to have "drinks all round".')

Every effort was made to try to preserve the unity of the fast-splintering party, and the nationalist deputation spent the whole of Friday, 5 December, toing and froing between Gladstone and Committee Room 15, passing new amendments to which Gladstone and Parnell might yet agree. (This was despite the fact that the Irish bishops had finally spoken out the previous day, issuing a public statement which said they must condemn Mr Parnell's leadership, not on political grounds, but on the moral issue as revealed in the London divorce court.) The results of the delegation's endeavours were nil; Gladstone told Labouchere, 'I have seldom spent a more painful hour or hour-and-a-half than that with the Deputation—my heart bled for them'; but his head adhered to the position that the question of a Home Rule Bill and the Irish leadership could not be linked and that he could only negotiate with their leader. By Saturday, 6 December, everybody realised that the vote on the leadership could not be postponed, though Parnell continued to try to stave it off by insisting that the delegates deliver a written report of their meetings with Mr Gladstone, and by using his powers as Chairman to quash the desired resolution. It was on this Saturday that Tim Healy made the most famous and cutting remark spoken in Committee Room 15. Argument was proceeding about the surrender to Mr Gladstone's dictation and John Redmond interjected acidly that the Liberal leader was now 'the master of the party', to which Healy responded, 'And who is to be the mistress of the party?' whereupon Parnell rounded upon him 'as the cowardly little scoundrel, there, that in the assembly of Irishmen dares to insult a woman.' Once the debate had descended to such personal acrimony, the decision on the leadership could not be postponed, and in the gathering gloom it was Justin McCarthy who proposed that the unprofitable, undignified debate be brought to a close and that those who shared his view should follow him from the room. Forty-five nationalists rose and silently filed out, leaving behind them twenty-six supporters of Parnell. Having filed out, the forty-five members went into conference and issued a statement which said that as an absolute majority of the Irish parliamentary party they declared that 'Mr Parnell's leadership of this party is hereby terminated.' They then elected Justin McCarthy as 'sessional chairman', solemnly declared that they remained true to the principle of Irish independence of action and obtaining the Home Rule desired by the Irish people. While the majority were clarifying their new position, in the fitful illumination of the oil lamps, Parnell was telling his supporters in Committee Room 15 that they had gained a victory, that he remained Chairman of the party, that the seceders had fled from the weight of Irish opinion throughout the world and stood in the contemptible position of men who had been false to their country, their party and their leader. Thus war was declared within the Irish party, and the simple issues were Parnell, Irish independence and the unknown future posed against Ireland, the will of the majority and the probable attainment of Home Rule through the Liberal alliance. Unfortunately, both sides were right in their battle cries; Parnell was the only man who could obtain Home Rule, but the only way it could be obtained was through the Liberal alliance.

Chapter Eighteen

After the dénouement in Committee Room 15 Parnell returned to his beloved Katie, and in the confines of Walsingham Terrace she provided warmth and reassurance, though not the moderate counsel which would have been helpful. The battlefield was now Ireland, not Westminster or any part of England, and on the evening of 9 December Parnell crossed to Dublin, but the figure of the woman immured somewhere in Brighton increasingly became a symbol of his disintegration, that is for his opponents, by his supporters she was ignored. It was Tim Healy who used Katie most venomously and scurrilously, and perhaps his seizing upon her as a method of wounding Parnell was occasioned by the reaction to his initial jibe in Committee Room 15—'Who is to be the mistress of the party?' It was recorded that when Healy made the riposte Parnell was shaken by a white-hot passion and trembled from head to foot, that momentarily everybody thought he would strike Healy and that it took several minutes of superhuman effort before he could control himself. Apart from the element of diablerie in Healy's nature which went unerringly and joyously for the victim's most sensitive spot, there was sound sense in attacking Katie and building up the image of the man whose career had been wrecked by a scheming woman. On the one hand, people could say Parnell was behaving in the way he was because he was under an ambitious woman's malign influence (a plausible excuse for those who did not favour the insanity motif); on the other hand, this semi-pitying attitude could be twisted into the patent unsuitability for leadership of a man who could allow himself to be dominated by a woman, and in a male-oriented society that was a damaging line of attack. Then there was the element of ridicule inherent in the picture of the hen-pecked Parnell, and it was again one which did not appeal to Victorian society.

Healy was not alone in focussing attention on Mrs O'Shea, and *Vanity Fair* was first off the mark on 22 November, with a piece entitled 'The Political Princess—O'Shea Who Must Be Obeyed' (the pun on Rider Haggard's best-selling novel tied in with the pronunciation *O'She*). By December the popular papers had joined in with comments that Mrs O'Shea was 'a woman not only of personal attractions but of intellect' who had undoubtedly 'taken considerable part in the intrigues and negotiations which have gone on with both parties during the last 11 or 12 years', while W. T. Stead weighed in with 'Not even the passionate efforts of the whole nation can save our sweyn from the grasp of Mrs O'Shea. The were-wolf woman of Irish politics cannot be shaken off.' Letters from respectable females were published: 'It seems horrible that the weakness of a woman old enough to take care of herself, and belonging to a class that should be refined and worthy of being called "the elite" should be able to ruin a career. . . . It is such women as she who lead men into the belief that we are weak frail dolls, virtuous only from fear or lack of opportunity or otherwise.' (What 'otherwise' might be was not specified.) And there were frequent references to 'the Uncrowned Queen of Ireland'.

The attack on the 'were-wolf woman of Irish politics' increased as the battle for the leadership of the nationalist party gained momentum, and from the moment of the split in Committee Room 15, when Katharine's role in Parnell's public as opposed to private life was brought out for inspection, she was popularly referred to as 'Kitty' O'Shea. No single person appears to have fastened onto the diminutive by which she had never been known; it seems to have been one of those spontaneous reactions. The lady's name was Katharine, which would not do popularly, she had to be reduced to everyday size, so 'Kitty' emerged with its suggestion of claws and coquettishness. In a letter to his wife written on 28 November, Tim Healy referred to 'Kitty's' involvement in proceedings, but by the time he started to launch his public attacks, newspapers had already announced to the world that 'she was commonly known as "Kitty" O'Shea'. The vilification of the woman he loved wounded Parnell, but he and Katie found some comfort in the fact that the detractors had not alighted on the correct diminutive, and after Healy's first vicious public outbursts he told her, 'It would really have hurt, my Queen, if those devils had got hold of your real name, *my* Queenie, or even the "Katie" or "Dick" that your relations and Willie called you.'

While Parnell led his cohorts from the centre of the battlefield, Katie remained at Walsingham Terrace, and in some respects her situation was worse than his. He had the excitement, stimulation and thought-deadening activity of actually being in the fight, while she was a virtual prisoner, with endless hours to fill, waiting for his telegrams, waiting for the newspaper reports, waiting for his return from Ireland, desperately worried about his health and safety. She did not have to be a prisoner in Brighton, she could have emerged from the house, but Parnell had always kept her away from direct involvement in the political fray (very few of the nationalists knew Katharine personally) and in the current circumstances he was even more anxious that she should not be subjected to personal insult or physical harm. When Katie wanted to get an urgent message to Parnell during the early days of Committee Room 15, she felt she must not appear personally and it was the faithful maid, Phyllis, who travelled from Brighton to the House of Commons bearing the letter. Now that the fight was showing signs of becoming ferocious, even less did Parnell feel that she should emerge and in Brighton she stayed, filling the role of anxious, watching, waiting woman, becoming more morally outraged and high-mindedly bitter as the attacks on her King—and herself—mounted.

Katie's moral indignation centred on her former idol, Mr Gladstone, an expected reaction from an emotional, subjective lady. In her opinion, he should have admitted openly that he had known about her liaison with Parnell, as should the dissenting nationalists who had similarly been aware for the past decade. (Towards the latter Katie adopted the full English racial stance, she pitied them, they were children who had no understanding of loyalty or of the true meaning of any cause or of Parnell's greatness.) She did not pity Mr Gladstone and she accused him of taking advantage of the known relationship between her and the Irish leader by using her as intermediary when it suited him (at whose initiative, one might ask). She further accused Gladstone of discovering that his religion could be useful to his country by overthrowing Parnell and Home Rule at the eleventh hour. It was untrue that he used *his* religion because Gladstone was a staunch Anglican and it was the Nonconformists who raised the outcry; but is there truth in Katie's assertion that the Liberal leader deliberately ditched Parnell because he was lukewarm about Home Rule? According to her, Parnell had never believed in the 'Grand Old Spider's' conversion and was convinced that Gladstone had denounced him because it suited his purposes. To a degree, this upholds the contention that the conversion was a matter of party politics and that Gladstone was doing little more than hold out the carrot of Home Rule to maintain his grip on his party. But it was not he who precipitated the divorce, nor did he engineer the British moral outrage, and after the defeat of the first Home Rule Bill he wrote to his son, 'We the promoters of Home Rule, continue in the certitude that the measure must and will pass' because, he said, he was convinced that the settlement of Irish grievances could only be realised by its implementation. He also introduced a second Home Rule Bill after Parnell was dead, at a time when the Irish party was still bitterly split and had no comparable leadership. While it seems true to say that Ireland never captured Gladstone's heart (in which feeling he was reflecting the emotions of the majority of his countrymen), after 1886 it also seems true that a reasonable portion of his mind was directed towards the implementation of Home Rule. Certainly the opposition, the bulk of the Liberal Party which had followed him on his Irish venture and the majority of the nationalists *thought* that he was trying to effect Home Rule for Ireland.

Whatever Parnell really thought when he landed in Dublin on 10 December for his first visit since the divorce, his tactical position was clear—attack Gladstone and bang the drum of Irish independence of action. On the head of the Liberal leader he poured his wrath and hatred; it was Gladstone who by the publication of his nullity letter had produced the present set of circumstances, it was he who had split the Irish party by refusing all offers of compromise and thus revealed himself in his true colours as the dictatorial leader of an English party which would only grant Ireland Home Rule on his terms and when he felt like so doing. In the moment of stress, Parnell showed how much of an Irishman he was beneath the cool English exterior, and if Katie rounded on Gladstone in subjective feminine fashion, Parnell turned on him with a bitterness that was as racially deep-rooted as was her noble pity for the nationalists. In Dublin the attacks were received with rapture, and Parnell's effort to regain control of *United Ireland*—the newspaper he had founded in 1881 but which under the long-distance urging of its former editor, William O'Brien, had within the last week switched allegiance—was accomplished by a pro-Parnellite Dublin mob invading the actual offices. No more than any capital city was Dublin representative of the rest of the country and Parnell could not rest on its citizens' rapture. Before he left to face his own constituency of Cork—not as simple a task as it sounded as his fellow MP in Cork was Tim Healy's brother—the passions already roused by the split became apparent. A group of anti-Parnellites tried to re-seize the offices of *United Ireland*, whereupon Parnell, just about to leave Dublin for Cork, rushed round with his supporters, and at one moment a pitched battle between the two sides seemed a possibility, but the numerically smaller anti-Parnellite group withdrew and a dishevelled but triumphant Parnell was able to appear on the balcony, announcing that he had regained control.

In Cork his reception was almost as rapturous as in Dublin, and there, apart from the obligatory attack on Gladstone, he further elaborated a theme which had appeared in his speeches in the capital—the appeal to the 'hill-side men'. Ironically, it was Willie O'Shea who had coined the phrase the 'hill-side men' when, in one of his convoluted explanations to the Special Commission about his Fenian friends, he had spoken of 'the men who thought the day might come when they could fight their country's battle on the hill-side against the British forces, and in the meanwhile objected to all outrages.' By an even greater irony it was now Parnell, the man who had rejected the Fenian aim of independence through force, who had created a strong, disciplined constitutional Irish party, who had not previously played on racial bitterness or chauvinism or bigotry but who had insisted on proper racial pride, it was he who made the dangerous emotional appeal.

The success of Parnell's new stance was swiftly put to the test, because there was a by-election in Kilkenny whose polling date was 22 December. Prior to the split, a candidate had been elected, Sir John Pope Hennessy, by the normal process of the nationalist party and with Parnell's approval. After the split, Sir John declared himself an anti-Parnellite and a loyal candidate to oppose him was hurriedly chosen. By 12 December platoons of influential nationalists from both sides had descended on the area and the next ten days saw the sad, unedifying spectacle of internecine warfare. From the start Tim Healy demonstrated that there were to be no holds barred; in his first speeches he mentioned 'Kitty' derogatively, and he also reopened the wound which had festered in him for a long time, by saying that in Galway in 1886 it had been known that Parnell 'was prostituting a seat in Parliament to the interests of his own private intrigue.' Two days later he warmed to the theme that Parnell had sold the constituency for the sake of his mistress's husband, and then he attacked both of them: 'Mr Parnell proposes to found a United Ireland . . . on the corpses of the majority of the Irish party, and then he will go through Ireland with a new banner constructed out of the petticoat of Mrs O'Shea. The green flag of Ireland with its sunburst is to be set aside. The sunburst and the harp are to be toned down and are to be replaced by the sign of the fire-escape.'

Having read Healy's attacks on his beloved Queenie, Parnell was not slow to respond in kind and he spoke of the miserable gutter-sparrows who were once his comrades, the chief gutter-sparrow being Tim Healy; he called Michael Davitt a jackdaw and he described long-suffering Justin McCarthy as 'a nice old gentleman for a tea party'. On 16 December verbal violence turned into physical violence when a scuffle broke out between rival crowds at a meeting and Michael Davitt was hit by a stick, and later in the day Parnell had a bag of lime thrown at his eyes. There was—inevitably by this time—argument as to whether it was flour, flour mixed with lime, or pure lime which could have blinded him that struck Parnell. Katie insisted that it was lime, and that had he not shut his eyes in the nick of time he would have been blinded; she underlined the isolated stress in which she was living by saying that having read a newspaper report of the attack, she nearly went out of her mind with worry until she received a reassuring telegram from Parnell. When the results were declared after the bitter campaign, Sir John Pope Hennessy had 2,527 votes while Parnell's candidate had 1,362. It was a resounding victory for the anti-Parnellites; it showed the validity of their claim that they represented the majority will, that the majority respected constitutionalism and the democratic process and rejected the autocracy of the morally and politically bankrupt Parnell. It was at Kilkenny that the spectre of priestly intervention in politics was resurrected, with assertions (not all of them coming from Parnellite sources) that priests were present in virtually all the polling booths, acting as personation agents for illiterate voters (and 25 per cent of Kilkenny voters were illiterate). It cannot be regarded as surprising that the priests should have come out in force, because the root cause of the present tragic situation was the divorce, and any good Catholic priest should have taken a moral stand thereon.

The idea that Parnell might retire now that he had been defeated in Kilkenny was fondly entertained in one or two quarters, but it was not one to which he subscribed. He knew that he was in for a long winter of discontent and Kilkenny was but a snow shower, and if anything the verbal and actual violence of the campaign stiffened his fighting instinct. On his way through Dublin, where he was received by as rapturous crowds as if he had won an electoral victory, presenting a wild figure with unkempt beard and hair, his eye bandaged from the flour/lime attack, Parnell passed College Green where stood the building which had housed Grattan's Parliament. He made no speech but merely pointed dramatically to the building and the crowd went wild with delight at the gesture which said Ireland would again have her own Parliament, with him at its head. From Dublin he sailed back to England and Katie, and perhaps the greatest irony was that at the moment when Parnell had repudiated England and all she represented in the shape of Gladstone and the Liberal alliance, when he was making his racial appeals to the hill-side men, he should at every possible opportunity travel to the archetypally English sea-side town of Brighton to be with the Englishwoman who had wrecked his Irish dream.

What Katie's feelings were when she saw her lover again just before Christmas 1890 she did not record, but many observers in Ireland (friend and foe) commented on how desperately ill he looked in these weeks, and one or two later said that he had the appearance of a dying man, with eyes burning from a skin of extreme pallor (whether this was hindsight is difficult to assess). The comments on his obvious ill-health were contemporary, and during the Kilkenny campaign he himself made the rare admission in a letter to Katie that he was feeling tired and unwell. She made little comment on Parnell's health at the end of 1890 or in the next few months, perhaps because it was a subject about which she had thirty years to torment herself. More than anybody she knew how fragile his constitution was, how much nervousness and in some areas sensitivity lay behind the cool exterior, how much his political battles consequently extracted from him, and how greatly she had had to nurse his health after the exertions of 1886. Should she have insisted that he lessen his efforts? While he was in Ireland, constantly on the move from hot stuffy halls into the bitterly cold air (and 1890/91 was a particularly bitter winter), making endless train journeys, stopping overnight in inadequate hotels, there was little she could do, other than pathetically provide him with the change of shoes and socks. But should she, or could she, have exerted her influence to ensure that the campaigning was less drastic? Should she, or could she, at least have prevented him from making the long tiring journeys to Brighton every week, visits which involved the crossing from Dublin to Holyhead, then the train journey to London, with the trek across the capital from Euston to Victoria Station, the further train to Brighton and the cab journey to Walsingham Terrace, and all the way back after only a brief respite. She recorded that she begged Parnell not to come home so frequently much as she personally longed to see him, but he said he must see her (and presumably young Katie and Clare, whom he loved). Further accusations of Katie's interference in Parnell's desire to retire were yet to come, but one wonders whether by the end of 1890 she could have restrained her lover. It was not, in fact, consumption of which Parnell died, but from December 1890 he exhibited the sort of frenetic, self-destructive energy which characterises a type of consumptive. He *had* to keep on the move, he *had* to keep fighting, and whether even the pleas of his beloved Queenie could then have slowed him down is a debatable point.

Before the end of 1890, even while the bitter Kilkenny campaign was being fought, further moves were afoot to try and effect a compromise between Parnell and his erstwhile unified party. They were set in motion by the delegates still in America, notably John Dillon, William O'Brien and T. P. Gill, and while three thousand miles had been a grave disadvantage in the days leading up to the split, it had some advantages in the aftermath. Distance lent a degree of perspective not available to those on the spot who were caught up in the personal bitterness and passions which overthrew reason, and Dillon, O'Brien and Gill were able to assess the news from Ireland with a certain detachment. Their position remained that Home Rule and the Liberal alliance were the paramount issues and that Parnell's immediate leadership was therefore untenable, but they saw that the internecine warfare would be disastrous, not only in Ireland but in its effect on British opinion, which, if recently favourable, was always only too ready to believe ill of the Irish. They drafted a compromise which they hoped Parnell would accept, and a very handsome document it was too; Parnell must retire temporarily from the chairmanship of the party but he was to remain President of the National League and joint treasurer of the party funds; declarations would be issued saying how much Ireland owed to him and efforts made to get the bishops to retract their denunciations; and he would be accorded a special position in the future negotiations on the terms of Home Rule with the Liberals. In effect, all they were asking Parnell to do was to retire from the titular leadership of the party while retaining the real power in the shape of control of the party machine, a veto on the use of funds and in the Home Rule negotiations. The snags to these magnanimous proposals were that they required the co-operation of Mr Gladstone, the virulent anti-Parnellites led by Tim Healy, and the Catholic hierarchy, but the American contingent was hopeful that these could be overcome and the proposals formed the basis of what became known as 'the Boulogne negotiations'.

These negotiations were conducted between William O'Brien, T. P. Gill and later John Dillon, Justin McCarthy representing the moderate nationalists who had been on the spot all the time, and Parnell and some of his supporters, notably John Redmond. They were held in France for the good reason that English warrants were out for the arrests of William O'Brien (who became the most eager conciliator) and John Dillon (more depressive in his hopes of compromise but nonetheless willing to placate Parnell). The negotiations lasted from the end of December 1890 until mid-February 1891 and were immensely complicated, with the terms of the compromise shifting, with Parnell travelling backwards and forwards between Ireland and Brighton and Boulogne, and with T. P. Gill (not under threat of arrest) providing the link with London. The terms, if altered from the original draft, remained extremely favourable to Parnell; compromise was extracted from the Healyites to the extent that they did not deliberately jam the negotiations; and guarantees on Parnell's earlier conditions for retirement— namely the future of the police and the land question—were extracted from Gladstone and the Liberals. Everybody bent over backwards to placate Parnell's honour, pride and retention of very real power, with the Irish overlooking the moral issues and his recent intransigence and with John Morley working like a Trojan against bitter opposition in his party to obtain the Liberal guarantees. (Harcourt's opinion of the Boulogne compromise was that 'it was really worthy of the Beggar's Opera'.) The assessment that Parnell never intended the negotiations to succeed, that his aim was to drive a wedge between the moderates and extremists in the Irish party and thus weaken the internal opposition, seems valid. But three months is a long time to waste on exhausting journeys between three countries in the hope of wedge-driving; the terms were so very favourable; and Parnell had not lost all political realism (John Dillon wrote: 'Men say here that Parnell is mad, but it seems to me that his astuteness is absolutely infinite'); various people insisted that during the course of the negotiations he seemed genuinely anxious for a settlement. So what changed him? for it was Parnell who in mid-February broke off the negotiations, officially saying that Gladstone's guarantees were insufficient.

The by now customary explanation was given that it was Mrs O'Shea who persuaded her lover that no true leader could agree to retire and that he must fight until inevitable victory. There was some truth in the charges of Katie's influence—the idea of Parnell's retiring from the leadership, if temporarily and in retention of much power, did not appeal to her—but as the whole or sole reason it is too simple. The explanation for Parnell's withdrawal from the Boulogne negotiations is perhaps that he was now convinced that he was the only man who could obtain Home Rule for Ireland (in which conviction he was right) because Gladstone was an old spider who would have to be forced to leave his web, but that the physical and mental strain of the last few months had begun to take their toll so that the clear outlines of the former political realist and master tactician who had known when to retrench, when to compromise, when to attack, had begun to blur. The failure of the negotiations meant that for the forseeable future, as long as Parnell remained, the unity of the Irish parliamentary party was fractured beyond repair, that Ireland herself split further and further asunder and it was war to the death. (John Dillon and William O'Brien caught the boat to England, where they happily gave themselves up to the police and retired to the temporary non-involvement of imprisonment.)

With the collapse of the Boulogne negotiations Parnell redoubled his efforts in Ireland, with the exhausting journeys therein entailed, the strain of addressing countless meetings, the stress of facing frequently hostile crowds. Katie said he was very happy in these months, that when he was away in Ireland he telegraphed her every morning and every night and that her only real worry was that he was beginning to show signs of extreme fatigue. This assertion appears in her chapter on the immediate aftermath of the divorce but in another chapter (much of her narrative is non-chronological) she mentions a violently stormy evening when she and Parnell made their way to the end of Brighton pier. From several allusions it can be placed in this period after the divorce and it sheds a different light on Parnell's mood. At the end of the pier, unable to stand upright against the force of the wind, drenched by the lash of the waves, Katie clung to Parnell, who suddenly lifted her in his arms, held her high over the thundering sea and said, 'Oh, my wife, my wife, I believe I'll jump in with you, and we shall be free for ever.' In that moment when she was poised between life and death above the ferocious surging of the English Channel, Katie clung even more tightly to Parnell and replied, 'As you will, my love, but the children?' Without a word he turned and carried her back along the wooden planks of the pier, and the moment had passed.

The next test of Parnell's position was another by-election, this time in North Sligo in March 1891, and by now the opposition was stronger, having launched its daily paper, the *National Press,* and having obtained greater support from the clergy. The campaign at Sligo followed the unedifying precedent set in Kilkenny, only more so; on both sides the language was more abusive and there were more actual fights between rival crowds. The result was another defeat for Parnell's candidate, with 3,262 votes for the opposition, 2,493 for his, but it did nothing to shake his determination or that of his supporters, and the internecine warfare became even more bitter. The acrimony deepened over the role of the Church; the anti-Parnellites insisted that the hierarchy was condemning only Parnell's moral unsuitability to lead Catholic Ireland, not him as a private individual or even as a Member of Parliament; the Parnellites (many of whose Catholic members were placed in a great dilemma) stated that the Church had no authority to challenge the political leadership of Ireland on any grounds.

However much the bishops and priests might claim they were condemning on a moral issue, they had become enmeshed (in many cases only too willingly) in the practical business of dethroning Parnell, and towards the end of May Croke of Cashel made a series of anti-Parnell speeches, in one of which he mentioned an essential ingredient of the nationalist party's existence—money. He said it was a great pity there was no public audit of the nationalist funds and he wondered what had happened to the vast sums contributed to the 'Parnell Tribute' in 1883, to the Defence Fund at the time of the Special Commission and to the cheque sent by Cecil Rhodes (for a cool £10,000). Archbishop Croke said he had no desire to insinuate embezzlement on anybody's part, but Tim Healy had no such compunctions and on 1 June he published the first 'Stop Thief' article in the *National Press.* (The articles were published anonymously but Healy wrote them.) Parnell had immediately replied to Croke's queries in a speech at Wicklow, saying the Tribute money was his own personal property so he did not have to account for it, the balance of the Defence Fund money was in his possession and he would use it for suitable public purposes when occasion demanded, while part of the Cecil Rhodes money had been given to the Plan of Campaign and the rest he retained. In his 'Stop Thief' article Healy said Parnell's replies were totally unsatisfactory, he referred to him as 'the burrowing adulterer' and 'the Elthamite' and said that for years he had been stealing money entrusted to his charge. The next day Healy returned to the attack—'We called Mr Parnell a thief. We now repeat the epithet . . . a wily thief is Mr Fox'—and for the rest of the week he continued his onslaughts against 'the faithful squire of Mrs O'Shea.'

Healy's inflammatory articles were in part just that—what could be more attention-catching than accusations of theft? But he had his suspicions that Parnell was using the nationalist funds under his jurisdiction to finance his present campaign (where else was the money coming from?), and while Parnell might successfully contend that as the elected Chairman of the parliamentary party he had every right to do so, to prove his point he would have to take Healy to court, and in the process explain in detail just what was happening to the funds, which would reveal a great deal about his present campaign. If he did not sue Healy for libel, then the anti-Parnellites could say he was guilty by default. Thus, if the articles were in one way unforgivable, in another they were a clever tactical exercise, and above all they showed how ferocious the enmity between the two sides had become. Within six months the split had widened to the extent that a leading Irish nationalist could accuse the recently revered 'Chief' of the theft of Irish nationalist funds. In the event, Parnell did not sue Healy, either from disdain or because he realised the cost, financial and otherwise, of a protracted lawsuit, and the legally unrefuted accusations did his reputation no good.

Whether Willie O'Shea enjoyed watching the spectacle of Irishman fighting Irishman (which he had helped induce) is unknown, but he had little else to give him pleasure in the months after the divorce. If he had hoped to emerge as the anti-Parnellite hero of the hour he was sadly disappointed, and almost from the moment of the divorce, attacks were made on him from various sources. The first notable person to query Captain O'Shea's position was Archbishop Walsh—this was before the hierarchy came out in denunciation of Parnell—and O'Shea wrote to Cardinal Manning about 'the extraordinary innuendo respecting my divorce case' made by Walsh, in which he had suggested that the Captain might have been politically motivated and might not be as innocent as implied. Forgetting that he had earlier accused Manning of making similar suggestions, a few days later O'Shea again wrote to His Eminence asking him to make His Grace retract his innuendoes 'immediately and unconditionally', but Manning was not interested. Some of the worst slurs on his character were made by Tim Healy during the Kilkenny campaign, and urged on by Chamberlain—whose name was also involved in the accusations about the Galway election—he rushed into print, denying that there was any truth in the statements that he had been elected for Galway because his wife was Parnell's mistress. This denial gave fuel to the anti-Parnellite press—the *Irish Catholic* said: 'Mr Parnell was reinforced by a new, or should we say, old companion in arms, no less a person than the redoubtable Captain O'Shea himself.' Although on the Galway issue he had Chamberlain's support—he wrote saying, 'Your friendship is worth having. You know how to stand up for a friend'—generally there was no scramble to defend Captain O'Shea's good name.

In February 1891 O'Shea was again publicly denounced by a member of the Irish Catholic hierarchy, this time by Dr McCormack, the Bishop of Galway. McCormack followed the pattern set by Healy, attacking Parnell's moral unsuitability for leadership as something which had not occurred overnight but which had festered since the notorious Galway election. In a published letter he said that Parnell, having failed to foist Captain O'Shea on other constituencies, 'had the effrontery of prostituting the Galway City constituency as a hush gift', that at the time Mr Joseph Biggar had supplied the missing explanation to the baffled, shocked citizens of Galway, and finally, having himself balanced the divorce court evidence against the accusations made in Galway, he had come to the conclusion that Mr Biggar's statements were corroborated. (Biggar was by now dead.) These were indeed strong words and O'Shea ran round in circles trying to get them retracted. He wrote dozens of letters to the Primate of All Ireland, to prelates in England, to contacts in Rome and eventually to the Pope himself; Wilfrid Scawen Blunt mentioned the 'huge correspondence' between O'Shea and various members of the Catholic hierarchy that he had seen in a London prelate's house. Finally in July 1891, O'Shea obtained a grudging private retraction of the worst slurs from McCormack, but nothing appeared publicly.

Back in the February he had more pressing problems than imputations against his honour; he was in dire financial straits. At the beginning of 1891 O'Shea had taken a lease on a house in Brighton, 12 Chichester Terrace, into which he moved with 'the children who share my fortunes.' They were Carmen and Gerard, for Norah had decided to stay with her mother at Walsingham Terrace and, as O'Shea told Chamberlain, 'the absence of my eldest daughter, Norah, is a constant trial.' (Norah was an extremely patient, long-suffering young lady and an excellent housekeeper; Carmen was none of these things.) Where O'Shea found the money to buy the lease is his secret, perhaps the Woods helped him but if they did, that was the extent of their largesse. At this period he still held the Woods in high esteem. He wrote to Chamberlain saying, 'Nothing could exceed—I ought to say equal—the care and affection lavished on myself and my children who are with me, by the family of the lady who was my wife.' But he was quickly in financial difficulties and asking Chamberlain if he could get him a job; immediately after the divorce he suggested that his friend find him a safe parliamentary seat—'If you want me back in the House, this is the moment to strike and extract a promise.' Neither Chamberlain nor anybody else wanted Captain O'Shea back in the House of Commons, and a fortnight later he was asking Chamberlain for the vacant Commissionship of Public Works in Dublin, a post which *must* be filled by an Irishman, but again Chamberlain failed to exert himself for this particular Irishman.

In mid-February he had to write to Chamberlain begging for money. He said that his lawsuits had so far cost him £5,300, which he had managed to pay as he went along without any help from anybody, but he now found himself 'in a corner, and a nasty one for the moment' because he needed £800, £400 immediately and £400 at the end of March, otherwise he would be 'at the mercy of a very dangerous enemy of mine'. (One would love to know who *that* was.) He said he was 'intensely mortified' at having to write to Chamberlain 'on a horrid matter of pence', but he had been unjustly treated before, during and since the divorce case, so could his friend possibly help? Chamberlain loaned the first £400 (not, as he told Willie, without difficulty) and O'Shea wrote back full of gratitude. It is apparent from the letters that O'Shea's feelings of persecution had not abated since his triumph in the divorce court; on the contrary they had increased. Everybody, with the exception of Chamberlain and the Woods, was against him (and the latter were obviously not willing to lend him £400) but with the money made available he temporarily retired from the scene.

Before Parnell faced the next test of his position—another by-election, this time in Carlow, caused by the death of O'Shea's old friend the O'Gorman Mahon—the event occurred which he said gave him greater happiness than anything in his whole life. This was his marriage to Katie, which took place in the Registry Office in Steyning, on 25 June 1891. The divorce decree was made absolute on 26 May, from which date Parnell and Mrs O'Shea were legally free to marry, and a local Sussex paper reported that the greatest possible anxiety was exhibited by newspaper editors, press agencies and politicians throughout Britain and Ireland 'to learn without a moment's delay news of the anticipated sequel to the most momentous divorce case of recent years.' Parnell and Katie wanted to be married in an Anglican church, and in the weeks after the divorce became absolute he spent some time approaching various vicars in the Brighton area, but none was willing to sanctify the union of the world's most notorious divorcee and her lover. Consequently they decided to marry initially in a registry office and hopefully to follow the legal ceremony by a church wedding. The gentlemen and at least one lady of the press quickly became aware that the wedding would occur at a registry office and worked on the correct assumption that it would be by special licence, in which case it would have to be performed by a superintendent registrar. Walsingham Terrace then lay outside the boundaries of Brighton and was part of Aldrington, which came in Steyning Union, and the superintendent registrar of this Union was a Mr Cripps, whose offices were actually in Steyning.

On 23 June, Parnell drove to Steyning and obtained from Mr Cripps a special licence which stated that a marriage between Charles Stewart Parnell, bachelor, Member of Parliament, forty-four years of age, of Avondale, Rathdrum, Ireland, but now of England, and Katharine O'Shea, formerly Wood, spinster, the divorced wife of William Henry O'Shea, of full age, 10 Walsingham Terrace, Aldrington, would take place in the Steyning registrar's office within three months of its issue. From that moment, as Katie herself recorded, Walsingham Terrace was besieged by reporters and she and Parnell laid plans to throw them off the scent (the idea of reporters attending the wedding was particularly hateful to him). Mr Cripps had shown himself kindly disposed towards the notorious couple and on 24 June, according to Katie, Parnell again drove to Steyning, where he obtained the superintendent registrar's consent to the ceremony being performed at an early hour on the twenty-fifth, although according to the *National Press* a jaunty Parnell was in London on the twenty-fourth and only bought the wedding ring at seven o'clock in the evening. Having settled the time of the ceremony, 8.30 a.m. on 25 June, Katie and Parnell informed their groom that they would require the carriage at 11 a.m. the next morning and his presence as witness to their marriage. The ruse worked, she recorded that 'the newspaper men soon had these instructions out of the discomfited young man', and consequently slightly relaxed their round-the-clock vigil on Walsingham Terrace. Two of Katie's servants, the faithful Phyllis and the children's nurse, were parties to the real plan, which was for the bridal pair to leave Walsingham Terrace by carriage at 6.30 a.m., with Phyllis and the nurse travelling by the workmen's train, which arrived at Steyning at 8.17 a.m.

According to Katie, 25 June dawned with the promise of being the most perfect of English summer days and she and Parnell were up to watch the sun spread a soft, glowing light across the sky (but according to the local Sussex paper, the early morning was oppressive, with thunder clouds menacing, although it agreed that the day later became brilliantly fine). Phyllis apparently fussed so much round her mistress, determined that Mrs O'Shea should look her loveliest on this happiest of days, that Parnell finally hustled her out of the room and into the waiting cab en route to the station. He himself then went to the stables, woke the sleepy groom, and returned with the phaeton hitched to Dictator, which Katie said was the fastest driving horse she had ever known. Normally Parnell never noticed what she or anybody was wearing, but Phyllis had performed her task well, and as he gave Katie the bunch of white roses he had personally selected for her bridal posy he said, 'Queenie, you look lovely in that lace stuff and the beautiful hat with the roses. I am so proud of you.' The 'lace stuff' was a shawl which Katie wore over a black silk brocade dress and the beautiful hat was also black, entwined with pink roses; as Parnell was in a black morning suit, they were a sombre-looking bridal pair.

Katie drove the phaeton, and as they set off on the nine-mile journey to Steyning they heard the clatter of hooves behind them and rightly deduced that the half-awake pressmen had leapt into life at the sound of the carriage's departure, and Parnell said to her, 'They are after us; let Dictator go!' which she duly did. She said it was a glorious drive, although the local paper again asserted that thundery rain spattered the air as the bridal couple made their way towards Steyning and that Parnell donned an overcoat to protect himself. The area round Steyning remains one of the more attractive corners of England, studded with copses and lanes banked by hedgerows, with villages nestling at the feet of the South Downs, whose ridges rear suddenly to form a barrier to the sea, and we will assume that the midsummer sun broke through the storm clouds as Katie and Parnell drove furiously along the coast through Portslade and Southwick to Shoreham, turning inland to follow the course of the River Adur, passing the hedges loaded with dog roses and the fields rippling with corn, urging Dictator over the undulations of the countryside through Bramber and into Steyning, with its cobbled High Street and its jumble of Mediaeval, Tudor and Georgian houses irregular against the sky-line.

The registry office was in the High Street, a comparatively modern building surrounded by thatched cottages and ancient tiled roofs, and Mrs Cripps had taken the trouble to decorate the bleak room which served for marriage ceremonies with sweet-smelling, many-coloured summer flowers. While Katie and Parnell waited for Phyllis and the nurse to arrive—for Dictator had beaten the train—she glanced in the mirror which hung on one wall of the small room, Parnell followed her gaze, looked at both their reflections and, blowing kisses to her in the mirror, said, 'It isn't every woman who makes so good a marriage as you are making, Queenie, is it? and to such a handsome fellow, too!' Shortly thereafter the witnesses arrived, the brief ceremony was performed and early in the morning of 25 June 1891, in the arche-typal picture-postcard English village of Steyning, Katharine O'Shea, née Wood, became the legal wife of Charles Stewart Parnell, MP. Immediately the ceremony was over, Mr and Mrs Parnell thanked Mr Cripps for his kind services, jumped into the phaeton and drove as furiously as they could back to Brighton. As they left Steyning they passed the newspaper men, but Dictator was going so swiftly that there was no hope of a chase, and the reporters descended on Mr Cripps, who stayed true to his promise to Parnell and revealed nothing; as the local paper reported, 'Throughout the day he declined absolutely to say that the wedding had taken place at all.'

At Walsingham Terrace the newly married couple had to force

their way through a further crowd of reporters, but Parnell insisted that they must let *Mrs Parnell* pass and if they did so he would later grant them an interview. Reluctantly, the reporters agreed but they camped on the doorstep, one man managed to bribe the cook and penetrated through the basement, and the most enterprising of their number—an American lady reporter—somehow got into the next-door house which the Parnells owned and crept through the interconnecting door to Katie's bedroom. Her enterprise did her no good, as Parnell was furious that she had entered Katie's bedroom and refused to see her, but she could claim that she had entered the house and she let her imagination run riot. Katie commented that the resulting article had the demerit of being almost totally inaccurate but the merit of being distinctly bright, including an artist's impression of the newly-weds, with Parnell in a fur coat and herself in 'a dangerously décolleté garment, diaphanous in the extreme, and apparently attached to me by large diamonds', seated in a bedroom which would not have done disgrace to the most ornate bordello, with the sedate Phyllis cast in the role of fluffy French maid. The article and the illustrations gave Katie great amusement (though Parnell was less amused), and they may illuminate how some sectors of public opinion—not only in America—viewed Mrs Parnell, namely as an old-style courtesan.

Later in the morning, as promised, Parnell saw the reporters and, apart from telling the assembled throng that it was the happiest day of his life, he said it had been impossible to obtain a licence to marry in a church, so he and Mrs Parnell had married in the registry office but they hoped soon to have a church wedding in London. He also said that he hoped to visit the United States some time in the autumn, and when questioned about the forthcoming Carlow election replied that he thought his friend would win the seat and that he expected to be in the area soon himself, but he could not say whether Mrs Parnell would accompany him, as she was a bad sailor and furthermore she had to attend to the matter of a probate action between herself and her brothers 'with regard to the Eltham property recently left to her by her late Aunt, a matter which was expected to come into court very shortly.' Having satisfied the reporters, Katie and Parnell went for a walk, wandering across the fields to Aldrington, where they stopped at a brick-works. Parnell enjoyed himself chatting to the workmen and after the men had gone for lunch he made a couple of bricks, which he and Katie solemnly put into the kiln with special marks on them. They then continued their walk, dropping down to Shoreham harbour where they sat on the shingle in the full glow of the midsummer sun (which everybody agreed was now shining) and talked of the future, of the day when Parnell would have won Home Rule for Ireland and could abdicate, when they could perhaps live in a warmer and kinder climate than the English and they would be together for always without the interruption of politics. It was a dream they entertained from time to time, the picture of cosy retirement with Katie playing the little wife and Parnell immersed in his hobbies. It was one they could afford to entertain, literally that is, for whatever happened in the probate action Katie was bound to obtain a share of Aunt Ben's fortune, and it was one they might have enjoyed in reality for a while, but the idea of the nearly forty-five-year-old Parnell and the forty-six-year-old Katie, both possessed of pride, ambition and restless bursts of energy, retiring permanently from the political arena is hard to swallow.

Later in the afternoon Katie admitted that the atmosphere became oppressive, the sky darkened and a thunderstorm broke. She and Parnell sheltered under the breakwater and she wished that on this day of all days the glorious sun had continued long into the soft summer night. Parnell apparently read her thoughts and told her that no storm could hurt them now, for there was nothing in the wide world greater than their love, and she was comforted because death was something she had forgotten.

Chapter Nineteen

For a couple more days the Parnells were able to enjoy the satisfaction of having made their love legal. Katie took pleasure in reading the telegrams and letters which poured into Walsingham Terrace and she said the friendly ones far outweighed the abusive. But on Saturday, 27 June, Parnell had to leave for Ireland to fight the Carlow by-election and hopes that his marriage might have softened the bitterness were swiftly despatched. It was in Protestant England rather than Catholic Ireland that such hopes had been entertained in some sectors, for in the former country divorce was recognised (if mostly with abhorrence) and by making Mrs O'Shea his wife Parnell had demonstrated that his love was genuine. In Ireland the bishops denounced the marriage, quoting the Gospels, 'Whosoever shall marry her that is divorced committeth adultery', while Tim Healy's paper, the *National Press,* expressed popular Catholic sentiment. On 26 June it informed its growing readership that 'the hero of the divorce court duly wedded at old Steyning Parish Church yesterday', an inaccurate statement but the meaning was clear and with many exclamation marks it wondered whether the honeymoon would be spent in Carlow!!! The next day it had an article headed 'Mrs O'Shea's Husband' which stated that 'if the hero of the fire escape' imagined he had bought himself new credit or a useful coat of whitewash by his marriage he was sorely mistaken; 'legalised concubinage' would do him no good whatsoever in Holy Mother Ireland, which was sickened to learn that Carlow was to be honoured with the presence of 'Captain O'Shea's divorced wife'.

In the event, Katie did not appear in Carlow, but as the election campaign swung into thrice-bitter gear, Tim Healy renewed his attacks on Mrs O'Shea—and no anti-Parnellite newspaper ever paid her the compliment of addressing her by her new legal name. In a speech made on 5 July he asked the question: What had changed Mr Parnell from the leader Ireland had known to the present despicable specimen of humanity? It was a rhetorical question and he answered, 'One bad, base, immoral woman. Parnell broke his pledge to Ireland, Kitty broke her vow to her husband. The person at the bottom of the whole business is Mrs O'Shea. . . .' At this point he was interrupted by a voice from the crowd shouting, 'Kate the First,' and a counter-voice shouting, 'I will follow Parnell . . .' but this loyal voice was drowned in shouts of 'Down the fire-escape.' The exchange was typical of countless meetings, with Healy stoking up the contempt and derision for the base, immoral woman who had ruined Parnell and for the man who had allowed himself to be thus ruined.

The Carlow by-election followed the pattern already set, with the added incentive for rowdyism in the fact that Parnell's candidate was Andrew Kettle and the banging of kettles to drown Parnellite speakers became a feature of the campaign. The result was a more decisive defeat than had been Kilkenny or Sligo, with Andrew Kettle receiving just over 1,500 votes while the anti-Parnellite candidate had nearly 4,000. The marriage—and the Church's firm denunciation of it—had turned more of Catholic Ireland against Parnell, and it was also losing him the support of the *Freeman's Journal,* which so far had stood firm behind him (the paper did not finally repudiate his leadership until September, but it started wavering from the end of June). Disaster at the next General Election stared Parnell in the face but he stared back at it unblinkingly, telling his supporters that if only a handful of his candidates were returned he would still fight on, and that all he needed to regain control of an independent Irish party was time, which was obviously on his forty-five-year-old side.

During the last two months of Parnell's life, efforts were made to try and heal the increasingly jagged split in the Irish party by John Dillon and William O'Brien, who emerged from the sanctuary of imprisonment in August. Their hope was that if they threw their weight against Parnell they could gain control of the opposition, stifle Healy's extremity, and thus wean away the more moderate of Parnell's supporters and re-form a unified party. This time the negotiations were conducted without Parnell's direct involvement, there was no longer thought of his retiring temporarily and retaining real power and it was on this aspect that the talks foundered, for the 'faithful few' would not repudiate him. For the man himself the last two months of life were consumed by meetings in Ireland to rally the few until they once more became the many, and he was beset by financial difficulties. Politically Parnell needed money to found a newspaper—as it became obvious that the *Freeman's Journal* was deserting him, it was essential that he have a new medium of mass communication to propagate his views. Personally he needed money to pay the costs of the divorce action; the court order had been served on him in April, at Victoria Station as he caught the train to Brighton, according to Katie, but with the utmost discretion.

In August he was writing to 'Queenie' from Avondale asking if she could arrange with the solicitors to defer payment of the costs until the end of the year, when he thought he would be in a position to clear the debt. At the same time, he and Katie were considering renting a house in North Wales, which again required money, and as if the journeys between Brighton and Dublin were not sufficiently tiring, early in September he wrote to tell her that he would make a detour from Holyhead in order to inspect the Welsh house they had in mind (they did not take it). He also went to see the vicar in Steyning about their marriage in the parish church there, but the vicar said he disapproved of divorce and therefore he could not personally officiate. However, under the terms of a remote Act of Parliament he could lend them the building if they could find another Anglican vicar willing to perform the ceremony. Even if the willing outside vicar were found, permission was required from the Bishop of the diocese, the Bishop of Chichester, and apart from being known to abhor divorce he was currently out of the country, so this plan was abandoned. Parnell persisted, and in London he discovered the Reverend James Penfold, the Anglican incumbent of a church in Marylebone whose conscience did not forbid him to marry a divorcee, and Parnell was intending to sanctify his union in church as soon as he had established the necessary residential qualifications in Marylebone.

When he returned to Brighton in the middle of September, Katie began to be really alarmed about his health. In repose, as he lay on the sofa in the comfort of Walsingham Terrace, his face had a look of absolute exhaustion, with deep-grey shadows under his eyes, and she tried to persuade him to see Sir Henry Thompson, who after the introduction to 'Mr Stewart' in 1886 had become his personal physician. Parnell refused, saying he was not ill, merely a little tired, and that there was no point in bothering Sir Henry. But Katie was deeply worried and asked if he could not rest temporarily, for if he became too tired then he would be ill. Parnell replied, 'I am in your hands, Queenie, and you shall do with me what you will; but you promised'—a reminder of her promise never to make him less than the man she had known and loved. He added that he would die rather than capitulate to the howls of the English mob, and she grew somewhat metaphysical, recording that she realised 'that in the martyrdom of our love was to be our reparation.' What she did not realise towards the end of September 1891 was that her martyrdom was to be his death, and had she truly appreciated that his stocks of energy had almost run their course, she would surely have prevented the last journey. As it was, her blend of feminine submissiveness and headstrong pride combined to wave her husband good-bye as he left on 25 September for yet another long, tiring journey to Dublin. As Parnell drove off in the phaeton to Brighton Station, he raised the customary white rose in his button-hole to his lips before the carriage rounded the corner and disappeared.

On his arrival in Dublin, Parnell's rheumatism was so bad that he had to carry his arms in a sling, and Dr Kenny (one of his most devoted supporters) begged him not to proceed to the unimportant meeting in the remote village of Creggs in County Galway, but all meetings, however remote the village, however small the crowd, were now important to Parnell, and he insisted on going. Sunday, 27 September, was an appallingly wet day in Creggs and he stood bare-headed in the pouring rain to address the small crowd and was then unable to change his soaking clothes for several hours because the bag in which Katie had packed his dry socks, shoes and other garments was mislaid. For the first and last time the exhaustion from which Parnell was suffering became apparent, and in the opening minutes his speech was so halting and inaudible that no reporter could transcribe his words. As he continued, he rallied his ebbing reserves and in this last speech he ever made, in the remote Galway village of Creggs, he said that he would continue to fight because he was fighting not for faction but for Ireland's freedom. On his return to Dublin, he was in acute pain from rheumatism in his left arm but he refused to rest, spending three days attending to the launching of his new paper, the *Irish Daily Independent*, before sailing for England and Katie on 30 September, telling his friends that he would be back on Saturday week.

On arrival in London, Parnell did not immediately catch the train for Brighton but decided to have a Turkish bath, in the hopes that it would relieve his rheumatic pain, and by the time he finally arrived at Walsingham Terrace he was so weak Katie had to help him from the carriage. Southern England was experiencing an Indian summer so the weather was particularly warm, but Katie had to stoke up a blazing fire before she could get the circulation flowing in Parnell's veins. For the first and last time, he admitted in person that he was feeling ill and said he would stay at home and rest for a while, but he still refused to see Sir Henry Thompson. For several hours that evening he and Katie sat before the blazing fire, she nestling at his feet with her head on his lap while he stroked her hair, then fell into a doze, woke and stroked her hair again, and finally asked for his stick as he wanted to go into the next room. When he stood up, his legs collapsed under him and it was only by leaning on Katie that he managed to get upstairs, having agreed that he should rest in bed. She had to undress him as he had not the strength to take off his clothes, and once he was in bed she rubbed him with fir-wood oil and packed wool round his left arm and made him agree to see the local doctor the next morning. During a restless night he talked of rheumatism as the Irish disease from which thousands of peasants had died, and grew excited when she suggested telegraphing Sir Henry Thompson—'No, the fee would be enormous at this distance.' The next morning he seemed better, sitting up in bed, smoking one of his favourite cigars, making notes for his next speech and writing to Sir Henry Thompson for his advice rather than paying the enormous fee for a personal visit. As he was feeling and looking brighter and was in less pain from the rheumatism, Dr Jowers, the local doctor whom he liked and trusted, was not sent for that day. Katie had her daughter Norah to assist her (apart from the staff), and Norah had already shown herself to be an efficient and devoted nurse.

By Sunday morning Parnell's condition had abruptly worsened, he was feverish, in agonising pain from the rheumatism, and his body temperature was alarmingly high. Katie accordingly sent for Dr Jowers, who found his patient 'in a very bad state' and called in his father, who was a leading Brighton physician, but there was little either man could do except advise constant nursing, prescribe a few medicaments to relieve the acute pain and trust that their patient would ride the crisis of fever which was approaching. Katie still wanted to telegraph to Sir Henry Thompson but in his lucid moments her husband, comforted by the letter he had received from Sir Henry, refused to let her do so. Later, Katie was so troubled by her failure to get Sir Henry down to Brighton that she published a long letter from him in which he said that he doubted there was anything that he or any living physician could have done to have saved Parnell in the last week because his constitution was worn out, and that she must not reproach herself for any one act or omission to act.

Parnell was a dying man from the moment he made that last speech in the pouring rain in Creggs and continued to behave as if he were in possession of glowing health, but as Katie sat by his bedside in that first week of October 1891, relieved occasionally from her vigil by Norah, it is doubtful that she appreciated the fact. In the face of the approaching death of a loved one, hope continues to spring eternal in the human breast and Katie had a capacity to ignore reality because up to a short while ago she had always managed to shape it to her pattern, and that there were forces outside her control had not yet penetrated her mind. On the Sunday night Parnell had not slept, and one of his many superstitions was that if he passed two sleepless nights in succession he would die during the third. On the Monday night he again did not sleep, but by the Tuesday morning he was too feverish to appreciate the implications of his own superstition, being only intermittently lucid and babbling not of green fields but of sunny lands and the Tory party. The Drs Jowers, father and son, paid several visits on the Monday and Tuesday. During a visit on the Tuesday afternoon Parnell appeared calmer and they left saying there was no hope for improvement for at least two days and they would call again the next morning. During the early evening Parnell mostly lay quietly, smiling at Katie whenever she touched him, begging her not to send the dogs from the room, at least not Grouse, his favourite, so Grouse and Katie kept their vigil. The Indian summer had fled, and as the evening wore on and Katie watched by the bedside, a gale blew up in the English Channel, the wind shrieked round the exposed end of Walsingham Terrace, the rain lashed against the windows and on the nearby beach the waves crashed and moaned. Late in the evening Parnell opened his eyes and said, 'Kiss me, sweet wifie, and I will try to sleep a little' and as she pressed her lips against his 'the fire of them, fierce beyond any I had felt, even in his most loving moods' startled her. Then, as she drew gently back from the embrace, Parnell gave a small sigh and slipped into unconsciousness. Katie immediately sent for the doctors, who arrived as quickly as possible, but Parnell never recovered consciousness and shortly before midnight on 6 October 1891, in the month which he had always loathed, in the presence of Drs Jowers, Norah O'Shea and his beloved Queenie his heart stopped beating.

At this point Katie's memoirs stop too, with the reiteration that the last words Parnell uttered were, 'Kiss me, sweet wifie, and I will try to sleep a little', not, as stated in the newspapers, 'Let my love be conveyed to my colleagues and the Irish people. I hope they will be as well cared for in their sickness as I have been.' One believes her. The attributed words sound extraordinarily unlike Parnell, and the bit about being cared for in sickness, unlike any dying man (this latter sentence was swiftly dropped from the authorised version of the last words). Katie's account of her husband's death has a poignancy and simplicity of style which is notably lacking from her earlier chapters, and there was no need for her to invent his dying words, for if Ireland had been the driving force of Parnell's adult life, since 1880 its mainspring had been Katie and his every action had proved his fierce love and need for her.

As the news of Parnell's death spread on the morning of 7 October, as the agencies transmitted it, the telegraph wires chattered and the cables hummed, and as it penetrated to the furthest corners of the earth, the reaction was shattered, stunned disbelief. The news was particularly stunning because nobody outside the smallest circle in Brighton had known that he was even ill. True, he had looked unwell in recent months and those closest to him had been worried about the strain on his constitution, but he had been ill in 1886 and 1887, when he had displayed amazing powers of recovery and had seemed to possess inexhaustible reserves. Now, at the age of forty-five, he was dead and it was unbelievable. The reporters descended on Walsingham Terrace, some of whom but three months previously had waited for news of his marriage, the crowds streamed out from Brighton and stood in the pouring rain and gusting winds staring at the house with its drawn blinds, watching the telegraph boys toil up with the piles of telegrams and the visitors calling to leave their condolences. The number of people actually admitted to the house was minimal, for inside Katie was in a state of dazed shock and after the isolated years with Parnell she had few close friends or relations. Mrs Emily Dickinson, Parnell's sister, travelled to Brighton on hearing the incredible news, as did several members of the shrunken Parnellite party, including the young Henry Harrison, for it was at this moment that he emerged on the scene.

Harrison was then in his early twenties; born of Ulster Protestant stock and educated in England, he had abandoned his degree course at Oxford University to follow the star of Parnell, whom he met for the first time during the days in Committee Room 15. If Parnell's star was then in the descendant, for Harrison it shone with the magic of yesteryear and he became—and remained for the rest of his long life—a devoted Parnellite. On hearing the news of his leader's death, Harrison was the only outsider who thought of Katie, of the agony she must be enduring and her need for friends in this terrible hour. The other Parnellites travelled to Brighton because they wanted to pay their condolences to the widow, but having done this their concern was for the funeral arrangements—the funeral must be held in Ireland—and for reassessing their position in the blackness of 'the Chief's' death. But the young Harrison telegraphed to Katie offering his personal services in any manner that might help, an offer which was not immediately appreciated by the prostrate widow but was accepted by Norah O'Shea onto whose even younger shoulders—she was only nineteen—all burdens were falling.

With the news of the death having been such an enormous shock, with the widow incommunicado inside Walsingham Terrace and in the immediate absence of hard news—how long had Parnell been ill? of what had he died? where was he to be buried?—the rumours started to shoot up like a newly sown lawn in spring and grew into some very rank weeds. The most persistent rumour was that Parnell, worn down by the stress of the recent fight, had committed suicide, and the parallel was drawn with the career of General Boulanger, who had similarly been the French people's idol, who had also fallen from grace, if for different reasons, and had committed suicide only the week before. There was the other rumour that Parnell was not in fact dead but had been spirited away to recuperate from a severe illness and would re-emerge when the time came to lead Ireland to freedom. The rumours were sufficiently strong to force a reluctant Dr Jowers to issue a statement which said: 'Mr Parnell died from rheumatic fever, with an excessively high body temperature and failure of the heart's action. He had a naturally weak heart. It is as plain a case as I ever attended, and there is not the least ground for the doubt that has been expressed in some quarters.' When the rumours, particularly of suicide, persisted, *The Lancet* entered the fray with an article about Mr Parnell's health which explained the effects of hyperpyrexia.

Having obtained as much information as they could, by 8 October the newspapers began to fill with comment and assessment on Parnell's life and death. Joseph Chamberlain and Captain O'Shea were interviewed; the former said Parnellism was now dead, a united Irish party might emerge under John Dillon but nothing was certain in politics; the latter, reported to be looking very grave, thought reconciliation in the Irish party was unlikely and made that reconciliation less likely by stating that in his last conversation with the dead leader (when could that have been?) Parnell had agreed that John Dillon was the falsest nationalist, Tim Healy the lowest, T. P. O'Connor the most contemptible and Justin McCarthy a mere figure-head; neither O'Shea nor Chamberlain had anything to say about Parnell personally. Most of the Tory papers compared Parnell's life and career with that of Mr W. H. Smith, the son of the founder of what has become Britain's most famous chain of bookshops and leader of the House of Commons, who had died the same day, with Mr Smith cast as a pillar of Victorian honour, probity and rectitude and Parnell as Lucifer fallen into the pit. *The Times* embroidered its theme that it had been right in suspecting Mr Parnell's character long before the divorce court revelations and that he had been patently unfit to lead any country, but it granted that he had also been one of the most remarkable men of the nineteenth century and it printed page after page of tribute and comment from other English papers, from Irish ones, from French, German, Canadian, Italian, and above all the American papers, for in the United States the reaction to Parnell's death had been overwhelming. His mother was in America and it was reporters there who apparently broke the news to her. She immediately asked if her son had shot himself (which added fuel to the suicide rumours), then said he had been killed by the lies and calumnies of his enemies, produced his last letter in which he had written, 'I am weary, dear mother, of these troubles, weary unto death', and asked that somebody should say a mother's last blessing over the grave.

Among the English and overseas newspapers there was a remarkable consensus of opinion about the effects of the sudden death, however different their views about the life. It was that Parnell's demise would heal the breach in the Irish party, that the bitterness would now be forgotten, that a reunified party would emerge under the leadership of John Dillon to realign itself with Mr Gladstone and the Liberal Party and obtain Home Rule for Ireland. In the Irish papers, as in Willie O'Shea's piece, there was an ominous lack of such hope, and on 10 October the optimism of the non-Irish journals was shattered by an article which appeared in the *Irish Catholic*. This article, which John Dillon described as 'un-Catholic, un-christian . . . a disgrace to Irish journalism', persisted in referring to the widow as *Mrs O'Shea* and contained the following statements: 'The death of Mr Parnell is one of those events which remind the world of God . . . so far as the world knows Mr Parnell has died unrepentant for his offences against God and his country. . . . The evil that men do lives after them, and the weeds which grow upon the grave of a dead cause are often more rank and noxious. To Catholics the close of the career of Mr Parnell will present itself with horrible significance. Death has come upon him in a home of sin . . . his memory is linked for ever with that of her whose presence seems to forbid all thought of his repentance . . . never a sign of sorrow for the insult he had offered to morality . . . against the anointed prelates and ministers of God's chosen church.' One can only say that no visitor from Mars on 10 October 1891 would have known that charity was one of the highly extolled virtues of God's chosen Church.

Fortunately Katie was in no condition to be hurt by these words although Parnell's supporters were and immediately launched into bitter counter-attacks which augured ill for Ireland's future. Indeed, Katie's condition was such that for a couple of days it was difficult to obtain sense from her, particularly on the subject of the funeral. Her instinct was that Parnell should be buried in Brighton in the town which held so many happy memories; her wish was for a quiet funeral attended only by herself, the few faithful friends and members of his surviving party. It was an impossible wish and eventually she allowed her instinct to be overruled and agreed that her husband should be buried in his native land. Her reluctant assent to a public funeral in Dublin, with burial in Glasnevin cemetery, was conveyed to Parnell's supporters and thereafter to the press by Norah O'Shea at a conference in the Hotel Metropole in Brighton. It is doubtful that Katie ever considered travelling to Ireland to be present at the funeral as she was in no fit state to undertake the journey, but if the idea crossed her mind she was assuredly advised not to appear. The decision to allow her husband to be buried in Dublin therefore meant that she could not follow the beloved body to the grave but that in death, as so many times in life, she must stay in Brighton, and grieve alone.

On Friday night, 9 October, Parnell's body was put into an unusually large oak coffin in the bedroom at Walsingham Terrace, but at Katie's wish the coffin was not sealed until the Saturday morning, when she took the last look at her beloved King and placed some very personal souvenirs beside the body, including the faded rose which had fallen from her bodice on that July afternoon in Palace Yard in 1880. On Saturday morning the coffin was closed, without many people having seen the body, which added fuel to the rumours that Parnell was not really dead or that he had committed suicide and was badly disfigured, and Katie's wreaths together with those from the children were placed on top. Her wreaths bore the inscriptions 'To my own true love, my husband, my king', while those from Norah O'Shea and 'little Katie' and 'little Clare' had the words 'To my dear mother's husband'. The coffin was then carried out of the house to the waiting hearse and the waiting crowds, and as it was the most dismal of days, grey and overcast with a persistent drizzling rain, it emerged to a forest of black umbrellas. The hearse and the mourners' carriages proceeded slowly through the dripping dankness of the grey October day, through the streets of a silent Brighton to the station, where coffin and mourners transferred to a special van attached to the scheduled train for London.

At East Croydon the special van was detached and hitched to another train for Willesden Junction, where it arrived about six o'clock and where Londoners, and the many Irish people in London, were able to pay their last respects. Then the boat train from Euston steamed into the junction, the van was attached thereto and Parnell's body set off for the last time on the journey to Holyhead which it had known so well in life. The Irish Sea was crossed by night and the mail boat sailed into Kingstown (now Dun Laoghaire) harbour at daybreak on the Sunday morning, and the weather was even worse than it had been in Brighton, with a thick mist, high gusty winds and squally showers. From Kingstown the van proceeded to Dublin by train, then the cortège wound through the city streets, stopping at St Michael's Church for a brief service before arriving at the City Hall, where the coffin lay briefly in state, surrounded by black drapes and a banner bearing the already truncated 'authentic' last words 'Give my love to my colleagues and the Irish people'; and some thirty thousand people were estimated to have filed past for the few hours it remained there. In the early afternoon the coffin started on its very last journey through the streets of Dublin from the City Hall to Glasnevin cemetery. It lay on a hearse drawn by six horses, with Parnell's own horse, Home Rule, following immediately behind, boots and stirrups reversed. Then came the mourners' carriages, then the long lines of representatives from most ranks and societies of Irish life. The procession wound through the streets, the rain poured down and the crowds were strangely silent, only the slither of marching feet, the wet clatter of the horses' hoofs and the mournful strains of the 'Dead March' from *Saul* breaking the eerie silence. There was no sign of the bitterness which divided the nation, and apart from a minor incident when a horse tried to bolt and in the temporary panic rumours spread that Tim Healy was present, all was orderly. The cortège reached Glasnevin cemetery about 5.30 p.m., with the light fast fading from the skies and the moon already risen, and after the burial service had been conducted Henry Harrison placed Katie's wreaths back on the coffin to be buried with the body. It was he who represented the woman to whom Parnell had given his love and his life but whose presence at the funeral would have been unacceptable to most of those who thronged the streets and pressed round the grave-side to mourn for the dead 'Chief'.

Parnell's burial did nothing to lessen the Irish bitterness, if anything it was exacerbated, the vicious attacks on the man and on the woman he had loved mounted, and less than a month after the funeral Tim Healy made one of his most notorious onslaughts against the widow. The nationalists were then wrangling about the 'Paris Funds', and in a speech at Longford at the beginning of November Healy said that Mrs O'Shea was trying to obtain control of the Irish money in conjunction with certain Parnellites. He spoke of her as 'this abandoned woman' and said, 'No more shocking incident has been heard of than this alliance between so-called Irish patriots and a proved British prostitute. I mince no words'—indeed he did not—'and I tell you why. Because she has found a protector and a challenger in the person of a Parnellite two-year-old, Mr Henry Harrison.' Healy continued by saying that when the party had offered honourable compromise to Parnell it was she who would not let him accept, and if they were to have English dictation in Ireland it was not going to be the dictation of Mrs O'Shea; Mr Gladstone and Hawarden might effect future events, but not Mrs O'Shea and Brighton.

In this vicious attack there was one statement which had some truth, namely that Henry Harrison was becoming the prop on which Katie leant, although when Healy made his Longford speech Harrison had not in fact met the widow. He had established himself in a hotel in Brighton, he was visiting Walsingham Terrace daily and making his services freely available to the burdened Norah O'Shea, but for a month after the funeral Katie stayed in her room where, according to Harrison, she gave free vent to her emotions; he mentioned 'the collective nerve-tensity' which ran through the building like an electric current. When Katie finally emerged from her room she faced a bleak situation. Bereft of Aunt Ben's money, she herself had had no income for two and a half years and they had been living on Parnell's money, most of which had gone. He had made a will in which he had left everything to her and also recognised Katie and Clare as his children, but he had made it *before* the marriage and had not altered it afterwards and it was therefore invalid. Katie had no claim on Avondale and the money which might accrue from its sale or that could be raised on further mortgages. Henry Harrison said that when he first arrived at Walsingham Terrace there was a shortage of cash, and as the weeks went by, tradesmen pressed for payment of already large bills and refused to deliver further goods until the debts were cleared.

The probate action still had to be heard, and why it was deferred yet again when Parnell had spoken of its imminent hearing as a reason why Katie could not accompany him to Carlow in June remains a mystery. As a result of the action Katie must obtain something and further manoeuvrings started between Mrs Parnell and her ex-husband, for the terms of the divorce had altered the O'Shea marriage settlement and Willie had become entitled to half of her income or a life interest thereon. For Katie a most pressing need was to wrest from her ex-husband legal control of Parnell's children, Katie and Clare, and in the pourparlers, indeed in all the negotiations which revolved round the subject of money and custody, Henry Harrison proved of inestimable value. When he was first ushered into the presence of Parnell's widow he found her like a caged tiger, ready to spring without warning, and for some time his relationship with Mrs Parnell was strained in the extreme. He recorded that she spoke *at* rather than *to* him 'in a markedly ironical and minatory fashion', and that on one occasion she produced a revolver from underneath her handkerchief and, accusing him of being a spy, pointed it straight at him. When he finally persuaded her to relin-

[289]

quish the gun, he discovered that it was fully loaded and properly cocked and that she was a good markswoman. After a while Katie accepted that he was not a spy from the O'Shea or anti-Parnellite camps and that she could trust him, and Harrison participated in the many conversations at Walsingham Terrace. (It was at this period that he was given access to Katie's private papers and discovered documents which seemed to him to point clearly to O'Shea's connivance.)

O'Shea himself was living in Brighton. Carmen and Gerard were with him, and the two children (if not the father) became frequent visitors to the house, as did the ubiquitous Anna Steele, the sisters having apparently forgotten the acrimony of Katie's divorce court allegations. Henry Harrison described Mrs Steele as a small, plump, elderly lady with a frankly inquisitive manner, and said that a stream of gossip, of 'so-and-so says this' and 'father says that' became the order of the day at Walsingham Terrace. Before long O'Shea grew to resent Mr Harrison's presence and assistance to his ex-wife, rumours were spread that the young man was Mrs Parnell's lover (or if not hers, Norah's), and this state of affairs ended by Harrison issuing a challenge to Captain O'Shea. The more serious matters with which Harrison had to deal were finance and the attempt to obtain an agreement from O'Shea about the custody of Clare and Katie before the probate action came to court. By the end of February 1892 the financial situation at Walsingham Terrace had reached rock bottom, the threat of Katie's being made bankrupt was real, and if she were declared bankrupt *before* the probate action she might be unable to contest it and might lose everything by default. For almost the last time, for the sands of Katie's luck were running out, a fairy godfather appeared in the shape of Sir Edward Watkin, chairman of the South Eastern Railway Company, and Channel tunnel enthusiast. At his wit's end to raise hard cash for the temporarily almost destitute Katie, Harrison discovered that a recent law stated that in cases of intestacy the widow could claim the first £500 of her late husband's estate, and on the strength of this information Sir Edward Watkin agreed to loan Mrs Parnell an immediate £500. Katie was thus able to stave off her most pressing creditors and meet the mounting costs of the probate action, which was now set to be heard on 24 March 1892.

Katie needed expert advice—and with Henry Harrison taking charge of her affairs she obtained it in the shape of Sir Charles Russell—for arrayed against her in the probate action was a formidable galaxy of legal luminaries. The Attorney General led for the defendants, Sir

Evelyn Wood, vc, and Charles Page Wood, Sir Henry James, qc, for the interveners, Mrs Anna Steele and Mrs Chambers (sister Polly), Mr Lewis Coward for the interveners, Captain W. H., Miss Carmen and Mr Gerard O'Shea, and the Solicitor General for Anne and Irene Courage. (The Courages also intervened, on what grounds is unclear, but Willie O'Shea told Chamberlain that all the Wood expenses had been paid by members of the well-known brewing family.) The news of the probate action revived interest in 'Kitty' O'Shea, who must surely appear in court this time, and long before ten o'clock on the morning of 24 March the courtroom was packed to capacity with people anxious to see the notorious lady in the flesh. But they were to be disappointed, for as *The Times* reported, 'In legal circles it had long been an open secret that a settlement of the action was likely to be agreed at.' (*The Times* at least used Katie's legal name, Katharine Parnell, even if it spelled her Christian name as Katherine.) The Woods were perfectly willing to settle, as long as they obtained half of Aunt Ben's fortune. Henry Harrison wanted Sir Charles Russell to contest this settlement, as he thought Katie could and should obtain a much larger share, if not the entire fortune, for the last will and testament had been entirely in her favour. (There was also the murky business of the lunacy petition and the statement of Mr Gladstone's personal physician on Aunt Ben's sanity, although Harrison apparently knew nothing of the lunacy proceedings, or if he did he never mentioned them.) Sir Charles Russell said he dared not risk going into court, as the temper of the jury was uncertain, bearing in mind Mrs Parnell's notoriety (the case was due to be heard before a special jury) and *her* temper, once put into the witness box, was an even less predictable factor. But it was agreed that Captain O'Shea's share of his ex-wife's share must be dependent on his relinquishing custody of young Katie and Clare, and Willie himself intimated to Chamberlain that blackmail had been used against him in the matter. This might be called a case of the biter bit, particularly since he told Chamberlain that Katie's case against him (not specifically with regard to the custody) was based on letters written to her 'in absolute confidence by a husband to a wife regarding the pecuniary assistance which the late Mrs Wood had promised me in my political career.' For who had produced in the divorce court countless letters written in confidence by a wife to a husband? With concrete evidence in their possession of Captain O'Shea's past financial indebtedness to Mrs Wood (which he had denied in the divorce court), Katie's counsel were able to persuade Captain O'Shea to

[291]

relinquish his legal custody of the two girls, although up to the last minute he fought a strong rearguard action, post-dating a letter agreeing not to take the girls away from Katie until *after* the probate hearing.

While the crowds sat patiently in the courtroom on the morning of 24 March, in the judge's chambers much of the discussion between counsel was taken up with the question of custody, at least on the O'Shea side (it was not a question which interested the Wood lawyers). When the legal luminaries emerged from the chambers soon after midday, Katie's junior counsel was able to tell an anxious Henry Harrison that O'Shea had given up his claim to young Katie and Clare—'We've got the children all right. I don't know if Jeune [the judge] understood what he was doing, but he did it right enough.' These final manoeuvrings over the two girls would seem to underline that they were unquestionably Parnell's children and that Willie O'Shea knew they were (although if one is defending him, it can still be argued that he did not realise that he had been deceived until after their births in 1883 and 1884). The final settlement of Aunt Ben's money, as agreed basically in the chambers before the judge and then worked out in detail over the following months, was that the Woods received half the fortune, Katie the other half, minus the court costs, which had accounted for £14,000. From Katie's share, which in the end amounted to nearly £65,000, Willie O'Shea obtained an immediate £7,500 in cash, with the bulk being held in trust for Katie for life, and she and her ex-husband each receiving the interest on £25,000, which came to about £800 per annum. On Katie's death, Gerard O'Shea was to receive 40 per cent of the remaining fortune, Norah and Carmen 22½ per cent each, and Clare and Katie 7½ per cent each. In the event, Gerard who was by now twenty-one and like his father always in need of money, received an immediate cash payment of £9,000. Thus was divided the money which in my opinion was the root cause of the debacle, initially because it led Katie to avoid a scandal by all possible means, later because it led the Woods into the fray.

Willie O'Shea's opinion of the settlement was contained in a particularly long, rambling letter to Chamberlain, a letter more filled than ever with complaints. In O'Shea's opinion his and his children's interests had been 'sacrificed to the paramount political object in view', which was Mr Gladstone's reputation. If the case had gone before the jury, according to him, Gladstone's name would have been bound to have been mentioned and Sir Charles Russell was prepared to make any settlement with the Woods to avoid this catastrophe. Gladstone's only connection with Aunt Ben and her money was that he had responded to Katie's pleas and persuaded Sir Andrew Clark to see the old lady and testify to her sanity. Mention of this connection had been avoided in the lunacy examination, so it is hard to see why it should have been inevitably raised in the probate action. Apart from believing that his interest (i.e. Katie's share) had been wantonly sacrificed by Sir Charles Russell to the Woods (and O'Shea's opinion of them was by now zero), he further complained that he had spent the last three weary years fighting lawsuits without a friend to assist him, and asserted that the nasty hints about his conduct towards Mrs Parnell had no foundation. These particular nasty hints revolved round the custody of Katie and Clare and the innuendoes about paternity, and he told Chamberlain that the only reason he had allowed Mrs Parnell to assume official custody was because the doctor and Norah had told him that Katie might go mad if he did not do so.

If the contention that it was the Woods who persuaded O'Shea to bring his divorce action is accepted, he had reason to have turned against them by early 1892. Had he not brought the divorce action, Katie would almost certainly have inherited Aunt Ben's fortune *in toto,* and it can be assumed that in return either for his continued silence or for an agreement to a quiet divorce, the heiress would have seen that her husband (or ex-husband) was well remunerated financially. When the Woods persuaded O'Shea to file suit for divorce, apart from the satisfaction and advancement he thought he would gain from ruining Parnell, he was also surely led to believe that he and the Woods would emerge from the probate action with the lion's share of Aunt Ben's money. Now that he found himself with a comparatively minor sum, O'Shea's cup of bitterness was filled to the brim. With the exception of Chamberlain, everybody was against him; the Unionist Party and the Tories had shown no gratitude for the wreck of Parnell's career; his wife had descended to using private letters to try and intimidate him (unsuccessfully, of course; he had only granted the custody because of her ill-health); an Irish nationalist QC, Sir Charles Russell, had sacrificed him to Mr Gladstone and the Liberal alliance; the Woods had sacrificed him to their greed; lies and calumnies continued to circulate about his every action.

However, O'Shea did pay his debt to Chamberlain (the money borrowed in 1891) and in an unusual burst of frankness and self-criticism he admitted that over the years from 1880 (when Parnell had appeared on the scene) he had received a good deal of money from Aunt Ben, with Katie obtaining further sums for him from time to time because 'often and especially in the year 1882, I was in want of money, owing to political expenses and, if you will, extravagant personal outlay, and I certainly pressed my wife to keep her aunt up to her promises.' Having unburdened his heart to an unsympathetic Joseph Chamberlain, O'Shea retired with £7,500 in cash and an annual income of £800 to nurse his grievances, and from then until his death no more was heard of him publicly. It was not a high reward for the wreck of Parnell and Ireland's dream and of his wife's life; indeed, the only people who achieved exactly what they wanted as a result of the divorce action were the Woods, for if Joseph Chamberlain was also an instigator he never realised his ambition of becoming Prime Minister.

Chapter Twenty

Henry Harrison had devoted six months of his young life to helping
Katie in her hour of greatest need. How she would have fared without
him is impossible to say but probably badly. Norah O'Shea was capable
within the house, an unemotional, self-contained girl, quietly and
selflessly carrying on with the routine jobs, coping with the debts, caring
for young Katie and Clare, listening to her mother's grief, catering for
her every mood, but it is doubtful that she could have dealt with such
matters as briefing QCs and arguing settlements. While he remained in
Brighton, Harrison took as many burdens as he could from Norah's
shoulders, playing with young Katie and Clare and taking them for
walks, and Clare, who looked so like Parnell, was his favourite. Once
their mother had accepted his trustworthiness, it was during these
months that Harrison talked to her about Parnell and Willie and Aunt
Ben. Apart from the obvious factor that she needed a sympathetic ear
and they were in short supply, one of the reasons Katie opened her heart
to Harrison was that she wanted him to write an authorised biography
of Parnell in which the truth of their relationship, presumably *vis à vis*
O'Shea, would have been revealed. Harrison considered the request but
decided he was not then equipped to do justice to the task and suggested
John Redmond, but he too refused and the authorised biography fell by
the wayside. This is an immense pity, as what Katie had to say then

would have been invaluable because her mind had not disintegrated to any degree, she was soon to be in possession of a large fortune and she would not have been publishing for financial reasons (as she later did).

Katie's story as told to Harrison, and related to the world by him many years later (1931) in his book *Parnell Vindicated,* emphasised that O'Shea had known about the relationship with Parnell from the start, if implicitly rather than explicitly, and that there was no question of his being the deceived husband. It was from listening to Katie talk that Harrison realised how large a part in the deceptions and divorce proceedings Aunt Ben's money had played, and he was the first person to do so. He said that Mrs Parnell was frank in her conversations and that he did not doubt her truthfulness and sincerity, but in the year 1892 frankness did not extend to discussing sexual matters, and being a young Victorian gentleman Harrison accepted without question that Mrs O'Shea had ceased to live with her husband long before she met Parnell, that the three children born in 1882, 1883 and 1884 were his because after 1880 she was living with him and because she loved him. Nobody doubted Katie's love; even such committed opponents as Wilfrid Scawen Blunt said, 'The lady, however, was really in love with Parnell.' The question was—had her love embraced total fidelity to him from 1880 or had her desire to keep O'Shea quiet taken her to the connubial sheets in 1881, and perhaps again in 1882 and 1884? As it was not a question Harrison considered probing, it was not one he could answer with finality, but in his own mind he was certain that she had been true to Parnell (and nobody doubted that he had been true to her) and that O'Shea was the complaisant, conniving husband silenced by money. Henry Harrison was the sole person who talked in detail to Mrs Parnell about her ex-husband and her dead husband and thereafter published a book.

Having rendered Mrs Parnell great practical assistance, having listened to her revelations, by the end of March 1892 it was time for the young Mr Harrison to pick up the threads of his own life; he was a devoted Parnellite and a General Election was approaching. He performed what he thought would be his last service to Parnell's widow by arranging the signing of a lease on a house in Merstham, near Reigate in Surrey. (In fact, Katie and Parnell had found this house before his death and the lease was due to be signed as he lay dying.) Harrison then took his leave of Mrs Parnell, Norah O'Shea, Katie and Clare and the faithful Phyllis (he commented on Phyllis's devotion), and returned to the outside world, but only a few months later he heard that bankruptcy proceedings were being instituted against Mrs Parnell. Although Katie stood to inherit £65,000, the legal niceties were taking time, the money had not been released, and without somebody like Harrison to manage her affairs she had failed to satisfy the clamours of her creditors. Once again Harrison devoted himself to sorting out the problem; he approached two of Parnell's most devoted supporters, Dr Kenny and Pierce Mahoney, and between them they managed to raise £1,000. Harrison then contacted the most pressing creditors and they agreed to accept a stop-gap cash payment, with the balance as soon as Mrs Parnell received her aunt's money. Once again, this time finally, Harrison said good-bye to the Parnells, and nobody could have given greater service to the dead 'Chief' or service which would have been more appreciated by him than did 'the Parnellite two-year-old.'

When Harrison took his final leave of Katie she was nearing her forty-seventh birthday and was in full possession of her faculties—he described her as a highly confident if highly emotional lady. How soon the first breakdown occurred is impossible to say, because from the moment Harrison disappeared as her chronicler Katie's life vanishes into the shadows, one catches but the occasional glimpse of her existence from a letter here, a few lines in somebody's memoirs there, a few personal reminiscences by the wayside. With Parnell's death, the core had gone from Katie's life; at the deepest level, the love of the man who had wanted her above everything in the world, the total commitment, the total understanding, the total need had vanished; at another level, her interest in politics and causes had evaporated as if they had never been, and her general statement that she was not a political lady and her assertions to Gladstone that her only interest in politics was Mr Parnell have *some* validity. Katie was like a magic bucket in a fairy story. When filled she was capable of acting of her own volition, not always in the way her master might have chosen if left to himself, but once the spell was broken she had no reserves with which to fill the bucket. Parnell had been a spell beyond her wildest dreams, he had taken her to the heights of political life and of physical and mental satisfaction, with him she had lived on the peaks of adoration, with him she had fought in the valley of rejection, and now he was gone and there was nothing and nobody to replace him. While Katie had revealed her mother's intensity of passion, she had not inherited Lady Wood's stoic ability to accept the disasters and sufferings of life, to hang on, keep going, find a new outlet, nor had she her ex-husband's capacity to survive by twisting reality, and once she began to feel herself incapable of shaping (rather than twisting) it to her own design, her mind sought refuge on another level and she slipped into insanity.

According to one source of information, T. P. O'Connor, Katie spent two years in a home during the first breakdown not long after Parnell's death. He wrote of 'a chilling description of how she would get up in the middle of the night, in a state of wild alarm, and call on them to go downstairs to the hall, where, as she thought, Parnell and O'Shea were fighting and attempting to kill each other.' The devoted Norah wrote: 'She has never stopped mourning Parnell and I, knowing the misery of her heart and soul, have spent my life in keeping her from the follies of so many human ways of "forgetting for a little while" when I could; and when I couldn't in nursing her back to health and sanity. Her periods of delusion have always been Parnell, Parnell, Parnell.' Up to 1906, Katie's periods of delusion and her periods of lucidity were cushioned by the fact that she had plenty of money; on the former occasions Norah was able to pay for expensive special nursing-home treatment, and when her mother was of sound mind they were able to move house constantly; Katie's restlessness of spirit, the need to move physically when she was unhappy mentally, became more pronounced in these long, sad, aimless years. She was recorded as having leased houses all along the south coast, at Folkestone, Hastings, Sandgate, Havant, Bournemouth, Hayling Island and on the Isle of Wight, at Teignmouth in Devon and over the border in Cornwall, where she apparently lived in style in a castle outside Saltash, and was said to have kept herself very much to herself but to have invoked the hostility of the villagers who knew who she was. The theme that Katie kept herself to herself runs through the thin vein of personal reminiscences, but awareness of who she was seems only to have occurred in a few places. Mostly the name Mrs Parnell meant nothing because to the world she was 'Kitty' O'Shea, and the increasingly plump, untidy, ageing lady attracted less and less attention as she moved inland to Pangbourne and Maidenhead and eventually back to the south coast round Brighton.

In 1906 the solicitor who had been entrusted with Katie's (and her children's) fortune, in Norah O'Shea's words, 'absconded with as much as he could lay his hands on'. Although Katie's memoirs finish with Parnell's death, in the earlier chapters there is the occasional leap forward; she mentions moving house frequently after her husband's death and she says she lost many of his treasured possessions, including the whole of his correspondence with Cecil Rhodes, in the upheavals. She also mentions the solicitor who embezzled her fortune, saying that Parnell's solicitor (and hers, but unfortunately she dispensed with his services), by now Sir George Lewis, came to her aid and salvaged something from the wreck. What Katie does not mention in her memoirs is that the dishonest solicitor managed to sell her a sob-story about why he had stolen the money and that she insisted on paying the costs of his defence, thus considerably reducing the size of the sum salvaged by Lewis. In her periods of lucidity, Katie apparently remained as headstrong and generous as ever. After 1906 the pattern remained the same: constant moves (if into less expensive houses), the relapses into delusion, the periods of sanity when Katie tried to forget by means Norah O'Shea did not catalogue. Whether she took to the bottle or to the company of young men, as sometimes happens with ageing, lonely women who have once been attractive and in whose blood strong sexuality still flows, is unknown; or perhaps Norah, as a good Catholic, was merely referring to the spiritualism which became one of her mother's interests and solaces. At this period the study of spiritualism was a highly popular and serious occupation, with such eminent men as Sir Arthur Conan Doyle convinced that one should and could contact the next world. To Katie, the belief that she was communicating with Parnell, on whatever distant planet his soul might be, surely gave great comfort.

Whether Katie gained comfort from the growth of the Parnell legend, whether she was aware of the last flowering of the Anglo-Irish literary tradition which enshrined the legend, is again unknown. In life her husband had already become something of a legend, the lonely, proud, aristocratic figure leading the Irish people to the promised land, but after his sudden tragic death he swiftly acquired the true hallmark of the legend, becoming all things to all men. For those who believed in the democratic process, he was the constitutionalist who had shown Ireland that such processes could work, that the application of pressure could fall short of violence; he was the man who had created a viable democratic Irish party which had withstood its creator's last frenetic attempts to destroy it (attempts he would surely have abandoned had he lived). For the many supporters of the newly founded Sinn Fein and of the renascent IRB, he was the Irish patriot who had fought for Irish independence and had been destroyed by the English wolves, and who in the last months of his life had realised that constitutionalism was bound to fail against English imperialism and that the only answer was revolutionary violence. For the last group of writers to bloom in the framework of the English Ascendancy, Parnell was the Balder-figure sacrificed for the rebirth of the nation, with themselves as the prophets. For Yeats he was the man of genius or greatness destroyed by the fear, ignorance and jealousy of the mediocre; for James Joyce, like Yeats, he represented much that was best in man but he had been destroyed by what was specifically worst in the Irish people as opposed to people in general, in Joyce's view by bigotry, narrow-mindedness, chauvinism, intolerance and the stifling grip of the priests. (Joyce wrote, 'They did not throw him to the wolves, they tore him to pieces themselves.') It is doubtful if Katie heard of James Joyce but he showed some interest in her. His published notes to the only play he wrote, *The Exiles*, are dismissive: 'The relations between Mrs O'Shea and Parnell are not of vital significance for Ireland, first because Parnell was tongue-tied, and secondly because she was an Englishwoman. . . . Her manner of writing is not Irish, nay her manner of loving is not Irish. The character of O'Shea is more typical of Ireland.' One cannot say that these notes rebound with insight, the relations between Katie and Parnell had *some* significance for Ireland, and as she was English there seems no reason why her manner of writing or loving should be Irish. Joyce was sufficiently attracted by her character for Molly Bloom partly to grow out of it, and Molly's early days in Spain owed something to Katie's Spanish sojourn.

For the living Katie the outlook suddenly became very bleak again. However, before following the course of her increasingly sad fortunes, those of her ex-husband and her relatives should be examined, particularly Willie's, because he died in 1905. From 1892 until his death it has proved possible to trace only one mention of his activities, that being contained in a letter written to Joseph Chamberlain in 1898. At that time O'Shea had become involved in trying to float a company to build a railway from Zululand across Swaziland, and he wrote to ask whether Chamberlain would be interested in putting up the capital for this money-making project. From O'Shea's point of view it was a reasonable request, for Chamberlain was then at the height of his

Imperialistic grandeur and had been a leading supporter of the campaign to build the railway from Mombasa to Lake Victoria. But in a southern African venture involving Captain O'Shea Chamberlain showed no interest, and perhaps even Willie then realised that his dearest, most trusted friend was no longer concerned about him. This was the last time he wrote to Chamberlain. O'Shea died in Brighton, or specifically Hove, on 22 April 1905 at 19 Lansdowne Place, aged sixty-five, from chronic interstitial nephritis leading to cardiac failure. The demise earned him half a column or a column in the leading newspapers, but the incident on which most of them dwelled was Galway rather than the divorce case. None of them made comment upon the late Captain O'Shea's precise role in the sensational events, and all of them said he had disappeared from public life after 1890.

With his father dead, Gerard O'Shea took on the mantle of defending his reputation to all comers. Gerard inherited his father's charm and the need for and inability to keep money; from extant notes in his hand he also inherited the snobbishness and the schoolboy delight in making clever remarks which so riled the Irish nationalists during his father's days in the House of Commons,* but what he did not inherit was the talent as plausible talker and negotiator. Willie O'Shea had for varying lengths of time impressed Mr Gladstone, Joseph Chamberlain and Cardinal Manning—a not unworthy collection of scalps—whereas Gerard does not appear to have held down any job and made no such illustrious connections. He married his cousin, Christabel Barrett Lennard, according to one family source because he seduced her, got her pregnant and Sir Thomas Barrett Lennard forced him to do so, but the marriage was not a happy one and the only child was, alas, retarded. Gerard always retained contact with his mother—if he left the burden of caring for her to Norah—and after his father's death this was strengthened.

Carmen O'Shea married Dr Arthur Herbert Buck, who practised in Hove (it was he who signed her father's death certificate). From this

---

* In 1936 Gerard tried to prevent the play *Parnell* (written by an American lady, Elsie T. Schauffler) from being presented in London. It had already enjoyed a considerable success on Broadway and, apart from objecting to the theme that his father had condoned his mother's liaison with Parnell, he made endless minor objections and comments: 'Captain W. H. O'Shea would have asked his maid to "bring" and not "fetch" the whisky. He had not the misfortune to be educated in the USA but at Oscott and Trinity College, Dublin. He did not call himself O'Shay, neither did he pronounce the words "sea" and "tea", "say" and "tay".'

marriage there were three children, but in 1914 it collapsed, and the American paper *The World* carried the headline 'Mrs O'Shea's Girl Secretly Divorced'. To say that Carmen was secretly divorced was hardly accurate, but that the case was conducted with the minimum publicity was true. The co-respondent was Edward Lingard Lucas, who later inherited his father's baronetcy, and *The World* noted that he already had a twenty-six-year-old son, but Carmen was forty by the time of the divorce so there was nothing too surprising in this information. Mrs Buck and Mr Lucas committed arranged adultery in style at the Savoy Hotel, a decree *nisi* was granted after a brief hearing and *The World* virtuously, and to later twentieth-century eyes surprisingly, added, 'England still retains one record—the possession of the least exacting, quickest divorce mill extant.' How much contact Carmen and her new husband had with Katie is uncertain, but in her last years, according to a Lucas descendant, Lady Lucas was much addicted to the pleasures of alcohol.

Henry Harrison's favourite, Parnell's elder surviving daughter, Clare, also married a doctor who practised in the Brighton area, Dr Bertram Maunsell. Her all too brief married life was happy, but Clare died in 1911 giving birth to her first child, a boy, Parnell's only known grandchild. The boy survived and, according to Norah O'Shea, grew into 'a clever little chap. His head is just the shape of his grandfather's, like Clare's', but in the early 1930s, while serving in the British army in India, he apparently died, unmarried, and as far as one knows Parnell has no surviving descendants. Dr Maunsell later remarried but kept in touch with Katie—he was one of the few mourners at her funeral—so one hopes that she was able to enjoy the pleasure of the company of her and Parnell's grandson. What happened to young Katie is a mystery, as none of the few contemporary chroniclers mentions her. In 1936, when the play about Katie and Parnell was causing a storm in London,* one of the metropolitan papers ran a piece about a lady called Mrs. Katharine Moule, then living in some poverty in Camden Town, who claimed to be their last surviving child. Mrs Moule said she had been born at Eltham on 27 November 1884, that she was her father's

---

* *Parnell* was eventually produced, as Gerard O'Shea took off for Hollywood to act as adviser for a large sum of money on the film being made from the play, and in the circumstances the Lord Chamberlain (who then licensed all plays for public production in Britain) felt he could not continue to object to its London presentation.

favourite because she looked like her mother, whereas Clare resembled Parnell, that she remembered moving from Eltham to Brighton after Aunt Ben's death, she remembered the wedding on 25 June 1891 and the horror and sadness of the house when Parnell died in her mother's arms. She said that Parnell always looked grave and rather terrifying with his dark beard and sad, pale face but was kind to the children. She claimed that she had been a fluent reader by the age of seven and that when her father was ill she read to him *The Last Days of Pompeii,* and there were further reminiscences about Parnell's telescope and his pestle and mortar and Katie calling him by the pet named of 'Mister'.

The exact birth-date of young Katie had not then been published so the lady would have needed to have checked on that, but most of the information she gave was available in Katie's or Harrison's book, and the bit about her mother calling Parnell 'Mister' was an elaboration on a theme which had appeared in another lady's 1936 letter to the press. This lady was the one who claimed to have played cricket with Parnell and the O'Shea children at Eltham, and she said that it was the children who called him 'Mister'. However, Mrs Moule also provided the information that she had married Louis D'Oyléy Horsford Moule in 1907, that thereafter he had served in West Africa and that they had only returned to England permanently after her mother had died, leaving her £2,000. On the marriage certificate one has been able to check, and in July 1907 a Guadeloupe Katarina Flavia O'Shea, then aged twenty-two, married Lieutenant Moule of the East Lancashire Regiment, and her father's name was given as Henry William O'Shea, Captain 18th Hussars. It seems unlikely that a child who was christened Frances Katie Flavia O'Shea and always known as Katie should change her name to Guadeloupe Katarina Flavia O'Shea and be known as Katharine, but the Spanish name suggests the possibility that she might have been Willie O'Shea's illegitimate daughter and that in 1936, short of money and hopeful that publicity might bring her some, she decided that the connection gave her the right to the more romantic claim that she was Parnell's rather than O'Shea's daughter. There is no record of a Guadeloupe Katarina Flavia O'Shea born in Britain in 1884 or 1885 (the age rather than the exact birth-date on the marriage certificate would place her in either year), only of Frances Katie Flavia O'Shea, but if the claimant were Willie O'Shea's illegitimate daughter she was probably born in Spain. The lady certainly stated on her marriage certificate that she was the daughter of Captain O'Shea of the 18th Hussars, even if somebody put Henry William rather than William Henry, and that she had some connection with him seems probable. But that Mrs Moule was Parnell's daughter, the Frances Katie Flavia duly registered to the paternity of O'Shea in November 1884, is doubtful, particularly as her alleged mother had no money to leave to the devoted Norah. Other than Mrs Moule's claim to be young Katie, no information on what became of her has proved traceable. After Katie's death, Norah herself was penniless and was helped by T. P. O'Connor, who first found her a job as a governess and then assisted with her training as a nurse. According to O'Connor, she qualified at Queen Charlotte's Hospital in London, changed her name to Norah Wood, and had died of lupus before he published his memoirs in 1929.

Of the Wood family, Sir Evelyn lived into respected if increasingly deaf old age, dying in his seventieth year in 1919 and being honoured with a plaque in the crypt of St Paul's Cathedral—'Intrepid in Action, Untiring in Duty, For Queen and Country.' The old ages of Charles Page Wood and Polly Chambers were comforted by their share of Aunt Ben's fortune, while Anna Steele lived on at Rivenhall Place for many years until the upkeep was beyond her means, it fell into the same ruined state from which Sir John and Lady Wood had rescued it, and she too moved to Brighton. In her last years (she died before Katie), Anna became an eccentric recluse, surrounded by animals, monkeys in particular, with a favourite which consumed vast quantities of anchovy-paste sandwiches, and one of the few human beings with whom she kept contact was Christabel O'Shea, Gerard's wife. The need to explain her actions was not unfortunately part of Anna's character; unfortunately, because she possessed literary ability and the novelist's observant eye and her account of the triangular (or quadrilateral) relationship between her sister, her brother-in-law, herself and Charles Stewart Parnell would have been invaluable. If she stayed silent on the subject of the most notorious love affair of the nineteenth century, of which she had such intimate knowledge, in her declining years Anna occasionally wrote poetry and one of her last poems to appear in print, 'An Old Maid's Thoughts', contained the lines:

And I feel my life is bitter,
My days are barren and drear,
And I grieve there are none who will miss me,
When the shadows of death draw near.

Her sister Katie probably entertained the sentiments expressed in the first two lines, although she was not without a few faithful relatives to comfort her (Anna sustained herself with the thought that she had friends, her poor dumb animals). Katie had several more barren years to live, and in 1913, when she was nearing her sixty-ninth birthday, financial disaster again struck. The money salvaged from the dishonest trustee in 1906 had been sufficient for her and Norah to survive in moderately comfortable fashion, but unfortunately it was invested in the Grand Trunk Railway of Canada, which ceased to pay dividends in 1913, and it was because she was in desperate financial straits that Katie published her memoirs, *Charles Stewart Parnell, His Love Story and Political Life.* They were published in two volumes, with illustrations, on 19 May 1914, and they caused such a furore that they were reprinted on 25 May, with a further printing on 2 June. They were published under the authorship of Katharine O'Shea—Mrs Charles Stewart Parnell in minute letters underneath—but if she had to consent to the use of the name by which she was known to the world, she drew the line at the hated diminutive 'Kitty'. As already indicated, the memoirs appeared with a preface by Gerard O'Shea in which he said his mother would entirely repudiate the scandalous, slanderous insinuations recently made against his late father.

The particular insinuations to which Gerard referred had appeared in the *Cork Free Press* on 6 September 1913, in an article written by William O'Brien entitled 'The First Inner Light on the Parnell Divorce Case. What might have been if Parnell was examined.' O'Brien printed a letter he had received from Parnell—'If the case is ever fully gone into, you may rest assured that it will be shown that the dishonour and discredit has not been upon my side'—and then drew his own deduction that Parnell 'would have been shown to be rather a victim than a destroyer of a happy home, and the divorce would never have taken place.' In 1913 such statements were startling; Parnell might already have assumed the status of a legend in some quarters in Ireland, but for the public at large nothing had been stated which disturbed the divorce court image of 'Mr Fox of the fire-escape'. Gerard O'Shea ensured that the slanders against his father's name reached a wider public by sending a long letter to *The Times* which was published on 10 September 1913, in which he said that his mother, the widow of C. S. Parnell, would shortly be publishing a book containing letters from his father 'in absolute refutation of the allegations published by William

O'Brien', a gentleman incidentally of whom he had never heard. This was a typical Willie/Gerard O'Shea swipe, because William O'Brien was and had been for years a leading Irish politician.

It was Henry Harrison's contention that Katie had agreed to the publication of the book because she was in dire financial straits, but that in 1914 she was also in one of her periods of delusion and the memoirs were entirely edited by Gerard O'Shea without clear cognisance on Katie's part. One can appreciate how shattered Harrison was when he read Mrs O'Shea/Parnell's revelations, because they implied that she had deceived her husband and her lover over the birth of Claude Sophie, failed entirely to mention the births of his Clare and Katie and suggested that for ten years Captain O'Shea had been the deceived husband, all of which implications, omissions and suggestions were in opposition to the story Mrs Parnell had told him and such facts as he knew personally. With the added factor that one of the photographs of Parnell's dogs was mis-captioned—for how could a lucid Katie have forgotten which of his dogs was which?—Harrison came to the conclusion that the book had been worked over by Gerard O'Shea unrealised by his deluded mother and he therefore tended to dismiss it as hopelessly unreliable. That Katie's memoirs are inaccurate and of little value (apart from the publication of Parnell's letters) is the view which has become generally accepted by students of the period.

The memoirs are disorganised, not well written and so ambiguous and ambivalent in dealing with Willie O'Shea as to be contradictory and at times ridiculous, but placing the text against information which can be proved or corroborated, what Katie actually said (as opposed to the many vital omissions) emerges as suprisingly accurate. Not all her statements can be checked, but the rambling, roseate reminiscences about her childhood and early life stand up factually when compared to the well-documented information in a privately printed history of Lady Wood and her children.* As already indicated, her account of her involvement with Gladstone and in the Home Rule battle of 1886, if not a model of clarity and analysis, is again accurate when checked with the material in the Gladstone Papers. The style of writing, in the book and in the letters to Gladstone, is certainly consistent. Katie had what Sir Winston Churchill elsewhere described as an 'up with this I will not

---

* The book is called *A Century of Letters*; see 'Sources' for further information.

put' style, cramming as many prepositions and conjunctions into a sentence as possible, and this personal trademark is apparent in her memoirs and her Gladstonian letters. Thus, however freely Gerard O'Shea might have cut the original and excised references injurious to his father, one feels that the text as published was written by Katie, almost certainly over a long period of years rather than as a sustained effort (which would account for the disorganised narrative as much as would her son's editorial efforts), and one also feels that the information contained therein, if tinged with romantic hindsight in some areas and to be viewed with a dubious eye in others, is on the whole more accurate than has been allowed.

If Katie was tottering into one of her periods of insanity when the book was in preparation stage, it seems possible that she nevertheless retained sufficient understanding to appreciate the implications of Claude Sophie's birth and allowed this to pass because she had in this instance deceived Parnell. But Henry Harrison could be right, she may never have deceived him, the birth could have been included because a distraught Katie wanted the world to know that she had borne Parnell a child but did not then appreciate the implications and Gerard O'Shea thought one questionable birth would not harm his mother but mentioning all three of Parnell's children would be going too far. There is the final possibility that Gerard O'Shea was right, that Henry Harrison, this author, all those who believe that William Henry O'Shea was a conniving, consenting husband are wrong and that Katie deceived both men from 1880 to 1886. (What O'Shea was doing from 1886, when he admitted he ceased to live with his wife, and 1887 when he admitted he became aware of the adultery, until 1889 when he filed his divorce suit, has in this case to remain unexplained.) Jules Abels, who propounded his belief in O'Shea's innocence in *The Parnell Tragedy,* also decided that Katie could not have written much of her book, his reason being that she lacked the intelligence and comprehension to have penned such as the Home Rule chapters. If one examines her many long letters to Gladstone, they show that she had a very clear grasp of the political situation between 1882 and 1886.

In 1914 Katie's book—mutilated or not, then comprehended by her or not—burst upon the astonished world in its own right. Wilfrid Scawen Blunt wrote: 'We talked about the O'Shea revelations. Everybody is reading them.' The most startling information was that Mrs

O'Shea had borne Parnell a daughter in 1882 (the omission of Clare and Katie was not glaring as few people knew of their existence; Henry Harrison said that when he first arrived in Brighton he was astounded to meet them, as their births had been so quickly passed over in the divorce court as not to register, certainly not with the possibility that they were Parnell's). The second most startling item was the inclusion of Parnell's love letters which cast such an unexpected light on the proud, cold, aloof figure known to the world, and the third was Katie's reminiscences about her role as secret emissary to Mr Gladstone and the part she had played in the Home Rule negotiations. (The revelations could be placed in order of importance according to whether one was interested in the personal or political; for most people the personal won hands down.) All the many, lengthy reviews commented fully on all three aspects; the *Pall Mall Gazette* thought 'the tit-bit of Mrs Parnell's book . . . is the description of Mr Gladstone arming the lady up and down in Downing Street. . . . Really it was too bad of the lady not to come forward with these extremely interesting bits of information when Mr John Morley was writing his *Life of Gladstone.*' Opinion was sharply divided about the revelation of the baby's birth and the publication of Parnell's intimate letters; words failed the *Daily Express* reviewer at the thought that Mrs Parnell should have printed such 'bald, intimate, undistinguished letters'; the *Daily Mail* considered that they and the disclosure of the baby's birth were gross errors of judgement which provided information more damaging to Mr Parnell's reputation than had the divorce court revelations; the *Daily Telegraph* queried whether such artless letters should have been published; and *The Times* gave an accurate lengthy résumé of the book but refrained from judgement, commenting only that it threw a flood of light upon the strength of Parnell's passion and on the character of the woman who had attracted and subdued him. The attempt to redeem Captain O'Shea's reputation from the charge of connivance was generally accepted; the *Daily Express* said that the book at least succeeded in this stated aim but added, 'O'Shea seems to have been the only person connected with Parnell who did not know that Mrs O'Shea was his mistress from the autumn of 1880.' The nearest thing to doubt was expressed by the *Daily Telegraph,* which wondered if perhaps Captain O'Shea had suspected more than he had cared to reveal. All these comments came from the English papers; in Ireland and largely in America there was a silence about Mrs O'Shea's revelations, understandably, because the publication of Katie's memoirs coincided with the third and final reading of Mr Asquith's Home Rule Bill, and they provided a good amount of ammunition for those who were opposed to its being implemented and were therefore best left untouched by those who desired its realisation.

The upsurge of interest in Parnell and his love story subsided after a few months and the widow again slipped from public attention. As a result of the publication of the memoirs, Katie earned sufficient money to enable Norah and her to live in some comfort, though as the years went by, the degree of affluence lessened. From what information is available, after the publication Katie slowly regained her sanity, the rages of grief and loneliness and recrimination subsided and she accepted her barren existence; in her last years she was described as 'a sonsy, comfortable soul, not unlike the best type of theatrical landlady'. Nevertheless, she had her bursts of restlessness and a servant at a hotel in Brighton where she lived for some months said she was an eccentric lady who frequently got up at two o'clock in the morning to go walking along the sea-front. In daylight as well as darkness Katie became a well-known figure on the Brighton sea-front, a short, plump old lady, out in all weathers gazing at the sea or puffing her way along the promenade, probably dreaming of Parnell and the hours she had spent with him watching the waves or braving the storms. In the last years of her life Katie's physical health began to crack, but she made one final move from Brighton to Littlehampton, where she rented a small terraced house in an undistinguished road which lies back from the sea-front and the town centre, 39 East Ham Road. The old lady next door, when questioned in the 1970s, remembered Katie as a stout, rather jolly person who kept herself to herself, said there was a gentleman who spent a good deal of time at the house and people wondered whether or not he was the husband (it could have been Gerard); however, the old lady confessed that she had no idea who Mrs Parnell was until after she had died and the newspapers were filled with her story. By the time of the final move to Littlehampton, Norah O'Shea had begun to lead some life of her own and was resident in London, but she hurried down to Littlehampton on hearing the news that her mother had had a severe heart attack to nurse her through the last illness.

From Littlehampton, on 1 February 1921, Norah O'Shea wrote to Henry Harrison thus: 'On the strength of your having been such a "stand-by" and help to my dear mother (C. S. Parnell's widow) when Parnell died—in the days when you were known as "the stripling" of Parnell's party—I am writing to tell you that your old friend is dying, slowly and painfully, of heart disease. She was seventy-six last Sunday, and has been ill for some months. Now, the doctors say, it is only a question of how long she can keep up her fight against death. The heart attacks grow more frequent and she struggles back with more difficulty and pain each time. She has happy delusions that Parnell comes to her at night, when things are worst, and draws her "out of the black waves".' In the early morning of 5 February 1921, thirty years after the death of her King, Katie's own life ended. One might quote the words of Dr Arbuthnot on the death of Queen Anne, 'I believe sleep was never more welcome to a weary traveller than death was to her.'

The Saturday evening papers ran the news of 'Kitty' O'Shea's (Mrs Parnell's) death on their front page, writing of the woman who had 'thawed the coldest human icicle of this age' but who had later ruined him and thrown the Irish cause 'back into the raging cauldron of faction, fanaticism and murder'. Michael Collins and the IRA might view this description of their fight as inaccurate, but Katie's death coincided with the last desperate days of the Black and Tans, and the dramatic timing which marked the crucial phases of her life was apparent to the end. In most of the Sunday and Monday papers her death was removed from the front page but it had ample inside coverage, in Britain that was, in Ireland it received as scant attention as had her memoirs. Most of the British papers ran a résumé of her life with Parnell, with romantic emphasis on the story of the rose dropped from her bodice at the first meeting and buried with his body, and on his last words being, 'Kiss me, sweet wifie', and for the first time in British print Captain O'Shea's role was queried—'He was apparently wilfully blind to this intrigue, or else a fool beyond the common.' In the brief Irish notices, the *Irish Times* (in fact quoting from the London *Times* obituary) said, 'To her destiny allotted the terrible role of Delilah'; the Dublin *Evening Mail* said that next to Queen Victoria she had done more to make history than any Englishwoman of the nineteenth century; while the *Freeman's Journal* said, 'Little was heard of the deceased lady after Parnell's death until she once more came into the limelight by the publication of two unsavoury volumes which purported to give the whole history of her relations with the Irish leader', and that her death

[310]

had not been unexpected 'by the few people who associated with her in her declining years'. Most American papers gave the news of the death of 'the former Kitty O'Shea' fair column space, and *The World* ran it as the front-page story, with a highly coloured and highly inaccurate review of one of the world's great love stories. It wrote of Katie as 'handsome, wistful, winsome, vivacious, with a brain as keen as Becky Sharp, yet as honest as Amelia' and said she had first met Parnell through the good offices of John Dillon when she was a member of 'Ruskin's St George Society and had outlined a plan to sell the handicraft products of true Irish homes', which conjured up an interesting picture.

Unless one believes that life is a vast cosmic joke without meaning or that its course is preordained, then Katharine Parnell, née Wood, formerly O'Shea, played a cataclysmic role in Anglo-Irish history. Even if one disbelieves in free will and like Parnell accepts the uselessness of mortals contending against fate and the inevitable working of a historic process, it has to be admitted that most human beings, including Parnell, do not while they are on earth behave as if it will all be the same in a hundred years; mostly, like Parnell, they struggle and strive and fight. By deciding to approach the Irish leader boldly in 1880 to add his scalp to her hostess's collecting, by being the lady she was, married to the man she was, Katie altered history. Had Willie O'Shea not divorced his wife in 1890—and his role is almost as decisive as hers—Parnell would almost certainly have been alive in 1893 when Gladstone piloted the second Home Rule Bill through the House of Commons. It was then thrown out by the Lords, and an ageing Gladstone (he was in his eighty-fourth year) rested on his laurels without trying to break their power, but had Parnell been the Irish leader Gladstone would surely not have been allowed to make the capitulation, and it is possible that the later Liberal fight to curtail the Lords' veto might have occurred in the 1890s. It would have been a titanic struggle, and the thought of Queen Victoria agreeing to create hundreds of Liberal peers at Mr Gladstone's behest (as George V later reluctantly agreed in principle if necessary) is hard to imagine. Assuming that the Lords' veto had been curtailed somewhere short of civil war by the combined weight of the Liberal Party and the Irish nationalist threat, Gladstone's version of Home Rule (amended from 1886, essentially with regard to the retention of the Irish MPs at Westminster) would then have received the royal assent and become law. Parnell would assuredly have wanted more autonomy than he had obtained, but it seems possible that he would have been willing to work within the framework of the United Kingdom (Cecil Rhodes, among others, was convinced that he would). The question remains whether the Fenians, representing the small but burning flame of Irish nationalism, would have allowed him to stay within the United Kingdom, or perhaps the question is, would Parnell have been able to dampen the Fenian flame? The answer would probably have depended on how economically successful his administration proved to be. But in the 1890s Parnell would have been dealing with Ireland as a whole because Ulster had still not organised herself to the point of being able to threaten rebellion as she did in 1914, and faced with the *fait accompli* she could have acceded to the situation. Parnell was a Protestant, he was not the cats-paw of the Catholic hierarchy and he was no radical in matters other than Irish independence. He was the last person who had any hope of carrying a *united* Ireland into any form of independence from England, and it is perhaps on this aspect that his love for Katie, and her headstrong, unquestioning buttressing of his position, has proved the most disastrous.

If in 1921 the world's newspaper-reading public had its memories revived of the Englishwoman who had done more to affect nineteenth-century history than any female other than Queen Victoria, in none of them was curiosity sufficiently stirred to attend the interment of her mortal remains. On the bleak Tuesday of 8 February 1921 the funeral car left 39 East Ham Road followed by two horse-drawn carriages, one of which contained the mourners, the other of which was empty, for it had been hired in case anybody from the past should decide to pay his last respects. Nobody came, and the cortège with its empty carriage drove slowly through the streets of Littlehampton to the municipal cemetery, unnoticed by the town's inhabitants. At the cemetery were two reporters, three press photographers and two policemen, and their presence attracted the attention of people tending their own graves and a few of them swelled the official mourners, who numbered four exactly, Gerard O'Shea and his wife Christabel, Norah O'Shea and the dead Clare's husband, Dr Bertram Maunsell. The burial service was read and Katie's body was lowered to its last resting place, and a few more flowers covered her grave than people attended the funeral, for in addition to the wreaths sent by the mourners there were those from a Mrs Elcho and a Miss Coles, from Sir Edward and Lady Lucas

(Carmen), a Mr Asheton, Mrs Bertram Maunsell and from Katie and Parnell's grandson, C. B. L. Maunsell. A simple cross was erected over the grave by Norah O'Shea with the inscription, 'To the beloved memory of Katharine, widow of Charles Stewart Parnell. Born 30th January, 1845, Died 5th February, 1921. Fide et Amore.'

Sources

Katie's memoirs, *Charles Stewart Parnell, His Love Story and Political Life,* in the two-volume edition published in 1914, provided a base for this book. For her family background and childhood a good deal of information was obtained from *A Century of Letters,* a substantial volume edited and privately printed by Mrs Bradhurst, the daughter of Katie's brother Charles Page Wood. In addition to details about all members of the Wood family, the book prints scores of Emma Wood's, Aunt Ben's and Anna Steele's letters to and from each other and their eminent correspondents, which letters were then in the possession of Mrs Bradhurst. Many of them have since been lost or sold (though a few, such as Anthony Trollope's letters to Anna Steele, remain in the possession of Mrs Christine Fitzgerald, Mrs Bradhurst's daughter); thus the book is particularly valuable and I am most grateful to Mrs Fitzgerald for loaning me her copy.

The bulk of Katie's letters to Gladstone is in the Gladstone Papers in the British Library, Add. mss. 44,269; Willie O'Shea's letters to the Liberal leader are the same catalogue number. Katie's letters to Lord Richard Grosvenor, and his to her, are in Add. mss. 44,315, which also contains letters about Willie O'Shea's unsuccessful bid for a Liberal seat in Ulster in the 1885 election. There are a couple of memoranda by Gladstone on the subject of Willie O'Shea in 1882 in Add. mss. 44,766, and the brief correspondence between Parnell and Gladstone about the Hawarden meeting in 1889 is spread among Add. mss. 44,507, 44,508 and 44,509. The letters from Parnell and Katie begging Gladstone to assist in the matter of the Lunacy Petition filed against Aunt Ben are in Add. mss. 44,503. Some memoranda by Gladstone on Parnell (his health in 1888, his Hawarden visit in 1889 and the divorce case in 1890) are in Add. mss. 44,773. The main Gladstone–John Morley correspondence about the divorce case is in Add. mss. 44,256, with the odd letter in Add. mss. 44,127. Gladstone's correspondence with Lord Spencer on the same subject is in Add. mss. 44,314, that with Cardinal Manning in Add. mss. 44,250. Some general correspondence with Lord Richard Grosvenor on the subject of the O'Sheas and Home Rule is in Add. mss. 44,316, while the earlier Gladstone–W. E. Forster correspondence in the Kilmainham days is in Add. mss. 44,160.

Apart from the material listed in the main catalogue of the Gladstone Papers, there are several interesting folders which were added in 1970 and which are separately catalogued. Of these, Add. mss. 56,445 contains letters from Gladstone to his son Herbert in 1886 about Home Rule, and a letter about the O'Sheas from Edward Russell of the *Liverpool Daily Post* written in 1890; in Add. mss. 56,446 there are further letters from Katie and Willie O'Shea written in the autumn of 1885; Add. mss. 56,447 contains letters written at the beginning of 1886, including Katie's request for a Colonial Office appointment for her husband and the correspondence about unauthorised communications and plots to trap Parnell and Gladstone into a secret meeting (the correspondence in Add. mss. 56,446/47 overlaps with the material in the main folder, Add. mss. 44,269). Add. mss. 56,448 contains some of the many letters and telegrams which poured into Gladstone from all over the country at the time of the divorce, including another interesting one from Edward Russell, and Gladstone's own notes on his position and the action he should take; Add. mss. 56,449 contains letters from Henry Labouchere about the prior knowledge of Richard Pigott's guilt at the time of the Special Commission, and some letters from Sir William Harcourt written at the time of the Boulogne negotiations.

Sir Charles Dilke's comments on the O'Shea/Parnell triangle are in his papers in the British Library, specifically Add. mss. 43,936 and 43,941. Willie O'Shea's correspondence with Joseph Chamberlain is in the Chamberlain Papers in the University of Birmingham, covering the period April 1882 to February 1898, reference numbers 8/8/1/1 to 8/8/1/167. Cardinal Manning's papers are in St Mary of the Angels Church, Bayswater, London, but they have had a sad history and are fragmentary. A few letters from Willie O'Shea survive on the subjects of Walsh's election as Archbishop of Dublin, Chamberlain and Home Rule, and O'Shea's indignation after the divorce; part of Manning's correspondence with Archbishop Walsh between 1886 and 1890 is also extant.

As my subject was Katharine O'Shea and there are no 'Parnell Papers' in Ireland, I focussed my research on England. (Parnell, unfortunately for future historians, did not possess the general Victorian habit of letter-writing or diary-keeping or of saving every scrap of paper that came his way.) Most of Parnell's lieutenants wrote their memoirs (some indefatigably) and the existing literature about Parnell, Gladstone, Home Rule, the effects of the O'Shea divorce case and Anglo-Irish relations in the last decade of the nineteenth century is large. My bibliography is by no means comprehensive, but I have tried not to omit any book to which I am indebted and/or which is necessary reading for anybody interested in the life of Katie O'Shea and the background against which she functioned.

NEWSPAPERS AND PERIODICALS

BRITISH

Birmingham Post
Brighton Gazette
Chelmsford Chronicle
Daily Express
Daily Herald
Daily Mail
Daily Telegraph
Essex Chronicle
Evening News (London)
Evening Standard (London)
Illustrated London News
Illustrated Sunday Herald
Labour World
Liverpool Daily Post
London Opinion
Manchester Guardian
Observer
Pall Mall Gazette
Penny Illustrated Paper
Review of Reviews
Reynolds News
Scotsman
Sheffield Telegraph

Star
Sunday Express
Sunday Pictorial
Sunday Times
Sussex Daily News
Times
Truth
Vanity Fair

IRISH

Cork Free Press
Dublin Evening Mail
Freeman's Journal
Irish Catholic
Irish Times
National Press
United Ireland

AMERICAN

Irish World
New York Herald
New York Tribune
World

Bibliography

MANUSCRIPT MATERIAL

Gladstone Papers, British Library (Main catalogue: Add. mss. 44160, 44250, 44256, 44269, 44314, 44315, 44316, 44503, 44506, 44766, 44787. Additional unbound: Add. mss. 56445, 56446, 56447, 56448, 56449).

Joseph Chamberlain Papers, University of Birmingham (O'Shea-Chamberlain correspondence).

Dilke Papers, British Library (Add. mss. 43936 and 43941).

Manning Papers, St Mary of the Angels, Bayswater, London.

OFFICIAL PUBLICATIONS

Hansard Parliamentary Debates, 3rd series (1830–1891) Vols 253, 255, 269, 303, 306, 313 and 328.

The Special Commission Act. Report of the Proceedings before the Commissioners appointed by the Act (London, 1890).

Pleadings in O'Donnell v. Walter and another and *The Times* (H.M.S.O., 1888).

ABELS, JULES, *The Parnell Tragedy* (London, 1966).

ASKWITH, LORD, *Lord James of Hereford* (London, 1930).

BLUNT, WILFRID SCAWEN, *The Land War in Ireland* (London, 1912).

—— *My Diaries 1884–1914*, 2 vols (London, 1919 and 1920).

BRADHURST, MRS, *A Century of Letters: Letters from Literary Friends to Lady Wood and Mrs A. C. Steele* (privately printed, 1929).

CHAMBERLAIN, JOSEPH, *A Political Memoir 1880–1892*, edited C. H. D. Howard (London, 1953).

CHURCHILL, WINSTON, *Lord Randolph Churchill* (London, 1906).

CLARKE, SIR EDWARD, *The Story of My Life* (London, 1918).

COOKE, A. B., and VINCENT, JOHN, *The Governing Passion: Cabinet Government and Party Politics in Britain 1885–86* (Brighton, 1974).

CORFE, TOM, *The Phoenix Park Murders* (London, 1968).

DAVITT, MICHAEL, *The Fall of Feudalism in Ireland, or the Story of the Land League Revolution* (New York, 1904).

DEVOY, JOHN, *Post Bag 1871–1928*, edited William O'Brien and Desmond Ryan (Dublin, 1948 and 1953).

DICKINSON, EMILY, *A Patriot's Mistake; being personal recollections of the Parnell Family* (Dublin, 1905).

ERVINE, J. G. ST JOHN, *Parnell* (London, 1925).

FRASER, PETER, *Joseph Chamberlain* (London, 1966).

GARDINER, A. G., *The Life of Sir William Harcourt* (London, 1923).

GARVIN, J. L., *The Life of Joseph Chamberlain*, vols 1 & 2 (London, 1932 and 1933).

GLADSTONE, MARY, *Her Diaries and Letters*, edited Lucy Masterman (London, 1930).

GLADSTONE, VISCOUNT, *After Thirty Years* (London, 1928).

HAMILTON, SIR EDWARD WALTER, *Diaries 1880–1885*, edited Dudley W. R. Bahlman, 2 vols (Oxford, 1972).

HAMMOND, J. L., *Gladstone and the Irish Nation* (London, 1938; reprinted 1964).

HARRIS, FRANK, *My Lives and Loves* (Paris, 1945).

HARRISON, HENRY, OBE, MC, *Parnell Vindicated: The Lifting of the Veil* (London, 1931).

HASLIP, JOAN, *Parnell* (London, 1936).

HEALY, T. M., *Letters and Leaders of My Day* (London, 1928).

HOWARD, C. H. D., 'Documents Relating to the Irish Central Boards Scheme 1884–85', *Irish Historical Studies*, vol VIII (March 1953).

——— 'Joseph Chamberlain, Parnell and the Irish Central Boards Scheme 1884–85', *Irish Historical Studies*, vol VIII (September 1953).

HOWARTH, HERBERT, *The Irish Writers 1886–1940* (London, 1958).

JAMES, ROBERT RHODES, *Lord Randolph Churchill* (London, 1959).

JENKINS, ROY, *Sir Charles Dilke* (London, 1958).

JEYES, S. H., *The Life of Sir Howard Vincent* (London, 1912).

LARKIN, EMMETT, 'The Roman Catholic Hierarchy and the Fall of Parnell', in *Victorian Studies* (Massachusetts, 1961).

LESLIE, SHANE, *Henry Edward Manning: His Life and Labours* (London, 1921).

LOCKER LAMPSON, GODFREY, *A Consideration of the State of Ireland in the 19th Century* (London, 1907).

LUCY, HENRY W., *A Diary of Two Parliaments 1874–1880 and 1880–1885* (London, 1885 & 1886).

——— *A Diary of the Salisbury Parliament 1886–1892* (London, 1892).

——— *Memories of Eight Parliaments* (London, 1908).

LYONS, F. S. L., *The Fall of Parnell 1890–91* (London, 1960).
——— *Ireland Since the Famine: 1850 to the Present* (London, 1971).
——— *John Dillon* (London, 1968).
MCCARTHY, JUSTIN, *Reminiscences* (London, 1899).
——— *The Story of an Irishman* (London, 1904).
——— *Irish Recollections* (London, 1911).
——— *Our Book of Memories—Letters of Justin McCarthy to Mrs Campbell Praed* (London, 1912).
MCCARTHY, MICHAEL J. F., *The Irish Revolution* (London, 1912).
MACDONALD, JOHN, *Daily News Diary of the Parnell Commission* (London, 1889).
MACDONAGH, MICHAEL, *The Home Rule Movement* (London, 1920).
MAGNUS, PHILIP, *Gladstone* (London, 1954).
MANSERGH, NICHOLAS, *The Irish Question 1840–1921* (London, 1965).
MILLS, J. SAXON, *Sir Edward Cook* (London, 1921).
MORLEY, JOHN, *The Life of William Ewart Gladstone* (London, 1903).
——— *Recollections* (London, 1921).
O'BRIEN, CONOR CRUISE, *Parnell and His Party 1880–1891* (Oxford, 1957).
O'BRIEN, R. BARRY, *The Life of Charles Stewart Parnell* (London, 1898).
O'BRIEN, WILLIAM, *Recollections* (London, 1905).
——— *Evening Memories* (Dublin, 1920).
——— *The Parnell of Real Life* (London, 1926).
O'CONNOR, T. P., *The Parnell Movement* (London, 1889).
——— *Charles Stewart Parnell: A Memory* (London, 1891).
———*Memoirs of an Old Parliamentarian* (London, 1929).
O'DONNELL, FRANK HUGH, *The History of the Irish Parliamentary Party* (London, 1910).
O'FLAHERTY, LIAM, *The Life of Tim Healy* (London, 1927).
O'HARA, M. M., *Chief and Tribune: Parnell and Davitt* (Dublin, 1919).
O'HEGARTY, P. S., *A History of Ireland under the Union 1801–1922* (London, 1952).
O'SHEA, KATHARINE, *Charles Stewart Parnell, His Love Story and Political Life,* 2 vols (London, 1914).
PARNELL, JOHN HOWARD, *Charles Stewart Parnell* (London, 1916).
ROBBINS, SIR ALFRED, *Parnell, the Last Five Years* (London, 1926).
SHERLOCK, THOMAS, *The Life of Charles Stewart Parnell* (Dublin, 1882).
STEAD, W. T., *The Discrowned King of Ireland* (London, 1891).
SULLIVAN, MAEVE, *No Man's Man* (Dublin, 1943).
SULLIVAN, T. D., *Recollections of Troubled Times in Irish Politics* (Dublin, 1905).
THOROLD, A. L., *The Life of Henry Labouchere* (London, 1913).
WALSH, PATRICK J., *William J. Walsh: Archbishop of Dublin* (Dublin, 1929).
WEBB, BEATRICE, *My Apprenticeship* (London, 1926).
WILLIAMS, CHARLES, *The Life of Lieutenant General Sir Evelyn Wood, V.C., G.C.B., G.C.M.G.* (London, 1892).
WOOD, SIR EVELYN, *From Midshipman to Field Marshal* (London, 1906).
——— *Winnowed Memories* (London, 1917).

Index

last years of, 309
managerial abilities of, 29–30, 45,
126, 143, 144, 148–149, 153–154,
174, 175–176, 223
maternal qualities of, 45, 68, 94, 112,
113, 156
memoirs of, *see Charles Stewart
Parnell, His Love Story and Political Life*
mental condition of, 107, 153, 156,
286, 289, 293, 296, 298, 306
Molly Bloom and, 300
moral indignation of, 260–261
O'Shea family and, 16, 25–26
Parnell attacked through, 258–260,
262–263, 277–278
Parnell's meaning to, 297–298
Parnell seen as evil influence on, 209,
221
Parnell seen as victim of, 258–259,
278
as Parnell's political confidante and
aid, 77, 84–85, 103–106, 123, 131,
136, 138, 139–140, 153–154, 155–
156, 172–173, 175–176, 253–255
political interests of, 27, 77, 78, 104,
120, 254
political liaison role of, 77, 78, 103–
106, 111–112, 123, 127, 131, 136,
138, 139–140, 142–150, 153–154,
155–156, 157, 163, 172–173, 174,
175–176, 181, 254
pregnancies of, 30–31, 34, 80, 84, 88,
89, 106–108, 109, 110, 123, 125
promise not to see Parnell by, 189,
232, 236
public image of, 1, 258–260, 275, 291,
298
remarriage of, 272–276, 279
residence changes of, 36, 187–189,
212–213, 298, 299, 309
sister Anna and, 33–34, 59, 116, 219,
221–222, 232, 290
threats to Home Rule Bill by, 160
unconventionality of, 35, 71
wedding (first) of, 24–25
wifely abilities of, 112–115
William O'Shea's courtship of, 18–23
youthfulness of, 62

see also O'Shea, William Henry;
O'Shea divorce; O'Shea marriage;
Parnell, Charles Stewart; Parnell-
Katie O'Shea relationship
O'Shea, Mary, 16, 24, 25–26, 35, 217
O'Shea, Mary Norah Kathleen (Norah),
34, 42, 45, 68, 69, 107, 111, 115,
182, 213, 229, 240, 271, 281, 282,
283, 284, 286, 287, 289, 290, 292,
293, 295, 298–299, 301, 302, 304,
305, 309–310, 312–313
O'Shea, Thaddeus, 17
O'Shea, William Henry (Willie):
absences of, in marriage, 29–39, 32,
35, 36, 45, 46, 110, 123, 179, 230,
234, 235, 248
Anna Wood Steele and, 34, 74–75,
208–209, 221, 225, 232, 235, 237
attacks on, after divorce, 269–271
awareness of wife's adultery admitted
by, 183, 209–210, 235
business activities and ambitions of,
25, 43, 45–46, 73, 203, 300–301
Catholicism of, 16–17, 20, 35, 48, 83,
91, 151, 211–212, 269–271
Chamberlain and, *see* Chamberlain,
Joseph
children as concern of, 208, 210
condonation and connivance attributed
to, 43, 44, 69, 72–75, 80–83, 98–
99, 106–108, 110, 122, 124–126,
128, 130, 142–143, 161, 167, 183,
196, 211, 216–217, 219, 220–221,
229, 236–237, 238, 239, 290, 296,
305–306, 307, 308
custody settlement and, 291–293
death of, 300, 301
divorce proceedings and, *see* O'Shea
divorce
divorce threats of, 82, 98, 183, 184,
189, 196
education of, 17–18
extramarital activities alleged to, 44–
45, 82, 98, 220, 221
failure of, as provider, 35, 36, 43, 46
family background of, 15–17
Fenians and, 199, 200, 204, 262
financial problems of, 20–21, 30–31,
33, 35, 36, 46, 68, 174–175, 184–

O'Shea, William Henry (*Cont.*)
    185, 208, 210–211, 229, 271–272,
    293–294
  Galway candidacy of, 149, 150, 159–
    170, 178, 263, 270
  Gladstone and, *see* Gladstone, Wil-
    liam Ewart
  Home Rule vote and, 178
  horses and, 18, 28, 30, 31, 229
  in House of Commons, 102–103, 141,
    152, 178, 229
  inheritance settlement and, 291–294
  as intermediary between Parnell and
    Chamberlain, 132–136
  Irish nationalist views of, 140, 178–
    179, 270
  Katie's financial dealings with, 46,
    49, 98–99, 126, 127, 130, 174–175,
    182, 196, 201, 219–220, 224, 226,
    231, 291
  Katie's political aid to, 68, 80, 109–
    110, 111–112, 127, 142–150, 160,
    174–175
  as Kilmainham negotiator, 91–100
    passim, 108, 110, 132, 133, 150
  Liberal candidacy of, 141–152, 154,
    159, 160
  masculine code of, 74
  military career of, 18, 20–21, 25
  paranoia of, 222, 226, 231, 237, 271–
    272
  Parnell affair as public embarrassment
    to, 178–183, 204
  Parnell confronted by, 74, 75, 125–
    126, 147, 235
  Parnell's death and, 285, 286
  Parnell Special Commission and, 198,
    199–201, 203–205, 262
  as Parnell supporter and colleague,
    58, 63, 80, 81, 91–95, 102–103,
    109, 133, 142, 229–230
  paternity question and, 81, 91, 107–
    108, 110–111, 123–125, 127, 230,
    231, 292, 293
  political ambitions of, 47, 48, 58, 80,
    82, 92, 108–110, 126, 129, 130,
    133, 134, 141, 142, 150, 154, 159,
    172, 271
  political opposition to Parnell of, 142,
    199–201

  suspicions of, 72–75, 81–82, 106,
    124–126, 180, 230, 231, 232, 236
  Wood family and, 208–210, 221, 226,
    271, 290–294
O'Shea and Company, Madrid bank of,
  25
O'Shea divorce, 43, 99, 101, 111, 121,
    122, 129, 179, 183–185, 188, 189,
    215–241
  Chamberlain's role in, 210–211, 215,
    218, 220, 240, 294
  commercial exploitation of, 239
  custody issue in, 224, 237–238, 240,
    241, 254, 289, 291–293
  decrees in, 237–238, 241, 272
  delay in initiation of, 189, 209–210,
    236
  fire-escape incident in, 233, 237, 239,
    263, 277, 278, 305
  hearing of, 228–238
  Katie's counter-charges in, 220–223,
    228–229, 232, 235–236, 237
  Katie's efforts to buy off husband in,
    219–220, 224, 226
  Parnell's lack of defence in, 226–227,
    228–229, 237, 239, 254–255
  Parnell's optimistic views on, 223–
    224, 226
  political impact of, 238–257, 262–
    263, 265–267, 269, 277–279
  press coverage of, 216–217, 225, 233–
    234, 238–241
  summing-up of judge in, 236–237
  William's petition filed in, 214, 215–
    218
  William as witness in, 231–232, 235–
    236, 237
  witnesses in, 232–234
  Wood family role in, 208–210, 219,
    220, 221, 226, 293, 294
O'Shea family, 16–17
  religion in, 16–17, 24, 25, 35
O'Shea marriage:
  correspondence in, 129–130, 146, 179,
    180, 183, 189, 232, 235, 236, 291
  early problems in (before Parnell),
    29–30, 34, 36–37, 42–43
  first contretemps over Parnell in, 72–
    75, 99

Parnell, Charles Stewart (*Cont.*)
  as revolutionary, 63, 83, 262
  suicide rumors about, 284–285, 287
  threats to safety of, 123, 263, 264
  Times attack on, *see Times*
  Tories and, 137, 145
  as 'Uncrowned King of Ireland,' 59
  unifying role of, 78–79, 83
  William O'Shea's candidacies and, 143, 144–145, 147, 149, 150, 151, 152, 154, 159–170, 263, 270
  Wood family as enemies of, 208–210
  see also Irish nationalists; O'Shea, Katharine Wood; O'Shea, William Henry; Parnell-Katie O'Shea relationship
Parnell, Delia Tudor, 50, 51
Parnell, Fanny, 67
Parnell, John, 52
Parnell, John Henry, 50–51
Parnell-Katie O'Shea relationship:
  children of, 80, 81, 85, 88, 89, 90–91, 106–108, 110–111, 121, 127, 219, 224, 254, 291–293, 295, 302–304, 306, 308
  as described in divorce court, 229–234
  discretion and deception in, 67–70, 76, 82, 87, 106–108, 116, 121, 122, 123, 129, 180, 182, 184, 187, 188–189, 296, 305–307
  domestic life in, 112–116, 124, 128–129
  early meetings in, 59–63
  on eve of divorce, 224–227
  Gerard's antagonism to, 184, 188–189
  grandchild of, 302
  historical consequences of, 311–312
  Irish nationalists and, 63, 77–78, 96, 98, 145, 149, 159–170 *passim*, 217–218, 224, 258–260, 277–279
  Liberal party and, 97–98, 152, 217–218, 223–224, 241–242
  marriage in, 272–276, 279
  mutual passion in, 62–63, 181–182
  pet names in, 88, 260
  private vs. public life in, 97, 166–167, 218, 239, 255
  public and press reaction to, 167, 169–170, 178–180, 182–183, 187,

216–217, 225, 233–234, 238–241, 243–244, 259–260, 272–275, 277–278
  quarrels in, 71–72
  sex in, 65, 106
  Wood family opposition to, 191, 195–196, 208–210
Parnell Special Commission (1888), 142, 146, 191, 196, 197–201, 202–206, 208, 210, 215, 222, 228, 262, 268
Parnell Tragedy, The, 130, 307
Parnell Vindicated, 296
Penfold, Rev. James, 279
Pethers, Caroline, 232–233
Phoenix Park murders, 100–103, 119, 120, 190–191, 197, 203, 205, 246
Phyllis (Katie's maid), 76, 128, 260, 273, 274, 297
Pigott, Richard, 198–199, 204–205, 206, 210, 213, 216, 222
Plan of Campaign, 189, 243, 269
'Plymouth Hoe,' 9
Presbyterians, 213
Primrose League, 244
'Proposed Constitution for Ireland, A' (Parnell's draft for Home Rule), 131, 139–140, 154
Protection of Persons and Property (Ireland) Bill, 75–76
Protestants:
  English, 20, 277
  votes of, in Ireland, 144, 145, 146
Pym, Horatio, 184

Quinlan, Catherine, *see* O'Shea, Catherine Quinlan

Radicals, 97, 133
Rae, Mrs, 172–173
Redmond, John, 252, 256, 266, 295
Review of Reviews, 244
Rhodes, Cecil, 246, 268–269, 299, 312
Rivenhall Place, 6–9, 10, 11, 12, 14, 19, 20, 21, 23, 28, 30, 33, 36, 64, 304
Roman Catholicism:
  annulment in, 211–212
  in England, 24, 132, 134, 137
  as Irish political influence, 58, 78, 79,